THE ENDLESS AM[

Dispatches from

Essays by

CHRISTOPHER LORING KNOWLES

Twitter: https://twitter.com/SecretSunBlog
Blogger: https://secretsun.blogspot.com/
Patreon: https://www.patreon.com/user?u=9779701
Online Store: https://thesecretsunsecretstore.bigcartel.com/
Facebook: https://www.facebook.com/groups/100180000038118

ISBN: 9798692403704

INTRODUCTION

PART ONE • YOU MAY NOT BE INTERESTED IN PARAPOLITICS

PART TWO • TECH-NO-FUTURE

PART THREE • STRANGE CONTAGIONS

PART FOUR • ONCE UPON A TIME IN HOLLYWOOD BABYLON

PART FIVE • DISPATCHES FROM THE BEATEN GENERATION

PART SIX • POP CULTURE DECLINE AND FALL

PART SEVEN • ALL MY HEROES ARE DEAD

PART EIGHT • NOT SO POPULAR CULTURE

PART NINE • DREAMING OF ME

PART TEN • IT'S NO GAME

PART ELEVEN • IT'S ALL REAL

PART TWELVE • BENEDICTIONS

APOCRYPHA

AND THAT WAS THE GEEK THAT WAS

THE ILLUSIONS FALL AWAY

DREAMT OF IN YOUR PHILOSOPHY

TONIC FOR THE TROOPS

THE INFORMATION

PRELUDE: THE DARK MIDNIGHT OF THE SOUL

I HAVE BEEN WRESTLING WITH THE IDEA OF A SECRET SUN collection since I first started the blog. The problem was that I had so much material on so many topics, I could never puzzle out a way to collect it and have it make any sense. A lot of what I do is based on analysis of imagery culled from the media — imagery that wouldn't be available for me to use in a book — so I was already starting at a disadvantage. I'd also done a lot of posts on comics and movies and other kinds of pop culture that I consider to be completely irrelevant now, so that material was no good, either.

Even so, I began collecting material for a Secret Sun book back in early 2017. The problem was that it was all just random bits of this and that, without an overriding theme. Well, 2020 solved that problem for me. This past year has seen so many of the negative trends I'd been watching since the start of the blog reach critical mass that I can't even keep track of them all.

When I went back and read some of my old posts, I was stunned to see how many of the (dire) predictions I've made over the years come true, just over the past few months. Mind you, this isn't because I'm psychic or some great forecaster. It's because even my amateur grasp of history allowed me to see how things that had been set in motion over the past decade would play out. And that's because it's all happened so many times before. All of nature is cyclical, and that includes human nature.

So I decided to gather up writings that deal, directly or otherwise, with this dark night of the soul that America has been trapped in for the entire Twenty-First Century. Not just America, but most of the industrialized world as well. A lot of this analysis will be in the context of popular culture and the media, but we'll be hitting a lot of other targets too.

Given our immense technological power and abundant resources, it's clear that the night sea journey our society and culture are stuck on is a *spiritual* crisis. For many — if not most — people in the West, life has become completely devoid of meaning and purpose, and the young seem to suffer the worst. In a time of unparalleled material bounty, birthrates have cratered and suicide rates have skyrocketed. Economic inequality is such that Karl Marx himself couldn't have conceived of it, even on his worst laudanum and absinthe bender.

We've become trapped in this endless midnight for any number of reasons, but in many ways it's because we believed we were immune from the laws of nature and the lessons of history. And I will be arguing that that's because the way we've learned how to live has divorced us from the natural order of this world. More importantly, the *supernatural* order as well.

WHERE WE ARE AND HOW WE GOT HERE

THERE'S AN OLD SAYING THAT GOES SOMETHING LIKE, "That which cannot last, *will* not last." It came to mind because we're seeing one unsustainable arrangement after another collapse, just in the past year alone. Especially in mass market entertainment, which I've made my beat over the past thirteen years.

Generation X, History's neglected and forgotten cohort, was raised at a time when America's parents decided, almost *en masse*, to utterly abdicate their responsibilities. So they left the kids at home while they went off to discos and key parties, or abandoned their children altogether while they fucked off to California to "reinvent themselves." Because of this, Generation X formed a unnaturally tight bond with junk culture, all too often our only companions and/or guardians. This passionate intimacy ultimately changed the popular culture at large, for better or worse. At this point, I'm going with 'worse', seeing how junk culture worship has instilled an epidemic of infantilism seen all too often in adults today.

I'M SURE YOU ALREADY KNOW THAT THE MASS MEDIA, whether news or entertainment, is lousy with some of the most vile human beings ever to walk the planet. The only reason most of them have gotten anywhere at all is usually down to raw ambition and/or nepotism and/or a willingness to do absolutely *anything* to make it. Which entails doing things most people would never imagine doing to get inside, usually things of a sexual nature.

So what else is new, right? Well, the problem is that the fundamentals have shifted beneath their feet, and all the old tricks don't work anymore. Only they've all been too busy sniffing each other's vapors to realize it. This whole 'virus' business is just putting a well-beaten horse out of its misery. The patient has been in Karen Ann Quinlan condition for quite some time now. Especially since the very-profitable DVD market tanked with the rise of streaming.

The harsh reality is that no one else cares about Hollywood anymore, partly because of the high costs and poor quality of the product, and partly because of the raw, unfettered hatred people in show business have for their audiences. Or at least the *unprotected* parts of their audience, a hatred which is on full display, literally around the clock, on social media.

BUT THERE'S A MUCH LARGER PROBLEM. Our popular culture *has* been reduced to shit and garbage largely because we're no longer a nation, we're an *empire*. Nations can go on indefinitely, but empires are always born to die. And when they fall, they have a tendency to fall hard. And to my way of thinking, there are generally two surefire, can't miss ways for empires to prematurely implode: urbanization and materialism.

If 2020 has done nothing else, it's proven that the modern city is a death trap for the soul and the spirit of humanity. Granted, most of the people inside those traps don't believe in souls or spirits, but these cities are also making people mentally and physically ill. They also depress birthrates to the point of extinction, as you can see in wealthy, futuristic cities like Tokyo and Singapore.

The contradictions in urban America have been heightened all the way up to space, a Gilded Age inequality generously dolloped with a viscous glaze of insufferable and insincere Woke sermonizing. Cities like Boston, Seattle and San Francisco have been running a huge con for decades, talking like Socialists while walking like Social Darwinists. But their fabulous wealth has always been derived from defense and intelligence pork, and now the bills have come due. The riots that blew up in the late spring of this past year arose for a number of reasons, as riots always do. But it really doesn't matter who's ultimately to blame for them, because riots in an urban empire are as inevitable as the tides.

Urbanization was developed to centralize labor and maximize profit, and as such urban centers are, and have always been, fragile and unstable. Now all the big city political machines who'd grown fat and complacent are about to run smack dab into the same financial brick wall that their predecessors did in the Sixties and Seventies, as businesses and workers flee for the provinces. Only this time around it's going to be crazy worse, thanks to the decentralizing power of the Internet.

AND HERE'S WHERE THE MATERIALISM COMES IN. By definition, empires have always been heterogeneous, and materialism has always been the imperialists' go-to lowest common denominator. In other words, the only glue holding together a diverse population today is the accumulation of money and/or power. Without the ability to make lots of money, heterogeneous populations have always, and *will* always, descend into hostile tribal factions. The process is only accelerated by the unnatural and stress-inducing reality of living cheek-by-jowl in gigantic human filing cabinets with people you don't know and don't trust.

The kicker is that modern technology, along with a very, very large and essentially empty planet, offers plenty of everything for everyone who needs anything. But then you run into the problem of the people in positions of power, who only feel like they actually have something if they deprive someone else of everything. And the current technocratic regime lording over us gives unprecedented power to people with the poorest interpersonal skills and the lowest capacity for human empathy. There are all kinds of social and historical reasons for this, but I reckon it all boils down to materialism at the expense of spirituality. Which is why the Apostle Paul said that *the love* of money is the root of all evil, not simply just money itself.

T HE FOCUS OF MY WORK HAS ALWAYS BEEN the intersection of religion and spirituality with popular and unpopular culture. And that intersection has led to some very odd turns in the past thirteen years, with the intentional injection of what can only be called black magic: secret society symbolism, satanic symbolism, pedophilia and other transgressive fetishes. This all arose in the wake of the 2007 economic crash, which also brought scarcity and uncertainty along with it. Not that these nasty things weren't there all along, but they were usually hovering around the margins of the culture. They *became* the culture in many significant ways thereafter. And they're also an integral part of that tribalizing mechanism I mentioned earlier.

Fraternities and initiatory orders have been with us forever, but often gain strength in periods of social and economic uncertainty, such as what Europe experienced during the Industrial Revolution and America experienced during the Depression. Further, bodies like Freemasonry rose to the immense power and influence they have alongside the rise of the multinational corporation, as a way to instill loyalty amongst the strangers and foreigners they'd ultimately have to do business with. So, as sheer blind luck would have it, the transnational nature of Masonic-type fraternities was extremely useful to transnational corporations like the British East India Company.

The problem with these groups is that they're both exclusionary by nature, and intentionally divisive. They're about sorting out who gets to be in the in-group and who doesn't. In-group favoritism is an inherent part of the package. They usually require applicants to subject themselves to humiliating rituals, and some even require them to commit acts of transgression, if not actual crimes. Secret societies and exclusionary sects can also sow mistrust and paranoia, especially in heterogeneous populations held together by abstract ideals of civic virtue. The scuzzier ones will do this intentionally.

So, the wholesale injection of exclusionary secret society memes into the culture, in the wake of a devastating economic downturn and the collapse of organized religion, has had a negative impact on society on the whole. There are plenty of other factors involved in this. The moral authority of the Catholic Church collapsed under the weight of the sexual abuse scandals, and the hijacking and despoiling of American Evangelicalism by the murderous Neoconservative kill-cult, created huge rifts in the body politic.

It's not that the Neoconservatives on the whole have any interest in or affinity with Christianity, they just saw the Evangelical movement as a rich source of manipulable cheerleaders and cannon fodder for their real passion: war-profiteering. So they manipulated their idiot puppet-king Bush II to get all the disposable flyovers on-side. The inevitable disaster and Bush II's ineptitude tore huge holes in the Body of Christ, such as it was by that point, and sent millions of Americans into spiritual and tribal exile.

ASIDE FROM THE MASS INFUSION OF MASONIC SYMBOLISM and the occult into pop culture, an extremely well-financed cohort of born-again atheists flooded the market in the early 2000s. The new atheist movement was loosely allied to the Libertarian movement, which was given a huge boost by Ron Paul's 2012 Presidential run, as well as the internet-based 'Skeptic' movement, which was spearheaded by the Center for Scientific Inquiry, formerly known as the Committee for Scientific Claims of the Paranormal, or CSICOP (pronounced *psy-cop*, or 'thought police', if you will).

The Skeptic and Nü Atheist movements picked up speed in the wake of the 2007 crash and picked up followers from a generation of young white males who'd been reared on the Internet. A new strain of Victorian-era Scientism was seeded into the Borgsong and missionized a huge crop of Millennials, whose attitudes towards religion ranged from indifference to frothing hatred. The converts to the Skeptic, Atheist and Scientism movements were extremely aggressive in spreading the new dogma online, and would troll, gang-stalk, harass and brigade anyone who stood in their way. Things were going great guns — well, aside from the Atheism+ schism of mostly female social justice warriors — until around the mid-Teens, when all of the air suddenly seemed to come out of the tires and stop the movement dead in its tracks. How and why did that happen, you might be wondering?

Well, in 2014 *Jane Does vs United States* was filed in Federal Court, on behalf of the one-time teenaged sex-slaves of a certain celebrity swindler named Jeffrey Edward Epstein. Whom, as it turns out, was both a mastermind and a financial facilitator of the Skeptic, Atheist and Scientism movements. Imagine that. It turns out many of the high priests of the new godless order were tucked in Epstein's deep pockets, and that includes the Transhumanist movement, a raw-boned sci-fi shuck that preyed on the crippling anxieties and neuroses of the new Techno-Priesthood.

The Atheist+ schismatics made hash of the Epstein connections with people like Lawrence Krauss and Richard Dawkins, but it wouldn't be until Epstein's 2019 arrest (and subsequent murder in prison) that the full scope of the STEM community's betrayal came to light. But by then no once much cared, because a new pestilence had seized the reins of power in every single, solitary institution in America: the Woke hate-cult, which filled the vacuum left by the organized religions that Epstein's atheist toadies helped vaporize. This cult soon became the most destructive and corrosive threat the Western world had seen the 1930s.

Wokeness is the mimetic analog of the cancer cell: it grows and festers, consuming and destroying all the healthy cells around it until the host dies and takes out the invasive force along with it. Wokeness is, for all intents and purposes, a mass suicide cult. The pessimistic side of my nature tells me this is no accident, and that the materialist zeitgeist that lords over us all is old, sick and probably just wants to die.

A S YOU MAY HAVE GUESSED BY NOW, this book isn't going to be an easy read. It's not meant to be. A lot of these essays are essentially primal screams from the wilderness of Twenty-First Century American culture. Some were written when I was locked in the grips of a debilitating chronic pain condition - and a ferocious opioid dependency - that basically cut me off from the outside world for a very long time. But I got past that, with a bit of luck and lot of hard work, using my own neurology as a long-term science project.

Something fundamental in our understanding of reality is changing, but I don't think we're all done for. I don't think its hopeless. I don't think the patient is beyond saving. I see it more like one of those inspirational Facebook videos, where a kind-hearted soul finds a stray dog on the brink of death and nurses her back to full health and happiness. Like that poor little dog, I think our culture has been starved and neglected of something vital to its well-being: spiritual awareness.

Wait: don't throw this book away yet. I'm not talking about religion or whatever currently passes for it. I mean *awareness of the spirit world*. See, every living thing on the planet both projects and consumes spirit energy, as do many things that are no longer technically living. It's hard to describe exactly, so I'll just point out that our greatest thinkers took this for granted for millennia.

I'm all too aware how hippy-dippy it might sound, but it's actually very pragmatic: if we're oblivious to the spirit world, we can't draw any power from it. Without (beneficial) spiritual power, there's no vitality, and without vitality there's no passion. Without passion, there's no real art, and without real art there can't be any culture. Worse, the *less*-benevolent spirits — and you'd damn well better believe they exist — can suck power from *us*. Hence, 2020.

T HINK OF THE SPIRITS LIKE RADIO WAVES. You can't see them or sense them, yet they're all around you. You just need a receiver to make any use of them. Well, we are the receivers of those spirit transmissions, like it or not. Just like you have a range from pocket radios to radio telescopes, so it is with us. Only a lot of high-end spirit receivers don't know what they are, and can run into a lot of trouble because of it. And cause trouble for the rest of us, too.

You'd also better believe that a lot of secret orders, who so love to mock us with their public rituals, understand all of this. They don't perform those rituals for the lulz, they do so because *they draw spiritual power from them*. Same goes for all the symbolism and alignments and the rest of it. They know this stuff *works*, and they're energized by the spiritual pollen it kicks up. What we are looking at is a spiritual crisis, due in large part to these actions.

So just keep all that in mind as you journey through these pages.

YOU MAY NOT
BE INTERESTED
IN PARAPOLITICS

FAITH COLLAPSING

DESPITE ALL THE THEORIZING YOU MAY BE HEARING in the media about American interventionism, the riots in Arab countries over an amateur film trailer satirizing the Prophet Muhammad represent a profound, existential crisis in one of the most powerful religions in the world. We are seeing one of those epochal moments in history, when a major religious movement reaches the end of its road, the point of no return.

We're talking about a religion with world-conquering ambitions and a stark, totalitarian ethos. A religion that's caused nothing but violence and disruption since it first reared its ugly head on the world stage. A religion that wants to crush human individuality and cultural uniqueness, all in pursuit of an insane, utopian vision of worldwide uniformity.

It's a religion that's been the cause of endless war and sectarian violence all across the planet, and shows no sign of quenching its taste for human blood. And yet its contradictions are so immense, and its foundations so faulty, it can't help but implode when faced with the reality of Twenty-First Century life.

Yes, my friends, the religion of Globalism is collapsing. The question then becomes how many of us will it take down with it?

I REMEMBER QUITE CLEARLY WHEN GLOBALISM became the religion of the corporate elite: it was a few years following the end of the Cold War when American industry faced its own existential crisis. Other markets were expanding and formerly Communist and Socialist economies were liberalizing, creating a gold rush that threatened to leave the self-appointed Masters of the Universe behind. But the working classes weren't eager to let the old guard give away the candy store, so soon we had younger, more persuasive Satans like Bill Clinton and Tony Blair take the stage.

A fresh coat of make-up was daubed on the old Whore of Babylon, and national treasures were set to be auctioned off to the lowest bidder. We soon saw a number of treaties — NAFTA, GATT, MAI — that have done untold damage to the American middle and working classes, while they've turned the rich into the super-rich, and the super-rich into veritable gods.

The Elites envisioned a borderless, nationless Utopia, through which workers, resources, and capital flow without tariffs or taxes, and where mass immigration and outsourcing drove wages down to their lowest possible levels. A world where American brands and franchises were established in every village and city. Limited surgical warfare would remove any religious or nationalist-based resistance abroad, and American workers would be distracted into impotence with a never-ending bounty of bread and circuses.

If those didn't work, pseudo-religious movements such as the Prosperity Gospel movements (which a traditionalist Christian friend of mine says were "spawned from the pits of Hell") might do the trick. Any lingering resistance to the Global agenda would be diverted by manufactured tragedies, and overhyped hucksters, crying wolf with ridiculous fantasies that only the most gullible people could take seriously.

It's been only too successful. But the people who were supposed to lie down and die are refusing to do so. Chinese workers are increasingly restless, tired of bearing the brunt of the world's manufacturing burden for near-starvation wages. The politics of austerity are bringing people out into the streets in Europe, threatening the Neoliberal ruling class and its pet project, the European currency. Uncertainty reigns, threatening to topple the Globalist pashas from their pedestals.

One thing for sure is that the high priests of Globalism will cling to their illusions until the bitter end. That religion was born out of a host of short-term conditions — the end of the Cold War, the collapse of oil prices, the Tech Boom, the Nineties stock market boom — that everyone wants to relive, but which probably won't be repeated in our lifetimes. It will get increasingly more unpleasant to keep the rubes on the shuck.

But people's salaries and reputations are now invested in Globalist fantasies, so it's likely that many of them will double-down rather than admit that the world is not One. And of course, there's also the dream of endless profit, of planting your brand in hostile territory, and having the folks back home pick up the tab if there's any trouble. Since the super-rich have become completely unmoored from any sense of proportion or reality, don't expect that dream to fade any time soon, either.

THE ILLUSION OF CHANGE

I THINK I MIGHT NEED TO AMEND KNOWLES' FIRST LAW, or add a new paragraph thereto. The First Law has it that any controversy over symbolism in the mass media is created to disguise another symbolic message altogether. A classic example of this is the controversy over MIA's middle finger at Super Bowl XLVI, which disguised the grotesque display of pseudo-occult militarism of Madonna's halftime show.

I was waiting for the harsh reality that the gay marriage controversy was meant to distract everyone from. And now with the dismal employment numbers, the ongoing damage of the Sequester, and Obama's plan to sell out Social Security, the other shoe may well have dropped.

SINCE THE 2012 ELECTION, WE'VE HEARD NO END of crowing about the death of the Republican Party and the rise of the new Democratic majority and the inevitable triumph of 'social justice' and multiculturalism, and all of the other new and inviolate sacred cows. Obama is the 'New Reagan', who will form a new politics that will change America to suit the wish-dreams of hyper-privileged white 'progressives' in the media and academia, and we'll all live happily ever after. The only problem is that all of it, every jot and tittle, is bullshit: new window dressing on the same old scam.

The ultimate grail of the dictator is the illusion of change, the harmless controlled opposition that will generate lots of heat but no light. It's an old magician's trick, a deceptive diversion much like all the phony symbolism in the media. It's why 'Progressive' - a term copped from the Marxist concept of linear progression towards a utopian society - replaced 'Populist'. It's why 'Social Justice' - essentially a neologism for divide-and-rule tactics repackaged as identity politics - replaced the idea of *economic justice*.

You see, most of what passes for a Left in this country - entirely based in the university/NGO/media axis - are in fact the children of wealth, often *extreme* wealth, and privilege. Though they probably may be too stupid to understand it consciously, somewhere in their hollow heads they all realize that fighting for economic justice means money coming out of their own pockets.

BARACK OBAMA — WHOM ANY SANE, INTELLIGENT PERSON realizes is perhaps the ultimate Democrat in Name Only, a Wall Street-spawned Rockefeller Republican — offers up a diversion of symbolic social and cultural issues while doing every single thing that the billionaire hedge fund managers who own his very soul demand he do.

The scamsters rely on the identity-politics dodge to feed their left/right dichotomy. It divides people who otherwise might find common cause and unite against *economic* injustice, based in the rapacious and deliriously-corrupt securities exchange and banking rackets. Destroy the middle class so everyone is weak and powerless. Keep the working classes on the defensive through a bewildering host of hoops and hurdles.

Congress doesn't represent its voters, it represents its donors. Period. And the Republicans still have actual control of the House and *de facto* control of the Senate, thanks to the weak, semi-senile and compromised Harry Reid. And they have their mole at 1600 Penn, doing the work a President Romney could never have dared.

I got wise to this technique some years ago, when a British police chief was asked why bobbies don't carry guns. He explained that the idea was not to project a threatening image that people would react against, but to "make it look like you're losing when you're actually winning."

Recently, the bobbies borrowed LA police chief Daryl Gates' trick during their riots: let the yobs and the thugs run rampant. That way no one will stand up for them or their families when the budget ax comes down, which it most certainly did.

Pity poor *Salon* editor Joan Walsh. A virtual poster-child for the hyper-privileged white 'Progressive', Walsh keeps writing or commissioning impotent pleas for the GOP to roll over and play dead because Obama won the election. I actually truly believe that Republicans piss themselves laughing reading that stuff in the morning. If you see some Senator with a particularly amused grin on CSPAN, it could well be that he just read himself some fresh whining on *Alternet* or *Salon*.

Come to think of it, things *have* changed since the 2012 Election; they've gotten worse. Never mind all of the 'social justice' window dressing coming out of the White House. Divide 'n' rule and rape 'n' pillage proceed unhindered.

'Progressives' are constantly brainwashed, literally every single day, to accept everything that their favored media organs tells them is the truth. Questioning any of it — a single jot or tittle — makes you a 'conspiracy theorist'. That will surely earn you a dirty look or two down at the local Starbucks, which is all the discouragement status-conscious 'progressives' need. I'm sure questioning just whose interests the Democratic Party really serves is every bit as verboten. *Cui Bono?*

THE NEW SLEEPWALKERS

TWENTY-FOURTEEN MARKED THE 100TH ANNIVERSARY of the beginning of the First World War, hastening a lot of observers to mark the parallels between the world of the sleepwalkers of the early Twentieth Century and this strange fugue state the world finds itself in today.

1914 saw a world of fading empires - Austria-Hungary, Great Britain, the Ottomans, Czarist Russia - locked in struggle with rising powers such as the United States and the newly united Germany. 2014 sees the rise of a new power bloc, the so-called BRICS; Brazil, Russia, India, China and South Africa, all massive, resource-rich, (mostly) population-dense powers tired of living under the boot of the NATO alliance of North America and Western Europe. Whereas the powers of 1914 were interlocked through a Byzantine series of military and familial alliances, the entire world is operating today under a number of post-Cold War trade agreements, all of which were written to benefit the rich countries at the expense of the poor.

Another reality is a major population boom in the post-WWII era, thanks in large part to advances in medical technology (antibiotics, specifically) and food production technology (irrigation and fertilizers). Systems were put in place to manage the flow of capital, resources, commodities and labor. The assumption has been that as long as relative peace was kept and no major disruptions happened within the food supply, the world could basically run on autopilot.

The next order of business was Alexander's old dream: a single world state, in which the world went along its business sharing (give or take) a one-world government and globalized systems of culture, sport, finance, etc. We started hearing the term the 'International Community', as if it applied to a specific body, on news outlets such as NPR. As in, "*The International Community believes that the Iraq situation is...*" though who exactly comprised this community was never made clear. It's certainly interesting to note how many countries have Parliamentary systems, have football as the national sport, do business in English or Spanish, frequent the same fast food restaurants, etc etc.

Shocks periodically erupted, to the financial system, the job market, various regional conflagrations. Those were all manageable to a certain extent, or at least theoretically manageable. But then the Bush II Administration came along and decided the pace wasn't moving swiftly enough for the keyboard commandos that promised Bush the Lesser a new American Imperium, starting with Alexander's old stomping grounds in Afghanistan, and moving onto his father's arch-enemy Saddam Hussein in Babylon.

The pretext was that in the wake of 9/11, mustache-twirling Hussein couldn't wait to unleash waves of jihadis on the US, armed with WMDs and nuclear suitcases and all the rest of it. Of course, the fact of the matter was that Hussein hated the jihadis and they hated him. He didn't have any WMDs. His strong arm rule kept the jihadis on a leash, and gave the various religious minorities of Iraq relative sanctuary. So now the jihadis are running across Iraq like the maniacs, slaughtering the few Mandaeans, Yezidis, and Assyrians they haven't already driven out of the country.

Bush and his Neocon lunatics are ultimately to blame for this, but equally so is Obama, since he let a two-bit thug dictate the terms of US withdrawal. But that just leads us to wonder what the real agenda is behind ISIS, or ISIL, or Islamic State, or the Caliphate, or whatever the fuck they're called this week. Again, an entire blog couldn't unravel that mess. I won't even try here.

Obama seems to be sleepwalking himself, drifting from one elite golf course to another while Iraq burns and a civil conflagration unfolded on US soil. If the entire news media weren't in his pocket, I'd say Ferguson was his 'Katrina moment.' And 2014 certainly does feel a lot like 2005.

Black Americans have been getting squeezed like no time in my memory under Obama, driven from their neighborhoods by runaway gentrification and dealing with unfair competition in the labor market by immigrant workers. I don't think Ferguson was really all about a police shooting, and I don't think it's the last eruption we'll see. Which only goes to prove my maxim that when they put your guy in the White House, *look the fuck out.* Going back to at least LBJ, it means they're about to stick the knife in your back.

While America is focused on Iraq and problems at home, Russia is carving out chunks of Ukraine for itself, and all the toothless old women of Europe can do is wave feeble sanctions at Putin. They seem to be forgetting that whole BRICS thing, that a new power bloc is emerging in resistance to the Globalist powers of the EU. What's more, it seems that Germany is interested in cutting its *own* deals with Putin, a signal it's lost confidence in its own EU project.

Webster Tarpley ties all of this skullduggery back to the Masonic intrigues of King Edward and the Entente powers of Britain, France and Czarist Russia, even tossing the activities of our old friends Mesdames Blavatsky and Bailey into mix, citing them as Edward's agents. I have some trouble with Blavatsky, given her work with the Indian Nationalists, but Alice Bailey is a gimme. She and her apostles such as David Spangler and Benjamin Creme were all tied up in the United Nations for reasons never made clear, but they did recruit at least one top-ranking UN official at one point.

My guess is that the Alice Bailey organization was a dry run for what would later bear fruit in California, with the Presidio Russia project, Esalen, and The Zen Center. The Baileys were too weird and too crazy (Bailey said the bombings of Hiroshima and Nagasaki were, *"The greatest spiritual event which has taken place since the human kingdom appeared"*) but there was obviously an interest in some kind of syncretic spiritual movement that could take the place of the churches (most of which had become anti-Communist during the Cold War) for diplomatic purposes.

All of which plays a major role in the story we're trying to wrap our heads around today, since it was that axis of Rockefeller-funded New Age centers that first brought Boris Yeltsin to the US, thanks to the efforts of a Rockefeller agent named Rev. Jim Garrison. And it would be Yeltsin's kleptocracy that gave rise to Putin, and by extension, this new power bloc that is threatening to go off the dollar and adopt the Yuan as their new reserve currency.

Was the annexation of Crimea the new-model assassination of Archduke Franz Ferdinand? Are we all sleepwalking towards some kind of inexorable global conflagration? Will we see another global pandemic, similar to the Spanish flu pandemic of 1918? Already we're hearing scientists warn of the end of antibiotics. Let's all pray *that* doesn't come to pass.

Are tinderboxes like Britain sleepwalking towards serious civil unrest, especially if some shocking revelation of high-level official complicity in the Muslim grooming gangs emerges from within the Labour Party or the BBC? I grew up at a time when riots were a regular occurrence in England. There's a lot of people over there who've been swallowing a lot of rage for a long time. If there's a major terror event there, all bets are off.

AND SO IT IS HERE IN AMERICA TODAY. Obama has presided over the greatest upward movement of wealth this country has ever seen, and millions have left the workforce entirely for lives on public assistance. Most jobs created during his presidency have been low-paying service jobs, and most of those have gone to immigrants. The Democrats always dreamed of dethroning the Republicans, only to realize that the GOP was never running shit, except errands for the Globalists.

The economy seems to be growing, but for whom? Smart phones and social media seem to distract most people from all these problems, but what happens when the first major hole breaks open in the dam? What won't happen is what you saw in previous depressions, when Americans still had a sense of common identity and purpose.

Meanwhile, Democratic bastions like San Francisco, New York and Boston are like open-air laboratories in the study of rampant economic inequality, making the worst excesses of the Gilded Age look frugal by comparison. And futurists are all warning Americans that automation could do away with the very idea of employment itself. Americans may be sleepwalking, but it's not a particularly restful sleep. It's because of all this that I think the study of deeper truths is more important than ever. Perhaps changing the very way we think, even the way we use our minds.

A hundred years ago, people believed they lived within a constellation of fixed realities, only to see them all blown to shit, along with everything around them. The Old World died forever on the killing fields of the First World War, and I'm not sure we've even recovered from those shocks. I can't begin to imagine what a Third World War would look like, I can only imagine I never want such a thing to come to pass.

But I certainly don't want the robot world of the Futurists, and I seriously doubt the Transhumanist pipe-dream will ever escape the pages of bad science fiction novels, in my lifetime at least.

BUT PARAPOLITICS IS INTERESTED IN YOU

I HAD A NIGHTMARE A LONG TIME AGO, that there was a Presidential election and the candidates were Hillary Clinton and Donald Trump. Well, that's not actually true. Even in my most fevered, delirious states could I have imagined such a national tragedy. And the tragedy is just warming up out there in the cold driveway.

Of course, what may actually be happening is that the grown-ups, the men and women who risk life and limb in the oligarchic pursuit of Empire, may well have tired of all the freaks and sickos who are constantly fucking everything up and may well be in the process of taking the matches away from these political pyromaniacs. It may well turn out that whoever wins on Tuesday will be nothing but a figurehead, and will almost certainly be brought to heel by larger forces behind the scenes. We can only hope.

The email leaks we've been seeing have been blamed on a number of players — the Russians, Trumpkins, UFO hackers — but the smart money is on the Deep State. And the bookmakers would almost certainly bet the house that what we've seen is just the tip of the iceberg, the shot across the bow.

Although the Media — meaning the Democratic Party house organs and dis-information agents who make up what passes for a national mainstream media in this country — have kept the lid on the powder-keg, I very much get the feeling that both candidates (yes, I said both) are rattled. Why? Because I wonder if someone else has taken control of the wheel and let the ostensible top dogs know it. And let them know that none of their secrets are safe anymore.

One thing I will say for this farce of an election is that it's exposed how corrupt and complicit the so-called 'two-party system' is, how fatuous and empty the party platforms are, and how they endlessly screw the hardworking people who keep that dead horse propped up. There's no question now that the establishment media is just a propaganda arm for the Democratic Party, which itself is just the old Rockefeller Republican Party with a politically-correct facelift. There's no question that the fixes are all in, or that the power structure is one big happy club that despises the people they rule over. We've always suspected it, now we *know* it.

When I was a kid there was a whole thing about Richard Nixon, Hillary Clinton's spiritual antecedent. Everyone seemed to think that Nixon didn't do anything everyone else in Washington wasn't doing as well, he simply had the misfortune to get caught. It's amazing how common this opinion was, from adults down to teenagers, maybe even younger kids as well. The question then becomes *why* Nixon was caught.

I've heard the media complain that Hillary is the victim of a 'witch-hunt'. This seems to be the default explanation for why all this damaging information is coming to light. Funny, I don't recall them ever using that term during Watergate or Iran-Contra. But what if there's some truth to this? What if Hillary has been targeted? Is it because she's a "strong woman," or is it because she actually *is* a witch, with a documented interest in the occult? Or it just because she's a longtime ethics offender? Or is it because of something else, something that the Deep State doesn't want their Washington hacks getting themselves all worked up about?

In that light, let's look again at this:

Hillary Clinton Gives UFO Buffs Hope She Will Open the X-Files

'Hillary has embraced this issue with an absolutely unprecedented level of interest in American politics', said Joseph G. Buchman, who has spent decades calling for government transparency about extraterrestrials.

She has said in recent interviews that as president she would release information about Area 51, the remote Air Force base in Nevada believed by some to be a secret hub where the government stores classified information about aliens and UFOs.

Oh, I can just *feel* your eyes rolling. But bear with me here a moment. There's a very real and tangible issue at work here.

Former Nixon lawyer Douglas Caddy told YouTuber 'Dark Journalist' that E. Howard Hunt (the inspiration for the Cigarette-Smoking Man of *The X-Files*) claimed that JFK was assassinated because he wanted to open the secret files on UFO technology. Sounds crazy, right? The only problem is that there's a memo written by JFK ordering such a thing, less than two weeks before his death.

President Gerald Ford made a lot of noise about UFOs when he was Speaker of the House, and instigated actions that led to the formation of the Condon Committee (which turned out to be a whitewash). Ford remained active on the issue, in large part due to pressure from constituents. But when he became President he fell silent on the issue. It was during his Presidency that many of the documents that made UFOlogy such a focal point for conspiracy culture were prepared for declassification. It was also during his Presidency that the MK ULTRA program was revealed to the public.

And wouldn't you just know it, good old Jerry Ford was the victim of not one but *two* assassination attempts. Ain't that just a kick in the pants, Elmer?

One was by ol' Lynette 'Squeaky' Fromme, late of the Manson Family/Process Church axis, speaking of MKULTRA (and more importantly, MK OFTEN). The other was by Sara Jane Moore, who was fixated on Patty Hearst and the 'Symbionese Liberation Army', created by another of Joly West's MK OFTEN graduates, former Vacaville inmate Donald DeFreeze. Some interesting 'coincidences' there, no?

Ford's successor, Jimmy Carter, was even more activist on the UFO issue, promising, "If I ever become President, I'll make every piece of information this country has about UFOs sightings available to the public, and the scientists." Carter expanded the powers of the FOIA program in 1978, freeing up reams of previously classified documents, proving the long involvement of the US Government in the UFO issue.

Not long after that, an Islamic Revolution took place in US client state Iran. The US Embassy was seized, and its occupants held hostage for months. Carter ordered a rescue mission, but it ended in disaster. That, and the extended siege at the embassy, crippled Carter's Presidency. The later Iran-Contra scandal revealed that elements within the Reagan campaign worked with the hostage takers in an arms-for-ransom arrangement in order to prevent Carter's 'October Surprise', or the release of the Americans before the national elections.

That's *three* Presidents with interest in opening the files on UFOs facing three unfortunate outcomes, for those of you keeping score at home.

Ronald Reagan was another one, having had his own UFO sightings. After his re-election, he'd begin talking up the issue, claiming that alien threats would act as a uniting force in a world divided by politics and religion. Then Reagan lost the Senate. Then the Iran-Contra Scandal exploded. Undeterred apparently, Reagan continued discussing the issue, even raising it at the United Nations. But the Gipper wasn't in the loop any longer by then.

George Bush the Elder was much higher up the intelligence food chain than his predecessors and largely avoided the issue, even as it was becoming a hot topic in he media. His successor Bill Clinton stuck his hand into the hornet's nest and ordered an investigation into the Roswell event. Unhappy with the initial results, Clinton ordered another and had one of his lieutenants search the archives for information on the UFO issue. Then he was impeached.

At the same time, New Mexico Congressman Steven Schiff attempted to open an investigation into the Roswell issue by subpoenaing the Air Force's financial records. Then Schiff contracted an aggressive form of cancer and died at the age of 51. Or as I say, "Schiff contracted a terminal case of UFOlogy." Strange as it may sound to most folks, messing around with UFOs leads to a startlingly high rate of early mortality. Don't ask me why.

George W. Bush was in office during the largest expansion of the National Security State this country had seen since 1947 (shortly after Roswell, in case you wondering), effectively starving the UFO-Conspiracy coterie of oxygen, nearly for good.

Bush's successor, Barack Obama, made some vague noises about looking into the issue while campaigning. But, as he did with nearly everything else to do with national security, Obama followed in his predecessor's footsteps on the issue. And has enjoyed a largely scandal-free, two-term Presidency.

Hillary Clinton made it a point to announce her attention to look into UFOs, and more importantly, Area 51. Her campaign is being run by Washington power-player's power-player John Podesta, who also has a serious interest in UFOs. And you know the rest of it: the two of them were mighty embarrassed when their email accounts were hacked and plastered all over the Internet.

You don't have to believe in ET or anything like that at all for all of this to work. What we're really looking at are elected officials sticking their noses into the business of the *real* government: black projects, black ops, the secret space program and all the rest of it.

We're seeing the elected government going up against the real government and getting its ass kicked. Plain and simple.

Alex Jones and company are all over the email scandals, wringing a lot of mileage over what seems to be an invitation to Podesta by an artist named Marina Abramović for a "Spirit Cooking" party that was never RSVP'd. Even so, that email presented the masses with one of those moments when the veil drops and we get a hard look inside the moral sickness of the ruling cabals.

MARINA ABRAMOVIĆ IS A HARDCORE OCCULTIST who presents her rituals as performance art. Her work reminds me of nothing less than the 'art ritual murder' of David Bowie's Clinton-era comeback album, *Outside*. But a male artist could never get away with the hideous desecration of women and children evident in her work. Seriously, it's pretty sick stuff.

Abramović's CV is mostly filled with the tedious and pretentious nonsense that the art world has endlessly pimped in the wake of the CIA-spawned abstract expressionist movement and the ponderous puddle of puke it dragged in its wake. Just reading descriptions of her work is tiresome.

But somewhere along the way, Abramović discovered the occult. Specifically some black magic strain that we've probably never heard about, probably practiced by some rich psychotics in some remote castle in Europe somewhere.

During a Reddit chat, Abramović let it be known she takes the occult aspect of her work seriously:

> Q: 'What place do you see the occult having within contemporary art; can magick be made [not simply appropriated/ performed]?'
>
> A: 'Everything depends on which context you are doing what you are doing. If you are doing the occult magic in the context of art or in a gallery, then it is the art. If you are doing it in different context, in spiritual circles or private house or on TV shows, it is not art. The intention, the context for what is made, and where it is made defines what art is or not'.

We saw the ostensible fingerprints of MKOFTEN lurking behind the work of filmmakers like Roman Polanski and Kenneth Anger, and we've seen the connections of MKULTRA legates to the Satanic Temple. Is MKOFTEN's successor program now promoting the work of Abramović? You know what my guess would be.

What's perhaps even more disturbing than the Spirit Cooking revelation was Abramović's despicable dinner party-art exhibit based on a cannibalism theme, with various food items sculpted into ultra-realistic scale modes of human beings. It's all-too reminiscent of the work of the Chicago Ripper Crew, the Satanic serial killers who abducted, tortured and cannibalized women in the late 1970s. Only in Abramović's case, the guests were a Who's-Who of the A-list, with pop singers, movie stars and politicians gleefully participating in the carnage. To his credit, funnyman Will Ferrell looked a bit stunned by all the gristle. Unlike Lady Gaga and Gwen Stefani, who looked like they were having the time of their lives.

AND SO THE WALL OF DENIAL and normality-bias consensus, behind which this stuff is kept a very safe distance away from our public culture, is ripped open once again. Just like it was with Reagan's astrologer, or the Bush family's involvement in the weird rituals of Skull and Bones, or the mock sacrifice rituals at Bohemian Grove, or Bill and Hillary's voodoo, and on and on it goes. UFOs and the occult might seem like trifles to most people, especially Millennials, but once you get past the lower levels of society and start climbing the ladder, you soon find out that those people don't think the way you do, and have what you might regard as weird beliefs. Beliefs that ultimately shape how all of our lives are lived.

It's like my Grandma always used to tell me: "You may not be interested in parapolitics, but parapolitics are interested in you."

"BUT LATELY ONE OR TWO HAS FULLY PAID THEIR DUE..."

I HAVEN'T REALLY SAID MUCH ABOUT THE JEFFREY EPSTEIN case because I haven't had anything to say that hundreds of thousands of other people hadn't already said, and said far better than I could. I knew for sure there were all kinds of Sun-jacent plot points to the drama, but nothing I found particularly surprising. It's all played out pretty much like you'd expect.

But let me first say this: I really wish people would stop using the word *pedophile*. It's a grotesque distortion of our language, and totally inaccurate. I suggest we go back to the traditional term: child molester.

Child molesters don't love children, they *hate* children, and childhood itself. When you get past the normalizing nonsense that elements within the MSM are trying to slip into the conversation and look at investigative reports and case studies, you soon see that child molester fantasies very often escalate into violence, torture, and degradation, even murder.

Attraction to prepubescent children is a paraphilia, meaning that the object of lust is exactly that: objectified. Think about Jeffrey Dahmer's philosophies for comparison. Epstein wasn't even a pedophile, as the term is usually rendered. Technically, he was primarily an ephebophile, but more accurately a statutory rapist. And a Mossad asset. And a human trafficker. And an extortionist. And a money launderer. And God knows what else, I'd rather not.

This is also a nerd story. Sexual fixation on minors and children has always been a problem in nerd and geek circles, something I had to contend with when I myself was a boy circulating in those same circles. Being a latchkey GenXer from *goddamn-fucking-Braintree*, I developed a sense for predators very early on, but a lot of other kids did not.

The guy who owned one of the first comic stores in my area went down on a molestation beef, as did a local magic shop owner. In fact, not only was the A/V teacher in my junior high school a known child molester for decades, it would so transpire that a teacher who was very actively involved in SF fandom had a crush on me. I found this out because a kid who sat in the front of the class room stopped me in the hall one day and said, "I hope you know that that guy draws pictures of you all the time in class." I later found out that was indeed the case when I snooped the teacher's desk. I was 14 years-old.

So with the geeks now having inherited the Earth, it's no surprise that some of the more unsavory facets of the culture are now mainstreaming themselves. It's a very serious problem, and one that isn't going to be solved with hyperbole and hysteria. Hopefully, it — and other problems unique to nerd culture — won't ultimately collapse society on the whole.

It has to be pointed out that people like Epstein are able to insinuate themselves into places like MIT and Harvard because of the more troubling appetites in some corners of those communities. And judging from Twitter, the problem is getting worse and more open. I really hate writing about this stuff, and I'm uncomfortable with people who lose themselves in topics like Pizzagate, but it's a fact of life, more and more so. Especially in STEM circles.

It seems Epstein wasn't a minor groupie in the powerful cliques of modern science, he was a major player. Maybe even more than that. And given his, well, INSANE ideas and ambitions (like cryogenically preserving his dick and repopulating the planet with his offspring), he could well be more of a factor in the shocking collapse of credibility and integrity in contemporary science. Not only that, but maybe Epstein encouraged or inspired the weird bravado people like Richard Dawkins and Richard Stallman showed in their own creepy public stances on child molesting.

Aside from everything else, there's been a lot of discussion as to some of Epstein's bizarre beliefs and the weird symbolism seen everywhere on Little St. James. A lot of it has centered on the so-called 'temple', which looks like a set from an old Italian Hercules movie. You don't need a Harvard degree in Semiotics to realize what you're looking at here. The only debates are over the meanings of the symbols and the exact purpose of this structure. There's been a lot of speculation from more mainstream sources that this was Epstein's study or sanctum. I actually think there's something to that.

Epstein clearly saw himself as a god, and he moved in circles that are filled with folks who hold weird, syncretic beliefs. Beliefs derived from Babylon and Egypt, or more specifically, Nineteenth-Century Masonic mutilations of Roman misinterpretations of Greco-Babylon and Greco-Egypt. So if Epstein really saw himself as a god, why wouldn't he retire into a temple? That's where gods are housed, right?

The temple dome feels solar to me, and the stripes and rounded gold doors could be representations of the sky. And that statue near the door looks like a Hippocampus goddess, another icon that should be very familiar to readers. Solar-Phallicism is at the very core of many Mystery cults, as well as the secret societies that claim lineage from them. Readers are well-familiar with Mithras symbolism that seems to be a thing with the very top of the pyramid, and has been for a very, very, very long time.

There's no reason to believe that Epstein would be any different, given the solar temple and the giant sundial. As with all the Mithras iconography, I doubt this stuff is built on a whim. At some point you need to acknowledge what's in front of your face.

I don't want to go all Q or anything, but it is fascinating to me how all these sex cults and sex rings that had been operating with relative impunity for ages have been run out of business these past few years. My guess is that it's the result of investigative efforts on the part of law enforcement for quite some time, and not something Donald Trump initiated. But it seems that whoever is behind this is also using the circus American politics have become as cover for some long-overdue housecleaning.

We still don't know for sure who ordered the Epstein snuff, but I'd imagine that no one was shedding too many tears at Windsor Castle. We've all seen the snapshots of Prince Andrew with Epstein and his teenagers, so that was a problem that needed solving. It's well-known Randy Andy spent a lot of time at Little St. James, and it's well-known that's he's the dullard of the family. So let's just say I wouldn't fall off my chair if someone told me that someone rather high-up needed to tidy up after the priapic pinhead.

Which brings us to Kevin Spacey.

Kevin's had a remarkable run of good fortune as of late. The kid who kicked the whole Spacey shitstorm up had a sudden change of heart and dropped the sex assault charges against him. That seemed to have something to do with his mother having deleted text messages on her phone she thought might put her son in a bad light. Either way, I sure old Keyser is happy to take the W.

Spacey's winning streak extended when the masseur that accused the actor of sexual assault suddenly dropped dead, and rather mysteriously at that. There's been some grappling over the man's passing behind the scenes, but it doesn't matter who gets suicided, it's who drops the case, right? I think Vince Lombardi said that. I'll have to check.

The other big story this week was that weird viral video posted by Kevin Spacey. Portraying his character from *House of Cards,* Spacey is either letting us know he's lost his last remaining marbles or he's issuing a coded threat to his fellow BLs in Tinseltown. A threat stating, "If I go down, I'm taking all of you with me." My personal vote is leaning strongly towards the latter.

Spacey may be a sociopath, but he's a highly-intelligent and highly-motivated sociopath. He's also in very deep indeed with the Cryptocrats, and probably has quite a few tawdry stories to tell about them as well. I certainly don't want to impugn anyone's good character, I'm just pointing out the interesting connections between Epstein, Spacey and certain folks of high birth, folks who at least nominally command very large and very powerful agencies and forces that aren't generally known to be squeamish about punching anyone's ticket if the need should arise.

Who's the real evil genius then? Epstein or Spacey? And what was that commemorative mug all about? I guess we'll never know.

Maybe old Keyser picked up a few pointers from the only *House of Cards* that really matters (meaning the original British version, not the unwatchable shit-show Spacey starred in). If you've never seen it, for God's sake, what are you waiting for? I guarantee you'll immediately cancel your Netflix sub when you see what butchery was done to this work of Conspiratainment godhead.

Finally, West Hollywood political fixture Ed Buck is finally having to face the music after running what sounds like a lost *Millennium* episode LARP (or an all-male remake of "Loin Like a Hunting Flame") for who knows how long. After two fatal overdoses in his home and a near-third, whoever has been protecting Buck's fucked-up, drugged-out predations on black men finally ran out of patience with the psycho. Either that or got the whammy put on them.

The latter, hopefully.

POSTSCRIPT: Another interesting facet to Epstein's death is how the online parade of sub-comic book-level "science" stories came to a abrupt halt after he died. For several years before that, pop-science sites were filled with ridiculous stories engineered to cause gullible geeks to believe that all their *Star Trek* fantasies were about to come true. Every futuristic trope you can think of from sci-fi and Saturday morning cartoons was repurposed into a "news" story, in which the pie-in-the-sky headlines were almost always walked back below the fold (as it were) with mealy-mouthed qualifiers.

Given the fact that all those same sites went back to the usual boring science class stuff they'd before Epstein's death almost immediately after he died, we can only assume that he was using them to forward his agenda as well. Which makes for a nice lead-in to our next chapter…

WE INTERRUPT THIS SINGULARITY...

THE BEST SCIENCE FICTION — meaning nothing written in the past fifteen years — was cautionary. It was about projecting what was happening in the present, exaggerating it, then blowing it completely out of proportion so it can be better understood by the masses. In theory, at least.

The line between science and science fiction tends to blur in the Transhumanism movement, a psychotic/apocalyptic religion that promises an imminent future where Man and Machine will allegedly merge. Ray Kurzweil's Singularity, another technological eschaton in which machines which reach their apotheosis and become our new gods, is deeply embedded into the H+ movement as well.

A lot of scientists think Kurzweil and his Singularity are a joke — as do Jaron Lanier and William Gibson — the pipe-dream of a brilliant but demented flake so terrified of death that he's built a movement to try to stave it off. A flake who is also powerful enough to bring a lot of people along for his ride to the 'Nerd Rapture', as Gibson puts it.

SCIENCE AND TECHNOLOGY HAVE HAD A REMARKABLE RUN, but many people think we're nearing the end of their era. For instance, you may not have heard about it, but we reached the physical limits of computer power in the mid-2000s. Unfortunately, Big Tech's pimps, procurers and pushers never seem to acknowledge STEM's enormous dark side. Certainly, a lot of people in North America, Europe and Japan are justified in recognizing the stark diminishment of their livelihoods, thanks to Internet-enabled outsourcing. And technology has given a whole kitbag of tools to Wall St. And to the National Security State as well, to rip us all off and hem us in.

As someone who has worked with computers since the 1980s, I can safely say that the changes in the way I've worked with them have been largely cosmetic. I'm essentially doing the same things I was doing with them back in the Reagan Era, only faster, fancier, and prettier. I used to think computers and the Internet would lead to a Golden Age, now I know better. To be honest, I'm nostalgic as hell for the old AOL days. Those old 2400 bps days were like opium injected directly into my cerebral cortex and believe me, I would know how that feels.

I'm no Luddite, I still cling to those old Cyberpunk dreams. It's just that I'm a Jungian about science and technology, where the Transhumanists and their fellow travelers are Prosperity Gospel suckers who can't bring themselves to acknowledge the huge shadow side of STEM, because that would mean acknowledging the black, oily stain in their own dead hearts.

Transhumanism is nothing even remotely new: remember *The Six Million Dollar Man?* Or the Borg, even? Which raises the question: how far will we go with this stuff? How much of your soul do you want to surrender to Silicon Valley? How much time and money will we ultimately waste on some rich fool's pipe dream?

Gibson was probably thinking of Kurzweil when he wrote the *X-Files* episode, 'Kill Switch.' Not the creator of the Skynet-like AI, rather the mad genius who uploaded his consciousness to join it off-screen. But how will Kurzweil upload his consciousness to the Net when we still haven't a clue what the hell consciousness is, or how it works? Will he ever accept that we may never know in this incarnation? That maybe we're not *allowed* to know?

And, of course, one thing you never hear about in Kurzweil's fever-dreams is a catastrophic computer virus. Or glitches, meltdowns, sunspots knocking the entire grid out, electromagnetic pulses, or whatever disaster is lurking there on the shadow-side of his Brave New World. As we saw with the *Wired* wave of digital hype back in the early 90s, nothing ever seems to work out the way the Silicon Valley salesmen promise.

People like myself, who cut our teeth on sci-fi and comic books since we taught ourselves to read, have seen it all. We've seen it all play out, know all the angles, the scenarios and the outcomes. Nothing surprises us, except that the fact that everyone else always seems to be surprised when the worst-case scenario actually does come to pass.

For Mr. Kurzweil, I don't what to say. No one can deny his genius. But I've always said that genius shares a driveway with madness, and that that level of achievement always comes at the expense of something vital in their lives. And so it is with the Materialist mindset. Kurzweil's desperation is only unusual in that he doesn't want to surrender to the inevitable.

Most of Kurzweil's peers these days pride themselves on their stoicism and cynicism and atheism, blithely forgetting how the original Stoics and Cynics and atheists didn't lead the way to a glorious future for their native Greece. They were the harbingers of demographic collapse and cultural decay. Not to mention Greece's ultimate defeat at the hands of more vigorous, theistic enemies. I guess we're all supposed to forget that part of the story.

Maybe Transhumanism and the Singularity really are all playing out in secret in some lab somewhere, but I doubt it. Too many people who know better seem to only feel pity and embarrassment when the topic is raised.

THE TRANSHUMAN DELUSION STUMBLES ON

W E'RE BEING LIED TO, BY EVERYONE with any degree of power or influence. That's not news, that's just human nature. But what is new is a growing mythology that humanity is on some inevitable march to a glorious post-human (or *Trans*-human) future, one in which all of our longstanding problems will magically disappear beneath an avalanche of technological hoodoo.

It's essentially the same line we heard back during the (previous) Great Depression, that if we just tighten our belts and muddle through, everything will work out splendidly. Only now our intrepid scientists are laboring as we speak to create robot bodies and nanobrains. The kind of scientific evangelism we are smothered in these days has troubling precedents: both the Nazis and the Communists proffered Scientism as a salvational force meant to displace traditional religion. Scientism has the inbuilt advantage of turning all attention back to the State, which completely controls and dictates the course of science, both through its own infrastructure and that of its propaganda outlets such as *National Geographic*.

It all seems a little too late now. I don't know how much of this the rubes are buying. We all see how unfair and unequal society has become, all the more so over the past five years or so. No less a firebrand than Chris Rock said that if normal working people saw how rich celebrities lived, there'd be a revolution.

No one really believes that ordinary folk will ever benefit from all of this technology, and some of us don't really believe that this technology is ever coming to market. Certainly not in the form it's being evangelized. Even so, the New Dispensationalists are out there, telling us all we're inevitably evolving into technological super-beings. This nonsense from the Royal Society reveals the type of delusional thinking at work:

> British astrophysicist and cosmologist, Sir Martin Rees, believes if we manage to detect aliens, it will not be by stumbling across organic life, but from picking up a signal made by machines. Writing for *Nautilus*, Sir Martin said that while the way we think has led to all culture and science on Earth, it will be a brief precursor to more powerful machine 'brains'. He thinks that life away from Earth has probably already gone through this transition from organic to machine.

Make no mistake, this is *religion*. It's based on absolutely nothing at all, no science, no data, no observation. It's just an opinion based on a linear, progressive model of human history that is really not that much different than the Dispensationalist model of History unfolding towards Revelation.

But let's humor this credentialed fantasy for a moment. What happens to this glorious race of cyborgs when the Sun has a momentary case of indigestion and shoots a random solar flare at our shiny new Borgworld? We almost found out when we nearly hit by a devastating solar storm in 2012. Can you imagine all of the electronics in your body suddenly seizing up and shitting the bed? Bye-bye, Borgworld, Hello, Flintstones.

This is apparently such a concern that bogus articles are being pumped on search engines, reassuring tech consumers that all is well, resulting in headlines like this: *"Strong solar storm won't fry electronics."* But in a stunning example of how duplicitous the propaganda that consumers are constantly bombarded with is, the soothing headline was definitely contradicted halfway down the body text of the article itself: *"The US government regards the possibility of major solar storm as a 'black swan'. A event that could be calamitous."*

What's more, there's a growing body of evidence that technology in fact is having a *devolutionary* effect on human physiology. The published data is damning, but it's not being discussed in the major media, itself increasingly the property of the major technology concerns. Here's a headline for you: "How the Internet is making us stupid."

> In a recent experiment at Stanford University, researchers gave various cognitive tests to 49 people who do a lot of media multitasking and 52 people who multitask much less frequently. The heavy multitaskers performed poorly on all the tests. They were more easily distracted, had less control over their attention, and were much less able to distinguish important information from trivia.

The science is already in: our intellectual lives have already been decimated. And now we have more data to mull over: all across the board, all across the world, IQ levels are *dropping*. Now some clinicians are also wondering if smartphones are also making young people mentally ill, leading to an increase in suicides.

There is also an alarming rise in autoimmune disorders, including those effecting the nervous system. Aside from the usual culprits such as our horrible food, could electromagnetic pollution be a silent cause of this troubling epidemic? Some studies seem to point to that probability.

In the sales driven world of Technohype and Scientistic evangelism, everything is always looking brighter, and everyone's lives are always getting better. In the real world, nearly every negative trend you can wave a stick at is on the rise. Blind allegiance to Scientism will not save us, and the promises coming out of the hype machine are all looking increasingly hollow.

ALL OUR FUTURE YESTERDAYS

THE OPERATING PHILOSOPHY BEHIND MY WORK is that pop culture is always more resonant when it addresses spiritual issues or wields some variety of spiritual power. The more interesting the particular spirituality in question, the more interesting the art. Hence, Jack Kirby is more interesting than Steve Ditko, Led Zeppelin is more interesting than Deep Purple, David Bowie is more interesting than Elton John, Philip K. Dick is more interesting than Isaac Asimov and *The X-Files* is more interesting than *Law & Order*. And William Gibson is more interesting than all of his Cyberpunk contemporaries.

Nihilism is all the rage in hipster circles these days, which is why absolutely nothing new or interesting is coming out of that culture. 'Hipster' now basically refers to a subculture in which the empty obsessiveness of geekdom is applied to cultural artifacts once reserved for the 'cool' people. In that light, hipsters might want to make sure they don't take any time to investigate the world-views of their icons, lest they notice the conspicuous lack of Bill Nye/Amazing Randi-type thinking among their favorite artists. Even Beck, who arguably first planted the hipster meme into the mainstream back in the early Nineties, is a devout Scientologist.

Philip K. Dick is the hippest sci-fi icon going these days. But the very same people who carefully display unread copies of his books — alongside their unplayed copies of *Fun House* and *Sketches of Spain* — for their poseur friends go out of their way to mock his beliefs and experiences. Why? Because they can't even begin to understand them. Most of them have never darkened the door of a house of worship, and mocking non-atheists isn't just sport, it's one of the few genuine means of self-identification they have left. Their atheism isn't a philosophy of any meaningful sort, it's simply an empty status marker.

William Gibson isn't nearly as *de rigeur* as Dick, but his work is every bit as infused with spirituality, if not in a less-ostentatious fashion. With Gnostic spirituality as well, though far less self-consciously. Maybe even unconsciously: Gibson's had an enormous influence on the Transhumanist cult, most notably in the *Matrix* extravaganza, but the Wachowskis didn't really understand Gibson's gnosis. Gibson's cyberspace wasn't the prison, it was the *escape* from the prison. It was a place of endless freedom and possibility.

Which of course means that these stories were all written long before the Internet was available to anyone outside of university computer labs, by a guy who did his writing on a manual typewriter. But Gibson's obsession with dislocation and artificial environments ties into the Gnostic desire to escape the Demiurge's world. Preferably into the Pleroma, but escape into a self-created world would surely be a nice consolation prize.

And unlike the stereotypical image of the lone seeker often associated with Gnosticism (and common in Gibson's fiction), the deep feelings of alienation that the Gnostic harbor could also act as an epoxy for alternative community. Under the right conditions, at least.

In Gibson's *Neuromancer*, two AIs seek apotheosis, to become self-sustaining intelligences within the Matrix. Having achieved that, the AIs then take on the personas of Voodoo Loa in *Count Zero*, guises which allow them to interact with the alienated yet gifted outsiders the AIs need to further their evolution. In other words, memes taken from the ancient Mystery religions re-enter the Gnostic world via Gibson's Sprawl Trilogy, mirroring the ancient syncretism in which Abraxas and Horus and Hermes Trismegistus all morphed into one another, like some old Michael Jackson video.

That's all fine and good but who cares, right? Well, it may well turn out that constructing safe havens within Cyberspace might be the only escape available for the foreseeable future. Whatever the motivation, more and more people are living inside their electronics. That's a fact of life which you can love or hate, just like you can love or hate the tides, or the movements of the tectonic plates. For me the point is whether those devices are expanding or contracting their reality. The point is whether we are using these tools for liberation or enslavement.

Like the Loa in *Count Zero*, I see spiritual language as a useful code for a pragmatic rewriting of the human OS. I don't want to deny the laws of Nature, I just want to expand our understanding of them, and if necessary, hack them. In other words, Gibson's appropriation of the language of mysticism is useful to our assimilation of technology, and the mythology of his sci-fi can give your understanding and application of the Cyberpunk technology we now have access to a near *apotheosis* of a boost.

The problem isn't necessarily the technology, it's the human robots that are using it. If you believe you have a better way, it's up to you to prove it and deprogram those robots around you into fully-functioning human beings.

PRISONERS OF THE ATOM

I N THE 1960S, HUNDREDS OF THOUSANDS OF PEOPLE were employed in the state of California in and around the space program. These were very good paying jobs that raised families in upper middle class comfort, creating a new gold rush to a new American dream.

Today, California drags a screaming nation into a new Feudal nightmare, a bifurcated garrison state in which a small cognitive elite squat like gargoyles atop a vast ocean of poverty. The state has become so segregated by class and race that most upper-class Californians have no idea their duchy is the poorest in the nation.

It all began to fall apart in the early 1970s, when the Apollo program ended and NASA's sights were set ever lower. Thousands of jobs were lost, beginning a middle class exodus from California that rages on to this day. Apollo skeptics have gleefully pointed out that every mission since the moon landings were low earth orbit shuttle missions, the proverbial walk around the block in outer space terms. But the incredible cost (and danger) of space in relation to benefit — and the bludgeoning recession and oil shocks of the 1970s — made the numbing yet practical (*someone* has to maintain all those spy satellites) shuttle program a gimme for Congress.

Now PayPal billionaire Elon Musk is trying to rekindle the old rocket flames. His SpaceX startup has been making a fool of NASA, and has become the hottest name in rocket technology. Others are following his lead, most notably Jeff Bezos with Blue Origin. Musk realizes that you have to do something with all that hardware, so he proposes a Mars mission with all the Red Bull-fueled gumption of a Silicon Valley startup.

But there's a force not even a Valley whiz kid can resist and that's the power of entropy. We are so used to rapid-fire technological and scientific progress, we're not going to know what to do now that the rate of progress is grinding to a halt. Some believe we've picked all the low-hanging fruit, that all the big, breakthroughs have been made. And now humanity is like late-period REM or U2; continuing to record and tour long after the blockbusters have come and gone, watching the audience age, watching the returns diminish.

I recently read Jacques Vallée's memoirs of his time during the heady days of Silicon Valley and it was shocking to me how much of the great gizmos we see as modern triumphs were all in prototype long before most of you were born. What is touted as the apple of the American economy these days? Well, there's Facebook, which is just a souped-up America Online, itself just a fancier version of the old dial-up BBS systems in use for decades.

We've all seen the videos from the Sixties, showing off the prototypes of the Internet as we know it today. Forty years ago Silicon Valley was putting the basic architecture into place. What are they doing out there today? Besides creating hedge-fund pillage-ware and Facebook games, I mean?

THE TWENTY-FIRST CENTURY LOOKS NOTHING like I imagined it would back when I was a kid. But back then we didn't realize that gravity, entropy, and rapacity would get such a big megaphone in the big campaign. Another Internet whiz kid, Peter Thiel, has diagnosed the problem. We've had great success in the world of electrons, but not so much in the world of atoms: "*We wanted flying cars, instead we got 140 characters,*" Thiel says.

This speaks to a theme I've been banging on all along. Just because something exists on paper, doesn't necessarily mean it exists *off* of it. Science fiction films conditioned us to expect a lot of great things that require massive expenditures of resources that simply make them untenable. *Star Trek* can't exist without energy, not to mention light-speed travel that goes way beyond most physicist's wildest speculations. A lot of people want to believe that the technology exists, it's just being hidden. Maybe yes, maybe no. But it's of no use to us either way.

And then there's the inconvenient fact that we had a big, quick burst of creativity after a very, very long period of technological stasis (17th Century AD technology really isn't at all dissimilar to 17th Century BC technology), but now the default setting of 'painfully slow, incremental progress' seems to be reasserting itself. That's a place no one ever really wants to be.

Air travel is nearly identical today as it was in the 1960s; in fact many 1960s airframes are still in use. Some cars drive themselves, some use electricity, but they still don't fly, and electric cars were first conceived over a hundred years ago anyway. Hovercraft are still not consumer products. Some of the futuristic technology that actually does make it to market fails simply because it's simply unnecessary, or offers an awkward consumer experience. Google Glass has been discontinued, to name one example.

You may have noticed you don't hear much about Transhumanism lately. Again, another case of a concept failing when it got to the application stage. The Singularity certainly may come one day, but unless major breakthroughs are made — breakthroughs that require sums of money there's no real evidence are being spent — it will come and go without us.

And who really wants to go first when it comes to being carved up like a turkey in hopes of some theoretical digital immortality? I think we'll still be fragile bags of meat for the foreseeable future, subject to the same limitations that our ancestors were. And a few new ones, probably.

ARTISANAL APOCALYPSE

HAVE YOU HEARD ABOUT THE LATEST FAD TO HIT SILICON VALLEY? It seems that Transhumanist Singularity is out, and Y2K-styled doomsday apocalypticism is in. Yes, the overpaid *machers* of the Machine Age are suddenly hot on Survivalism. And they approach the art of Armageddon with the same zest, zeal − and cash − that they set about creating apps to destroy your jobs and futures. So are you ready for artisanal apocalypticism?

Before you answer, let's look carefully at what these people are doing. They're not uniting to save humanity and stave off the breakdown of society with all the vast wealth and political power and influence that this country has showered on them. They're fixing to take the money and run, because they believe the breakdown of society is imminent. At heart, they're still the same cowardly little nerds that they always were.

But what are they afraid is leading to the breakdown of society? Why, the very technologies that they are shoving down everyone's throats! They're afraid that all the good-paying jobs they've either destroyed or outsourced will lead to anti-oligarch sentiment and "a turn against technological innovation," as one well-known huckster put it. To which I'd say that the country has every right to turn against "technical innovation" if it takes away their livelihoods. Why shouldn't they?

What do people now see in Silicon Valley, from all these people who asked for our trust and promised a bright new tomorrow? A bunch of rats ready to jump ship as soon as their robots have destroyed our economies! How long do they think they can hide from what they've done to us? How long before the law of the jungle takes hold and they're cowering for mercy before their alpha-male security teams?

SILICON VALLEY SURVIVALISM COULD BE SEEN as just another fad of people with too much money and too much justifiable guilt on their hands. Transhumanism and uploading and all the rest of it went nowhere - like most sane people knew it would - and this might be the next escapist fantasy on the bucket list. Maybe it will all die down. Maybe that *New Yorker* piece will embarrass the survivalists to sanity, and Calexit will be the next big crusade to embark on (God willing, for the good of the rest of the country). But it should be noted that this movement comes at the tail end of an eight-year orgy of esteem for the Valley, when they essentially had the run of the White House.

All that unparalleled money and power and still they feel the icy breath of paranoia on their necks? How can this possibly be? They should be bathing in milk and rose petals, and lighting their bongs with $100 dollar bills, no?

But maybe the bigger issue here is the constant need to reinvent the wheel, to bow down to the false god of efficiency. Maybe we need to stop allowing the bottom line to drive the course of technology, and develop technologies that feel freeing and invisible, rather than overbearing and ubiquitous.

That's why I can't help but wonder if this rash of Survivalism is really just a manifestation of a collective guilty conscience. The Techlords' Tomorrowland never opened, and never will (outside of Dubai, at least). If AIs flush a lot of clever people like lawyers, doctors and accountants from the economy, do they really think those people won't seek revenge? Or, for Heaven's sake, *truck drivers?* How deep a hole do these neo-Survivalist rats really want to dig?

We don't *need* AI. We can get along fine without robots. This world ran perfectly fine before Uber, and AirBNB, and iPhones, and all the rest of it. Come to think of it, the world got along fine without computers and the Internet, as ironic as it may be for me to admit that. The laws of Karma still stand: bad actions lead to bad results. Technology hasn't changed that, and it never will.

THE MANDATE OF HEAVEN

A S I WRITE THIS, THERE WAS A DEVASTATING CAR BOMB attack in Baghdad, ostensibly blamed on Islamic State. This news comes while I've been reading countless texts talking about the *centuries* of slaughter that took place in the very same places we are seeing it today.

Thousands of years ago, in the very same place, a Babylonian court poet would call on the fire-god Girra in protest of similar types of carnage in a famous epic poem of the time. Despite the fiery connotation, Girra was not a devil, he was the "Firstborn son of God" and the "Shepherd of Mankind," who was "The Door," that blocked the gods of war. He was even called on *to drive out demons.* Yet, it so happened that this poet's petitions were never answered.

Reading all this historical material I am thunderstruck by how familiar it all seems. The Sumerians, Akkadians, and Babylonians all thought they enjoyed the Mandate of Heaven, perhaps more than anyone else in history. Until they suddenly didn't. Same way Rome was 'the Eternal City' until it wasn't.

And now a lot smarter people than myself believe that the current political, social, and economic arrangements are unsustainable. I think most intelligent people agree that if we continue on the roads we are on, all of these social and political trends are all leading us to wide-scale civil conflict. And possibly worse.

This is especially relevant in the wake of Brexit, which too many people seem to think was a populist uprising, and not the brutal calculation of British business elites chafing under the yoke of the EU's Byzantine regulatory regime. Either way, the Rubicon has been crossed and Europe's troubles have only just begun. Not to mention NATO's, which festers in the shadow of Russia and China's rise as serious military powerhouses, and the subsequent collapse of most of Europe's military capabilities. This at a time when serious questions are being raised about the rolling pork-fest that we call the US defense budget.

There are a lot of people predicting the dawn of a new Dark Age anyway, for many parts of the world at least, that systems are always inherently fragile and subject to collapse, and that there are simply too many pressures on them already, that breakdown is inevitable.

T HINK ABOUT THIS: AT SOME POINT, HACKERS, probably state-sponsored, are going to unleash not a virus, but an *Artificial Intelligence* on the Internet with one simple command: *"Crash everything you can."* I'm sure there are programmers working on algorithms designed to crash Facebook, Google, Apple, and Netflix as we speak. At some point, this is going to happen. It's inevitable. It may even work.

Similarly, I can't help but wonder if there is a force at work deliberately trying to crash the neoliberal Capitalist world order from within, attacking it from its Left rather than the Right, or if it's finally succumbing to its own contradictions. Maybe there's a very good reason hedge-fund billionaires are buying remote island getaways. I know we all want to believe that the elites know what they're doing, and it will all work out somehow. But maybe they don't know shit. Maybe they've been bluffing all along.

As intractable as many beliefs and attitudes might seem at the moment, or how powerful certain arrangements, institutions or alliances may appear, History teaches us that once open conflicts begin many of them will shift radically, and many will actually dissolve, literally overnight. What makes sense in an aura of relative peace and prosperity falls away when civil war and economic disaster strike. Or as Mike Tyson once said, "Everyone has a plan until they get punched in the face."

We're already seeing a return to an archaic kind of paganism, not the happy-funtime LARP variety of the alleged neopagans, but the grim paganism of Santa Muerte and the Wotanist sects. The old-time paganism where things get *killed*. This may be humanity's default setting. A careful reading of history probably backs that up. Suddenly, the demon-haunted nights of ancient Mesopotamia seem relevant again.

OUR MYTHIC HISTORY IS FILLED WITH MORALLY AMBIGUOUS figures offering us technology, particularly rebellious figures like Prometheus (a Titan) and Semjaza (an Angel), but even more established figures such as Hermes, Cadmus, and Osiris, the civilizing forces of the ancient world. But there's always been a shadow side to these figures, speaking to our desire to return to an Edenic innocence. The common denominator is that the figure who is a teacher of actual practical techniques with which to improve the human condition, not just abstract philosophies or spiritual dogma, *is never really completely trustworthy*. These characters are something we seem to have mixed feelings about, and always have.

But Osiris and Cadmus have a lot more in common with Prometheus and Semjaza than one might think at first. Osiris, the civilizer, got pretty messed up himself by Set, who came to represent authority when he took the throne. Afterwards, Osiris became a figure of eternal judgment, leaving all the nurturing to Isis. Another way of looking at it is that Osiris became *the King of Hell*. Similarly, Cadmus was punished by Zeus for killing the Dragon of Mars and condemned to spend eternity as a serpent, in much the same way as the Serpent in the Garden was cursed by Deus to crawl on his belly for leading Adam and Eve to the fruit of the Tree of Knowledge. The parallels between the two narratives could fill a really boring academic treatise.

Hermes himself would often use his bag of tricks against the gods' authority on *our* behalf. In some ways, Hermes could be said to be a rebel himself in that he was willing to bargain, to cut deals, to work magic with us, all away from Olympia's all-seeing eye. But at the same time Hermes was never to be entirely trusted. He had a devilish streak all his own. Then as now, there was an ambivalence about this process and an ambivalence towards science and technology in general. Which certainly don't have all that great a track record when it comes to creating human suffering.

TECHNOLOGY IS THE DEFINING STANDARD OF POWER of our time, and so the future struggles over the Mandate of Heaven will be over technologies, or more concisely, systems of knowledge. Yet somehow we're seeing that same technology having a devastating effect on human intelligence and competence. This is exactly what I warned Timothy Leary about back in 1993 when he was going around hawking virtual reality. I told Leary that the more people immerse themselves in virtual environments, the less they would be able to function in the real world. Leary got very angry at me over this, but this recent "adulting" theme has proven me right. Young people who are whizzes on their smartphones but can't boil an egg or drive a car have become kind of a joke, but it's not really funny if you want to sustain a functional civilization.

This ties back to the question of human evolution, which not only makes no sense in relation to all the other animals on the planet but has no actual internal logic either. Threats, intimidation and harassment help keep most biologists quiet but the gaps are there, they're glaring and only getting worse. We won't even go into the face-punching absurdity of cavemen genetically engineering wild wheat into a usable food crop, but there it is.

And perhaps most glaring of all, our science and technology seem to have an anti-adaptive aspect, in which they encourage us to de-evolve. And they also seem to discourage us from spiritual pursuits, which has a proven historical track record of demographic collapse for cultures that embrace the scientific at the expense of the spiritual.

This goes back to Ancient Greece at the very least, and probably long before. This too might be at the core of our ambiguity towards technology. It's certainly at the core of many traditional societies' briefs against Western Culture. And they have a point.

I also think a lot of powerful people have come to realize that the myth of the Technocratic Utopia that dominates Western thinking now is a mirage and trying to reach it will only end in tears. Actually, I *hope* they do. I'm afraid they don't, and we're going to end up riding their fantasies all the way down to the very last stop.

A DEMON HAUNTED WORLD AFTER ALL

CARL SAGAN'S LANDMARK MANIFESTO, *The Demon-Haunted World: Science as a Candle in the Dark,* marks its twenty-fifth birthday this year, an event it will probably be celebrating mostly by itself. Still, along with others like *The God Delusion, The End of Faith, God is Not Great,* and *Darwin's Dangerous Idea,* it was — for a brief moment — held up as the New Canon, the new Gospels for a worldwide Scientistic Utopia.

Look around you; see any signs of that Utopia out there? Yeah, me neither. In fact, it very much feels like the world is very much haunted by demons these days. In fact, demonic spirits seem to be having the utter run of the place. How did this happen? How did we get here?

Well, there are a lot of reasons for it. But a lot of it stems from a very powerful and very well-funded movement that set out to destroy established religion, yet soon realized it didn't have anything viable to replace it with. And you know what they say, Nature abhors a vacuum.

NÜ SCIENTISM (AKA NÜ ATHEISM) and its praxis Nü Skepticism made a huge splash in the late '00s and early '10s. The movement had a lot of money, a lot of star power, and a lot of media support on their side. *The Demon-Haunted World* was seen as a foundational text, and Sagan himself was seen as a Patriarch to the new faithless faith. Sadly, the crusade was short-lived. A major schism emerged almost immediately between the actual scientists and their camp followers (mostly *I Fucking Love Science*-type amateur bloggers) over the then-nascent/now-dominant Woke theocracy, ultimately resulting in the Atheism+Plus spinoff sect.

The cudgel the Atheism+Plus inquisitors used against their former idols was the Woke moving-goalpost of 'misogyny'. And soon many of the founding fathers of Nü Scientism found themselves dodging sexual harassment claims and others accusations of 'misogyny'. They didn't do so very effectively. Richard Dawkins even started making bizarre apologies for pedophilia (or at least started doing so in public).

There's a great temptation to dismiss all of this intramural drama as simply more entitled Millennial hysteria and the bitterness of disillusioned groupies, but the Atheism+Plus movement actually did the world a tremendous favor when it threw back the curtain on who was one of the biggest hands pulling the levers on Nü Scientism.

And that, of course, was none other than the late, unlamented Jeffrey Edward Epstein.

Epstein's money was the driving force behind Nü Scientism and its comic-book corollaries like Transhumanism. Along with Bill Gates and other paranoid billionaire sociopaths, Epstein funded Transhumanist associations and Transhumanist-adjacent research at major universities, to the tune of tens of millions of dollars. Epstein also courted and financed many of the leading figures in Nü Scientism, and held conferences to court Nü Scientismists and parties to raise cash for them.

This vast network of dark money and media influence fed a constant stream of propaganda to the credulous children who've been manning the science desks at major media outlets since the 2007 financial crisis swept away all the real journalists.

In that light, do notice that the Nü Scientism and Nü Atheist movements began to flounder when Epstein started getting hammered by lawsuits from his former sex-slaves around 2014-2015. Coincidence? Sure. I mean, if you believe in coincidences.

Before all that there was Carl Sagan and his *Demon-Haunted World.* The book got a lot of hype in 1995, but not quite so much love in the sales department. But it was a easy, breezy read and so was clung tight to the bosom of aspiring atheists and skeptics.

T HERE'S NO QUESTION THAT SAGAN WAS A BRILLIANT MAN. He possessed an extremely sharp mind and was an agile pitchman for Big Science® in the mass media. Ironically, his sales skills are actually a bit unlikely given that he originally plied his trade as an astronomer/astrophysicist/cosmologist, so-called "pure sciences" with zero practical use for anyone who isn't an astronomer, astrophysicist or cosmologist. Still, his *Cosmos* series was a big hit for PBS, and as long as there are school field trips, there'll be a market for that kind of thing.

Sagan took on a whole host of demons in his *Demon-Haunted* book, but UFOlogy seemed to be his primary bugaboo, since it was the biggest deal at the time. So much so that legions of his fellow Scientismists were trying to ride the gravy train by publishing anti-UFO books, some of which disguised their real agenda on the dust jackets. I doubt a lot of people were fooled, but a lot of kids probably got them as crappy presents from their least favorite aunts.

B ut Sagan also threw down with mediums, Cryptozoology, Psi, the Face on Mars, NDEs, hypnotherapy, channeling, and all the rest of the late-Eighties/early-Nineties catalog of New Age and Fringe beliefs and practices. Hard to remember a time when you could expect to get on the best-seller list going after such things, but Carl Sagan helped construct this timeline we're stuck in today. So, you know; *karma.*

M IND YOU, THE WORLD SAGAN WAS TALKING ABOUT was a much different world than our own. Christianity was certainly waning, but was still held in wide esteem, at least theoretically. You saw the rise of megachurches, the Promise Keepers and pseudo-Christian cultic movements like Prosperity Gospel, and most survey respondents would have claimed to believe in God. The average voter was generally more conservative, in large part due to the booming economy and childbirth rates. Baby Boomers were coming into power, but didn't quite have the maniacal death-grip they got on everything when they seized the controls in the Bush II-Obama Administration.

UFOs were peaking as a popular phenomenon: TV shows like *Sightings* and *Unsolved Mysteries* did regular segments on them, *The X-Files* was gaining ground in the Nielsen ratings, and UFO conventions were held all around the US on a regular basis. UFOs were also bleeding into the militia and apocalyptic cult undergrounds. Bill Cooper published *Behold a Pale Horse* in 1991 and it soon became a foundational text for a strange blend of religion, militarism and fringe politics brewing in Middle America.

Moreover, the New Age movement and its offshoots were still seen as weird and cultish by the mainstream, unlike today where the New Age is so inter-woven into the mainstream that no one even notices it exists anymore. You certainly wouldn't have *The New York Times* actively promoting witchcraft back then, like we do now. So Sagan might have been throwing a lot of shade, but could be reasonably confident the Establishment would have his back.

Moreover, events in the wake of the publication of *Demon-Haunted World* seemed to vindicate Sagan's thesis: the Solar Temple and Heaven's Gate mass suicides, Oklahoma City, the Aum Shinrikyo terror attacks, just to name a few.

U NFORTUNATELY, SAGAN WOULDN'T BE ALIVE to bask in a lot of this validation, dying of cancer in December of 1996. But by the same token, Sagan wouldn't be alive for what's going on now, with the rise of Woke, the mainstreaming of the occult and the beating that the science establishment has been taking about its trustworthiness and credibility. Nor would he see his first wife and son wander far off the Reductionist reservation when it came to hot-button topics like AIDS and 9/11.

Nor would Sagan have been alive for the Fall of the House of Epstein, which took a lot of his famous friends down with it.

STRANGE CONTAGIONS

EVERYTHING OLD IS NEW AGE AGAIN

THOUGH I DIDN'T REALIZE IT AT THE TIME, the New Age movement was my entry point into the World of Weird some 30 years ago. It was also an object lesson in how the sandblasting power of consumer culture can reshape everything into its own image. It may seem like a weird detour to be writing about the New Age in these apocalyptic times, but I hope to convince you that it's anything but.

First, the news: Despite decades of derision and scorn from the media and academia, the New Age population — classified in polls as 'Spiritual But Not Religious' (SBNRs) — now outnumber Jews, Muslims and the dying 'Mainline' Protestant sects, according to a new poll published in *The New York Times.*

This latest poll is especially fascinating because I distinctly remember Pat Buchanan triumphantly crowing about a similar poll back in 1987 that counted the SBNRs as being 'statistically insignificant', or at less than one-percent of those surveyed. My, oh my, how things have changed.

IF YOU READ THE MAINSTREAM MEDIA YOU'D THINK that Western civilization is on an inevitable march towards a bright, godless future. This may be true inside the hyper-privileged bubble that the media elite and their friends travel in, the bubble that insulates them almost entirely from the effects of the real world. Outside this bubble, religion is not only on the march, it's literally on the warpath. Its most certainly winning the war of the cradle; in fact, atheism seems to have surrendered that battlefield entirely.

The new New Age is filling the void left by a rapidly-aging Fundamentalist movement, now in steep decline in the US. George W. Bush's glorious promises of Armageddon in the shadow of Mystery Babylon itself gave the movement a jumpstart, but it all fell apart when his wars went sideways.

Today, most of the major Evangelical leaders are dead or retired, and the popular megachurch preachers are predominantly Prosperity Gospel hucksters who have no real interest in politics. The face of American Christianity is increasingly a brown face, and the face of American atheism is almost exclusively white, which leads one to wonder (though you don't have to wonder much) what motivations are being left unsaid. You can look at Tumblrs and Instagrams of atheist meetings — such as James Randi's Amaz!ng Meetings - and count the nonwhite faces on one hand, if at all.

But scandal and schism has shattered the skeptic movement, and many of its major stars being accused of rape and sexual harassment. The old line and the new feminist atheists are now openly at war with each other.

Jeffrey Epstein, one of the top bankrollers of the movement, was imprisoned for having sex with minors. A major skeptic celebrity was convicted in federal court on a huge eBay fraud rap. The list goes on and on (and on), but you get the point. What it all boils down to is that these movements were never going to be ready for prime time. They have peaked, despite their uncritical audience within the media itself.

SO NOW YOU'RE ASKING, what the hell does this have to do with a bunch of housewives noshing on quinoa and perfecting their lotus positions? The question is its own answer in a way, because the New Age is *everywhere* now. Yoga studios and health food stores are as ubiquitous as hair salons and hardware stores in middle class neighborhoods. Various New Age therapists and consultants can be found in professional buildings in more upscale burgs, advocating the benefits of meditation in the form of 'mindfulness'. Even Christian churches see the value in yoga, meditation and health food.

This latest incarnation of the New Age is ubiquitous precisely because it is amorphous and essentially doctrine-less. It's a somatic regimen disguised as a spiritual movement (and vice-versa). The New Age is less a coherent movement than a totalizing thought-contagion. Kind of a model for the current phenomenon of corporate giants who sell nothing but recycled data.

On the plus side, the new New Agers are middle-class, health-conscious and despite stereotypes to the contrary, politically engaged. On the down side, the new New Agers are prone to elitism, solipsism and an insufferably preachy neo-Puritanism, which I saw a lot of at Esalen.

The current state of the movement is the result of a deliberate colonization effort of a tiny, amorphous, post-hippie, neo-Theosophist subculture by the most important family in America. This process began in 1985 after the death of Esalen co-founder Dick Price, which was followed by the takeover of the institute by a clutch of corporate types, led by Starbucks exec Steven Donovan.

And as much as it's anyone's, Esalen is a Rockefeller project. Rockefeller money helped build Esalen, sustain it, and grow it. It helped rebuild it after various crises. The Rockefeller in question was the late Laurance Rockefeller, whose very, very deep pockets helped build a New Age Empire in California, including Esalen, the San Francisco Zen Center, the Lindisfarne Association, the Institute of Noetic Sciences, and the California Institute of Integral Studies.

This isn't surprising; nothing gets done in this country without people with deep pockets behind it. But it might explain why the New Age movement is so arid and inert and unthreatening: it was engineered that way. What remains to be seen is what course this movement will take in the future, particularly if current economic, social and global crises continue to worsen.

Despite all this money and pressure, I'm sure your Facebook newsfeed is filled with New Agers who, despite the dated stereotypes, leaven their Rumi and Eckhart Tolle quotes with memes about GMOs, chemtrails, the Federal Reserve, the NSA and so and so forth. And of course, New Agers are more open than the population at large to UFOs and ancient astronauts and all the rest.

There are some who believe that the New Age is simply a symptom of a self-centered, superficial culture. Certainly, the movement has cycled through a series of spiritual dabblings like kids through a toy box — Buddhist, 'Celtic', Native American, channeling, angels, *Da Vinci Code*-type neo-Medievalism — before stepping away from nearly all of it to concentrate on self-improvement, health, yoga and other purely somatic pursuits.

A REMARKABLY SIMILAR SITUATION TO TODAY was seen in the early Nineteenth Century, with proto-New Age groups such as the Transcendentalists and the Oneida Society. There were any number of weird sects, with strange notions about health and diet, that bought up tracts of land and formed short-lived communities across New England and New York. Most of these groups were small and weird, and had no real impact. It wouldn't be until the Apocalypse came in the form of the War Between the States that the first New Age movement — Spiritualism — would take off like a rocket.

It's said that Spiritualism became so powerful a force because so many Americans had lost loved ones during that horrific conflict that the need to 'commune with the dead' became too powerful for the Church to stand in its way. But it would be Madame Blavatsky who would understand that Spiritualism was nothing without a creed, and so was Theosophy was born.

Blavatsky attracted the cream of New York society (Thomas Edison himself was a Theosophist) and created such a powerful tidal wave that we still base all of our science fiction and fantasy on the work of people initially inspired the explosion set off by the Madame: Edgar Rice Burroughs, Arthur Conan Doyle, HP Lovecraft, Robert E. Howard and many, many more. It would be Theosophists who would bring Buddhism to the West, which would have a profound effect on culture to this day. So powerful was the effect of Theosophy that even Gandhi himself was drawn into its orbit (as were other key Indian nationalists). Still believe there's nothing to this?

So while New Age may seem inert, harmless and nearly meaningless, outside of describing a personal inclination, it has by its amorphous nature changed the world in its image in the past three decades. It's impossible to call it a religion in credal sense (remember 'Spiritual but not Religious') because there is no fixed creed, no theology, no doctrine. But there certainly is an infrastructure in place, thanks to the Rockefellers. And they seem to prefer a toothless, inert New Age.

I don't think the new New Agers will ever become the 'One World Religion' of Evangelical fever dreams, but I do think they have become a force to be reckoned with. Whether or not the movement breaks out of its current demographic is dependent on who emerges as a leader. Then all bets are off.

Having seen the Elizabeth Clare Prophet organization during its Eighties peak, I've seen how authoritarian Theosophy and the New Age can get when working in concert with fringe politics. With our present age serving no one but a tiny handful, the appeal of a 'new age' could be unimaginably powerful. The type of people who are now 'Spiritual but not Religious' are the kind of people who you could build a movement with. And perhaps once it begins to slake those vague spiritual longings with powerful religious ideas, they could use that movement to build an army.

Don't think for a moment history has no precedent for such a thing.

I'M NOT REALLY A HUGE FAN OF THE NEW AGE, but very few New Agers will ever admit to the label. It often seems like the hallmark of a New Ager is denying they're 'New Age'. Yet here I sit on this blog dedicated to topics that booksellers would put in the New Age section without a moment's hesitation, listening to ambient music on SomaFM, preparing and eating vegetarian food I bought at Trader Joe's and Whole Foods. Later, I'll take a break and do my daily meditations, not because they're 'New Age' or not, but because they work for me.

So even though I tend to shun the New Age movement for its lack of content and discernment (and the endless elite manipulations it's always been the medium for), I am forced to acknowledge its Borg-like power.

I'm certainly not alone, the Internet is full of people who occupy some corner of the New Age but will actually criticize or even outright attack the New Age. The Great Invisible New Age Mother Church doesn't seem to mind. You can slam the New Age one minute and then advance the cause of UFOs or alternative health modalities the next. Go right ahead. Actions speak so much louder than words. Namasté.

Resistance may very well be futile, given the New Age's whatever-it-takes pragmatism and seemingly-endless capacity to adapt and mutate. Its lack of recognized leadership, dogma, and creed make it hard to track but also very hard to *target*.

Which is to say that the New Age movement's amorphous nature and something-for-everyone variety make it immensely appealing for a culture tired of fifty years of hypocritical Evangelical hectoring, but not quite ready to follow so much of Europe into the nihilist graveyard.

IT MIGHT SEEM AS IF THERE ARE SERIOUS HEADWINDS for the movement, with the rise of Islam and campus radicalism and so on. But these aren't new phenomena either. Refugees from the collapse of campus radicalism in the Seventies and Nineties actually fed into the New Age's growth. And considering the fragile mental state of today's so-called 'social justice warriors', the New Age will probably find a new influx of adherents when these movements inevitably collapse to infighting and organized resistance. Some might argue the seeds are already being planted now.

The New Age seemed to grow and grow while nobody was looking and now it's literally everywhere, even implanted inside the sanctuaries of its former enemies. American New Agers are more numerous than any sect aside from Catholicism yet hardly any would identify themselves as such.

In a funny kind of way, it reminds me of *Invasion of the Body Snatchers*: people you've known and least suspect will become followers of some New Age practice or another, sometimes precipitated by a health or personal crisis. They won't see themselves as being any different, but over time they will inevitably become distinctly New Age (though some people might say this is a case of pot and kettle).

I should mention here that the scariest (and best) version of *Invasion of the Body Snatchers* — meaning the 1978 version with Donald Sutherland, Jeff Goldblum, and Leonard Nimoy — was in fact a dark satire of the original New Age movement.

THE FLAT EARTH AND OTHER STRANGE NEW REBELLIONS

T HE LONG-HELD PREJUDICE AGAINST SCIENCE FICTION literature is not totally unjustified. This is especially true of the kind of science fiction written before the reformist movements of the 1960s and 1970s, as well as later forms such as Cyberpunk. Mind you, I don't see SF as a viable literary form any longer. Like comic books, it's become a hobby-circle medium, mostly consumed by people who also produce it, or would like to.

And as much as I might have enjoyed some of the storylines and concepts of writers like Arthur C. Clarke, he was incapable of writing recognizably human characters. This is not to single Clarke out; he was a veritable expert on human nature compared to an Isaac Asimov, say, or a Ben Bova.

Even William Gibson misunderstands the reactions regular people have to the ubiquity of technology. The more ubiquitous and invasive technology becomes, the more most people *resent* it, not fetishize it. People are addicted to their iPhones and other gadgets, but they're just mediums; it's the content that most people fixate on, not the technology itself. In fact, studies have shown people are becoming increasingly technologically illiterate too, as our gadgets become more powerful.

One of the worries of the establishment media (which is to say the government, since outlets like the major networks, *The New York Times, National Geographic,* and major magazines and newspapers are merely echo chambers for the government) is the so-called 'Anti-Science movement'. This is a meaningless blanket term, since there are any number of divergent and mutually-hostile movements put under this umbrella.

But what the government's puppet-heads are *really* worried about are people who don't accept the dictates of government and/or corporate science unquestioningly. This is a particular concern since the stink of corruption in corporate and academic science has gotten so overwhelming — the peer review system has become a total joke, for instance — that the mainstream media can no longer ignore it.

In fact, many of the so-called 'Anti-Science' people have done a lot more actual science on their pet causes than the *I Fucking Love Science* drones, who usually don't do anything but post stupid memes on their Facebook. Most of them couldn't explain the scientific method to you if you held a gun to their heads. Science is just a substitute religion for them, which is to say *government* science.

Which itself is just another way of saying they actually worship governmental <u>power</u>, and a vindictive and totalizing power at that.

T HE TOTALITARIAN CONTROL EXERCISED OVER SCIENTISTS today is much worse than anything scientists had to deal with from, say, the Medieval Church. In fact, the whole notion that the Church went around smashing science down where ever it found it really is just a stupid myth. But go and question the party line on global warming, or any of the other new orthodoxies today, and your career in science will be destroyed in a heartbeat.

As government and corporate power exercise increasing control over science, they've branded any dissent or opposition as 'anti-scientific'. This has become one of the countless slurs you hear coming from progressives, who depressingly have become the absolute mirror image of the Religious Right of the 1980s and 1990s, only infinitely more powerful and vindictive.

As the mask comes off and capital 'S' Science reveals itself to be nothing but a submissive lapdog for Globalism, I think we can expect some strange rebellions from the status quo. Most of these will probably be totally marginal, but you never know what's going to pop up and strike a nerve. And so it is that I've spent the past couple of weeks trying to wrap my head around one of the strangest new rebellions, the surprisingly-vigorous revival of the old Flat Earth Movement, a fringe movement that's found a surprisingly large new audience.

Essentially, it goes like this: the Earth is a disk covered by a dome and surrounded a wall of ice that keep the oceans in. The Moon and the Sun orbit the Earth, and the planets are just 'wandering stars'. The space program is a hoax and satellites don't exist. The Apollo missions were faked because space travel is impossible. All the zero-G footage we've seen was done in high-altitude airplanes, the same ones the (fake) astronauts were trained in.

Flat Earth theory tends to be surprisingly Gnostic, in that the planet is a prison and there's no escape. And so the high altitude nuclear tests that the US and USSR undertook in the late 1950s — called Operation Fishbowl, believe it or not — were an attempt to punch holes in the dome but were unsuccessful. The movement also seems to be very anti-UFO, which seems a bit peculiar. If someone built the Earth as a prison, wouldn't they want someone to keep an eye on it?

E VERY MOVEMENT NEEDS A ROCK STAR, and the Flat Earth movement currently has Matt Boylan, a Canadian photorealist painter who claimed to have worked for NASA and been initiated into the secret of secrets at a party. Boylan doesn't offer any evidence for this and his credibility is a bit questionable, given the fact that he pushes the theory with a stand-up comedy act. During which he rolls out the world's worst Denis Leary impersonation. He seems to be a very talented painter, though.

You know me, I love a wild theory. But the main thing I got out of the Flat Earth material was further evidence that NASA is totally full of crap. Flat Earth makes no sense to me, seeing that that the other heavenly bodies are all spheres but the Earth is not. The entire model just didn't ring true to me. But maybe that's just my lifelong conditioning, right?

But I got some fuel for my own fires, namely my own nutty conjectures that if all this NASA stuff is faked, maybe it's because planets like Mars and Venus aren't what they say they are. But I'm the first to admit that's conjecture; I'm not making YouTubes about any of it. And at the end of the day it doesn't even matter if the Earth is flat or round. It doesn't change my experience of the world one single bit.

Flat Earth theorists believe that the globe model is used to diminish the importance of the planet and of humanity, but I didn't really find that argument very compelling, in the same way I don't find the materialist theories that human life is some cosmic accident and everything is meaningless compelling either.

Poking around, I saw a few conspiracy types protest that the entire movement is a psyop, meant to discredit 'Truthers' in general and Apollo skeptics in particular. Boylan's Vaudeville act didn't exactly dissuade me from that argument (one video has him expounding his views while slurping on wedges of grapefruit like a pig, as if he were trying to be as repulsive as possible) and such an operation is business as usual for the Cryptocrats.

But animals in captivity are known to display aberrant behavior and human beings are no different. I expect more of this kind of thing as our lives become more controlled and our horizons continue to shrink.

As to science, I'm old fashioned; I think it should be above politics. Scientists may come to rue the day they all threw in with the Globocrat partisan agenda, no matter how emotionally satisfying it might be to use science as a brickbat against their imagined enemies. And by extension, their schoolyard tormentors.

WHY I AM NOT A MYTHICIST

THE INTERNET HAS SPAWNED AN ENTIRELY NOVEL ECOSYSTEM of autodidactic thought contagions. It seems that when freed of the interference of the gatekeeping power of the mainstream media, ideas that once seemed too weird to even consider can bite down and take a big chunk out of the outer culture.

'Mythicism' or 'Jesus Mythicism', which argues that Jesus never actually existed, is one of those ideas. It's a fringe concept that was taken up by Internet researchers very early on and has made major inroads in this era of 'Nones'. Mythicism is a follow-on of sorts on the work of groups like the Jesus Seminar, liberal theologians who took a scalpel to the Gospels and declared them to be almost-entirely fabricated, based not on collections of Jesus sayings but on literary invention. A kind of one-upmanship, if you will.

On the face of it, the Mythicist argument is pretty compelling. There are no contemporary news accounts of Jesus, and very few independent references in the immediate period following his purported death. Most of the information we have on him comes from biased sources. The accounts in the Gospels are filled with obvious parallels to earlier stories in the Bible and pagan religions. And the dates in the Gospel stories can't always be squared with what we know from recorded Roman history.

But you'd be shocked to find out how little we actually know about many, many historical figures, especially figures from Antiquity. Noted Lovecraft scholar (and former Minister Robert Price) sums up the Mythicist arguments thusly:

> 1. There is no mention of a miracle-working Jesus in secular sources.
>
> 2. The epistles, written earlier than the gospels, provide no evidence of a recent historical Jesus; all that can be taken from the epistles, Price argues, is that a Jesus Christ, son of God, lived in a heavenly realm, there died as a sacrifice for human sin, was raised by God and enthroned in heaven.
>
> 3. The Jesus narrative is paralleled in Middle Eastern myths about dying and rising gods; Price names Baal, Osiris, Attis, Adonis, and Dumuzi/Tammuz as examples, all of which, he writes, survived into the Hellenistic and Roman periods and thereby influenced early Christianity.

No offense to Mr. Price, but I really don't find any of these arguments very compelling. Why?

Let's go in order.

> 1. Scholars will tell you that the region was filled with itinerant preachers and miracle workers. There's no particular reason for one or the other to be recorded, except that he was noticed by a someone who could write. 'Someone' usually being a Roman bureaucrat, who probably couldn't tell any of these characters apart anyway. And there's good reason to believe that Jesus was also leading a *political* rebellion. That alone would be reason for him to be written out of history.

> 2. What this says is that Jesus was the Elvis of his day and was instantly mythologized as soon as he died. This in fact speaks to the power and effectiveness of his ministry, seeing that he was deified even before the Gospels were written.

> 3. Well, of course. He died. And rumors soon spread among his followers that he rose from the dead, a common reaction to such a trauma. And having studied the Mysteries in earnest, I can tell you with utter certainty that the Gospel stories and the Mystery dramas really aren't that similar at all.

Which leads us in an oblique way to perhaps the best-known proponent of Mythicism these days: Joseph Atwill, author of *Caesar's Messiah*. Atwill argues that the Flavian Roman imperial family created Christianity to pacify the militaristic opposition to their rule. Even more incredibly, they placed a literary satire within the Gospels to mark their handiwork.

There's no doubt the Flavian dynasty were deeply involved with the development of Roman Christianity and its eventual elevation as official cult of state, probably from very early on. It's also possible that they took the Gospels — under the sole control of Rome for ten centuries — and worked in a number of in-jokes that spoke to their interference with this religion. However, there were all kinds of other Gospels, stories and collections of Jesus sayings that were not included in the Bible. There was even a major schism in the Jesus movement that is recorded in the Bible itself. We are conditioned to believe those other stories are apocryphal because the Church says so, but we have no other reason to believe they are any less authentic than the Gospels themselves.

Scholars generally tend to dismiss Atwill's arguments that the Judean insurrection was such a military threat that Rome would need to construct a religion to handle them. What the Romans were probably more concerned with were the large number of Jewish converts within the Empire (10% of the population, reportedly) and the reaction they might have to the Judean Wars.

Even so, the Flavian project certainly wasn't universally appreciated in the Roman hierarchy. Though the accounts have been wildly overstated, there were periodic (and often brutal) crackdowns on Christians, right up the beginning of the Fourth Century. So how do we square that? Jesus was clearly mythologized, there can be no argument about that. Real people are mythologized all the time. It doesn't mean they don't exist.

Another prominent Mythicist is the late Dorothy Murdock, AKA Acharya S. Murdock was a brilliant Classical scholar and prodigious writer, but she was also a polemicist who took the work of some extremely questionable historians like Gerald Massey too seriously. Murdock thought that the Apostle Paul was a myth too. In fact, from the apparent coincidences between his life and that of Jesus, it has been suggested by not a few people (including Murdock) that Jesus Christ is a fictional character based in large part on Apollonius of Tyana.

The Jesus-Apollonius parallels are well-known in Biblical studies, and parallels between the two figures have been commented on throughout history (no less a luminary than Voltaire weighed in on the issue). The problem is that Apollonius' story wasn't actually written down until 230 CE or so, and the Jesus stories had been very well-circulated for a long time by that point. Moreover Apollonius' biography was commissioned by Julia Domna, wife of Septimus Severus, AKA the Empress of Rome.

Julia's husband was having a lot of problems with Christians at the time, which I still believe wasn't just a case of the Romans being meanies (Severus seemed to be well-disposed to Christians) but of Christians engaging in acts of sedition against the State (acts which later copyists just happened to overlook in Roman histories). Given Julia's background — and the mess the Empire was in — she may have thought it advantageous to offer up an alternative religion to Christianity for the masses.

F OR A GUY WHO AN INCREASING NUMBER OF PEOPLE believe never existed, Jesus sure has inspired a K2-sized mountain of books claiming to "solve the Jesus mystery." And all that stands atop a couple of thousand years of orthodox theology and Christological exegesis. You can really get yourself very quickly lost in the parade of PhDs who will publish endless editions on the most trivial details of Jesus' life, ministry and influence before you even get to the various volumes explaining that he was actually a Buddhist, or a Pharaoh, or an Essene, or a proto-Muslim, or a proto-Marxist, or a proto-Scientologist, or a space alien, or a light being, or… ugh. No wonder there are so many atheists nowadays.

Me, I'm not a Doctor of Theology nor a Urantian mystic. I'm just a guy who… *notices* things.

So when it comes to getting to the truth of the New Testament, I follow Occam's Razor: "We consider it a good principle to explain the phenomena by the simplest hypothesis possible."

Wait, that's not Occam, that's actually from Ptolemy. What Occam really said was: "Nothing ought to be posited without a reason given, unless it is self-evident or known by experience or proved by the authority of Scripture." *That's* Occam.

Now, how I approach this is rather radical. Instead of getting out my x-ray goggles or my secret decoder ring, I simply read the text itself and try to arrive at a working theory that requires the fewest number of moving parts. I find the story is interesting enough without coloring outside the lines.

You see, the big problem with the 'Jesus Myth' crowd is that hardly any of them know anything about magic, and subsequently fail to look at the Gospels through a magical lens. All those mysteries are essentially solved once you accept that this story is in fact part of a very ancient tradition that brings us back to the earliest known civilizations in the Middle East.

ONE OF THE BIGGEST GUNS IN THE MYTHICISTS' ARSENAL is the fact that we have no contemporaneous documentation for Jesus' existence. But there would only be two primary sources for that information, right? Jewish or Roman scribes. But we have to ask ourselves, why would they notice Jesus at all? Because if we take the Gospels as a rough roadmap for the Jesus story, this omission from history isn't surprising at all.

A holistic reading of the Gospels leaves us with the strong impression that Jesus led a fairly small band of disciples, nearly all of whom abandoned him at his arrest. Luke names seventy disciples in one passage, but Mark — the earliest Gospel — does not, so we can probably assume there's probably some confusion here over humous and posthumous followers. Only a small handful of his entourage — his mother and her friends, it seems — were said to attend his crucifixion and burial.

It's a cinch that Romans weren't exactly champing at the bit to document every trouble-making Jew who popped his head up and proclaimed himself Messiah, especially one whose followers all hightailed it as soon as trouble arrived. It's simply not the way things worked back then. I doubt the Jewish authorities were worried overmuch, either. And it's really not odd that we don't have Jewish sources considering that the entire country was, y'know, *leveled to the frickin' ground* some 40 years after Jesus' reported death.

It's not like you had an internet to back up your files on to. If you lost a text written by some Temple inquisitor chronicling Jesus' arrest and execution to a fire set by marauding Romans, tough shit, you lost it forever.

That's why most of the information we have from Judea at the time is from Roman sources. And that includes Josephus.

A S FAR AS THE ARGUMENT THAT EVERY DETAIL OF THE GOSPELS can be traced to a precedent in the Hebrew Bible, there are three arguments I can offer in response. First of all, the Hebrew Bible is actually rather huge and documents the purported story of an entire people over a span of centuries (how many centuries exactly is a matter of debate). There wasn't an enormous variety of human experience (no one was jetting off to Maui or bungie jumping from skyscrapers, for instance) to draw on at the time, so it's inevitable that something Jesus did would have been done by someone before and recorded in the Bible. Hell, there are probably precedents for crap you or I do in the Old Testament, too.

Second, you're dealing with a culture that lived and breathed its religion. There was no separation between 'church and state' because the two were entirely contiguous in their eyes. A lot of what went down was almost certainly an intentional attempt to retrace the steps of the ancient prophets that Jesus wanted to emulate. This is the same impulse that had ancient conquerors trying to recreate the lives of Sargon of Akkad or Alexander by following in their literal footsteps.

Third, a lot of the examples cited as New Testament plagiarisms cited by atheists are just plain weak. I mean, they're stretched like taffy. Like this:

Jesus Consorts with Sinners: Matthew 9:12 - Hosea 6:6

'For I desire mercy, not sacrifice, and acknowledgment of God rather than burnt offerings'.

OK, you could *conceivably* stretch that passage to its breaking point and cite Hosea as precedent for Jesus' consorting with sinners and tax collectors, but only if you're feeling extremely generous. Moreover, Hosea is pretty harsh on sinners in the verses in the very same chapter Mythicists *don't* cite, so the parallel just crumbles to dust in your hands.

Escape to Egypt: Matthew 2:15 - Hosea 11:1

'When Israel was a child, I loved him, and out of Egypt I called my son'.

This passage says nothing about an escape to Egypt, but is about the alleged Egyptian captivity. Again, none of this is to say there are not parallels between the Old and New Testaments. In fact, the Gospel writers often *strain* to make parallels in order to establish Jesus as the true king of Israel and fulfillment of the Prophets and so on and so forth.

But let's take Occam's Razor to its strop and see if we can't carve our way out of some longstanding logjams when it comes to Jesus' earthly existence and ministry (or *magical* work, if you prefer). You see, recently I've noticed that there was a tradition of Jewish magicians, trained in ancient Babylonian magic, whose stock in trade was exorcism and spell-craft against demons (Babylon had a big demon infestation issue). And I can't help but notice that Jesus' show-stopping routine was usually exorcism. Winding back to that Matthew passage:

> Then they brought him a demon-possessed man who was blind and mute, and Jesus healed him, so that he could both talk and see. All the people were astonished and said, 'Could this be the Son of David?' But when the Pharisees heard this, they said, 'It is only by Beelzebub, the prince of demons, that this fellow drives out demons'. - Matthew 12:22-23

Beelzebub is believed to mean 'Lord of the High Places', or 'Lord of Things that Fly'. He is said to be identified with Ba'al, who is in turn identified with the Babylonian Bel, aka Marduk, in whose name exorcisms were performed. This in turn was an art Jewish mages learned during the Babylon Captivity and brought back home.

Now I can practically hear your thoughts here: this guy is no different than the rest. Just leaping to one conclusion after another to hammer the evidence into his own favorite little cubby. But let me add this: according to *Jewish Mysticism and Magic: An Anthropological Perspective*, a common practice among Babylonian magicians was to write incantation texts on earthenware bowls. Why is this significant? Read this:

> A team of scientists led by renowned French marine archaeologist Franck Goddio recently announced that they have found a bowl, dating to between the late 2nd century BC and the early 1st century AD, that is engraved with what they believe could be the world's first known reference to Christ. (The) discovery may provide evidence that Christianity and paganism at times intertwined in the ancient world.
>
> The bowl reads: 'DIA CHRSTOU O GOISTAIS', which has been interpreted by the excavation team to mean either, 'by Christ the magician' or, 'the magician by Christ'.

See? A to B to C. No channeling or Reticulans necessary.

ONE OF THE REASONS I NOT ONLY BELIEVE JESUS was a real person, but was also a charismatic preacher and leader, are a number of thorny problems the Gospel writers feel they needed to address. Contemporary writers may not have recorded Jesus at the time, but I strongly believe that stories about him survived past his death in oral traditions, at the very least.

What is especially unusual about the Gospel accounts is that Jesus is almost universally scorned by Jewish authorities, who hardly offer even a grudging admiration of the man or his work. Not only is he attacked as a sorcerer (which you'll find was the majority opinion on him among Jewish and Roman commenters in the years after his death), he's called a glutton, a lunatic and a drunkard, and is attacked for the company he keeps (sinners, probably meaning sexual sinners of various types, and tax collectors). Ouch. Remember, this is the Son of God they claim to be writing about here.

I've seen various explanations for these embarrassing details, but they feel a bit too raw for me. They feel as if Jesus was the target of unflattering gossip in his time, gossip that long survived him and was enough of a problem that the Gospel writers were forced to deal with it. I'm sure entire volumes have been written about all of this by scholars with credentials running up and down their bony legs, but I'm just calling it like I see it.

M ORTON SMITH WAS A PROFESSOR AT COLUMBIA and the author of the controversial *Clement of Alexandria and a Secret Gospel of Mark* and the equally-controversial *Jesus the Magician*. The book raised a huge firestorm of controversy but what Smith did was actually very simple: he read the Gospels and the various commentaries on Jesus and Christianity from Antiquity and compared them with what we know about ancient magic. And he found the evidence to be frankly compelling.

From a *New York Times* review:

> I t was his reputation as a magician that caused him to be thought of as a god, the Jews went out of their way to emphasize Jesus' humanity, calling him illegitimate, ignorant, ugly, dishonest, and blasphemous. Smith constructs a picture of Jesus as the opposition saw him: the bastard son of a soldier called Panthera, he was reared as a carpenter, but went to Egypt and learned magic, returning to Galilee tattooed with magic spells...

Smith argues that Matthew, in sending the infant Jesus on an unnecessary trip to Egypt, was apologetically toning down the truth, which is that he went there much later to learn magic. I think Smith was onto something. But one thing I might quibble with is the interpretation of the alleged 'flight into Egypt'. What if this story were concocted or embellished to account for the fact that Jesus was an Egyptian Jew, or even a Jewish Egyptian (ie., a convert)?

There was a large and prosperous Jewish community in Alexandria — the super-metropolis of its time, and probably more recognizably modern than we would like to admit — and Jesus may well have come from that community and made *Aliyah*, as it were, in order to fulfill his religious destiny.

It works like this: followers of Jesus are going hither and yon spreading his message to Jew and Gentile alike. But communal memories are long enough that some people remember Jesus as an Egyptian, an ethnic group that had a thorny reputation with Jews and Syrians and so on. People hear of Jesus and say, "You mean that Egyptian who was crucified way back when?" That's a big problem. So the authors of Matthew take a bit of poetic license and have Jesus born in a manger in Bethlehem, but escaping to Egypt to pacify the xenophobes. I mean, their very souls are at stake, no?

In that light, I'm not really sure his name was ever actually 'Yeshua' or variants thereof. His name could actually have been 'Jesus', a logical product of the vigorous Hellenization of the Jewish community in Egypt. There's actually no record — none at all, in fact — of his name being anything other than the Greek 'Jesus'. Note all of the New Testament texts were originally written in Greek, a detail of history I always found a bit revealing.

You see, people today don't realize how porous the borders between religions were in Alexandria, something the Emperor Hadrian commented on when discussing the matter to a friend named Servianus. In fact, his letter might tell us a lot about many of the issues we're dealing with here, namely Egypt, magic, identity:

> The land of Egypt, the praises of which you have been recounting to me, my dear Servianus, I have found to be wholly light-minded, unstable, and blown about by every breath of rumor. There those who worship Serapis are, in fact, Christians, and those who call themselves bishops of Christ are, in fact, devotees of Serapis. There is no chief of the Jewish synagogue, no Samaritan, no Christian presbyter, who is not an astrologer, a soothsayer, or an anointer. Even the Patriarch himself, when he comes to Egypt, is forced by some to worship Serapis, by others to worship Christ.

Some have claimed the letter is spurious, but the actual fact is that it doesn't tell us much we don't actually know from other sources. And it gives you a good idea why Jesus might wanted to have hidden his true nationality, if in fact that was the case.

So did Jesus really come back to Israel as a child as some of the Gospels claim? Or did he in fact go there in order to join a major religious movement, one that the Bible acknowledges he submitted himself to? Did he go to Israel to follow a leader so important that Jews would later claim the sack of Jerusalem was God's judgment and wrath for this man's assassination? Note that Mark — generally acknowledged as the first Gospel to be written and the gospel that places the greatest emphasis on his magical work — begins with the words of John the Baptist and immediately proceeds to tell of Jesus' Baptism by John, skipping Jesus' birth narrative and childhood stories completely.

T HE PRIMARY ARGUMENT OF THE MYTHICISTS — whether they're talking about Jesus, Paul or any of the early Church Fathers — essentially boils down to this: because there are elements in the biographies of these figures that bear similarity to myths associated with other well-known figures in pagan religion and/or Judaism, the Gospel stories are also mythological.

So because we can find parallels for some — *some*, mind you — of Jesus' miracle stories in the stories of pagan fertility gods like Adonis and Osiris, or in the solar savior canon of god-men like Hercules, this is definitive proof that Jesus is also a mythological figure. The fact that ancient Roman and Jewish authorities — who were universally hostile to Jesus and his movement — took it for granted that he was a real person (and a sorcerer of some ill-repute) is dismissed out of hand. On what grounds exactly, I'm not entirely sure.

But believing Jesus or Paul were real people doesn't mean you need to buy into the tenets of orthodox Christianity, or any other kind of Christianity, for that matter. Look at it this way: in 1966, a movie was released called *Jesse James Meets Frankenstein's Daughter*. As far as I know, the real Jesse James never met Frankenstein's daughter, because I'm pretty sure "Frankenstein" was a fictional character. Do we assume then that Jesse James was also a fictional character?

That same year the same production company also released *Billy the Kid Meets Dracula*. Now, Billy the Kid was a real-life outlaw who became the object of a number of shall we say *apocryphal* stories, in the Pulps, in comics, in serials. Dracula was a real-life warlord who became a vampire in the famous novel written by Bram Stoker, and from then on unleashed a torrent of fictional narratives in various media. Do we assume Dracula never existed? After all, he wasn't a vampire and didn't live in the Nineteenth Century. He never met Billy the Kid either. Are they both fictional characters?

Of course, the obvious argument is that all three of these men were recorded (and in Billy the Kid and Jesse James' cases, actually photographed) during their lifetimes. But I would argue — again — that there really was no reason for anyone to take notice of Jesus, who authorities would see as nothing more a small-time troublemaker with an insubstantial following who was summarily executed as soon as he got in someone's hair.

Jesus was a mystic and a magus, preaching an explicitly spiritual message during an intensely political time. First-Century Judea was a powder keg of conspiracy and rebellion, and would explode into full-scale insurrection a few decades after Jesus' apparent execution. There was no shortage of would-be messiahs, and a lot of them probably had much bigger followings than Jesus. And again, I think Jesus was probably not a native Judean, was apparently rejected out of hand by Jewish religious authorities, and was not very highly regarded during his lifetime.

EVERYONE HAS THEIR THEORY, AND MINE IS THAT JESUS was a mage, part of a very ancient tradition that literally dates back to Sumer. He was quite possibly an Egyptian Jew (or even a convert, of which there were millions) who came to Palestine to follow John the Baptist, didn't necessarily speak Aramaic (or spoke very little of it), and ultimately became a reluctant revolutionary, whose flirtation with rebellion got him arrested and executed.

The interesting thing about Jesus' use of Aramaic is that it always seems to be used in a ritual or magical context, seeing that the rest of the text is written in Greek. So in other words, there seems to be a big show made that Jesus is speaking Aramaic, because he seems to be doing it in the context of spell-craft. A famous example:

> Taking her by the hand he said to her, 'Talitha cumi, which means, 'Little girl, I say to you, arise'. - Mark 5:41

Why break the fourth wall, as it were, to point out Jesus is speaking Aramaic here? It seems a bit incongruous, don't you think? Well, it makes perfect sense if you place it in the context of spell-craft and the use of grimoires and so on. It especially makes sense if Jesus didn't usually speak Aramaic, which an Egyptian citizen probably wouldn't.

Speaking of Egypt, there's also the ritual connecting to the resurrection of Osiris that you've probably seen other researchers point out, with the name Lazarus acting as a cipher for *El-Osiris* in the Hebrew ('Osiris the God'), and Mary being roughly homophonic with *Meri*, which is one of the epithets of Isis.

> Now a man named Lazarus was sick. He was from Bethany, the village of Mary and her sister Martha. (This Mary, whose brother Lazarus now lay sick, was the same one who poured perfume on the Lord and wiped his feet with her hair.) So the sisters sent word to Jesus, 'Lord, the one you love is sick'. John 11:1-3

There are two other interesting things to note if we're looking at, if in fact we're looking at a conscious mythologizing. First of all, Martha ('Mistress of the House') is essentially the same name as *Nephthys*, who accompanied Isis in her lamentations. Second, Bethany — a name which has confounded historians for centuries — could be derived from *Beth-Anu*, or 'House of the Sky God', Anu being the Babylonian equivalent of Yahweh. Since there is so much Babylonian magic in these stories, we can't dismiss the possibility out of hand.

So there are all kinds of reasons to believe that Jesus was a magician and a mystic, who combined a message of a transcendent 'Kingdom of God' with demon-banishing rites dating back to ancient Mesopotamia. There's reason to believe this because that's exactly what the available evidence tells us.

So I think we're looking at real people who got mythologized, plain and simple. And I think Jesus was, first and foremost, a follower of John the Baptist who began his own ministry after John's arrest by Herod.

T HE CRITERION OF EMBARRASSMENT COMES THROUGH yet again when looking at how the Gospels treat John. Mark acts as if Jesus never existed before he met John, but dispenses with the matter fairly quickly, adding to the possibility that Jesus may have only come on to the scene to follow John. Luke, however, spends a LOT more time with John's story, and acknowledges that John wasn't quite sure that Jesus was all that.

Luke seems to be aware that he is writing for a people that believed that John, and not Jesus, was the Messiah. Some believed that Luke was writing before the fall of Jerusalem and before the death of the Apostle Paul, and that a first draft might have been produced circa 64 AD. Therefore, the first chapter of Luke acknowledges the supremacy of John in his audience's mind by telling his story first. And John's teachings, as spelled out in Luke, are basically Jesus' teachings. All of this speaks to the fact that Luke was trying to sway a large and skeptical audience that was intimately familiar with John's teachings and that saw Jesus as a poseur at best, and a usurper at worst (see Luke 4:24).

Most importantly, John does not identify Jesus as the coming Messiah in the Book of Luke. This is remarkable for a Gospel story, and stands in direct contradiction to the accounts of Matthew and John. Could it be that that John's large Jewish following was very familiar with his messianic prophecies? Given the detailed account of John's biography and actions in Luke's Gospel, it's very likely that there were once written records of John's life and works from which Luke is quoting, particularly in the third chapter.

None of this would have been necessary if Jesus were a wholly-invented character. Luke could have spun the same kind of fables the John writer did, who was writing in Alexandria long after anyone who would have known either man had died. Luke seems to be struggling to kosher Jesus with John's remaining followers, who might have known (or known of) both men, and probably not going over very well at that.

John was clearly the better known of the two at the time. But Jesus obviously won out in the long run, thanks in large part to Paul and his writer friends. But I also believe that Jesus' mysticism struck a special chord following the fall of Jerusalem, also thanks in large part to the religious genius of Paul. Even Jesus' own brothers thought he'd gone off the grid, theologically. Note in John 7:5, Jesus' brothers may have come to Judea, either to join him or on other business, if they too were Egyptian Jews. Egypt and Judea were both Roman provinces with large Jewish populations and there was a lot of travel and trade between them.

There's also a passage in Acts that is quite curious, because it tells of an Egyptian Jew who knew Jesus' teachings, but was in fact a follower of John the Baptist (whose style of ministry also quite literally dates back to Sumer). This passage tells us a lot, and following the 'criterion of embarrassment':

> Now there came to Ephesus a Jew named Apollos, a native of Alexandria. He was an eloquent man, well-versed in the scriptures. He had been instructed in the Way of the Lord; and he spoke with burning enthusiasm and taught accurately the things concerning Jesus, though he knew only the baptism of John. Acts 18:24-25

The wording here is a bit ambiguous, almost *deliberately* so. Apollos was instructed in the 'Way of the Lord', and knew Jesus' teachings, but only knew 'the baptism of John'. Since baptism is a defining sacrament of the Christian faith, is the author of Mark trying to confuse the issue of whether Jesus was actually a student of John's teachings? I very much get the feeling that the early Christians were addressing an audience familiar with John and his teachings, but not so much when it came to Jesus.

Now, I'm not trying to debunk the Mythicist arguments here, I'm simply doing what the title says; explaining why I am not a Mythicist myself. Take it or leave it, it's all the same to me.

IN A STRANGE WAY, JESUS REMINDS ME of The Velvet Underground. Pretty much everyone hated the VU at the time, preferring instead to groove to the Jefferson Airplane or The Mamas and The Papas. But it's been said that everyone who saw the Velvets went out and started a band, ultimately leading to Punk and New Wave. I'd argue everyone who saw the Velvets went out and became a rock critic, but you get the picture.

And so the Velvets ended up playing to tens of thousands of people by the time did their reunion tour, because their influence had seeped into the culture over time through indirect means. The Jefferson Airplane were probably working the country fair circuit with a bunch of replacement members that very weekend, and there was probably an ersatz Mamas and Papas driving everyone to suicidal despair in a hotel lounge somewhere.

I think Jesus is a particularly fascinating example of a significant ancient magician and moral teacher, as is John the Baptist. I think a lot of people are turned off to learning about him because they don't like some (or all) of his fans, in the same way I let the burnouts in high school turn me off to The Doors. It wasn't until I read Jim Morrison's poetry that I realized he was one of *us*, and not one of them. Just something to think about.

I'll let you know if I have any other sacrilegious analogies to share later.

GIVE 'EM ENOUGH WOKE

TO THE SURPRISE OF ABSOLUTELY NO SINGLE LIVING SOUL on the planet Earth, the latest reboot of *Charlie's Angels* is an unmitigated towering-clown-orgy-inferno of a financial and artistic disaster. Worse, it followed hot on the heels of an even greater wipeout for *Terminator: Dark Fate,* the latest in a string of box office catastrophes for post-#MeToo Hollywood.

Even in the context of 2019 Hollywood, the casting for *Charlie's Angels* is utterly inexplicable. The original Angels were idealized adult beauties of the traditional variety, and the movie versions were more girlish GenX hipsters. This bullshit looks more like a high school gym teacher posting evidence of her Mann Act-violating getaway with her two favorite sophomore volleyball players on Instagram. Seriously, are those two no-named nothings co-starring in this turkey even old enough to *drive?*

You all know how exasperated I am with Hollywood pimping 85-pound sprites as action heroes, but this really reaches a new low. See, the one thing I hope to all the stars in Heaven or Las Vegas I never witness is any of these sylphs engaged in a real fistfight with the kinds of hulks Hollywood has them battling. Even the most mediocre semi-pro boxer would literally cave these poor pixies' faces in with a single punch, if not actually knock their heads off their necks. Superhero movies are one thing, but this moronic insanity borders on incitement to mayhem.

THE UNSPOKEN PROBLEM IS THAT HOLLYWOOD is in very, very serious trouble, no matter what you hear to the contrary. Big stars don't work anymore, time-honored franchises don't work anymore, giant CGI budgets don't work anymore. And if anyone in that town has an original idea in their brains, they are terrified to let anyone know it exists.

More and more movies are losing more and more money, and no one has a single clue how to turn it around. To make matters worse, the deluge of cultural studies majors flooding into town has brought with it a particularly virulent strain of hot, steaming Woke.

And so we've had a hate-fueled epidemic of one-way race and gender-swapping, and feminists destroying various established properties, as well as the very weird tactic of lashing out at internet straw-men when plugging your costly hijacking of someone else's creative work.

For the most part, this tactic has led to financial cataclysm. Which, of course, means that it will be utilized in perpetuity. Financial failure is *never* punished in Hollywood. If you lose hundreds of millions of dollars for the right reasons, you will never want for work.

And so it was with this turkey, in which pseudo-feminist rhetoric was breezily spouted by privileged Hollywood hotties falling out of their designer dresses, while payola-loving shill reviewers drooled over every syllable.

This is the *quintessence* of late Capitalist prerogative. Contradictions are not exceptions, they are hidebound diktats, brutally enforced by career-crushing punishments. But being a player in Hollywood means you never — *ever* — have to take a single shred of responsibility for losing hundreds of millions of someone else's money. As we see with Elizabeth Banks being handed a new franchise to bankrupt, one mere week after utterly bankrupting the *Charlie's Angels* franchise.

Take *Charlie's Angels star* Kristen Stewart, for example. She's blown untold millions of studio dollars since the *Twilight* series ended, and will probably flush another $50M with this bomb. Does it matter? Of course not. Hollywood never seems to tire of burning hundreds of millions of dollars trying to make this shrill, charmless harpy a superstar.

Stewart's unbroken string of calamitous failure since the last *Twilight* movie has done nothing to humble the actress, or to tame her compulsions to alienate potential movie-goers. And why should it? She's deliriously wealthy, never needs to work another day in fifty lifetimes, and knows that there will always be a daisy-chain of producers on her doorstep, just itching to piss their investors' millions down a bottomless rathole.

And what does it really matter anyway? Most of the industry is biding time before the Chinese buy up most of the studios, a process that is already well underway. Why not enjoy the party before it all comes to a screeching halt?

This got me to thinking: there are all kinds of debates and arguments about Woke on the Internet by a lot of people much smarter than I am. But what if they're arguing about the wrong things? I've long wondered if Woke — or PC, or Identity Politics, or whatever you want to call it — isn't actually some vast, insidious, self-replicating counter-intelligence operation, ingeniously designed to not only sabotage but to utterly destroy and disintegrate the businesses and institutions of those who suck on the Woke pipe from within. Because if it isn't, it sure as hell acts like one.

And now, the rotten foundations are beginning to crumble. So what if Woke isn't some spontaneous eruption of revolutionary fervor, or even some insidious plan by secret Sorosoids to color-revolutionize America?

What if Woke is a kind of mindless virus, concocted, purified and unleashed by parties unknown who wish to collapse all the opinion-forming institutions in America? What if Woke was really engineered to *destroy* Hollywood, the news media, the universities and Silicon Valley from within?

Consider that while some Americans might see these institutions as bastions of liberalism, many other people around the world see them as nothing more than propaganda farms for the brutal US war and debt-making machines. Sounds crazy, right? Well, it only sounds crazy until you look at the K2 of crushed corpses Woke has left in its wake.

L ET'S START WITH THE PRIMORDIAL SPAWNING GROUND of Woke, the liberal arts colleges in the northern US. It was at this network of schools that unhinged Sixties radicals were allowed to find sanctuary — and tenured positions with very fat paychecks — after COINTELPRO turned its gimlet eye towards the movement. And it was literally at these very institutions that the groundwork for intersectionalism, postmodernism and all the other proto-Woke contagions first festered, like maggots inside a bucket of puke.

Things were going great guns for a while, but the piper always comes to collect his/her/their/xer due. And now most of these far-left 'liberal arts' schools — including bastions of extreme mental sickness like Oberlin, Antioch, and Evergreen — are succumbing to utter bedlam on the quad and financial oblivion on the books. The so-called 'Mainline Churches' were also early Woke adopters, and the results have been uniformly Hellish. Nearly all of them — Episcopal, Presbyterian, Methodist — are at knocking at Heaven's door, having sacrificed tens of millions of parishioners on the pagan altar of Woke.

Then there's the primary vector for the Woke virus in the past few years, online media sites. Get your galoshes on, because the blood is flowing like a river for these Wokelords and Wokeladies. Thousands of jobs have been slashed in the past year or two, and dozens of these sites have become digital zombies. And it will only get worse as whatever's left of the VC funny-money dries up.

More recently, we saw the collapse of the once wildly popular *College Humor* site, which died of an aggressive case of self-induced Wokeicide. Maybe they should have stuck to goofy viral jokes, and not insincere and hypocritical social justice pandering. Similarly, the once wildly-popular *Cracked* has succumbed to the inevitable consequences of Wokeification. Have you been there lately?

Just kidding, no one goes there anymore. It's like visiting a hospice for dying Millennials.

This is all just a tiny sampler of the slow-motion Jonestown known as Woke. I hate to say so, but despite the endless carnage of Wokeness, I can't see an end in sight. Pandemics have their own genius and burn their own paths. Worse still, America's cognitive elites have proven themselves to have neither the cunning nor the wherewithal to stand up effectively against Wokeness. Ironically so, since they unleashed the virus in the first place, believing it would decimate their enemies and leave their own citadels standing.

It didn't work out that way. Wokeness is memetic Ebola, and everything Woke even casually brushes by eventually explodes into a puddle of blood, pus and diarrhea. The virus is inside their city walls now and has infected nearly the entire managerial class, present or aspiring.

I think Woke has a lot more destruction and division to sow, but I think we may be looking now at the beginning of the Woke end-game, when even the torrent of vast, countless billions that many of these Wokeified entities are either endowed with or are laundering begins to slow to a trickle. The hell of it all is that it's like applause during a Stalin speech; no one dares running the risk of hopping off the suicide express train first.

There is such unbearable pressure amongst the gentry classes to not only adhere to every single, solitary Woke dictum that any random blue-haired, body-positive shut-in on Twitter conjures up, but to make such a interminable display of Woker-than-thou'ness, that no one dares point out that the entire opinion-making infrastructure of the Western world is throwing hundreds of millions — if not *billions* — of dollars down the Woke sewer.

I don't know about you, but I'm not optimistic the fever will break any time soon. Hollywood is so awash in funny money, and is such a self-enclosed, hypocritical hothouse of near-Maoist Woke orthodoxy, that catastrophic failure for the right reasons is only rewarded with opportunities to piss away even larger sums of investor's money. The silver-spoon set, that are the primary subscribers and promoters of Woke, are gambling not with their own money, but with the livelihoods and well-beings of the working people who do the actual rowing for their ships of fools.

THE INSANITY ASSASSIN

IF YOU'VE BEEN LIVING DEEP IN THE WOODS — or just wisely avoid social media — you probably didn't hear about Ricky Gervais' scorching monologue at The Golden Globe Awards on Sunday night. Gervais absolutely *dunked* on the phenomenon of hyper-privileged Hollywood millionaires — whose combined wealth, luxury and sheer ease of living has no precedent in all of human history — passing moral judgment on tens of millions of ordinary Americans struggling to scrape by.

It was made doubly delicious later when aging 90s sexpot Patricia Arquette got up and began rambling incoherently, her own matronly golden globes hanging out of a designer dress that probably cost more than most people watching at home make in a month.

That in turn was made triply-delicious when Arquette — not generally regarded as one of show business' leading intellects — smashed her young costar in the face with her award, leaving a huge welt. Gervais' manager could never buy better publicity. It was a beautiful thing. But in the cold light of day I can't help but think Gervais was simply a hired assassin, working on orders from much higher up to slay Wokeness. "Woke" meaning boutique fake leftism for high earners and their idiot children, which is fast becoming the Heaven's Gate cult of the 21st century. Heaven's Gate writ impossibly huge, that is.

The Heaven's Gate allegory is quite ingenious — if I don't say so myself — in that it was both the name of a suicide cult and one of the worst box office disasters in cinema history, pulling in a paltry $3.5M against a $44M production budget.

Which brings me back to Ricky Gervais. For reasons that are not entirely clear to anyone anywhere, Hollywood went all-in on Wokeness a few years back. Then it decided to offer up nearly all of its golden geese on the altar of the nonbinary deity of Wokeianity. I'm not sure what the thought process was. My current hypothesis is that the not-nearly-as-bright-as-you-think movers and shakers of Tinseltown never got the memo that Internet metrics are faker than fuck, particularly on Twitter.

And so they were fooled by the scammers and sock-puppets, and deliriously overestimated the audience for Woke-scoldery. The results have been uniformly awful. Especially so in the merchandising sectors, which Hollywood has become increasingly dependent on in the past decades. Just look at Toys 'R Us.

Wait: you can't. They went out of business, thanks in part to taking a bath on unsold Star Wars merchandise.

The alchemical sorcery of Hollywood accounting is hiding the damage — and massive subsidies from the MIC are helping staunch the bleeding — but Wokeness is absolutely *slaughtering* franchise after franchise, *The Terminator* and *Charlie's Angels* being just the two most recent casualties. This is especially fool-hardy, given the collapse in birthrates worldwide, translating to a smaller and smaller customer pool in the coming years for youth-oriented properties.

The problem is how do you stop the rot? Thanks to all the Millennial lib-arts majors who are now deluging the media industries like fecal filth from a broken sewer, Woke is more entrenched than ever before. And while social media wokelords and woke-ladies might be a tiny demographic, clickbait hungry media outlets are all too happy to exploit their cancel crusades, which in turn affects inattentive normies. Especially the hyper-status-conscious upper middle class mothers who generally control the family entertainment budgets, and live in mortal terror of violating the ever-shifting dictates of Woke.

So say you're a studio head or hedge fund manager watching your sexiest assets bleed out, what do you do? Well, you probably have to get an anti-Woke campaign up and running, post-haste. But you need spokespeople with solid liberal credentials. Bill Maher has dipped his toes in the anti-Woke water, but his appeal and audience are limited. JK Rowling has played footsie with anti-Wokeness, but that's probably her own prerogative given the batshit insanity gripping the UK these days.

Ricky Gervais seems like a good pick. He's English, so he won't come across as a Trumpster even if he was an outright Tory, which I don't believe he is. Plus, he's the brains behind *The Office*, one of the biggest moneymakers in Television history. Best of all, he's an outspoken atheist, so he won't come across as the reincarnation of Fred Phelps.

Now, the odds that Gervais slipped his monologue past all the gatekeepers involved in a major awards show are slim to fuck-all. There are kinds of camera and lighting cues to be choreographed with these things, so it's certain that every punchline went through a committee.

What else might be at work is similar to what we saw with #MeToo clearing out a lot of overpaid deadwood. Hollywood has been bleeding an ocean of red ink for years now, and not all the drug cartel money-laundering in the world can balance the books. So #MeToo and the other ops run out of Creative Artists Agency were great cost-cutting mechanisms. You could not only cut salaries but pensions and severance of the *alter kockers* marked for elimination. But debt is only one of the industry's problems, and not even one of the top ones.

Movie stars don't mean anything anymore. A star can't "open" a mediocre movie anymore, never mind a shitty one. Your local Redbox is filled with movies you never heard of filled with big stars you're sick to death of. Streaming pays pennies on the dollar, compared to windfalls of yore. The inflated salaries one-time 'A-listers' still demand are a major liability, a vestige of a Hollywood that's long since dead.

Having a very smart comic like Gervais make all these overpaid celebrities look very, very stupid is an excellent way to kick off the next round of budget melting. There's been some impotent sniffing from shills on Twitter, but as far as I can see it's only making matters worse for the celebrities whose pads these people are all on.

Hollywood will always and forever be very liberal, but it can no longer afford the hefty price tag of radical chic. I don't know if it can truly recover from Stage 4 Wokeinoma but it's got to do *something*. And I can't help but wonder if that 'something' is exactly what we saw on Sunday night.

**ONCE UPON A TIME
IN HOLLYWOOD BABYLON**

THE MIDNIGHT MAN

I'M NOT ONE OF THOSE "MANSON GUYS." To be perfectly frank, I actually find the guy and his so-called Family to be boring and depressing. But in the broader context of what I see as a long-running occult war on the American people, being waged by powerful lunatics within the intelligence community, the story gets a lot more interesting.

In his book *Chaos: Charles Manson, the CIA, and the Secret History of the Sixties*, author Tom O'Neill tracked down documentation of the involvement of high-placed creepy-crawlers in the whole Manson saga, which other writers had speculated on for years. And lo and behold, a lot of very familiar names to longtime parapolitics watchers popped up, like the odious Louis Jolyon West and his sidekick, David Elvin Smith.

However, missing in O'Neill's treatise was any mention of the Process Church of the Final Judgment or the Solar Lodge of the Ordo Templi Orientis, without which the Manson story makes no sense, at least to me. These occult orders rubbed up against Manson a number of times in San Francisco and Los Angeles, and preached much the same kind of apocalyptic visions Manson later would pass on to the messed-up kids he pulled into his orbit.

MKULTRA, THE CIA'S ALLEGED 'MIND-CONTROL' program, obviously plays a major supporting role in the Manson drama as well. But where I split off from a lot of other people who've written about this case is my conviction that the 'mind-control' rap was merely a cover story for what was an infinitely more ambitious black magic working. Specifically, a working to create suitable vessels for mass entity possession.

I know how ridiculous that may sound to a lot of people, but bear in mind that the techniques to create Manchurian Candidates, deep-cover sleeper agents, and chemically-augmented interrogation have been well-known for at least a thousand years (and were all used extensively during the Second World War). Moreover, a number of scientists who've looked at the actual MKULTRA programs — particularly the work of Ewen Cameron — have dismissed them out of hand as worthless pseudo-science. Remember also that the nickname of project leader Sidney Gottlieb was 'the Sorcerer.'

The methods used by men like Cameron — sensory deprivation, induced coma, endlessly repeated words and phrases, massive doses of hallucinogens — may have had no actual basis in science, but they've been used for a very, very long time in ritual magic and shamanism. And they've been used for a very long time because they *work*, as evidence from any number of traditional societies bears out.

No less a luminary than The Grateful Dead's LSD guru Augustus Owsley Stanley told *One Flew Over the Cuckoo's Nest* author Ken Kesey exactly that when the former MKULTRA test subject took the program's mind-fucking methods public with the so-called "Acid Tests." As recounted in a *Rolling Stone* interview, Owsley told Kesey, "You guys are fucking around with something that people have known about forever. It's sometimes called witchcraft, and it's extremely dangerous. You're dealing with part of the unconscious mind that they used to define as angels and devils." Stanley added, "All the occult literature about ceremonial magic warns about being very careful when you start exploring these areas in the mind." Needless to say, nobody listened to him. And here we all are today.

The Manson story is also a drug story and the same can be said about the Process Church, to my eyes at least. But so is MKULTRA, and so is shamanism, witchcraft and ritual magic. Drugs, particularly hallucinogens, have been used to facilitate spirit contact, both good and bad, for millennia. And powerful drugs like DMT have produced reports of experiences with nonhuman entities so specific and consistent they can't be dismissed as simple hallucinations.

Something to think seriously about as an over-medicated populace begins to show widespread symptoms of traditional demon possession, and powerful hallucinogens are being decriminalized, if not legalized. MKULTRA Mark II is well underway, my friends, and it's an open question as whether we can survive the onslaught of malevolent spirits it will inevitably drag in its wake.

I dug into the Manson saga back in the early 2000s when I was trying to trace the weird path the Kenneth Anger film *Lucifer Rising* would take through the history of Parapolitics and High Weirdness. That film would not only connect to the Manson Family (specifically Bobby Beausoleil), but The Rolling Stones, Anton LaVey, Led Zeppelin, the John Lennon assassination and even the Loch Ness monster, believe it or not.

Researching the whole story showed me that ritual magic was real and it produced real results, just not in the way you might see in a Harry Potter film. It also showed me how dangerous ritual magic really is, mainly to the people who practice it. So it confirmed the reality of the occult, at the same time it totally tore away any lingering delusions I might have had that it was something to mess around with. Ultimately, the people who practice the black arts are looking for short-cuts and unfair advantage, and that inevitably lands them on the wrong side of the laws of Karma.

We should keep all this in mind as the entire world falls under a dark spell the likes of which has never been seen before.

"YOU ARE LUCIFER."

The following was my original pitch for the Lucifer Rising cover story in *Classic Rock*. Putting the final article together took over a year, but I'm proud to say it was their best-selling issue ever.

NINETEEN SIXTY-NINE WAS THE YEAR THE UTOPIAN DREAMS of the Aquarian Generation all came tumbling down to Earth. The false dawn of the Woodstock festival was book-ended by the horrific Tate-LaBianca murders in Los Angeles, and then by The Rolling Stones' catastrophic free concert at the Altamont Speedway. And a new band called Led Zeppelin, sporting a harsh, stripped-down new sound and a dark, occultic worldview, crashed the flower-people party and set the stage for a parade of imitators.

Like a demonic sprite summoned to chronicle his master's handiwork upon the Earth, underground film-maker Kenneth Anger released his land-mark short film, *Invocation of My Demon Brother*, a work dedicated to British occultist Edward Alexander 'Aleister' Crowley. *Invocation* made use of jump-cut editing, unleashing a montage of black magic ritual imagery, along with footage of the Rolling Stones' free concert in Hyde Park, commemorating the death of Brian Jones on July 3rd of that year.

Anger had inserted himself into the Stones' orbit, just as Mick Jagger's ego had mushroomed to such mammoth proportions that he imagined himself as the earthly incarnation of Lucifer, the rebel angel of Christian folk mythology. Jagger was (allegedly) commissioned by Anger to create the soundtrack for *Invocation* and constructed a tuneless 12-minute suite of electronic farts on a brand new device called the Mini-Moog Synthesizer.

The history of *Invocation of My Demon Brother* was nearly as malevolent as the film itself. The project started life in 1966 as *Lucifer Rising*, Anger's paean to the spirit which he saw manifested in the social unrest and upheaval of the time. Anger cast Bobby Beausoleil, one-time guitarist with legendary acid rock band Love, as Lucifer.

A falling out would result in Beausoleil allegedly fleeing to Los Angeles with the 1600 feet of film shot for the project. And a curse apparently put upon him by Anger would result in Beausoleil falling into the demonic clutches of Charles Manson and his desert-dwelling 'Family'. Following the success of *Invocation*, Anger set to work re-conceptualizing *Lucifer Rising*.

Ejected from the Stones' orbit after Jagger renounced the devil and all his works in the wake of Altamont, Anger had the good fortune of meeting Jimmy Page, guitarist for Led Zeppelin at an auction of Crowley's possessions.

A three-year drama would follow with Page agreeing to compose the soundtrack to *Lucifer Rising,* only to face Anger's wrath after only 28 minutes of music had been recorded. Like Jagger's work on *Invocation*, Page's soundtrack sounded utterly unlike anything Led Zeppelin had recorded.

Using his guitar run through an ARP synthesizer, Page composed a series of nightmarish dirges, portions of which were used for the intro of 'In the Evening' from Led Zeppelin's final album, *In Through the Out Door.* Following a break with Page, Anger would reconcile with Beausoleil, who was now serving time for his role in the Manson killings. Beausoleil eventually composed the soundtrack for *Lucifer Rising,* from his prison cell, possibly a historic first.

INTERVIEW WITH BOBBY BEAUSOLEIL

T HIS INTERVIEW WAS CONDUCTED VIA TELEPHONE IN 2006. Bobby Beausoleil is currently incarcerated for life in California for the murder of a drug dealer named Gary Hinman. I found Bobby to be a charming guy and compelling storyteller. By all accounts he has successfully rehabilitated, but will die in prison for horrific crimes that he had no involvement in. Meanwhile, multiple murderers get a fraction of his time inside. Such is the potency of the Manson myth, and such is the lingering power of the people who orchestrated it all, using Manson and his wet-brained whores as patsies.

Chris Knowles: *Let's talk about the recording of the soundtrack itself. Kenneth said that (criminal psychologist) Minerva Bertholf acted as a go-between on that?*

Bobby Beausoleil: Yes. She was a schoolteacher at Tracy. She'd been there for about 25 years and she just kind of took a shine to me. She made a deal with me that she would sponsor my project, this project that I wanted to do, and help me to create some inroads with the superintendent if I would get involved in education. So I made a deal with her, struck a bargain. I held up my end and she held up hers. She was an eccentric old lady. She'd been in the system for so long that she just didn't give a shit anymore. And she didn't really have to do all that much. She just let the superintendent know that she would act as my sponsor, which made it possible for me to get equipment in.

CK: *Now, was there a music program in effect at the time?*

BB: No. When I first got there, there was no music program. There were a couple of guitars, electric guitars, and a couple of small Fender Champ amplifiers. No drums. Maybe once a month the guys would be able to get some time in the chow hall and play the guitars.

And guys would bring in Bugler cans, you know, tobacco cans. Anyway, they'd bring in Bugler cans and use those for drums.

CK: *But you had a full kit on the album.*

BB: This is before I even started working on the soundtrack or even negotiated with Kenneth. I started negotiating with the administration at the prison to get a real music program, and I was able to get some support for it. We secured a room, which was an old barbershop, and we started putting together a music program. I made a nuisance out of myself, I really, really hammered on it and was able to, through perseverance and a lot of good luck, and a climate at the time which was looking for alternatives to violence [in the prison?].

CK: *Were there a lot of problems in the prisons at the time?*

BB: Oh, yeah, there was a lot of gang violence. Of course, we were trying to create an alternative to that, and that's how the administration saw it. So they were looking for ways to introduce alternatives to that sort of activity, something positive and pro-social. So I was able to get a little bit of funding, and gradually we built that music program, which ten years ago was still functioning, so it may still be functioning today. I have a feeling it probably is. But we got our little former barber shop and turned it into a music room. We got better amplifiers. I got a few things donated. Mostly we were able to get a little bit of additional funding through the recreation department and bought some better amplifiers and a drum kit.

CK: *Well, let me just clarify: this was because of Kenneth's approach to you? Or this was before?*

BB: This was before I had even negotiated with Kenneth. So I had already been on this mission to be able to have bands, and we did, we stepped that up. We had my own band, which later became - I can't remember what we called my band, Magic Theater something, I don't know what it was. I can't remember. Magic Theater Studios. And we also set it up where there would be a kind of ethnic balance. In other words, several different ethnic groups representative bands in the band room in alternating time slots. So my band got two nights a week, and we were considered the white band, you know, then there was the black band, the soul band, which had a couple of nights a week, and then there was a Mexican band that had a couple of nights a week. And then there was one night a week for a country band.

CK: *So were these basically just loose jam sessions, or did you play for other prisoners?*

BB: Yes, mostly. I've always liked playing my own stuff. So we did some covers at first, Santana, Allman Brothers type stuff. But I've always pushed the original material, so we did kind of a blend of both at first.

CK: *Let's talk about when Ken approached you at Tracy.*

BB: Well, he didn't approach me. I approached him. I got his phone number from a mutual friend, an artist in Los Angeles who I had maintained contact with, a guy by the name of Kenneth Kendall, who Kenneth had introduced me to back in the Sixties, back in '67. We had made one trip to Los Angeles and met the former wife of Jack Parsons, you know…

CK: *Marjorie Cameron.*

BB: Yeah. And he took me to his favorite haunt, the graveyard, you know, with the… I can't remember. At Universal, I think it is.

CK: *Oh, the one with all the stars? With the mausoleums and stuff?*

BB: Yeah, he took me through that. It was one of his favorite haunts. So anyway, we had made that trip down there and I met Kenneth Anger and maintained contact. And so through that I was able to get Kenneth's phone number, and I talked to him on the phone, and we kind of reestablished a relationship. And I had him send me a letter requesting that I be able to do the soundtrack, that I could then take to the super-intendent.

I met with him, I put in a request to meet with him, and Minerva helped me out with that a little bit, let him know that I was wanting to talk to him. So he calls me up, and I made my little spiel, showed him the letter from Kenneth, and said I would really like to have an opportunity to do this. And he says, 'Well, I'm not going to stand in the way of a guy wanting to make a buck'. Which was not what it was about at all, but I was happy that I had his endorsement. So I was able to get the equipment in. I ordered the equipment, it was sent to Minerva, and she brought it in.

CK: *How many musicians did you work with in all?*

BB: I can't remember offhand. I think it was about a dozen that are actually on the recording, though there were more that passed through at different times. You know, there was always kind of a transitionary thing that went on with the band, too, in the fact that we were a prison band. You know, guys would get in trouble and then they would go to the hole, or guys that get transferred to another prison for some reason, or they were paroled.

So people were going in and out of the band all the time. There were several different bass players, there were several different drummers, and a couple of different keyboard players. Most of the guitar players stayed throughout, myself and Steve Grogan pretty much all the way through.

CK: *Let's switch back to 1968 just for a bit. Lucifer Rising in its first incarnation became Invocation of My Demon Brother.*

BB: Right.

CK: *What was your role in the totality of that? You were in a lot of the footage yourself, and at the same time you were working with the band The Magic Powerhouse of Oz. Was this more a collaboration between you and Ken, or were you being directed by him? How exactly did that go?*

BB: He never directed me except for when we were filming. I made a deal with him, and it went like this: Kenneth saw me perform with the orchestra at the Invisible Circus, which was an event that was staged by a group of people comprising the Diggers, the Mime Troupe, the Sexual Freedom League, a number of different groups. And it was, like, supposed to be a love-in free-for-all in this big cathedral. There was a church complex called Glide Memorial Church and it was, like, little auditoriums in it, and then there was the main tabernacle, what you would call that cathedral area…

CK: *The sanctuary.*

BB: Right. And there were various little rooms, areas. Anyway, the pastor, who was really liberal and didn't know what he was getting in for, okayed this thing. And they eventually had to move it out after 24 hours They finally, they moved it down to Golden Gate Park down by the beach. But it was supposed to have been a three-day event. And we played the first night. We were at the Glide Memorial Church during the event called the Invisible Circus. Kenneth was there. We were the band that was kicking off the whole event. People had shown up earlier in the afternoon, and there were a lot of people milling around, and there were conga players, you know, the black guys from the Fillmore district and all. Grooving, you know? But we had set up a false wall was set up in this little auditorium next to the main church area, and there was to be a poetry reading in it. And they'd set up a false wall made of paper, but that nevertheless looked real from the other side, where they were having the poetry reading. My band set up behind the false wall. We had, I think it was about eight or nine topless girls belly dancing.

CK: *Playing the part, yeah.*

BB: Yeah, they were young chicks, and they were liberated young chicks. You know, the whole idea was that everybody, they wanted to get everybody making love. The promoters just wanted everybody just to, you know…

CK: *Let it all hang out.*

BB: Let it all hang out, be creative, be musical, be Bacchanalian, you know? So we set up, we had our equipment set up behind the false wall before the poetry reading began, and then on cue we started playing one of our pieces, and the girls busted through the paper wall and started dancing with the people that were in the audience. It was pretty wild. It was a pretty wild scene. And I did a little performance with one of the girls. Not a sexual performance, not a real sexual performance, although it was certainly implied. You know, playing my guitar to her dancing. I had her stood up on a chair next to me as I was playing, we were doing this sort of thing.

And Kenneth, he really tuned into that. He saw me then after the gig, he accosted me out in the parking lot. I was out there with my band smoking a joint with them, and he came up to me and he said, 'You are Lucifer!' I didn't know what he was talking about. I didn't know who this guy was, y'know? Anyway, so he explained himself and explained that he was making a film called *Lucifer Rising* and wanted me to star in it.

CK: *Let me ask you another question. What was he trying to get at, do you think, when he was doing that film? The reason I ask is that I know in late '67, '68, the scene in San Francisco started to get a little heavy.*

BB: Things started to go south, yeah, right around that time. Which, it was inevitable that it happened that way.

CK: *Now, what was Kenneth's reaction to that? Was he excited about that? I mean, did that play into what he wanted to do on the film?*

BB: Well, he saw the youth culture as the emergence of, closed prophecy of the child of Horus being represented, the changing of the gods from the ages of Isis and Osiris to the Age of Horus, which was their child. So it was the age of the child, and so he saw this as the emergence of the Aquarian Age, which is the Age of Horus or the Age of the Child.

And I was to be representative, iconic of that in the film. So there was no script. If you look at his films you'll see that there is a lot of symbolism, there is a lot of gesture, things done, it's like a dance. And if you look at it like that, as a dance, and don't try to make too much sense of it, it's really, he's done some remarkable things.

It really communicates something. If you're trying to find a story, you're going to miss the point, I think.

CK: *So you guys kind of fell out at one point in time. What happened with that?*

BB: Well, The Magic Powerhouse wanted to play a gig, so I started lining up a gig at the Straight Theater. Kenneth got involved, which was fine with me, but it was kind of like at the last minute, and he wanted to have it be the Equinox of the Gods celebration, that's what it was called, an event at the Straight Theater, but he was a big help in one respect.

He paid for posters to be made, and some props, rented scrim for the special light show effects that we were doing, even had a projection of portions of the film on the scrim, and it was like the band was playing inside the film because the scrim is kind of translucent, like the effect of having one video playing over another, the two of them kind of mixed. That's the effect of scrim, only this was live, you know? Like we're inside a light show. So it was a great effect.

And he had a programmed ritual as part of it, and right in the middle of it, the tape broke. And his part of the ritual, which he had prerecorded that day reading from Crowley's *Book of the Law.* The tape broke and he just kind of like started improvising. Things didn't go well, and we ended up blaming each other.

In retrospect, from the audience viewpoint it went great. It was really interesting. It just wasn't the way we had planned it. The band's gig was good and it was weird and people dug it. Everybody was in costumes. That was kind of the thing. It was 'everybody show up in costumes'. We didn't have, a dance license, so we used the dance floor at that point at the Straight Theater, so we used the dance floor as an extension of the stage and added to the band.

And there was this guy that played a huge, huge set of gongs. It's like, y'know, a set of gongs like 25 feet long or something, at least 20 feet long. Some as tall as a man, down to dishpan size.

And so he played along with us, he joined the performance. We used the dance floor as his platform as well as Kenneth Anger's platform for his ritual, which we had props from the movie lit up using lighting, using some of the film lights, the spotlight and so on, to make the dance floor sort of an extension of the stage. And then everybody just showed up in costumes. It was really a very colorful event.

But there was bad blood afterwards and we had a falling out, and I wound up leaving San Francisco shortly thereafter after the ritual funeral of the Haight-Ashbury.

CK: *That was with the Diggers help?*

BB: There was a conflict between the Diggers and the Haight Street Merchants, because the Haight Street Merchants had publicized Haight-Ashbury as the Mecca for the movement, and it just overwhelmed that little community to such a degree. It brought in the criminal element and it brought in the predatory element, and it just kind of destroyed the whole thing that we were doing by just having just too much, and too many people coming from all over the country into this little place, this little village. Runaways attracting hard guys, you know, predators.

CK: *So what was going on down in LA when you got there?*

BB: Not much. I mean, there was a lot of the same type of stuff. There was a lot of strife, a lot of conflict between law enforcement and the youth movement. It was a lot of crank, you know, which… When the crank came in, the crank and the heroin came in, things were really starting to get bad. So I kind of started withdrawing from the scene. I did some studio gigging, and I fell in with Charlie. He was trying to record an album of his music.

CK: *Was that with Terry Melcher?*

BB: Yeah, Terry Melcher and Dennis Wilson. Dennis was a friend of mine, and he and I and Gregg Jakobson, a friend of Dennis' and his personal manager. And Terry Melcher was kind of like the kind of distant producer that we were trying to pander to to get these things done. And we did get recording time with the Brothers Recording Studio, and did some recordings. Charlie was not the focus, though. It was really hard to do this. And I thought he had a lot of talent. I mean, I thought he was unique.

CK: *A lot of people have said that. I mean, Neil Young said that.*

BB: Really? Well, that's good to hear, because Charlie did have something to offer. If you heard him when he was really on, he was amazing. He was amazing. I mean, he could flow, you know? Just off the top of his head sometimes, he would just like get into… He would be able to almost channel it, y'know? He just kind of, his stream-of-consciousness stuff poetry was amazing. His musical poetry was amazing. And being an improvisational musician, myself, and always wanting to play in the moment, letting music create itself in the moment, there was a commonality between the two of us that I was hoping to recording, and hoping to be able to get it out in the world and let people hear this kind of unique thing that was happening.

So, I mean, you know what happened, and I got, you know. [sighs]

We all sort of kept withdrawing and withdrawing to the fringes, and things got dicey and I ended up killing a guy. So that sent me to prison.

CK: *Well, it seems that there was just so much negativity in the air at that point in time. I wonder if it was because you had this great thing with these special people, these artistic people, and then the hordes come in, and you had all the shysters and the bikers and just all the troublemakers and all this kind of stuff.*

BB: Yeah, well, you get into that mode and you start thinking 'outlaw'.

CK: *All right, so let's get back to the situation with the recordings, Dennis Wilson, Terry Melcher, and Charlie.*

BB: I began hanging out more with people like bikers. You know, the hippie thing had just become... I don't know, man, it just died, you know, and it didn't know it was dead, you know? You couldn't tell, at least initially, who was for real, if it was a cop.

CK: *There was a lot of paranoia.*

BB: Yeah, there was a lot of paranoia, and there was a lot of hard drugs in use, which I never got into. I never got into heroin, never got into methedrine. I didn't like what it did to my friends. And, you know, when they got into that, I couldn't trust them anymore.

So I withdrew from them, and the hippie thing became more fashion rather than a real shift in consciousness. So I just kind of withdrew and I got into the biker thing just trying to find a way to stay free, to stay free, and I kind of romanticized what they were about.

And what they were really about wasn't what I was imagining, you know, but I had it in my mind that I could live on the highway and...

CK: *So you rode with them?*

BB: Yeah. Well, I was building a bike at the time I got arrested. I had built one, actually, I had built a trike, and I was rebuilding it at the time I was arrested. I had a trike because I usually had more than one chick with me, so I had to have something I could pack at least a couple of girls with, so I chose to go with a trike. Which I got razzed about, but I didn't give a shit.

CK: *What was it, they called you a sissy or something?*

BB: Well, Danny DeCarlo is the guy, one of the guys who ended up testifying against me, *the* biker, actually, who ended up testifying against me. His thing was, I remember his remark, 'You know, trikes are for meter maids'.

CK: *Let me ask you a question, because this is something that I've always thought about. What kind of effect do you think just that whole psychic backdrop of Vietnam was having on all this? I always see it as just creating so much stress and anxiety among people, you know.*

BB: Well, that *was* the backdrop. I mean, that was it. And I was drafted, and I tricked my way out of being inducted. This guy that worked in Spahn Ranch before Charlie or any of those guys showed up, this guy had worked at Spahn Ranch for a number of years. And he was from Arkansas, and he was just cornpone. You know, he had about fourteen kids and a big, fat wife, but they didn't live together, they just came to visit him every once in a while at the ranch. I looked around and
I said, 'Okay, who won't they take to Vietnam?' And I saw this guy and I borrowed his clothes and I went to the induction center when was my time to go, and they didn't want me. I just went as him and tried to *be* him. Y'know?

CK: *Do you think that what was happening affected what was going on with your scene?*

BB: Well, we were seeing pictures of it. You know, this was the first war that had ever been displayed in that way by the media. You know, we didn't see it so much on television, although there was a little bit of that. In fact, there was probably a lot more than we were seeing because we didn't really watch that much television, we didn't trust it.

CK: *Was there a lot of violence against the hippies at that time down in LA, with some of the Okie types down there?*

BB: Well, yeah. There were places you couldn't go. You had to really be careful. Yeah. There was a lot of that. There was a lot of conflict, you know, flag-wavers, you know the guys with the-hard hats, the guys with the gun racks on the back window of their pickup truck and the American flag decals.

CK: *Were you playing parties at that time down in LA?*

BB: Well, no, I was doing a little bit of studio gigging. I was really trying to withdraw from all that. I moved out to Topanga Canyon, which is where I was when I met Charlie. I was living out there and I had a dog and a couple of girls with me.

CK: *Let's switch back up to the Lucifer Rising stuff.*

BB: We're almost out of time, I've got to tell you. We've got maybe three or four minutes.

CK: *Yeah, exactly. I just wanted to get a couple bits on this. When you were, finished the soundtrack, did you have problems with Ken again?*

BB: Well, yes. As soon as I finished the soundtrack, he had another interview shortly after the film was debuted, and he went back to that old story about me having stolen a film, which I never did. I mean, he tells that story, and I've gotten to the point where I don't really care if he does or not. I mean, he may actually believe that I stole some footage.

CK: *He didn't bring it up with me, so...*

BB: Yeah And the thing is, he and I have patched things up recently. It was my letter to him, it was after my letter to him that he agreed to do the interview, by the way.

CK: *Oh, thank you! Because that was really the linchpin, you know. Kenneth was very hard to get to commit.*

BB: Well, I really wanted him to be a part of it, so I just kind of said, 'Hey, you know, that's water under the bridge, man. Let's patch this up and preserve our legacy, here'. So he did. He agreed right after that to do the interview.

PART OF THE PROCESS

T HOUGH ANTON LAVEY'S CHURCH OF SATAN grabbed all the headlines, 1966 would be a pivotal year for another notorious Satanic cult: The London-based 'Process Church of the Final Judgment', formed by two disgruntled former Scientologists named Robert and Mary Ann Moore, who would soon change their surname to DeGrimston. Oddly, for such a small group with no visible means of support, the Process had themselves a big old mansion in ultra-ritzy Mayfair, and were able to buy an $80,000 yacht and decamp to Nassau. $80,000 could buy one hell of a lot of yacht in 1966.

In June of that year, the cult settled in Xtul, Mexico and lived the getting back to the garden hippie dream. As times in Eden are notoriously short-lived, their idyll was disrupted by Hurricane Inez, which had pulverized the poor fishing villages in the area. The Process were somehow spared, which convinced Robert DeGrimston that he was the new incarnation of Christ come to bring his very weird gospel to the masses.

On their return to London, the Process morphed from hippie peaceniks to black-clad thugs, often seen traveling in packs with German Shepherd attack dogs, as their black and red Dracula capes billowed in the breeze behind them. DeGrimston announced the impending apocalypse and replaced the Holy Trinity with a quadrinity of God, Satan, Jesus and Lucifer.

Like so many of these instant cults, the Process seemed to have an awful lot of money at their disposal. Enough to open up a lecture hall, cinema and book shop, all preaching their violent new evangel. Enough dosh to publish a slick magazine (magazine publishing is not only costly, it's a notorious loss-maker) filled with graphic, bold-type invocations to the dark forces of violence, dominance and mayhem.

G REAT EFFORT IS NOW BEING MADE to rehabilitate the Process Church and attack their critics, but what if the Church were just another front for other, more troubling activities, including drugs, mind control and political extremism? What if the Church's congregants had no idea what other players were actually doing behind the curtains while they went about their zany cultic business?

Perhaps we'll never know, but we should look at their travels in 1966 anyway. They apparently went from Nassau to the Yucatan Peninsula to New Orleans.

That's a very interesting path indeed, wouldn't you say?

First, Nassau. From a 1981 *Christian Science Monitor* article, entitled 'Bahamas: an island paradise for drug traffickers':

> Tainted cash flowing in from drugs smuggling has permeated every sector of the economy. The story is much the same in Nassau, capital of the Bahamas, where many new commercial ventures funded by drug money are changing the face of the inner city.

Then Yucatan. From a STRATFOR report on drug cartels in Mexico:

> While some South American drugs come into Mexico on land at the Guatemalan border, most are shipped via air or boat along two main routes. The first route enters the Yucatan Peninsula by either remote airstrips or the port of Cancun and then goes across the border into Texas by land, air or sea along the Gulf of Mexico.

Then New Orleans:

> 'As a port city, New Orleans was a gateway for drug smuggling well into the 20th century, and the city's historic tolerance for gambling, drinking and other behaviors proved conducive to drug dealing and addiction', state museum historian Karen Leathem said.

What exactly were this English cult — who'd later also set up branches in other coastal cities such as Boston and San Francisco — doing, hopping around these smuggling hotspots like that? And why exactly would they later get mixed up with a series of bloody murders in Los Angeles?

I guess we'll never know.

Oddly enough, 1966 would be a pivotal year for Scientology and for its founder, former Naval Intelligence agent Lafayette Ronald Hubbard. In March, Hubbard and his wife created the 'Guardian's Office', which was basically the Church's secret intelligence branch. By the end of the year, Hubbard had acquired a fleet of ships and created his own private navy, the so-called 'Sea Organization'.

1966 would see yet another famous occultist move to San Francisco. Flush with cash from the American publication of his salacious, muckraking book *Hollywood Babylon*, Kenneth Anger set to work on a motion picture tribute to his personal savior, Lucifer. Anger set up shop at a famous city landmark, The William Westerfeld Mansion, also known as the 'Russian Embassy'.

Which, rather suspiciously, was the base of the city's first hippie commune before Anger moved in.

It was at the Russian Embassy that Anger began work on *Lucifer Rising,* but the young, semi-feral boy he cast in the lead fell through a skylight to his death. Anger replaced him with future Manson Family member Bobby Beausoleil, though Anger would claim Beausoleil took off with the negatives for the film when he split for LA.

Royalties from *Hollywood Babylon* weren't Anger's only source of income, however. He was also flush with grants from the Ford Foundation, which by that time was just another CIA cut-out. Anger was also getting money from the Getty Foundation as well. Awfully powerful friends for an obscure producer of short art films to have, wouldn't you say?

Anger's focus on the *Lucifer Rising* project was erratic, and he ultimately assembled scraps of footage and a recording of Mick Jagger pressing random keys on his new Moog synthesizer in *Invocation of My Demon Brother,* Anger's tribute to Aleister Crowley.

Ritual magic would reemerge in earnest in San Francisco in 1967, with the establishment of the 'New Reformed Order of the Golden Dawn'. Two years later, a former Army Lt. Colonel named Grady McMurtry would re-establish the Ordo Templi Orientis in America, claiming right of succession through Crowley himself. Coincidentally, Church of Satan bigwig and Temple of Set founder Michael Aquino was also a Lt. Colonel in the US Army.

With media-darling Anton LaVey and his lascivious Church of Satan, the mysteriously-flush Process Church, and Ford Foundation and Getty-funded Kenneth Anger all up and running in 1966 ('Year Zero', according to Roman Castevet), another pawn would be put onto the board, one who'd frame the counterculture in an entirely different light for America's Silent Majority.

In 1967, lifetime con and aspiring singer-songwriter Charlie Manson had been let out of prison and immediately made a beeline for the mass open-air party taking place in San Francisco. He would find himself living in an interesting neighborhood. A block and a half away from Manson's crash-pad was a parish of the Process Church. Impressive that the tiny London-based cult could be planting churches on the other side of the word so soon after their founding, don't you think?

Manson apparently crossed paths on occasion with another famous San Francisco occultist, Bobby Beausoleil, then living with Kenneth Anger on the Haight. Beausoleil and Manson were part of an itinerant circle that seemed to drift on the California coast, sometimes living in SF, sometimes in LA. Beausoleil would head for Los Angeles when things went sour with Anger, who put a curse on his young protege.

There Beausoleil would move in with a school teacher and part-time drug dealer named Gary Hinman. Of course, it was in LA that all Hell broke loose. But let's save that story for later.

REPORTS VARY AS TO MANSON'S INVOLVEMENT with the Process, but I'd say the proof's in the pudding: Manson would go from being just another drifter and ex-con to a mind-controlling, apocalyptic-predicting ideologue preaching a remarkably similar cosmology to DeGrimston's own, after living cheek by jowl with the Process Church.

Another OTO lodge — the scandalous Solar Lodge — would start operations in Los Angeles around the same time as the other OTOs. They'd make headlines for child abuse and other offenses at the same time the Manson Family was in the news. Reports are sketchy as to whether Manson was involved with them, but the Solar OTO covered a lot of the bases that Manson later would.

Apocalypse, race wars, and mind control were the order of the day, but the Lodge also traded in sexual repression and violent child abuse. A scandal over the OTOs brutal treatment of children hit the papers and the group's founders high-tailed it to Mexico, never to be heard from again.

THERE'S FAR TOO MUCH SMOKE HOVERING AROUND THE PROCESS to dismiss them as just another nutty but harmless cult. And there is certainly more than enough evidence to speculate that the cult were a front for a much nastier operation, as these groups so very often are.

Manson quit San Francisco and made his way down the coast, eventually hooking up with Beach Boy Dennis Wilson, who set up recording sessions for Charlie with producer Terry Melcher. Soon, stars like Jimi Hendrix and Neil Young were coming around to check out this crazy street freak and his improvised song-poems. Manson gathered up an entourage of mostly young, fucked-up street kids along the way, but ran into the same hassles in LA that hippies were facing in San Francisco.

Manson then somehow finagled a gig for himself and his 'Family' at the Spahn Movie Ranch, where Hollywood producers used to shoot Westerns. More recently, TV shows like *Gunsmoke* had used it before it fell into disrepair.

Interesting place for a drifting ex-con and his street-people friends to crash. Coincidentally, the Process Church of the Final Judgment, would open a chapter in Los Angeles shortly after Manson and his entourage arrived in the area. Even more coincidentally, the Process would end up moving in some of the same circles as Manson and would, like Manson, also try to recruit Terry Melcher to their cause.

B Y 1969, HELL HAD WELL AND TRULY BROKEN LOOSE IN AMERICA. A deeply-divisive and increasingly-futile war, assassinations and race riots that crippled major cities, widespread violence at the Democratic National Convention and a growing epidemic of hard drugs like speed and heroin were leading the country to the tipping point. And increasingly, seemingly 'random' and horrific acts of violence from 'serial' and 'spree' killers would fill the headlines.

Pop culture would be increasingly dominated by themes of horror, black magic and Satanism, everything from movies to bestselling fiction to television and to comic books. Concurrently, Dispensationalist Apocalypticism would rise from the Fundamentalist margins into the mainstream, with best-sellers like Hal Lindsey's *The Late Great Planet Earth*. It was as if the entire country had fallen under a particularly malefic spell.

Largely coinciding, strangely enough, with the creation of the CIA's Project MKOFTEN.

Yet Manson was reportedly still preaching his race-war apocalypse, at least according to some of the testimony that emerged during the trial. One account had it that he took matters into his own hands; over drugs, significantly. Manson would end up shooting a black drug dealer whom Family enforcer Tex Watson had locked horns with.

Drugs would play a starring role in the killing of Gary Hinman by Bobby Beausoleil, which was apparently ordered by Manson as another act in the Helter Skelter ritual (the killing was supposed to blamed on Black Panthers by Manson's tortured logic).

Manson was himself acting on the orders of the Straight Satans outlaw biker gang, who felt that Hinman had burned them with a bad batch of LSD. Beausoleil was ordered to get all the Satans' money back from Hinman, to the amount of $1000, but was then ordered by Manson to kill him when Hinman said he didn't have the cash.

A SLOW-MOTION NIGHTMARE WOULD BE UNFOLDING at Cielo Drive, just a few days before Watson and his accomplices showed up to murder Sharon Tate and her friends: The murders at Cielo Drive shocked Hollywood (Manson: "*Write something witchy*" in the victims' blood), followed by the murders of the LaBiancas. Later, rumors would circulate that Rosemary LaBianca had been involved in meth dealing in her former life as a biker moll.

However, *Ultimate Evil* author Maury Terry later asked a curious question: if 'Helter Skelter' was the true motive, then why did the killings stop after La Bianca? A drug hit — which became all too common in the years that followed — is the obvious answer, especially when the victims are taken into account.

But here's another log to be thrown on the hellfire…

HIPPIE COMMUNE RULED BY 'BLACK MAGIC'

LOS ANGELES, Dec. 5 – 'Black magic.' 'He believes that he, and all human beings, are God.' 'There is no crime, there is no sin.' 'The women were the key to everything'.

Three friends of Charles M. Manson used those words Thursday to describe him and the way they say he ruled a clan of nomadic hippie-types on a commune near Death Valley.

'The whole thing was held together by black magic', said Watkins, who has followed Manson since they met two years ago in the Haight-Ashbury district, then the hippie Haven in San Francisco.

'You don't believe it? Well, it really exists, and it is powerful', Watkins said.

'He (Manson) believes that he, and all human beings, are God and the devil at the same time. He believes all human beings are part of each other', said Poston, a Manson follower for two years.

As you can plainly see, all of Manson's hocus-pocus was very much in synch with the teachings of the Process. Their *public* teachings, at least.

SO THE MANSON PICTURE BECOMES A LITTLE CLEARER. He wasn't just some random ex-con, he had contact with Scientologists in prison and the powerful, apocalyptic cult mind-control of the Process and the Solar OTO when he got out. That goes a long way in explaining what he became. And the sulfurous waft of high-level spookery hovers above it all like a shroud.

You don't need to fall in with some of the more extreme theories about the Process Church or the OTO's involvement with Manson to recognize the toxic power of the propaganda they were pumping out (in especially powerful form, in the case of the Process), or the effect it had on marginal characters like Manson or the dodgier details of their CVs.

In one of those zany, wacky, loony coincidences you can only chalk up to kismet, the Process Church would fall apart in early 1974, shortly after Air America, the CIA's airline widely reported to have been involved in drug smuggling from the Golden Triangle in Southeast Asia, had its operating authority canceled by the Civilian Aviation Board.

And as sheer, random happenstance would have it, DeGrimston was stationed in Southeast Asia when he served in the British Army. Malaysia — which was later plagued by drugs and gang violence — to be exact.

Weird, wacky coincidences there.

PERHAPS ANOTHER KIND OF RITUAL

R ITUAL OF EVIL (1970) WAS THE SECOND OF TWO PILOTS for an unaired series called *Bedeviled*. Inspired by the success of *Rosemary's Baby*, the pilot films featured French legend Louis Jourdan as a psychiatrist named David Sorrell who moonlights as an occult detective. The pilots were also remarkably well rendered, all the more so considering they were TV movies. The first — *Fear No Evil* — dealt with an occult secret society within a cutting-edge laser research lab (whose head was played by Carroll O'Connor, of all people) and the second dealt with kinky cults and the idle Hollywood rich.

Ritual of Evil is by far the more interesting of the two, all the more so given that its plot is rife with parallels to the Manson Family case, though none of the details that people might normally focus on. Instead, it seems to be encoding details about Sharon Tate, the Process Church and the bad news party scene on Cielo Drive, details that didn't begin to go public until Ed Sanders' muckraking expose *The Family* was published in 1971, more than a year after this film aired.

In *Ritual*, a rich young woman named Aline Wiley is discovered dead on a beach, and investigation into her death reveals that a LARPish satanic cult called 'Capricorn' has been making the rounds in LA, spicing up the local orgy scene with mock human sacrifices and black masses.

At first, suspicion for Aline's death falls on a folk singer (played by Georg Stanford Brown) who is lodging on the Wiley estate, since he recently spent time in prison on a drug rap. The folksinger here is black and Manson is a racist hillbilly, but it doesn't take a rocket scientist who we're looking at here. And damn, if the songs Brown's character don't remind a lot of Manson's own meandering, preachy compositions. Brown is also shown recording demos in the aging movie star's guest house in the film.

David Sorrell is treating Aline's younger sister who bears the same childish, sing-songy malevolence seen in Squeaky Fromme, Susan Atkins, Patricia Krenwinkle and the rest. She is plagued by dreams in which she becomes Aline, which couldn't help but remind me of Manson-isms like, "By killing you, I'm killing me," and all of the rest of his beatnik-convict hoo-ha.

But Sorrell soon learns that Aline was mixed up with Capricorn, and used to bring hippies to her parties and subject them to nasty, satanically-tinged S/M games. These games then climax in the ritual sacrifice of a Charles Manson-lookalike as sacrificial lamb and Aline's own death.

W HOEVER WROTE THIS THING KNEW THEIR WEIRDNESS. Several details pop out at you while watching *Ritual of Evil*.

• **First of all, the actress who plays the Sharon Tate character** (Carla Borelli) is in fact a dead ringer for Sharon Tate. Her name is odd: *Aline*. But in light of Tate's involvement in *Eye of the Devil*, note that Alex and Maxine Sanders, celebrity witches and creators of 'Alexandrian Wicca', were hired on as technical advisers for *Eye*. **AL-ex and max-INE= ALINE.**

• **There's a washed-up female screen star** running around the house in question, which is actually a lush beachfront property in Malibu. This seems an obvious (and unkind) reference to Doris Day, whose son Terry Melcher was renting the house on Cielo.

• **There's some genuine occultism dropped into the script,** some *Book of the Law* references and call outs to Astarte and other figures you wouldn't hear cited in your usual dopey Hollywood Satanist potboiler.

• **The Proce… sorry, *Capricorn* is presented an organization** with a decadent but essentially harmless front, and with a more diabolical force operating behind the scenes. The male leader of Capricorn is a poseur and a buffoon, and the real power lies with its female leader. Similar to what the public would only find out much later about the Process Church.

• **Just in case you didn't get the hint** that they actually were talking about the Process in this film, they include a subplot about a German Shepherd that's used in Capricorn's rituals.

And this is perhaps strangest of all: having met and spent time with Jacques Vallée, I can assure you that Louis Jourdan is doing a dead-on impersonation of Vallée in *Ritual*. That in fact makes me wonder if this and *Fear No Evil* started life as UFO-themed series about Vallée or a Vallée-like character, and that Jourdan studied film and video of the UFOlogist to prepare for the role. Remember also that Vallée was close friends with Anton LaVey at this time as well.

NEEDLESS TO SAY, THIS FILM HAS EERIE PARALLELS to the bloody goings-on the previous summer in the real Los Angeles. Sharon Tate traveled to England in 1965 to appear in *Eye of the Devil*, one of many occult thrillers produced in the 1960s and a kind of prototype for *The Wicker Man*. Tate won the role in a very *Rosemary's Baby*-like fashion: actress Kim Novak had originally won the part but fell from a horse and couldn't complete the film. Tate was hired to re-film her scenes.

Tate and Polanski would have another disturbing encounter, this time with dogs allegedly belonging to the Process Church, who were reportedly in the neighborhood as part of an estate-cleaning deal they arranged with an LA real estate baron. Polanski and Tate had been asked to take care of neighbor Patty Duke's dog. One night it escaped off its leash, sending Polanksi running to catch it. As he ran down the hill in pursuit, Polanski was suddenly surrounded by a fearsome pack of German Shepherds, which Ed Sanders would later claim belonged to the Process.

The omens kept on coming. Shortly before her death, a pregnant Tate had an affair with an actor named Christopher Jones, who would later recall a disturbing encounter with the actress:

> "One night we went to visit the Trevi Fountain, and I looked at her and had the strongest feeling she was going to die'. Another time I was looking over at her and asking her what she was thinking about, and she suddenly came out with: 'The Devil is beautiful. Most people think he's ugly, but he's not'."

THE SCENE AT CIELO DRIVE WOULD GET VERY EXTREME, even by Hollywood standards. *The Daily Mail* later described it as "a revolving door with celebrities dropping by, unknown people flitting in and out, and orgies fueled by cocaine and hallucinogens like mescaline." Bobby Beausoleil had told British journalist Barney Hoskyns that, like the fictional Aline in *Ritual of Evil*, "Sharon Tate and that gang …picked up kids on the Strip and took them home and whipped them."

Dennis Hopper told *The LA Free Press* that Tate and her circle fallen into 'masochism and bestiality' and that they recorded it all on videotape. Similarly there is also a strange and somewhat oblique relationship to a dog in *Ritual of Evil*. We learn that the dog attended all of Aline's parties (nudge, nudge). Hopper also claimed that three days before the murders, twenty-five people were invited to a mass whipping of a Sunset Strip dealer who'd sold them some bad dope. I seem to remember that twenty-five people attended the black mass referred to in *Ritual of Evil* as well.

Producer Terry Melcher — the son of aging Hollywood sweetheart Doris Day who had previously rented the house on Cielo Drive — hinted that Tate and her circle were dabbling in Satanism. Like Hopper, Melcher reported that the new tenants shot homemade S/M porno movies with Hollywood players in starring roles. The goings-on in *Ritual of Evil* also take place in the home of an aging Hollywood movie star, played by Ann Baxter.

Were the activities at Cielo being filmed for blackmail purposes? Were they being filmed for private collectors? Police were rumored to have found a large stash of homemade porn featuring Hollywood stars and players in Polanski's house. Were these films somehow linked to the murders?

Stories would later emerge that Manson and right-hand man Tex Watson hired themselves and the Family out as a murder-for-hire outfit. Before the murders, Manson was casing out the Cielo Drive property. Someone seemed to be worried about their face appearing in one of those films.

There'd be even darker rumors about the scene at the house and the films being made there. Many years after the Tate/LaBianca murders, Manson had told an interviewer, "Don't you think those people deserved to die? They were involved in kiddie porn." Sammy Davis, Jr., who'd have his own flirtations with the dark side, later said of the Cielo Drive scene: "Everyone there had at at one time or another been into Satanism."

Given the blatant Process clone and the number of Manson stand-ins in *Ritual of Evil*, what does this tell us about Manson's own connection to the cult? I would argue it's ironclad evidence Manson was mixed up with them, given that the public had no idea about the links until after *Ritual of Evil* aired. And despite the many denials of their association, *The Process* magazine would later publish a piece by Manson:

> In the *Death* issue of Process from 1971, a brief article by Charles Manson appeared, entitled "Pseudo-profundity in Death," which Charlie penned during the course of the Tate/LaBianca trial. In this article, Manson described death as "total awareness" "Coming to Now and Peace from this world's madness and paradise in my own self."

The Process Church *hired* Manson to write the piece, meaning they certainly had contact with him while he was in prison. And that certainly seems to speak to a deeper and earlier connection, in this writer's opinion.

S O WHAT DOES THAT ALL MEAN? Given the time it takes to write, prepare and produce even a made-for-TV movie, it means it must have been written before Charles Manson and the rest of his family had been arrested for the Tate-LaBianca murders. It was certainly written before the public knew anything of the connections between Sharon Tate's murder and the Process Church. That means the connections between the Process Church, Charles Manson and the orgy scene at Cielo Drive were known by someone in Hollywood, long before the public or even the police knew anything about it.

Telling tales out of school indeed.

GOODBYE CHARLIE

C HARLES MILLES MANSON, AN EARLY BETA-TEST for the now-familiar Joker archetype, has died at the age of 83. A lifetime convict and two-bit grifter, Manson was accused of masterminding two horrific murder sprees, ostensibly in hopes of triggering a race war he called 'Helter Skelter', so named after the famous Beatles song from Manson's beloved 'White Album'.

You probably know the official version of Manson's story, and I'd wager quite a few of you are very well-read in the non-official versions as well. But to me, Manson was just a charismatic jailhouse punk whom certain parties found useful for a time. He did what he needed to do, was paraded around in front of the television cameras, and then was thrown back in the can, where he felt most comfortable and secure.

Three hots, a cot, and a parade of credulous journalists to dump his bullshit on from time to time? A never-ending stream of fan-mail from mentally-ill dip-shits? Charlie achieved a level of grifter-nirvana that the most adept swamis and mystics would kill for.

As he himself once admitted, Manson was absolutely nobody, and probably would have remained so had he not shown up among certain circles in San Francisco at a time when a grand and ambitious new Project had been launched. This Project would round up a host of charismatic fuckups like Manson, give them whatever they needed so far as money, dope, whatever they liked to fuck. And of course, scads and scads of media attention.

So a bullshitting bottom-feeder like Howard Stanton Levey was reborn as Church of Satan founder 'Anton Szandor LaVey'. When not spreading the hackneyed Satanic gospel on any number of high-profile media outlets, LaVey was essentially a host for kinky sex parties. All of which were almost-assuredly filmed recorded by the city police, for whom LaVey was a paid informant.

You also had Kenneth Wilbur Anglemeyr — AKA Kenneth Anger — a onetime filmmaking prodigy gone to seed, whose fringey, fetishy work was openly financed by J. Paul Getty Jr., the Ford Foundation and other real-life Bond-villains. And you had a ditzy hausfrau-turned-shopkeep like Sybil Leek recast as the Wondrous Witch of the West and feted like royalty on American talk shows. It was all part of the Project, all part of the Overarching Agenda.

And a no-hoper like Manson — whose life trajectory would have inevitably landed him nowhere but back to punking and snitching on the block — rubbed elbows with big-time showbiz types, rock stars and movie producers. People who otherwise would never piss on a Charles Manson if he was on fire.

MANSON AND HIS RAGAMUFFIN BAND of privileged but homely suburban girls in the middle of their first schizophrenic breaks found themselves sheltered on a TV-set ranch, looked after by a psychopath named Tex Watson, a success-track frat-boy who apparently suddenly chucked it all to 'find himself'. Or something. The Family supported themselves by whoring and dealing, and I'd guess by any number of blackmail or shakedown schemes.

Manson quite correctly points out he never killed anyone. Stone-cold killers like Watson and Susan Atkins probably didn't need much prompting, and it's generally agreed upon that the murders were committed to convince the cops that Bobby 'Cupid' Beausoleil — a musical prodigy caught up in a bummer drug deal with some angry bikers — was in fact innocent of killing music teacher-drug dealer Gary Hinman.

Who exactly was targeted for the spree — and *why* — is of course another conversation altogether. And what certain parties knew about it all is yet another conversation even still. Suffice it to say it all reeks of the stench of a certain unique bouquet known to be exclusively cultivated in the meadows and fields of Fairfax County, Virginia.

DISPATCHES FROM THE
BEATEN GENERATION

HISTORY'S LATCHKEY KIDS

THERE'S A NEW THEME DEVELOPING IN THE MEDIA: the supposed 'Baby Boomers vs. Millennials' war. You've probably seen it floating around. It's the kind of thing journalists love to write about and whenever possible, try to referee. Pretending they can referee the generation gap makes journalists feel important. Not much else does these days.

This apparent struggle has emerged as an issue in the workplace, with Boomer management expressing their frustration with flabby Millennial work habits. In turn, Millennials have shot back arguing that it was a lot easier to find and keep a job when the Boomers were coming up — in other words, before Globalism began systematically dismantling the middle class — and that life was easier and cheaper back then.

Indeed, within the fictitious media construct known as the 'post-Recession recovery', the Baby Boomers were said to have 'won' the great struggle in the job market, continuing to hold a larger proportion of plum gigs than their children. I'm not sure how this excuses some of the work habits or the overall lack of preparation that managers complain about, but that's not my fight.

Some in the media have tried to smooth over the conflict, assuring the two opposing generations that they're more alike than they might think they are, with their privileged idealism and all the rest of it. One study even highlighted the two cohorts with the title, *Two Special Generations: The Millennials and the Boomers*. As in "Hey everyone, don't fight. You're all in this together. You're all, you're all… so special!"

And who gets left out of this equation, again? Why, the *Not*-so-Special Generation. History's latchkey kids, those born between 1965 and 1984, commonly known as 'Generation X'.

You know who I mean: the ones who had to fend for themselves while their parents went off to find themselves. The generation who were raised on TV dinners while their parents were off at TM class. The latchkey kids left at home while their parents were slipping off to key parties. The generation that grew up knowing all too well how much better everything was for their parents and older siblings.

But it was also the generation that, for ever-so-brief a time, were at the cutting edge of technology and culture. If Generation X had a theme, it was chafing at the arbitrary restrictions it saw, not only in culture and business but in the business of culture as well as the culture of business. So many of the innovations that have been made in the workplace — the ones Millennials have now come to *expect* — were put into place by GenX'ers.

It was Generation X that embraced the Internet and became its first great wave of both users and entrepreneurs (I mean, *blogging?*). So much is said now about video games and the power of the industry, but it was Generation X that first truly embraced the medium and became its pioneering engineers and programmers. Having seen the Oculus Rift webinar, I can safely say that I didn't see anything shockingly unlike what I'd seen in gaming 20 years ago. Maybe more bells and whistles, but the same basic chassis.

It was Generation X that got fed up with the music industry monopoly and built its own scenes — punk, metal, hip hop, jam bands, rave — often dealing with a lot of legal and criminal hassles to do so. The window would open only for a frightfully-short time, but long enough to break down a lot of old ways of doing business.

Of course, no one realized that the music business itself was going to be written off as an expendable asset for the mass marketing of cellphones and other consumer electronics: a *loss leader*, if you will. Least of all those GenX'ers who thought they could carve out niches for themselves as independent musicians. But at the same time there's also a whole range of viable alternatives to corporate pabulum for listeners, and that came in large part out of the independent spirit of the Eighties and Nineties.

Generation X would make its mark on cinema with the Independent boom in the 1990s, and they would do so not by embracing high art, but by reframing the junk culture that babysat them in its latchkey days. GenX auteurs would use pulp and teen trash as their medium, and in irony of ironies, be embraced by the same kinds of critics who never gave the source material these filmmakers grew up on the time of day.

Which brings us to comics and superheroes. Everything we're seeing now, all the big hit movies and TV shows, owe their success to the material that Generation X comic fans embraced and/or created in the Eighties and Nineties. There hasn't been anything of any real significance done since that incredibly fertile period. All the storytelling conventions we're seeing now in films were established back then. That was also a period when you saw a lot of self-publishing, a lot of self-starting on the retail end. But it would be — and to a shocking extent, it *remains* — Generation X who embraced and supported and militated for that work. Many of them would go on to work in the film and TV industry, then fight to get their favorite mythologies on the screen.

So why do the media care so little about Generation X? Why does everything they accomplished seem to be forgotten all of a sudden? Why are most of what we see are pity stories, despite the fact that some of these writers are GenX themselves?

Well, maybe it's because of that independent streak, that rebellious nature that formed the GenX stereotype. While you can't generalize about Sixty+ million people, GenX'ers on the whole do tend to be quite a bit more skeptical of government and authority than most Boomers, and most certainly more so than the Millennials.

That tendency towards autonomy is not something that people in power much care for; look no further than the small business tax codes. Hell, look at everything everywhere these days. Autonomy and independent thinking don't seem to be on the menu, do they? Unless, you mean to be eaten.

Millennials can't be stereotyped either, but we are seeing many of them embrace all kinds of trends and technologies that are inhibiting personal freedom, individuality, independent thinking and complexity. Maybe some of these Millennials — a *vanguard*, perhaps — would argue that these are necessary sacrifices, that it's all leading to a more fair and just society.

To which I'd argue to them, are you *sure* about that? I mean, are you really *certain?* It's a hell of a thing to be wrong about.

Have there ever been any examples were people are lured into giving something — or perhaps, *everything* — up in exchange for some promised better thing that in fact never actually arrives or comes true? Or in fact what arrives is actually the *opposite* of what was expected or promised?

Maybe GenX has become inconvenient because they learned a few lessons about trusting the System from their parents' and elder siblings mistakes, lessons that the Panopticon seems hellbent on deleting from the Borgsong.

I'll end this by advising everyone to not count Generation X out yet. You're talking a cohort that grew up with diminished expectations already, and has already dealt with two major economic downturns in the adult lives of its senior members. And a cohort whose vanguard made their mark by rewriting the plans laid out for them to their own liking, or at least *tried*. It may still have a few tricks left up its collective sleeve.

Let's hope someone does.

LET ME TELL YOU A STORY

I'M NOT REALLY A BIG FAN OF DONALD TRUMP, never have been. I don't hate him, certainly not like I hate Hillary Clinton (meaning 'passionately'), and I don't hate him like I hate the neocons, neolibs, and other various scoundrels, rapscallions and mountebanks that do hate him.

But I'm still not entirely sure this year hasn't all been a bad dream I'm having because that chicken sandwich I had last night wasn't cooked well enough. Trump may not exactly be a low-rent gangster from Queens who got lucky and hit the big time, but he sure likes to act like one. But do I think he's the bastard lovechild of Adolf Hitler and Squeaky Fromme? Come on. Get real. This is a guy who's spent his entire adult life doing business in New York real estate, big money casinos and television. He's pretty much been vetted. Real Nazis have a very hard time hiding it.

Trump is a boor, and has a remarkable penchant for saying all the wrong things at the wrong time, but if you think he's a Neo-Nazi, then you've never had the misfortune of dealing with a *real* Neo-Nazi. I don't mean a bigot or a LARPer Nazi, or a 4Channer. I mean an honest-to-God *Neo-Nazi*. I have, and it's kinda like looking into the shark tank at the New England Aquarium. You realize that you're encountering something entirely alien to your experience.

Let me tell you a story.

I was deeply involved in the Boston Hardcore scene in the early Eighties. The skinhead look was fashionable but we were all actually punk rockers. Things could get pretty violent and obnoxious, but it was pretty much kids just having fun while they were young enough to get away with it. But there were Nazi punks in the woodpile, no doubt about it. And they liked to hurt people.

They weren't always skins, and they weren't always local. I remember some Nazi punk band somehow got an opening slot at a show at The Channel and they all looked like Beavis and Butthead's stupider older brothers. But things got pretty ugly pretty quickly. During the melee, the lead singer of the band hurled the microphone stand into the crowd, nearly killing a girl. Then they got chased back to New Hampshire, or wherever the fuck they came from.

But there were also some scenesters who started in with the Nazi shit, too. I was seen as suspect not only because I liked verboten bands like Van Halen and The Clash, but also because my best friend was Jewish and my high school sweetheart was a black girl from Brookline. I remember going wandering into the wrong room and encountering a clutch of Nazi punks getting all weepy over an LP of old SS marching songs.

It was like… yeah, I'm going to just go *not-here* now. But that was nothing compared to these Neo-Nazi skins who showed up one night, from God knows the hell where.

The New York punk band Kraut was in town (*not* a Nazi band, incidentally) and local Clash cosplayers Stranglehold were the opening act. Some Neo-Nazi skins I'd never seen before were milling around, pretty much minding their own business. They weren't really physically imposing, but goddamn, they were scary. They had all kinds of tattoos, including the spiderweb and teardrops. In fact, that's what struck me. Tattoos weren't really a punk thing yet, so I'd never seen the teardrop tattoo before and didn't know what it meant.

So anyhow, Stranglehold comes on and the crowd all gets into it. Boston moshing was considerably more violent than other scenes, since these were essentially a bunch of prep school jocks who liked to throw elbows. A fun night ended with bruises, maybe a black eye or bloody nose. Whee.

Then my friend Dave got pushed by someone into one of these Neo-Nazi skins. Faster then the eye could see, the skin clocked Dave with a right hook. One of his friends gave him a couple more shots and pushed him down. The Neo-Nazis wore giant signet rings, and at first it looked like the punch took Dave's eye out. It was a bloody fucking mess.

The dance floor cleared. Like an idiot, I leaped into the middle of it and started yelling, "Come on, let's fuck these guys up!" and so on. To this day, I don't know what the fuck I was thinking. I doubt anyone heard me but they certainly saw me waving my hands around and pointing as these Neo-Nazis. The band played on, seeming a bit confused by what was happening.

The Neo-Nazi who punched Dave looked straight at me, and I will never forget his eyes. I didn't see a glint of human recognition in them. Nothing. Nada. Zip. Zilch. He seemed to have already sized me up and determined I wasn't anything he needed to waste his time on. My foolish show of bravado fell on deaf ears anyway. The legendary punk rock warriors of Boston all backed off. *Brotherhood! Unity! The Scene!* Maybe later.

The moshing started up again (only nobody called it 'moshing' then), but there was a very wide berth between these Neo-Nazis and everyone else. I heard people say later they were carrying, but I don't believe that. I just think everyone looked into those eyes and realized that any fight with these guys was not going to end with the usual bloody nose and bruised knuckles. These Neo-Nazis gave you the unmistakable impression that they took their violence very seriously. Very, *very* seriously.

I mean, these guys were ready to take on an entire club. In Boston. They didn't seem fazed by the prospect.

Some friends and I ended up leaving halfway during Kraut's set to take Dave to the emergency room at Mass General. At some point I imagine those Neo-Nazis probably joined some mercenary force and went on to commit war crimes in El Salvador or somewhere.

So the Great Trump Panic has gotten to the point that there's an ongoing crackdown not only on actual Nazi websites, but on some non-Nazi conspiracy sites and YouTube Channels and Facebook pages and on and on. You're seeing a lot of attacks by establishment voices, not only on 'conspiracy theory' (well, any conspiracy theorizing aimed at the Establishment), but also the slightest deviation from the consensus you'd encounter at a dinner party in the Hamptons or Pacific Heights. This is an elite backlash, believe it.

The ongoing but markedly-diminished 'Pizzagate' phenomenon is a major impetus for this backlash, especially after some actor (no, seriously: he even has an iMDb page) showed up at Comet Ping Pong with an assault rifle and shot up their computer. The big problem is that the whole Pizzagate thing is predicated on the assumption that you can crack a global criminal conspiracy by looking into symbolism and coded language. Unfortunately, that's not really how it works. You can tell quite a lot from symbolism, but when building an actual legal case you need actual physical evidence. *Habeas corpus,* they call it.

But by the same token, you're seeing a lot of people try to pretend that there's nothing amiss in Washington whatsoever, all the evidence to the contrary. *The Washington Post* reported that child sex trafficking was in fact a major problem within the Beltway in early 2016, and we've seen thousands of people arrested for such all over the country this year alone.

There are two problems here. First, the all-consuming toxin of partisanship turns everything it touches to shit and garbage. It became an Us-Against-Them thing and actual truth be damned. The second is that most decent people can't even picture themselves engaging in that kind of activity, and henceforth can't picture anyone else doing so either. Big mistake.

Let me tell you a story.

I used to do appearances at conventions in the Nineties, and probably got to know a little more than I wanted to about the seamy side of Fandom. You'd see a lot of really sketchy shit on perfectly reputable dealer's tables. A lot of it seemed to come from Japan for some reason.

So, at a couple cons I ended up sitting next to a guy I will call the 'Canadian Cartoonist', who has since passed away. I'd vaguely heard of him, some controversy in *The Comics Journal* dealing with some offensive racial caricatures in a book he worked on. So my guard was up a bit when I met him. But as it turned out, he was a really nice guy.

The Canadian Cartoonist was very funny, very talented, quite charismatic and good-natured, and extremely knowledgeable about comics. Just a good guy to be stuck at a crappy con with. And then I looked at his artwork and thought, *Oh my God: this guy is a total fucking pedophile.*

Now, the creepy stuff you'd usually see at cons was neckbeards fantasizing about pubescent girls in Wonder Woman costumes or something, maybe a protruding nipple or camel-toe here and there. That's not what the Canadian Cartoonist was into. He was into drawing *very* young boys in the most compromising positions you'd never want to see. He rationalized drawing eight year-olds in bondage by claiming they were actually elves. Or something. *That* was an eye-opener.

The Canadian Cartoonist disappeared after *The Comics Journal* article for a couple years. I learned he went to Asia somewhere (I believe he spoke one of the languages) in the interim. I also heard rumors that it was a kind of 'get the hell out of Dodge' situation. Around the same time he left, there was a fairly well-known comics artist he was tight with who got busted for, *y'know.*

Now, I'm sure some of you are saying what do you expect, this was some overgrown babyman fanboy. This had nothing to do with the government or any conspiracy.

Let me tell you a story.

I grew up in Braintree, as many of you know. And oftentimes growing up in Braintree in the Seventies was kind of like a mashup of *Twin Peaks: The Return* and *Lord of the Flies.* In fact, the more I think about it now, the more insane it seems. I was only vaguely cognizant of it at the time, but notorious Boston gangster/MKULTRA subject Whitey Bulger had one of his cronies bumped off across from the park we all played in. Shades of *Blue Velvet.*

Now, I'm seeing a lot of demeaning armchair Freudianism during this big psychological warfare operation being waged against 'conspiracy theory'. It's always something to do with 'persecution complexes' and 'delusions of grandeur' and this, that, and all the other bullshit. Someone should add, *'plus, growing up in Braintree'* as a disclaimer. What could I possibly mean by that?

Read this, from *The Boston Globe* in 2008:

Prostitution sting charges 7 as FBI puts focus on youth

Seven people face prostitution-related charges as a result of a law enforcement sting in Braintree, part of a nationwide effort by the FBI to rescue children forced into prostitution.

> Although none of the people arrested locally in 'Operation Cross Country' was underage, one told authorities that she had been working as a prostitute since she was 14. About one-quarter of adult prostitutes started when they were juveniles, officials say. The stings were carried out last month by local police and the FBI. Most of those arrested were from Boston, and were using Braintree as a base of operation.

OK, this operation was broken up in 2008. Do you know when I first heard about this going on in Braintree? In <u>1982.</u> I heard about it from a guy who I knew was friendly with a town cop. He said they were using girls from the high school to pick up men from the subway station, then take them across the street to the Motel 6 to get laid. I couldn't believe it when I heard the names of some of the girls involved. They were all *very* young.

That no underage prostitutes were arrested in an FBI operation targeted at rescuing them is not surprising in the least. Someone almost certainly tipped someone off. I mean, this is *Braintree* we're talking about. What exactly do I mean by that? Well, the Braintree Police apparently carried out a similar sting in 2005. It couldn't have been terribly successful if the FBI felt they had to take over three years later, wouldn't you say? Bear in mind that this operation was focused on major cities like cities like Phoenix and Denver. Plus, *Braintree*.

Let me tell you a story.

I went to East Junior High (now East Middle), and sometimes it felt like *Sin City* as performed by the cast of *Bugsy Malone*. Unless I wanted to walk a good half-mile out of the way, I had to navigate through Monatiquot Village on my way to school, a Section Eight apartment complex which then was filled with Aquarian casualties and their feral kids.

You could choose one or two paths to East, both of which had open-air drug bazaars going on before and after school. High school kids would meet up with sixth-graders and sell them pot, speed, acid, you name it. I mean, I already knew what 'microdot' and 'windowpane' meant when I was ten years old. I wish I were exaggerating.

The Big Path, as it was known, became a Thunderdome after school. Fights would be arranged and scheduled, Don King-style. No, I'm not kidding. Everyone knew who was going to be fighting there after school. It was like a boxing card. Sometimes there'd be two or more fights going on at the same time. You never, ever saw a teacher or principal come to break it up, even though this was all in clear eyeshot of the front door of the school.

There was also a teacher at East who was an *open* pedophile and used the A/V room as his recruitment office. He was also a foster parent. And a Boy Scout troop leader. Yep, that's Braintree in a nutshell.

Everyone knew what was going on. Everyone knew the kids this guy was fostering (and nobody messed with them; they were pretty tough). The guy set them and some other boys up with minibikes, stereos, BB guns and the best sneakers. I remember standing in art class in sixth grade, watching one of these boys doing donuts in the courtyard on his brand-new Honda mini. He eventually got bored when no one came out to chase him and drove off.

This teacher would stand in the hallway between periods and hit on passing students. All *prepubescent* students, mind you. I only had a social studies class on that floor, so I only had a few run-ins with him. He had really greasy long hair, acne scars and the most disgusting leering smile you ever saw. I mean, child molester straight from Central Casting.

So you're thinking, this was all just schoolyard rumor, right? Nothing more to it. I mean, if there was how the hell did this guy get away with it? Well, he didn't. He was eventually arrested. Off the coast of Florida, in a yacht sitting in international waters, if memory serves. I do remember reading about that in *The Patriot Ledger*.

Like I said, this wasn't a secret. Everyone, and I mean *everyone*, in school knew about it. So how the hell did he get away with it? I have my theories, but it's worth mentioning we're talking about the Boston Archdiocese here, where hundreds of priests got mixed up in the sex abuse scandal. You may have heard a thing or two about it. Two of the most notorious priests (Shanley and Geoghan) served in Braintree at one time or other. You also had to contend with perverts approaching you in the streets now and again. That was just part of the landscape. So again, how the hell did this guy get away with it for so long?

Well, it helped that he was plying his trade in Braintree. He picked the right town for it, say that much for the guy.

Let me tell you a story.

LONGTIME READERS REMEMBER THE UNIVERSITY OF ALABAMA Shooter, Dr. Amy Bishop, and that I went to school with her and her brother Seth. I was in at least one class with her (a sci-fi lit class) and maybe more in my first go-around in ninth grade. I wasn't exactly friends with her brother, but I did talk comics with him in the lunchroom from time to time. Amy and I spent a lot of time in the same hospital for the same reason, but I don't think our paths crossed there.

Anyway, I've been reading a book about Amy Bishop (*A Professor's Rage*) since I'm trying to get a handle on mind control and so on, pertaining specifically to children of my generation. Why?

Well, I got kind of weird notion about it while researching the Grunge scene and the phenomenal rate of attrition it's engendered, and it proceeded from there. There's a lot of material to sort through when dealing with mind control, most of it rubbish. I keep remembering why I've spent so many years steering clear of that particular thicket. But our Ms. Bishop shows all the hallmarks of being a real-life, honest to God Manchurian Candidate, and I need to find out how and why.

Let me just give you the *Reader's Digest* version. One fine December night — according to the single newspaper account this rather extravagant episode earned at the time — our Amy was trying to unload her father's shotgun, which she'd being messing with upstairs. She came down to the kitchen and asked Seth to help her. But as cruel Fate would have it, the weapon accidentally discharged into poor Seth's chest and he died. Just a freak happenstance. The family were understandably crestfallen and the Braintree Police determined it was an accident and Amy went on to enjoy a sterling career in science.

Except what *really* happened is that after reading an account in *The National Enquirer* of the shotgun murders of *Dallas* star Patrick Duffy's parents, Amy blew two holes in the walls of the house, charged downstairs, blew her brother away, ran out into the cold night with shotgun in tow, and went on a rampage Quentin Tarantino would find excessive.

She waved her loaded Mossberg at passing motorists, then attempted a carjacking or two before finally engaging in an armed standoff with two Braintree patrolmen. There were any number of felonies to book this young woman on but the Chief of Police rushed down to the station, declared it all an accidental shooting, then ordered his staff to forget about the rampage and kick the girl loose.

Somehow this was all fine and dandy with Norfolk County DA William Delahunt, his prosecutor, and a special State Police investigator. Yes, it was all fine and dandy until one chilly winter's day when Amy gunned down her comrades in the University of Alabama Biology Dept.

Then-current Braintree Police Chief Frazier, who was extremely pissed off about the cover-up (which included the relevant police files and logs being removed from the station and hidden in the home of a retired captain) called the Alabama cops and told them all about the Seth snuff. One of the reasons Frazier might have been so pissed off was that he was mysteriously suspended four days before Seth's murder and Amy's subsequent rampage.

As Fate would have it, there was *another* Tarantino rampage in Braintree that ended with Frazier gunning down some nutjob after a high-speed chase. Frazier was the shop steward at the time, meaning he was the one guy the aggrieved officers could appeal the Chief's decision to.

It gets worse. It gets so much worse that I keep putting my iPad down and muttering incredulous sounds to myself every time I try to dig into this book. I thought I was pretty jaded by now but this is like… *fuck*.

Let's put it this way: if I read the Amy Bishop story in a novel, I'd find it all too unbelievable to finish. As far as I'm concerned, pretty much everything is on the table now. Reptilians, Monarch, Pizzagate? Hey, whatever floats your boat. If this shit went down, the sky's the limit. Treat yourself.

H ERE'S HOW IT GOES: young Amy fires a shotgun inside her house, shoots and kills her brother, goes apeshit on Washington Street, waves her rifle at passing motorists, car mechanics and paperboys before engaging in a Mexican stand-off with two of Braintree's finest. I couldn't even tally the number of major felonies she committed that night.

No charges.

Some years later, the now-Doctor Amy punched out a soccer mom in a crowded International House of Pancakes, in front of dozens of witnesses.

No charges.

Then our intrepid Doctor Bishop allegedly sent not one but *two* letter bombs to her lab supervisor at Boston Children's Hospital, who was also a big deal at Harvard, allegedly. He pissed her off in a particular way, allegedly. Care to guess what happened next?

The FUCKING UNABOMBER TASK FORCE swooped in and took over the case. We're talking FBI, ATF, Postmaster General, Federal prosecutors, so many agencies that your head spins.

No charges.

Bear in mind that these guys managed to put *the Unabomber* in prison but couldn't do the same with Amy Bishop. It was then kicked over to an ATF unit, who gathered some pretty incriminating circumstantial evidence.

No charges.

The lead investigator was so disgusted he took retirement. I'm not even done with the book, and I've literally lost count of the number of law enforcement agencies that were ordered to lay off Amy Bishop. Literally everyone from the Braintree Police all the way up to the FBI. If all that wasn't bad enough, Doctor Amy kept getting plum gigs, in labs and classrooms, even though the general consensus seemed to be she was both a crappy scientist and a useless teacher.

Some of Amy's students at Huntsville actually started a petition asking the school to replace her. And pretty much everyone she worked with was absolutely terrified of her. Later, it turned out that her house-husband did a lot of the actual science while Amy ran off to writing workshops in hopes of becoming the next Michael Crichton. From all accounts, she sucked at that too. And it seems all the books featured protagonists heavily based on Amy herself. The third and final manuscript dealt with a herpes epidemic.

All that transpired before Amy went into some kind of trance and opened fire during a faculty meeting, which was staffed by microbiologists. In fact, teaching staff were in a panic because somehow they believed Amy had planted a bomb designed to spread the *herpes virus*.

Mind you, biology professors and instructors at one of the leading schools for genetic science were convinced of this. People who understood the science. According to the police, they were mistaken. We all make mistakes, I suppose.

Amy was in a trance after the shootings and seemed totally unaware they even happened. She denied she had anything to do with it and that the other professors were still alive. Yeah, it's like that. You know the drill.

Operation Paperclip — y'know, that time when the Truman Administration imported a couple thousand of the most committed, most ideological Nazis and giving them plum gigs in corporate America — initially called Fort Strong its home. That's on an island a few thousand feet away from Wollaston Beach, which Amy could have walked to from her house if she wanted some exercise. I did it a few times myself.

And in the craziest darn coincidence you could ever imagine, Amy ended her career (and her colleagues' lives) at Huntsville, just a short walk away from the Marshall Space Center, where Wernher Von Braun (and pretty much his entire staff) wound up after leaving the fine shores of Boston Harbor. You just gotta love those coincidences.

So; remind me *again* why I shouldn't believe in conspiracies?

LET ME TELL YOU ANOTHER STORY

I N 'LET ME TELL YOU A STORY' I talked about the ongoing psychological warfare operation being waged on 'conspiracy theory', a buzzword used to demonize anyone who doesn't believe everything they see or read in the mainstream media. We're seeing all kinds of armchair philosophizing from journalists, who at this point in the game are being existentially traumatized by the collapse of the print media, the overwhelming competition for gigs, and all the politically-correct struggle sessions.

To these undiscovered psychiatric geniuses, 'conspiracy theory' is just some kind of coping mechanism for losers and borderline psychotics. If this all sounds suspiciously Soviet to you, it's because that's precisely where this line of thinking originally came from. You see, I happen to perceive history and current events through a conspiratorial lens for a number of different reasons, but it basically boils down to the fact that I grew up in Braintree, Massachusetts in the 1970s and 1980s.

I left Braintree as soon as I turned 18 and never moved back. Don't get me wrong: I had a *blast* in high school. My teenaged years were essentially *Repo Man* as directed by John Hughes. But there was something wrong there. Like some subliminal signal or inaudible hum I could never seem to shake. And I couldn't escape the feeling that Braintree hated its children. The amount of abuse, neglect and predation I personally saw continues to stagger me when I look back on it. I didn't realize until later that it wasn't supposed to be this way.

A FRIEND OF MINE DUBBED BRAINTREE 'TWIN PEAKS EAST' back in the day, and it's an apt metaphor. It's also very, very much like Lumberton in *Blue Velvet;* a more or less normal suburban facade built atop an army-ant nest of corruption. But there's something much, much worse at work in Braintree. Most people — even people who live there — have no idea. And this is not ancient history, this is now.

The Braintree Police were mired in a major scandal in late 2016 in which large amounts of money, firearms and illegal drugs went missing from the evidence locker. How large? An audit of the Braintree police evidence room found that more than 4,000 pieces of narcotics evidence, 60 firearms and $400,000 in seized cash was missing. I mean, this is *Serpico* stuff we're looking at here, only it's now and not New York City in the Seventies.

The Chief and Deputy Chief were forced to retire, and hundreds of cases may have to be thrown out, including the drug case of a lunatic who was caught on camera trying to abduct a baby from a Braintree store. And of all the crap luck, a case against a major drug trafficker has also been affected.

Strong suggestions were made that the evidence locker clerk was responsible for what is not only grand larceny but official corruption on a scale that suggests collusion with larger criminal forces, of which there are many operating in Braintree. The clerk, a 21-year BPD — veteran, mother of one and stepmother of three from an old-line Braintree family — 'committed suicide' two days after the investigation began. Vague and completely unsubstantiated rumors of misconduct were duly fed to local media.

The clerk's married name was Susan Zopatti, but I knew her as Susan Lawson in high school. If you asked me back then the last person I would picture getting involved in a criminal conspiracy when she grew up, Susan Lawson would be near the top of the list. I mean, she was on the *track team*.

B RAINTREE'S MOST FAMOUS FAMILY TODAY are the Wahlberg's, but they moved to East Braintree from Dorchester after Donnie signed his first New Kids on the Block check. They live a block away from my old house. They bought the old Moline place on Pilgrim Road (I was friends with Robbie Moline. He was an excellent drummer).

Braintree is best known for being the birthplace of the two President Adams, but also as the site of the robbery that resulted in the infamous Sacco and Vanzetti trial. In case it doesn't ring a bell, two anarchists were blamed for the robbery and murder of a security guard and paymaster of a shoe factory. This all went down in the wake of the Palmer Raids, and became such a global *cause célèbre* that luminaries such as HG Wells and Albert Einstein. Hell, even Benito Mussolini got involved.

Braintree was an industrial suburb in the old days, dotted with factories. Most were either abandoned or in ruins by the Seventies. Me and my buddy Charlie used to play 'Planet of the Apes' in the ruins of the old Michigan Abrasives factory, a door down from the Sacco and Vanzetti crime site. The Monatiquot River ran through the ruined foundation. The border between East Braintree and Quincy was straddled by the old General Dynamics shipyard, from whence the slogan 'Kilroy was Here' came (in honor of James J. Kilroy, a ship inspector during World War II). The shipyard was once the largest private employer in the South Shore area, and built battleships and destroyers for the Navy, as well as some of the first LNG tankers. It closed in 1986.

About a half mile up Quincy Ave is the Citgo Fuel Terminal. For several years, Citgo was the property of the government of Venezuela. Robert Kennedy Jr. could be heard on radio commercials a few years back, praising the Chavez government for giving heating oil allowances to lower-income families in the area. Chavez ultimately died of an aggressive cancer, after which his ruling junta collapsed. Venezuela has since collapsed into near-total anarchy. Citgo was bought back for a song.

Do you want me to sum up my brief in a single sentence? In Braintree, someone thought it would be a good idea to install a major petrochemical facility a few blocks away from a public beach and a large recreational and sporting facility for children. Or vice versa, depending on the exact timeline. And now soil samples have shown that benzene, a ferociously-dangerous chemical solvent, are 200 to 300 percent above mandated safety levels, according to a recent study.

N OW, I PREVIOUSLY MENTIONED THE A/V TEACHER AT EAST who was openly molesting a number of prepubescent boys. This was not a secret. Ask anyone who went to East before the guy's arrest and they will tell you all about it. But since I hate to make a public claim without evidence to back it up, I actually spent cash money to track down the news story on the arrest. Here's the *Globe* story in its entirety:

BRAINTREE MAN ARRAIGNED Feb 16, 1980

A 44-year-old former Braintree junior high school teacher and scoutmaster pleaded innocent yesterday to 20 counts of rape and sexual assault against two Braintree boys. Robert Galowicz of Braintree was arraigned in Dedham Superior Court yesterday after a Norfolk County grand jury handed down the indictments last week.

Galowicz, a recipient of the 'Outstanding Young Man Award' from the Braintree Jaycees, is accused of having committed the acts over a period from 1976 through 1979, according to Norfolk County Dist. Atty. William Delahunt. The two youths involved, both students at East Junior High School in Braintree where Galowicz taught for 22 years, are now 11 and 16.

Galowicz was being held on $50,000 bail and $5000 cash surety. He resigned from his job at the junior high school on Jan. 21. And was arrested a week ago in Ft. Lauderdale, Fla., aboard a 52-foot cabin cruiser.

Assistant Dist. Atty. Charles Hely told Dedham Superior Judge Thomas E. Dwyer yesterday that he sought high bail for the defendant because Galowicz had resigned his job, put his house up for sale, and left the community 'when he got wind of the investigation'. Galowicz was being held last night at the Dedham County House of Correction, Hely said. The investigation into the case has not yet been completed, Delahunt said.

Delahunt.

You've heard about this guy before (he declined to pursue murder charges against Amy Bishop), and you'll hear about him again. I'm not exactly sure what Delahunt's relationship was to the Bulger Brothers, meaning the tag-team of Whitey Bulger, crimelord and drug kingpin, and Billy Bulger, State Senate leader and most powerful political figure in the Commonwealth. But you couldn't do business in Boston without dealing with at least one them.

Whitey is one of the better-known MKULTRA test subjects, and was living openly in Squantum — literally right next door to Fort Strong of Operation Paperclip fame — the entire time his brother and FBI handler told authorities he was hiding out in Europe.

So there's a lot to unpack with the Bob Galowicz story. First of all, 'got wind of the investigation' is Braintreeish for 'tipped off by the cops'. That's just how it works in Braintree. Remember how I talked about that prostitution ring operating out of the T station using high school girls? I haven't found any clippings on it yet, but I did find this *Patriot Ledger* story from 1991:

POLICE ARREST FOUR IN PROSTITUTION RING

State, local, and federal law enforcement officials arrested four people yesterday and broke up what they said was a $60,000-a-month Braintree-based prostitution operation, with more than 4,000 customers. 'This is a very organized and sophisticated operation', said Cassidy, who is the head of the attorney general's narcotics and organized crime unit.

(Two) men were charged with deriving support from prostitution and were held at the Braintree police station until their arraignment at Quincy District Court today. Two women were also arrested. Officials said they are among the 30 prostitutes who worked for the ring. Two alleged principals in the operation were still at large yesterday, said officials.

"Two alleged principals in the operation were still at large" means the guys who actually ran the operation — and their best girls — were tipped off by the cops on their pad. You see this over and over again with these prostitution rings in Braintree. I don't know if the reporters writing these articles have that sussed out, but it seems to pop up a lot. And then there's this recent headline:

"The shooting of a police officer and the suspicious death of a 19-year-old woman has Braintree officials considering tougher rules for hotels."

This is just a joke. The Mayor of Braintree announced he was going to clean up the hotels only *after* a scathing report in *The Patriot Ledger* in 2016 about the rampant sex trafficking going on in Braintree. So over a year and a half ago, they had an "agreement" with the hotels and now they are considering "tougher rules." Amazing. Sex trafficking has been going on in Braintree hotels since they built them. I remember seeing very nice-looking whores milling around the lobby of the Sheraton Tara at my aunt's wedding in 1980. And now they're *really* putting the fear of God into the pimps; watch your step or the Mayor's gonna consider tougher rules! See what I'm getting at here?

Now, from what I've gathered from someone familiar with Galowicz, he only did a three-year bit. For *twenty* counts of rape.

Only raping two boys twenty times is probably what Galowicz did in a week, not a three year period. And he was at East for 22 years. I don't know about you but I really don't think he got out of bed sometime in 1976 and said, "You know what? Today's a good day to start raping sixth-graders."

Everyone knew — and *saw* — that Galowicz spent a lot of money on his boys. He offered expensive gifts as part of his lure. And if you find that hard to believe, note that he was arrested on a 52-foot cabin-cruiser, which I am told he owned. That's a hell of a lot of boat for someone pulling in a junior high school teacher's salary in the Seventies, even on layaway. My mother taught at a junior high in Milton at the same time, so I know what I'm talking about.

So how was all of this allowed to happen? Well, I'll tell you what. Let's do a simple bit of arithmetic. Schoolteacher, stable of young boys, inexplicable cash flow, "got wind of investigation." I think you can do the sums.

If not, do a little reading up on the sexual abuse scandal of the Boston Archdiocese. Eight of the publicly named offenders served in Braintree at one time or another, including the notorious 'NAMBLA Priest', Paul Shanley. Of course, no one really knew about the priests then but kids had other things to worry about at the time.

Let me tell you a story.

My elementary school buddy Charlie lived off Pearl Street. Charlie's parents had money and he was the best kid ever to play with. His folks gave him every toy you could think of. In fact, his room was filled with toys he didn't even take out of the packages. His older brothers collected comics but left for college, so every time I left Charlie's house I was carrying a grocery sack full of them. It was like Christmas, especially since my family were dirt poor.

Charlie and I were coming back from South Braintree Square one day, sometime late June, early July 1976. We just passed the Michigan Abrasive ruins when this yellow Pinto pulls up to the sidewalk. This guy, maybe early-mid 20s, gets out and says, "Hey guys! Do you want to go to this youth meeting at church? It's going to be great, everyone is going to be there."

Not, "This youth meeting at All Souls, or this youth meeting at Sacred Heart." Just "church." No one talks like that. The whole thing was a bit too *Mystic River* for my young palette. There were two other guys in the car, same age. I remember neither of them looked at us. None of these guys looked like they'd been to church in years.

I was like, FUCK THAT. I started to back off. I knew we could book it through Michigan Abrasives and lose these guys if we had to. Charlie stayed, and started to talking to this guy.

I was at least a hundred feet away and yelling, "Charlie, let's go! Come on." Luckily, he eventually got the message and took off.

NOW, THIS WAS BY NO MEANS AN ISOLATED EVENT. Kids in Braintree had to deal with this shit, probably in your town too. It's hard to explain now, but this was a time when parents seemed to suddenly abdicate their duties to their children and let them run rampant. Some of you probably know what I'm talking about. It wasn't just Braintree. There was also an enormous amount of child abuse, the kind that older people justified by saying it 'toughened you up'. It didn't. It just made kids angry and self-destructive.

It usually ranged from mildly abusive to really, really fucked up violence. And the neglect could take horrible forms. There were these three brothers (who we'd now describe as 'being on the spectrum') at East who were so filthy and uncared for that the nurse had them bathed and supplied with new clothes. The old clothes were burned in a metal can outside the cafeteria. Mind you, I didn't hear about this second-hand. I was in the Vice Principal's office (which I was a lot) when all this went down.

That was the static. Young kids fighting and using drugs on the edge of the school grounds (if not inside them), open pedophiles recruiting and pimping eleven year-old boys in school, parents going out and leaving their kids unattended all night, stepping over passed-out drunks on your way to buy candy in Weymouth Landing; this was every day. And you took it for granted. No biggie. Kids are tough. Wasn't it always like that?

But then one day a horrible, horrible signal burst through the static. This might be a good time for some of you to stop reading. Because I'm about to tell you about Dianne DeVanna.

THE FOLLOWING IS AS MILD AS YOU CAN POSSIBLY PORTRAY the systematic rape, torture, humiliation and beating death of a young girl that absolutely traumatized a town that already wasn't exactly paradise for kids. At the hands of her father, stepmother and another relative.

> Nearly 30 years ago, the murder of a young girl reverberated far beyond the South Shore and resulted in wholesale changes in the way the state deals with child abuse.

> Eleven-year-old Dianne DeVanna was found dead in her Braintree home on Sept. 23, 1978, the victim of shocking cruelty at the hands of her father and stepmother. The little girl had been tortured, including being hanged by her feet from a staircase with her hands tied and mouth gagged. She died from a blood clot in her brain, caused by a blow to the head.

That doesn't even begin to describe it. Believe me, Medieval inquisitors were kinder and gentler to heretics than Dianne DeVanna's own family were to a small, defenseless child. What she endured was as cruel and sadistic as it gets.

Dianne had originally been given up for adoption by her father after her mother died and he remarried. She was returned home in 1978, by order of a Family Court judge. For the next three weeks Dianne was beaten, raped and tortured every single day by the adults in her home, and possibly the other children as well. I've read the actual reports and they really are too horrific to detail here. Seriously, you really don't want to know.

Then one night, Dianne suffered a series of brutal beatings over eight hours. Dianne's father, stepmother and some degenerate relative took turns kicking her to death as she lay on the floor naked, hands bound with duct tape. But it actually gets worse. Like rainfall, the coverup started almost immediately.

A S IT HAPPENS, NO CAN QUITE FIGURE OUT WHY Dianne DeVanna was returned to her family at all. Golly, wouldn't you just know that all the professionals claimed they'd argued against her going home? A special state-wide panel was called to investigate, that's how big a story this was. Yet, all of the very high-paid doctors and lawyers and bureaucrats just couldn't explain it. Why, she must have "slipped through the cracks."

And sure enough, William Delahunt — good ol' 'Kick 'Em Loose Billy', who'd later let Amy Bishop skate and Bob Galowicz do an easy bit for two decades of child molesting — gave the male relative immunity from prosecution in an open-and-shut case that didn't need a stoolie. Even *after* that same relative admitted to taking part in Dianne's murder, and even *after* he admitted to raping her every day.

Of course, it was surely a total coincidence that not long after Dianne was returned to her abusive family to be tortured and murdered, reports of sexual abuse at the Catholic group home she'd been living at in Jamaica Plain began to surface. This would turn out to be one of the earliest priest sex-scandals. And wouldn't you know it, the house the DeVannas lived in just happened to be a rental property across from St. Clare's Parish.

I'm sure it's just a total coincidence that one of the biggest property owners in Braintree was also the single biggest patron of the Boston Archdiocese. In fact, when the Church was forced to sell off its headquarters in Boston, this same billionaire donated one of his office buildings for them to move into.

Where? Why, in *Braintree*, of course.

STRANGER THINGS: (REAL LIFE) EIGHTIES HORROR

N ETFLIX'S NEW SERIES STRANGER THINGS is practically a checklist of Secret Sun standbys, from remote viewing, to alternate realities, to human experimentation, to OG geekdom to the friggin' *Clash*. Suffice it to say, it's been a sync motherlode.

The story starts off with a *Twin Peaks*-type mystery: a young boy named Will Byers goes missing after riding his bike home from a friend's house one night. He comes from a broken home with a single mother who isn't entirely stable and has a low-paying job as a department store cashier.

Will's obsessed with *Lord of the Rings* and comic books and *Star Wars* and the rest of it, loves to draw and likes The Clash. He and his friends get bullied a lot by the 'mouth-breathers' at school, who all think he's gay. Yeah, you could say I related to young Will. Except I was downright *obsessed* with baseball when I was his age.

I didn't play *Dungeons & Dragons*, mostly because it wasn't really big when I was his age, and by the time it was I didn't have anyone to play it with. The comic store I worked in didn't even sell any D&D stuff at the time, just to give you some historical context. If you've watched the show and have read this blog over the years, you've probably picked up on some of the other connections, like the peculiar nature of the Byers' living room. That seemed awfully familiar.

So was the general theme of bad shit happening to kids, something else I was all too familiar growing up with. Actually, just this past week I was talking with a fellow Masshole about a tragic death at a local quarry in 1983, and sure enough, that very theme pops up in *Stranger Things*.

Anyhow, after Will goes missing a strange young girl appears, who has apparently escaped from a secret government lab. Will's friends take her in and soon discover she's no ordinary kid. We soon learn she's a super-psychic byproduct of the MKULTRA program.

S TRANGER THINGS HAS BEEN CALLED A PASTICHE, AND to be sure it wears its influences on its sleeve. There are a lot of licks lifted from *E.T.*, *The Goonies*, *Firestarter*, *Akira*, *Altered States* and a whole host of other Eighties classics. There's a healthy dose of *X-Files* and *Outer Limits* in evidence. But there's also a lot taken from lesser-known films such as *Beyond the Black Rainbow* and *Wavelength*, a decidedly obscure movie Secret Sun readers are probably familiar with.

Speaking of MKULTRA, *Stranger Things* stars Timothy Leary's god-daughter Winona Ryder, whose father was one of Leary protégés. Winona's had a hard go of it the past several years, having fallen from grace several years ago after being arrested for shoplifting in 2001. Which means she's perfect for the role here, and adds a spiritual connection to the source material that helps complete the circuit. In more ways than one: she'd offered up ransom money when Polly Klaas was kidnapped in 1992.

Stranger Things works a lot of well-tilled plots, tropes, and familiar riffs from countless Eighties horror and sci-fi films. But it also taps into real-life horrors that were playing out in the media in the early 1980s; the highly-publicized abductions of children, the rise of conspiracies over child trafficking, organized pedophilia, government cover-ups and the role of 24-hour TV news in feeding the fear over what seemed like a new plague descending over the country.

This is the unspoken backdrop that animates the tension over Will's disappearance, just in case any of you might think that Winona's performance was a bit over the top. And if you look carefully, the producers inject some none-too-subtle symbolism in the scenes surrounding Will's captivity in the Upside Down, symbolism that perhaps signals to more salient horrors than extradimensional tulpas.

S O IF YOU WONDER WHY SO MANY AMERICAN PARENTS seem over-protective and paranoid these days, realize that many of them were kids during the early 1980s when the media firestorms arose over the series of shocking kidnappings and/or murders of young children. These took place in an already-heightened atmosphere of social anxiety, in large part fed by an endless deluge of slasher and serial killer movies, not to mention a series of Satanically-inspired crimes and serial murders.

There was also the fact of Satanism popping up again and again in crimes and abuse cases. While there is an ongoing controversy over the existence of 'Satanic Ritual Abuse' on a widespread and organized scale, experts generally agree that it's common among individual abusers. So the next time some halfwit starts shrieking "Satanic Panic! Satanic Panic!" just tell them to shut their stupid fuck-holes and do some actual reading.

Or just remind them that the Manson-linked Process Church of the Final Judgment would mysteriously resurface in the New York metropolitan area during the Son of Sam killings, and again a few years late with the so-called "Cropsey" child abductions (and in one case at least, abduction and murder), which would haunt the streets of Staten Island in 1980s.

Like Zodiac and the Son of Sam, the culprit convicted for two of the abductions — one Andre Rand — liked to write cryptic letters.

Rand even went so far as to write a collective valentine to the 'mothers of Staten Island', filled with unsubtle intimations of early death.

> 'Happy Mother's Day (to)all the ladies on Staten Island who supported 'prosecutorial vindictiveness' against an innocent person!

> 'Should I become a millionaire, it would be my true nature to grant all of you with each, an envelope full of seeds, to plant and cultivate a rosebush [shrub] that produces roses every season, as a token of my heartfelt forgiveness [year after year], rather than bouquets of rosebuds which blossoms and shortly dies out.

> 'It is only a tiny 'rosebud' - A flower of God's design; But I cannot unfold the petals with these clumsy hands of mine. The secret of unfolding flowers is not know to such as I - The flower, only the 'Spirit of God' opens, in my hands would fade and die'.

Yeah, I get the strong impression that Rand was taunting these mothers (not to mention law enforcement) with these letters of his, which seem embedded with clues, perhaps as to where his victims are buried. I especially get that vibe with the letters he sent to the makers of the *Cropsey* documentary, and generally get a heavy Zodiac vibe from the guy.

The *Cropsey* film is rife with hints of cultic involvement, but the producers never bother to follow up on them. They seem to be of that mindset that such things are not possible. Media conditioning is a powerful thing.

In a strange twist, a local Catholic mystic would write to police claiming that a sect of the Process Church were involved in the abductions. There would be evidence of cult activity around the area but nothing would emerge publicly as to its connection to the crimes. However, there would be some evidence emerged that the one victim that had been found may have been moved to her burial site from another location. By sheer dint of coincidence, Process Church of the Final Judgment leader Robert De Grimston had moved to Staten Island in the early Eighties and was living there during the Cropsey abductions.

Staten Island. What a fascinating path that man has traveled. And such bad luck to be in the midst of so much mischief and mayhem over the years.

Some investigators involved in the Cropsey case believed that there was ritual aspects to it and other high-profile abduction cases in the New York metropolitan area in the 1980s, including the widely-publicized Etan Patz kidnapping and murder. A particularly horrific hospital for the severely mentally-handicapped, euphemistically named the Willowbrook State School, enters the story as well. In fact, it plays a very crucial part in the entire Cropsey drama. The appallingly-inhuman abuse and neglect at Willowbrook would be exposed by an ambitious young reporter named Geraldo Rivera in the 1970s.

There was also the steady stream of Satanic-themed movies, books and records following in the wake of the creation of the CIA's Project MKOFTEN, coinciding with the rise of emotion-based, anti-intellectual movements within Evangelicalism, which were also fed and financed by elements in and around the intelligence community. Many of these movements fed their congregants a steady diet of paranoia and staged 'exorcisms', creating a heightened climate of fear and vigilance. What inevitably resulted was an explosive social tension, a culture being buffeted by powerful internal pressures. To top it all off, there was the constant ratcheting up of tension between the governments of the United States and the Soviet Union in the early Eighties, instilling widespread nuclear anxiety all across the world.

So when kids began disappearing, and often doing so under the specter of clandestine Satanic forces (many of which hinted at much greater conspiracies), the panic that followed was inevitable. One such case was the 1981 abduction and murder of six year-old Adam Walsh by the serial murderer — and avowed Satanist — Ottis Toole.

Toole had lured Walsh from a department store, repeatedly raped then decapitated the boy, then incinerated the body. He discarded the severed head, which was later found by fishermen. Toole was the sidekick of Henry Lee Lucas, a prodigious serial killer whose death sentence was inexplicably commuted by Texas Governor George W. Bush. Lucas and Toole were the inspiration for the 1986 thriller, *Henry, Portrait of a Serial-Killer*. Adam Walsh's father would later become an anti-crime crusader and host of the long-running TV show, *America's Most Wanted*.

T HERE WAS ALSO THE CASE OF RACHEL RUNYON, a small child who was kidnapped from a playground in Utah in 1982. Rachel was raped and murdered, and her body was eventually found three weeks later. Two years later, a message was found in a laundromat bathroom. It read, *'I'm still at large... I killed the little Runyan girl! Remember! Beware!'* and was decorated a 666 and an upside down cross. Criminal profilers came to the conclusion that the note was very likely written by Rachel's killer.

Then there is the long-running enigma of Johnny Gosch, well-known to most in the conspiracy and parapolitics communities. This case would become a major news story, thanks mostly to the tireless work of the boy's mother, and Johnny would become one of the first kids to appear on a milk carton. Gosch was abducted in September 1982 while delivering newspapers in West Des Moines, Iowa.

Two years later, 13-year-old Eugene Martin was also abducted from a Des Moines street while delivering newspapers.

The local police's behavior while investigating the disappearances was so phenomenally, so *stultifyingly*, inept it couldn't help but feed into coverup theories. The chief of police was so willfully obstructive, so much so that the Gosch family would later accuse him of involvement in the kidnapping. The chief was eventually fired.

The FBI wasn't any better. The Feds' stonewalling, as captured in the documentary film *Who Took Johnny?*, is so blatant you can't help but wonder what exactly is lurking beneath the surface there. Ultimately, the Gosch family were so frustrated by the lack of cooperation from law enforcement that they hired private detectives to help find their son.

But nine years after the boy's disappearance, there'd be a major break in the case. A convicted sex offender named Paul Bonacci came forward in 1991 and told investigators that he was an accomplice to the Gosch kidnapping. He claimed to have chloroformed the boy, and said he was still alive. Bonacci would also testify that he was forced into crimes against children by a shadowy figure called "the Colonel," who was kidnapping children and supplying them to a nationwide pedophile underground.

Bonacci then provided the Gosch family with information about their boy's abduction that the police had not released to the media. He also revealed that Johnny had been held at a remote ranch before the Colonel sold the boy off to a rich child molester. Bonacci also revealed the Colonel's full name: Lt. Colonel Michael Aquino.

A QUINO WAS AN ARMY PSYCHOLOGICAL WARFARE (or 'psyops') agent in the US from 1968 until 1990. He was discharged in the wake of investigations into his alleged involvement in the ritual abuse of children at San Francisco's Presidio Day Care Center. Aquino is also a devout Satanist and self-confessed neo-Nazi. He was also a high priest in Anton LaVey's Church of Satan in 1969. Accusing LaVey of going soft, he left to start his own Temple of Set in 1975 which has been in operation ever since.

For his part, Aquino would assiduously deny all of these claims, going so far as to write a book to refute them. Granted, Aquino is a relatively public figure who makes for an easy target, but for my money there's far too much sulfurous smoke around him for there to be no hellfire. Aquino's involvement in all of this may actually have been to play the designated villain, a visible target meant to draw fire away from offenders who might compromise players further up the chain of command. Note that the original target in the Presidio scandal was a Baptist minister named Gary Hambright.

Furthering his credibility as a witness, Bonacci would later take a camera crew from *America's Most Wanted* to the ranch where he claimed the kidnapped kids were being warehoused.

There they found a pit dug beneath the home, where Bonacci says Gosch was stowed away for safe keeping until the next buyer showed up. Bonacci also showed messages carved into wooden beams, which he claimed were cries for help by the other abducted boys. Another victim known simply as 'Jimmy' was able to describe the house in minute detail. Jimmy also corroborated Bonacci's claims that the kidnapped boys had been branded, which he'd been himself.

A LL THIS TIED INTO ANOTHER EIGHTIES HORROR, in which priests at the famed Boys Town (in Omaha, Nebraska) were allegedly supplying vulnerable young children to local businessmen and politicians for sex parties. This in turn dovetailed into another investigation, namely the embezzlement arrest of Lawrence King, the head of a local credit union and a rising political star who was closely tied to the Bush Sr. White House.

King's trial was rocked by accusations that he'd been bankrolling the Boys' Town procurements, leading to the involvement of state investigators. Their involvement was stymied by obstruction and cover-up, largely because of the high-placed local citizens whose names kept popping up during the case. Remember that this scandal — as well as the Presidio scandal — was a long time before the wave of abuse scandals that would rock the Catholic Church. For many, sex abuse by members of the clergy was unthinkable.

Consider this: what if a highly-visible, visually-distinct and unforgettable cartoon villain like Michael Aquino was injected into the Presidio and Boys Town cases to draw fire away from all the more respectable figures, ensuring that the boat would not be rocked and that business would carry on as usual? Meaning that the supply chain of vulnerable children to rich abusers would not be disrupted. After all, most Satanists don't have ready access to kids. Clergy do. Well, they did back then, at least.

In any event, nothing much would come of the accusations against Aquino, and he'd later be able to shrug it all off as the product of scapegoating and witch-hunting. Remarkably-effective diversionary tactics, when all's said and done. You'd almost think it was all the brainstorm of someone involved in psychological warf… Oh.

Speaking of diversionary tactics, the so-called 'Satanic Panic' of the 1980s and 90s directly coincided with a growing panic within the Catholic Church over priestly abuse. In fact, a decades-long study produced a 1985 report that warned Church leadership that they were sitting on a time-bomb. The Satanic Panic not only helped to divert attention away from the abuse cases that were beginning to emerge in local media in the Eighties and Nineties, it would also discredit the use of hypnosis and recovered memory. That in turn would also intimidate many legitimate victims of abuse into silence.

Cui Bono? indeed.

Present-day Satanists reactively chafe at any mention of this sort of thing, dismissing any discussion of satanic crime as hysteria and sensationalism. They'll insist they're rationalists and atheists, and that the *sturm und drang* ritualism and is purely symbolic. Which is *exactly* what Anton LaVey said 50 years ago. Unfortunately, it didn't take very long for it all to filter down to Satanic serial murder back then either, once devil worship oozed out of the smug and smarmy precincts of upscale San Francisco.

T HE PROBLEM WITH SATANISM isn't the privileged hipsters flirting with it for the shock value, the problem is when its inherent implication of license and transgression crosses over from irony to action. More often than not, this happens with the marginal and less-educated, but there's all kinds of evidence that Satanic depravity can effect the rich, jaded and bored with equal intensity (see *Abramović, Marina*). And there's all kinds of evidence that Satanism often dovetails with and feeds into extreme right politics as well. Most of the Satanists I've ever come across were also Neo-Nazis. I'd guess a lot of the current crop are too, they're just more discrete about it.

Unfettered license is embedded into every scrap of Satanic symbolism, iconography, scripture and lore. This is what the unconscious mind actually processes. It's why I personally find Satanic imagery so hard to digest. Ignore LaVey's or Lucien Greaves' half-hearted bromides and just look at the satanic track record.

I'm not talking about 'the Occult' (Satanism has never really struck me as particularly occultic, actually), or witchcraft, or whatever else gets tossed into the Satanic woodpile. After all, nothing gets labeled as 'Satanic' by amateur devil-hunters more enthusiastically than what's going on in that other church across the street there. I'm not even talking about 'Luciferianism', whatever exactly that means (and it can mean anything because it doesn't objectively exist). I'm talking about *Satanism*.

You see, what I'm trying to say is that in an atmosphere of economic decline, war, social disintegration, terrorism, racial tension and general pessimism about the future, maybe this mainstreaming of Satanism - after-school clubs and all the rest - isn't really what we need to be playing with right now. It very much feels as if someone is pouring kerosene on a pile of well-cured kindling. Plus, old newspapers and oily rags.

It's just itching for you to strike a match.

LESSONS LEARNED IN A MODERN MYSTERY CULT

WHEN I WROTE THE SECRET HISTORY OF ROCK 'N' ROLL I spent a lot of time worrying that some might see it as a major detour from the work I was doing on *The Secret Sun*. I also had to contend with younger readers, who were justifiably cynical about the music industry, which took total control over the creative process for major label acts sometime in the mid-90s. How could I explain that once upon a time things were different, and there was a scene that kids built from the ground up without realizing they were actually recreating the ancient Mithraic cults? Or that everything I needed to know I learned from punk rock?

My hatred of Seventies soft rock (which was impossible to get away from) was one of the reasons I embraced Punk so passionately. And not only Ramones-type punk; I was especially keen on the post-punk scene: bands like Wire, Joy Division, Killing Joke, Bauhaus and the like. Bands that took the energy and subversion of punk and applied them to a larger canvas.

This was the music I listened to when I wasn't at a Hardcore show. But those bands were out of reach for the most part. I do remember sneaking in to see Killing Joke at The Channel (I never paid to see a show unless it was at a big venue like an arena) by creeping in during the soundcheck and hiding beneath the PA riser until the doors opened. I saw Motörhead by grabbing an amp and walking through the front door while the opening act (Helix, for those keeping score at home) was breaking down. But for the most part, it was all-ages shows or bust. But the all-ages shows were where the action was.

And when I say Hardcore punk was a revival of the Mithraic Mysteries, I'm not trying to be cute. I mean it *literally*. It was an unconscious revival and the connections were not explicit (aside from the Straight Edge X icon, that is), but that just means it was all the more powerful and sincere for being so.

Hardcore bands weren't much different than the Kouretes or the Cabeiri: thrashing, aggressive, militaristic noise meant to alter the consciousness of the listener. There was the same masculine, militaristic ambiance and same puritanical morality; the Straight Edge ethos frowned on drinking, smoking, and drugs, and promiscuity. Mind you, Straight Edge orthodoxy has always been heavily mythologized in Boston Hardcore history. I went to a lot of scene parties back in the day and there was plenty of drinking and drugging going around, believe it.

Like any good mystery cult, it was all about *experience*, first and foremost. Listening to Hardcore records at home was kind of ludicrous and extremely pointless. The music was made for movement, extreme and immediate. It never sounded right on your stereo.

I had a different view of the scene than most, having been part of the inner circle of the Braintree HC bands Jerry's Kids and Gang Green. I ended up as a roadie (if you can call it that, since the only road was usually the one from Braintree to Boston) lugging amps and drum cases and setting up and breaking down. And it was a privileged view to a scene that was largely self-created. It taught some vitally important lessons. I learned to distrust not only the authorities — the first show I ever attended was shut down after 15 minute simply because the cops didn't like punks — but also the media. I saw how the big local fanzines picked favorites and blatantly rewrote history simply based on the personal whims of their editors.

I also saw how movements can grow, based almost solely on the conviction of their adherents. Hardcore shows went from being small affairs at offbeat venues to taking over major venues like The Channel and The Paradise. I'd see regional Hardcore bands who even college radio wouldn't touch fill large venues, while bands with hit singles struggled to fill small clubs. Alas, I'd see how movements could go terribly wrong, too. Hardcore sure did.

BUT I ALSO GOT A FULL BLAST OF THE PHENOMENA that would ultimately lead to the work I do here, documenting how spiritual consciousness can give art a visceral punch lacking in strictly materialist art. The Bad Brains' Boston debut was a powerful object lesson in this. I did the 'I'm with the band' amp-lugging routine to get into that show only to get my teeth loosened during Negative FX's set. Even with a bloody mouth full of loose teeth, the sheer electrifying power of the Bad Brains was impossible to deny. Their story would get complicated thereafter but when it mattered, the Bad Brains delivered.

It's a shame then that more bands back then didn't tap into that source, that spiritual power. New York's Cro-Mags did so; they were/are involved in the Krishna Consciousness movement, which ingratiated itself to homeless punks by offering free vegetarian meals on weekends. But most bands shunned such things. Especially in Boston, where so many people on the scene were trapped in stifling, all-boy Catholic prep schools like Don Bosco and Xaverian Brothers. Spirituality was the last thing they wanted.

ALTHOUGH HARDCORE FADED AS A VITAL MUSICAL FORCE rather quickly, the DIY spirit and rule-breaking that it inspired was a major influence on the developing alternative rock scene. Many of the big stars of the 1992 grunge explosion got their start playing in Hardcore bands, and Hardcore remained a yardstick with which alt.rock integrity would be measured. So in many ways, Hardcore would take over the mainstream within ten years of its emergence, based almost entirely on the utter conviction of its followers.

Something to seriously think about. Think about very seriously, indeed.

POP CULTURE
DECLINE AND FALL

MYTHS AREN'T FOREVER

HAVE YOU EVER SEEN THE HAROLD RAMIS REMAKE of *Bedazzled?* It's not a museum piece by any means, but it's a very clever comedy with a charm all its own. It helps that the Devil is played by Elizabeth Hurley in all her splendor and glory. She's a talented comic actor, a gift I think some people have overlooked in favor of her more apparent attributes.

The remake doesn't bother to retrace the steps of the classic original, but instead casts Brendan Fraser as an uber-awkward IT nerd pining after a pretty but otherwise-unremarkable secretary. After an awkward encounter with co-workers in a bar, Fraser meets Hurley. She then takes him to her nightclub which seems like a roiling bacchanal filled with the beautiful people, all having the time of their lives.

Only later do we find out they're all damned, and the party will never, ever stop. The beautiful people are condemned to go through the motions for all Eternity, as if trapped in some horrific Depression-era dance marathon. With musical accompaniment by Slayer.

It felt like I was in a LARP of that *Bedazzled* scene a couple years ago at the New York Comic-Con. The show was dangerously oversold, and every face I saw looked exhausted, miserable, and trapped in some pantomime they didn't really understand. The place was so packed that no one could even get a look at any of the tables. The vendors, who were paying an arm and a leg for their trouble, were crestfallen. How oversold was it? It took me a half-hour to walk a single aisle. It was like something out of *Soylent Green.*

Finally, I and several thousand other patrons escaped to Artist's Alley, located in an entirely separate wing of the enormous Jacob Javits Center. Of course, in the old days meeting the artists and creators would be the whole point of a convention. But the con industry has metastasized into something entirely different. In many ways it's just a giant costume party now, much to the chagrin of people trying to earn a living selling at the increasingly costly tables.

I went to another con yesterday, in the middle of an enormous industrial park in Central Jersey. It was *very* sparsely attended, perhaps a sign that the market has been oversaturated. New York Comic-Con was just a few weeks ago, and Christmas shopping starts in earnest by the end of this week. So perhaps it was an aberration. geek culture *is* mainstream culture now, so it's not like it was twenty years ago when everyone was worried the bottle was finally running dry. But in a way it has: it's run dry creatively. We're talking about a situation where the big story this year is yet *another* sequel for a film franchise that's nearly forty years old.

I have no doubt the new *Star Wars* will do gangbusters at the box office. Tentpole films and football are the last vestiges of a common culture we have left in America's increasingly-fractured populace, thanks to technological narrow-casting and Globalist social engineering. But will it have the effect the original had in 1977? No, of course not.

Star Wars was such a blockbuster because it was such a pure distillation and amplification of the most intoxicating tropes in sci-fi and fantasy, in much the same way that Van Halen's first album was a distillation and amplification of Sixties and Seventies hard rock tropes. Both hit so hard because they felt so new, yet drank deep from rich mythic streams that had stood the test of time.

It's also worth noting that both emerged out of a California that doesn't exist anymore, meaning a land of social and economic mobility. Today's California is a Feudal hellhole, the poorest and most economically unjust state in the union, where a rapidly expanding underclass and a rapidly-dwindling middle class are ruled over by a sociopathic, technocratic elite nursing totalitarian ambitions not seen in almost a century. The *Empire*, in other words.

It's a strange feeling to see the pop culture of my youth have such staying power. But those icons were created by a different class of artists, with a different understanding of the world. *Star Wars* was deeply spiritual, at least in its original incarnation. But it was also a celebration of the old 'just war' doctrine, deeply unfashionable among intellectuals in the post-Vietnam era.

The Marvel icons were the offspring of men whose heads were filled with ideals, Stan Lee with his sunny humanism, Jack Kirby with his AstroGnostic obsession with aliens and gods, godlike aliens and alien gods, and Steve Ditko with his passionate political idealism clashing wildly with his personal paranoia and unresolved sexual issues.

The early superheroes were the offspring of the Pulps: Batman was a wafer-thin reworking of the mystic vigilante The Shadow, and Superman heavily borrowed from strongmen like Doc Savage. Superman's creator Jerry Siegel was well-versed in pop occultism and UFOlogy: his next major creation after Superman was the occult superhero The Spectre, and his last major creation was The Starling, an alien hybrid whose origin clearly showed that Siegel had been boning up on abduction literature.

THE QUESTION NOW BECOMES HOW LONG can you keep re-selling these old stories? At some point you need a generational cohort to stand up and create new ideas of their own. I don't think this generation is going to be the one, certainly not if the auto-erasing convulsions ripping through our college campuses are any indication.

Unfortunately, what may be the deciding factor is war. Many of the pulp creators were World War I vets and many of the comic creators served in World War II, as did crucial pop culture figures like Rod Serling (*Twilight Zone*), Leslie Stevens (*Outer Limits, Battlestar Galactica*) and Gene Roddenberry (*Star Trek*). Maybe these stories didn't actually arise out of those men but instead were *forced* upon them by history.

Globalism hasn't created a world of sunshine and candy canes, it's created a world of endless war, social chaos, and mass population transfers. China and Russia are just two of the many countries tired of US unipolarity, and are building up their militaries to do something about it. All it takes is one brutal economic crisis and it's Katie, bar the door.

Myths grow out of times of crisis and upheaval, in one way or another. The current vogue for superheroes is a symptom of the powerlessness felt by a populace under assault by the realities of Globalist social engineering, war-making and economic redundancy. Yet we still live in the post-conscription era, where war is a distant anxiety for most people.

If war does come, it will be a new kind of war, unconventional, asymmetric, civil. The way things are going, it may well come sooner than later. Given the ubiquity of technology, it may be impossible for myths to arise immediately as they did during past wars, when the distribution of information wasn't so instantaneous and the news-cycle wasn't so short.

But myths *do* die. They aren't immortal. The next war or financial crash may in fact sweep away the myths of the Twentieth Century entirely. The wars may send people reaching back to far older myths, as civil wars can rekindle the bonfires of identity, sending people back to the myths of ancestors. This has always emerged in times of close conflict, particularly in conflicts seen as struggles against occupying powers.

The time may well come when our descendants look upon our pop culture as nothing more than postmodern bread and circuses. Our current conceptions of popular culture will then be seen as antiquated and redundant, a mass self-indulgence of happier days gone by.

WOODSTOCK AFTERSHOCKS

S O MUCH HAS BEEN WRITTEN ABOUT WOODSTOCK, I'm not sure whether anything of value is left to take from it. Despite all the hype, it was the death-knell of Aquarian idealism, at least as it's generally understood today.

A lot of these great musicians got their start playing all-night raves in small dancehalls and clubs; a truly underground phenomenon. In San Francisco and other cities, the music was the spear's tip of a multimedia experience that united a relatively small, well-educated and culturally-aware vanguard who were just naive enough not to see the wolves at the gate, or to realize that most people don't *want* to be enlightened.

Personally, Woodstock wasn't really my scene; I would have rather been at Monterey Pop. That was before all of the *really* bad vibes set in; the bad drugs, the assassinations, the Mansons, the Weathermen, the Panthers, the Angels, you name it. At Monterey, kids still believed that if only the rest of the world could feel what they felt from their music, then their lives would be changed too.

Of course, this was the naïveté of a pampered generation that had no experience with real want or hardship, and to this day sees itself as the apex of galactic civilization. But once the Establishment started to push back in 1968, things quickly changed. And the lovefest at Woodstock was soon followed by its its mirror-universe inversion at Altamont.

From what I've read and been told, Haight Street and Sunset Strip were nightmare zones by early 1969, besieged by runaways and thrill-seekers, then quickly followed by an army of thugs, sickos and pushers ready to feed on the sheep. According to Mikal Gilmore's article, "Summer of Loss," it had been headed that way since 1967. The Diggers, who represented the original SF freaks, went so far as to declare 'The Death of Hippie' mere weeks after the Summer of Love ended. Their oasis had been spoiled and the real party was over.

It's become a truism among certain alt.researchers that Hippie was all a setup from the start, but that's not how it works. The countercultures that resonate arise from a handful of marginal types who can't find a place in mainstream culture. So they coalesce and build one all up from scratch. Several attempts at doing so have failed, but the ones who succeed often become easy targets for the rip-off artists. And if they're *really* unlucky, fodder for the spooks.

At the very least, yesterday's rebels often become today's superstars and tomorrow's establishment. Those are just the facts of life. If you're smart and talented and charismatic, someone is going to try to make a buck off of that.

Very few artists can resist the siren call of success forever, particularly when they have expensive drug habits to support.

A lot has been made out of the military and intelligence lineage of a lot of these artists' fathers, overlooking the fact that the entire country was effectively fully militarized twenty years before, and pretty much every Boomer's father was in the military. And if your dad was even mildly smart or media-savvy, he ended up in intelligence or in the officer corps. Beat crawling through the frozen mud in some ass-end of France or somewhere, right?

Which is not to say that they were not wolves set among the sheep; that's been going on since countercultures first appeared. But reducing the entire Sixties counterculture to 'psyop' status just doesn't wash. There were a lot of people who were honest, genuine and motivated, not to mention independent. Of course, these were also the rebels who the System usually came down full-force upon.

I resented the hell out of the whole Woodstock phenomenon and the generational mythology around it when I was a young punk rocker. It seemed like one great big party that didn't bother to pick up after itself, and left behind a whole ton of cultural trash. And being a student of counterculture history, I was always irritated that the Baby Boomers acted as if they created all of it, when they basically just consumed what the media provided them with.

And most of the vaunted social experiments of the time ended in failure. The lip service paid to starry-eyed idealism — and flat-out *bullshit* — you see everywhere in the *Woodstock* documentary is as wince-inducing as seeing these kids roll around in septic mud. And tragic, in light of where it often led. But for better or worse, the Sixties equal 'Counterculture' to most people. And the last gasp of it, since what we see now are just endlessly mutating subcultures.

In the end, the Sixties counterculture left us a lot of great music, and not just the overplayed old standards you hear on classic rock radio (I've been listening to a lot of Sixties Psych, and the depth of talent even in bands I'd never heard of is mind-blowing). We'll probably never see that kind of embarrassment of riches again, but it's worth working towards a building a culture that at least has the potential to do so, even if just an exercise. That's going to be a lot harder in this technocratic surveillance state we're all trapped, but not impossible.

Potent countercultures are *always* powered by spirit, even if it's a spirit other people wouldn't even recognize as such. Mind you, I don't mean ghosts and I don't mean religion, I mean a power that's as ephemeral as it's invigorating and motivating. A power that ties people together in a common purpose, even if they have no idea it even exists. You know, the kind of powers they created the Borgsong to suppress.

THE NIGHT GREEN DAY STRUCK OUT

I REALLY SHOULD HAVE KNOWN BETTER. As the nation reels from the worst natural disaster in its history and wakes to the nightmare of the criminal incompetence of its so-called leaders, *some* sort of emotional relief was expected. But there wasn't any to be found at Giants Stadium when Green Day took the stage.

It was a gorgeous September evening. Spirits were high and the tailgate parties were in full effect. Yet, the coming nightmare this country is facing was already in evidence, as gas prices were well into the three-dollar range, even along the bargain gasoline corridor of Route 46. I'm not necessarily opposed to Stadium shows, they can be a lot of fun if the performers in question are up to it. These weren't.

Jimmy Eat World, the painfully earnest Emo band, opened the festivities. They were tight, polished and utterly forgettable. They saved their two hits for last, which were the only songs that left even the slightest impression. But they went over well and got the little teeny-boppers dancing.

After Jimmy finished their set, the DJ played a set of Green Day's sources: The Clash, Cheap Trick, Queen, The Beastie Boys and so on. Maybe that was a bad idea. Most of those acts jumped their own sharks after hitting the stadium circuit, and hearing them at Giants Stadium acted as a foreshadowing of the disappointment to come. All of which is to say that I was hoping against hope that maybe this kind of success wouldn't spoil Green Day.

Boy, was I wrong. Wronger than I ever dreamed.

Green Day's set started off pretty well. They launched into an energetic version of 'American Idiot', and then segued into 'Jesus of Suburbia' and 'St Jimmy'. But something has obviously gone south with Billie Joe Armstrong. He worked the crowd like a wedding singer, and every corny stadium cliché you can imagine was pulled out of his kitbag.

Billie Joe spent more time working the enormous audience than singing. Giant video screens, flash-pots, KISS-styled pyro, and the most elaborate fireworks display I've ever seen almost totally overshadowed the show. To cement the wedding vibe, Armstrong led the crowd in numerous 'day-o' chants. Yes, that's right: *DAY-O CHANTS*. It was douche chilling.

A cringe-worthy run-through of the Isley Bros' 'Shout' was pulled out of Armstrong's bag of tricks, a bag he seemed to have stolen from David Lee Roth's Las Vegas revue dressing room.

Yet those old riffs — all time-tested and utterly predictable — were charming in comparison to hearing Armstrong shout *'New Jersey!'* in his best WWE voice every three seconds. Mother of fuck already, Billie Joe.

Green Day played fairly well, and their run-through of their earlier numbers was competent, if not a bit rushed. But the ultra-simple Punk Rock Pop that they traffic in doesn't seem majestic enough to warrant a stadium gig. It's not as if Green Day have the composition chops of The Who or Paul McCartney, and Billie Joe is certainly no Freddie Mercury.

Semiotic mindfucks ruled the day. Although Green Day's new look is lifted wholesale from The Clash — right down to their choice of red, black and white graphics and clothing, and the stencil lettering on some of their t-shirts — none of the anger or purpose of The Clash was anywhere in evidence.

I was reminded of Joe Strummer's transcendental show in New York shortly after 9/11. To honor the dead, Strummer started the show with his reworking of the old Irish folk song, 'Minstrel Boy', a lament that was being played at the funerals of New York City Firefighters. Nothing in Green Day's musical kitbag could rise to the occasion, and their cover of Queen's elitist 'We Are the Champions' didn't jibe with a band purporting to speak for the underdog.

As the undeniably charismatic and energetic Billie Joe worked the crowd for laughs and endless cheers, those kinds of worries were probably the last thing on his mind. But perhaps the giant video screens revealed more than they were intended to.

Whenever the cameras focused on bassist Mike Dirnt, a sour note of dissonance to Billie Joe's puppy-dog enthusiasm was sounded. Dirnt looked bored, frustrated, fed up. He's the Punk true believer in Green Day, and you can't help but wonder if he wonders what on Earth he is doing there. Even the effervescent drummer Tre Cool seemed to tire at the shtick at points, though the only sign was a slightly-furrowed brow providing a strange contrast to his trademark toothy grin.

In the end, Jon Pareles put it best in the headline for his *New York Times* review of the show: *"A Band Turns Into What It Once Parodied."*

MISSING FOUNDATION, OR BONO SCRAPES THE BOTTOM

I 'M A BIG FAN OF THE FILM BEDAZZLED, both the Cook/Moore original and the Fraser/Hurley remake (shut up). Both films riff on the old Faust routine — the proverbial deal with the Devil — in order to show you that the house always wins and you always get the shite end of the stick.

The basic takeaway in *Bedazzled* is that the Devil isn't just enormously powerful, he's actually the greatest legal mind in history. There's a reason Satan is introduced in the Book of Job as the Adversary (or essentially, Jehovah's Attorney General). He knows the law like nobody's business, and he's here to make sure you choke on it. It doesn't matter how clever you think you are, there's always gonna be a line item on page 5,682 of Appendix Z, written in maddeningly ambiguous language, that will wreak havoc on all your hopes and dreams.

Another of my favorite films is *The Devil's Advocate* (no, seriously; *shut up*), the 1997 supernatural potboiler that pits a scenery-gobbling Al Pacino against an outmatched and bewildered Keanu Reeves, with a young, pert Charlize Theron caught in the middle. In a climax so over the top it practically bounces off the Chrysler Building, Pacino's Satan unloads his great secret on Reeves: he doesn't make anyone do anything. He just puts that delicious cheese in the trap and lets all the hungry little rats discover it on their own. He insists that he loves humanity, only problem being that we shaved apes are too stupid to play his kind of chess.

The reason I bring this all up is that Paul David Hewson — better known to the world as 'Bono Vox', lead singer of U2 — made his own deal with the Devil back in 1980 or so, when he chose riches, fame and glory over the Gospel. This certainly isn't a value judgment on my part, it's how he frames it himself.

You see, before the release of their first album, three-quarters of U2 were mixed up with Shalom, a Charismatic Christian sect (or *cult*, if you prefer) run by an Englishman named Chris Row. For those of you who can't tell one batch of holy rollers from the next, Charismatic Christianity can get pretty intense, and is often *intensely* sexually-charged. It's a bonafide Mystery cult in all but name, essentially a stock-and-barrel rebirth of the old Attis Mysteries. Only without the drugs and sex orgies. Well, openly, at least.

Some Charismatic services, like Pentecostal Holy Ghost rave-ups, make most rock concerts these days seem like slumber parties. Which is probably why Fundamentalists tend to hate Charismatics, seeing their churches as estrogen-drenched pits of heresy, hysteria, wife-swapping and sodomy. The thing is, the critics are more or less correct in that assessment. And by, "correct in that assessment," I mean, "jealous."

One of my old girlfriends used to take me to Charismatic meetings at Sacred Heart and they could get pretty intense. And since this is *my* life we're talking about here — a never-ending fugue-state in which Death and Chaos seem to have been constantly hovering overhead since birth — my very first Charismatic meeting came a few hours after I watched police divers pull the body of a fifteen year-old girl out of the water and onto the beach of the Quincy Dam behind the South Shore Plaza. Not a great start to the summer. But as much as I hate to admit it, the trauma really amped up the experience at the prayer meeting.

My point is that it's not like U2 were sitting around with the hairshirts and cat-o-nine-tails, moaning into the gloom over their sins. But neither was it like rockin' in the free world, with dollars falling from the heavens and American nubiles throwing themselves at their feet. At least I don't *think* it was.

I've heard tell that Charismatics can get pretty wild (wife-swapping, the down-low, etc), but it's an all-or-nothing deal. It's not like being a Presbyterian. When you're a Jet, you're a Jet all the way. Backsliding only goes in one direction. This lifestyle can get so intense that U2 were seriously considering chucking in all that beat-combo business and throwing down for the Paraclete, even after their first album made a big buzz in the States.

But seeing how this fallen, irredeemable world is Satan's Kingdom, Island honcho Chris Blackwell threw big devil-dollars in U2's faces in order to lure the young Dubliners away from the Narrow Gate. Blackwell was desperate: his top earner (Bob Marley) died from a mysterious bone cancer while U2 were barnstorming around on their first US tour. Most people would probably say the band made the right decision, seeing how things panned out and all.

But there's no doubt it left them with nagging feelings of guilt, especially young Master Bono. This guilt shone like a beacon to Diablo E. Satannas, Esq., Attorney-at-Law. And so it was that the Prince of Lies came a'calling with his can't-miss grift: *world-saving.*

After spending U2's salad days telling interviewers how corny and square bands like The Clash were with their soft-boiled socialist politics, Bono immediately stepped straight into Joe Strummer's Doc Martens and began penning his own 'anthems'. Mind you, these were mostly vague and uncontroversial toe-tappers about world peace: *Don't bomb us, Mister Reagan, Tra la la. Hey.*

Bono and the band seemed able to chase the guilt away with some newly-minted World Council of Churches social gospel sloganeering, singing straight out of the grand Rockefeller hymnal. But at some point, it all went pear-shaped and Bono morphed into the Oligarchy's go-to court jester.

Since — I don't know, 1993? — there hasn't been a neo-colonial con that Bono didn't sign off on, a pseudo-cause from which he paused, a Globalist gambit that he didn't ambit. Admit it; any time you're reminded of the sickening puddle of Globalist shills the MSM is constantly ramming up our collective pisshole, you can't help but picture Bono, in his hepatitis-yellow shades, mugging and preening as if he's baptizing we great unwashed in his all-powerful Bono-sauce.

And it was fun while it all lasted, certainly. It always is, until the Devil sends you the bill. And boy oh boy, should our Paulie-boy have read the fine print. This bill came with a *motherfucker* of a past-due notice.

See, the Devil isn't just the world's greatest legal mind, he's also its Master Salesman. He may well have strung poor Bono along the Road-Paved-with-Good-Intentions until the Irishman found he was in over his head in brimstone. You know how it is; a compromise here, a compromise there, then all of a sudden the Devil's loading all your valuables — along with your immortal soul — into a U-Haul. Satan's a *closer*, doubt it not.

So before Bono even realized what was happening, some crazy bitch he tapped to helm his ONE Foundation racket was busy whoring off her female employees to the Junior Assistant to the Associate Water Commissioner of Nowherenia Province, Deepest Africa.

Mind you, I don't know if our Bono ever *really* believed that these foundations and charities that the filthy rich launder their money through were ever anything but rawboned shucks and scams. But you get the sense that Bono's so smitten with the waft from his own taint that he just might have.

But that ONE nonsense, that's Children of God-level shenanigans here. MI6 honeytrap shenanigans, even. But as if that weren't bad enough, Bono then did the most chuckleheaded thing you can imagine in the Twittermob Era: the dumb fuck *apologized*. Not only *apologized*, but queefed out the lamest, saddest, cringiest apology you've ever heard. And as if there wasn't enough blood on the tracks, the poor bastard *admitted fault and foreknowledge.* Needless to say, it only encouraged more attacks.

Proving yet again he's no Dylan, the Great Wordsmith then pinched out this cringey wincer: '*In fact, if they would agree, I would like to meet them and apologize in person*'. Mother of God, Bono: maybe you can meet with those disgruntled employees after you fix your wife's boyfriend's supper. By the way, they're fresh out of Astroglide; be a dear and fetch some at the chemists?

Cheers.

That humiliation went down just a few weeks before Bono cringe-bombed the globe with a week-late 'shithole country' mic-drop while he and the boys stunk up the Grammys with their latest low-T bopper, titled who gives a fuck.

Prancing on some platform on the Hudson River, U2 did their legendary impersonation of a bunch of half-in-the-bag exurban dads getting the old band back together for someone's stepdaughter's second wedding. And instead of playing any songs anyone wanted to hear, the dads sharted out a set of their originals, which kind of sounded like U2 music would sound if played by people who'd never actually heard any U2 music.

In this case, the real U2 looked extraordinarily tired and haggard, and seemed to regret this stupid idea of playing out there in the freezing-fucking-cold-what-the-hell-were-we-thinking-of-anyway. And just because Bono was desperate to top the legendary cringe-monsoon of U2's 1997 'surprise gig' at the Astor Place K-Mart, he pulled out a star-spangled bullhorn and started yelling out two-week-old DNC talking points.

You could just feel everyone in the audience being deluged by a Category 10 cringe-attack. Douches *were* chilled.

The irony here being that Bono was sharting out all the right goodspeak on the Grammy's at the same time his little ONE scam was squeezing workers — *disadvantaged female workers* — in poor countries by doing crap like screwing them on taxes and whoring them out as bribes to local muckety-mucks.

I'm trying to work out the math here: maybe U2 signed their first pact with Satan in 1979, when they were still up-and-comers. Then they re-signed in 1998 after the execrable *Pop* laid a big goose-egg. If we presume Hell's calendar goes by the 19-year Metonic Cycle, I'd say U2's contract was up for renewal round about, let's say *November of 2017*. Bingo.

Sure enough, the once-pliant Irish press then took aim at U2's legendary and long-standing tax piracy, the bloody ingrates sensing metaphysical blood in the water. Maybe one day the press will train their sights on Bono's cozy relationship with the United Nations, whose systematic sexual abuse of children is so egregious that there's even a Wikipedia entry for precisely that. Wikipedia not being exactly keen on manning the hustings against organized pedo-rackets, I might add.

POP (CULTURE) HAS EATEN ITSELF

A LOOK AT THE 2011 TOP 20 GROSSING FILMS IN THE US should send spasms of terror down the spine of any Hollywood mogul. The number one film was a *Harry Potter* sequel, the last in the series. Number two was a *Transformers* sequel everyone agreed signaled the death knell of the franchise. *Twilight*, another franchise that's ending soon, was number three.

Going down the list you have a *Pirates of the Caribbean* sequel (based on a 50 year-old theme park ride), the fifth *Fast and Furious* film, a *Mission: Impossible* sequel (a franchise from the Sixties), a *Sherlock Holmes* film (created over a century ago) a *Planet of the Apes* reboot, three movies based on Stan Lee/Jack Kirby comics from the early Sixties, a couple comedies, a drama, a *Smurfs* film (another ancient franchise), some kiddie flicks (including *Puss in Boots*, based on an Medieval fairy tale) and God help us all, an *Alvin and the Chipmunks* movie.

Given that nearly all of these films could have been made almost fifty years ago, it's more than safe to assume there is an absolute drought of creativity in Tinseltown, which is merely a microcosm of the drought in creativity in the larger culture. A look at what's been released so far in 2012 is even more depressing: a list of mostly forgettable castoffs, with only two films having broken that crucial $100M mark.

We keep hearing how massively huge and awesome geek culture is, but the numbers don't bear it out. Sure, most of these movies have some connection to geek culture, but more importantly, they appeal to *chronological* children. And taking your kids to the movies is one of the few affordable sources of entertainment available to families these days. There's a *very* big difference between geek culture and mainstream culture that geeks also consume.

Hollywood actually tried making a film solely for the geek market, and spent a fortune on production and promotion doing so. That film was called *Scott Pilgrim Vs. The World*, a cute little romp based on a popular series of graphic novels. They pulled out all the stops on this one, spending upwards of $85,000,000 on production and God knows how much on promotion (you couldn't turn on SyFy or Cartoon Network in 2010 without being hammered by ads for the film).

Let's be conservative and say they spent $30M on promotion; that's an investment of $115M on a film that grossed $48M worldwide ($30M US, $18M int'l) and did a paltry $15M on DVD.

Given that the exhibitors and the retailers get half, and there are always random legal fees to worry about, this film needed to hit the $250M mark to break even (being conservative, again) and barely grossed a quarter of that.

Then there's this: *John Carter* is expected to take a $115M write-down, making it one of the biggest money-losers in Hollywood history. My theory on the backlash to this film has less to do with the quality of what's on the screen and more with what it represents; a pre-postmodern America of the Pulps and the frontier, an America of possibility that's lost to us now. *John Carter* is definitely not a postmodern superhero, and can't be revised to postmodernity the way Guy Ritchie's *Sherlock Holmes* was.

'John Carter' is also an unwelcome reminder of an America in which mystically-minded creators like Edgar Rice Burroughs actually *created things*. You know, had actual *ideas*. An America where movies weren't built around goddamned board games.

Then there's TV, the great hope for auteurs and science fiction and fantasy fans. With the success of *Lost* (and the critical success of *Battlestar Galactica*) networks trotted out a parade of series meant to recapture that lightning in a bottle — *Flash Forward, Invasion, The Event, The River* — but all of them failed.

Nerds will lecture you until the cows come home as to how *Fringe* is superior in every way to *The X-Files,* but *Fringe* is limping to its death at a time (its fourth season) when *The X-Files* was romping, and garners ratings (just above a dismal one-share) only a fraction of *TXF* at it's lowest, final-season ebb. Fox seems reluctant to announce its cancellation because its already-catastrophic ratings would collapse to *Dollhouse* levels, but when your show-runner is talking doing a 'fifth season' as a comic book, you know which way the wind is blowing.

SyFy — which is to actual science fiction what MTV is to music — recently put the kibosh on a new *Battlestar Galactica* series, after unceremoniously slaying the *Caprica BSG* prequel. *Ringer* (starring geek goddess Sarah Michelle Gellar) is limping to cancellation, and most of the geek-friendly CW lineup (*Vampire Diaries, Nikita*) struggles to hit a one-share. Fox also killed Steven Spielberg's *Terra Nova,* and JJ Abrams' *Alcatraz* and a *Napoleon Dynamite* cartoon are not the sure-things they should have been.

We'll leave aside the dismal spectacle of pop music, because it's been so terrible for so long that I really have to wonder about people who can still be bothered to get upset about it. What I'm hearing on Top Forty radio sounds like an endless late Eighties tape-loop, so much so that I'm almost expecting Exposé, T'Pau and Taylor Dayne to be brought back from obscurity any minute now.

American comics — which should be a beehive of pure, unbridled creative madness — are puttering along, catering largely to an audience of middle-age men (superhero comics) and a much smaller audience of hipster creator/readers (indie comics). The big headline on geek industry site *ICV2* was that February's sales were up over Feb. 2011, an impressive feat until you see how flat-out *disastrous* 2011 figures were. DC's recent reboot rules the Top Ten, but that's simply a Nineties vintage makeover of a late Fifties makeover of early Forties superheroes. A endless nostalgia loop.

Having been involved in fandom since the mid-Seventies, I can say that I've never seen the ideal of true creativity have a lower cache in comics than it does today. Sure, all these old, wacked Kirby concepts took a good twenty years or so for the rest of fandom to warm up to, but even then you had your mystic madmen like Steve Englehart and Jim Starlin, your Robert Crumb's and your Richard Corben's and your Doug Moench's, your hippie phreaks spiking the funnybook punchbowl with four-color blotter.

In the Eighties and Nineties you had your British Invasion, which gave us mystic madmen Neil Gaiman and Alan Moore and Grant Morrison and Warren Ellis. I doubt any of these guys would get their feet in the door the way things are going. The readers simply wouldn't tolerate it.

With Borders gone, graphic novels aren't as welcome in the more conservative environs of stores like Barnes & Noble. A look at what's selling at B&N.com doesn't fill my heart with hope: most of the graphic novels in their top 1000 are *Walking Dead* volumes, whose success is surely fired by the overwhelming success of the TV series. But *Walking Dead* is not really a series that most people associate with comics, it's just a George Romero knockoff. Well-crafted, but I mean, *come on.* Pay the guy royalties already.

And no matter how hard the sociologists apologize, the zombie meme is a warning sign. It's a symptom of surrender, of collapse. I wonder if zombie stories — or something like them — were popular in late-period Rome. I'll have to look that up.

WHAT ALL OF THIS IS SYMPTOMATIC OF is the ongoing process of Disenchantment. This, in the end, is a conscious process. And for all of the brave talk about science, rationalism and reason, Disenchantment is an auto-destructive process for societies. History teaches us nothing else.

I'm hearing how successful Skeptics and atheists have been recruiting geeks to their cause, so the withering of creativity in geek culture in the past ten years makes perfect sense: the repetition and remakes, the superficiality, the so-called 'hard science' which exists only on paper, the imposition of identity politics which repels most readers outside of the incessantly fractious in-groups.

Because *true* creativity is neither rational nor scientific, as Alan Moore will tell you and as our immersions into Jack Kirby's weird worlds have proven. Even though Lovecraft and Gene Roddenberry gave lip service to science and rationality, it seems motivated more by Lovecraft's aristocratic loathing of the superstitious masses he saw in Red Hook and Roddenberry's loathing of his own Southern Baptist roots. True rationalists write forgettable hard sci-fi crap that no one reads anymore: authors like Asimov, Niven, Bova, Clarke. Guys whose brave predictions of our future have yet to come to pass and probably never will. In other words, to approach creativity with the rational mind is profoundly *irrational*.

And I've talked about how *MythBusters* and the Skeptic® movement is inducing a kind of pissy, reactive reductionism in the world of Fandom that is directly antithetical to the attitudes of the creators of their favorite franchises. It's all a kind of *armoring*, a retreat to the cold comforts of reduction for its own sake. It's a profound form of cowardice. As time goes on and this armoring fails to deal with the psychological dysfunction that used to be channeled into creativity, we'll see a lot of meltdowns in public, like the jerk on *Mythbusters*, Penn Jillette, the Amazing Atheist and much, much more.

I can't help but notice how bitter and angry so many of our skeptic friends are, or how all that rage addiction ends up carving ruts into their faces. I also can't help but notice how the armor so many people wear online seems to be oxidizing into a virtual iron maiden, the classic case of a weapon turning against its wielder.

I also can't help but notice how all of this reduction-worship is playing havoc on geek culture, which is stuck in an endless rut of remakes, revamps and reboots. Your average blockbuster movie is created by committees who consult sales charts and graphs and digitally-composed test surveys, which they use to endlessly bombard the creatives with revisions. Most big-budget production exists in a totally digital environment, with actors reduced to puppets hitting marks in sterile green-screen rooms under the thumbs of dictatorial technocrat directors.

Ironically, given the mania for 'science', or the fetishization of a Humanist religious ideal people refer to as 'science' (true science can be as visionary and mystic as art, as Newton, Tesla and Crick taught us), the absolute parade of sludge that we're seeing in pop culture is the direct result of the imposition of scientistic principles on the creative process.

You want science? Look at what's playing at your local multiplex. All of it is test-marketed according to scientistic principles in front of sample audiences who are required to fill out excruciating, scientifically-designed questionnaires, which are then fed back into the system for the requisite changes.

Even the productions of most comedies and dramas are as spontaneous as the construction of a lawn mower. That no one loves this stuff is a given. Hardly anyone remembers most of these films after a few months.

What you're hearing on the radio might as well be created by guys in lab coats, it's almost completely electronic. Even the vocals are becoming robotic with the use of Auto-Tune. 'Artists' are interchangeable, aside from a handful of superstars or genuine talents whose voices can't be simulated by technology. Yet, I mean.

So come on, science nerds; you own the Top Forty. It was made for you. Hell, it's all made *by you;* by people who view the world as a dumb, mindless machine meant to be fucked to death, the same way you do. There's your 'Science': in our pop culture. Own it. You made it. Take a bow. Such is the price of reduction. Always has been and always will.

M UCH KEENER MINDS THAN MY OWN have wrestled with all of this, particularly Max Weber:

> The fate of our times is characterized by rationalization and intellectualization and, above all, by the 'disenchantment of the world'. Precisely the ultimate and most sublime values have retreated from public life either into the transcendental realm of mystic life or into the brotherliness of direct and personal human relations.
>
> It is not accidental that our greatest art is intimate and not monumental, nor is it accidental that today only within the smallest and intimate circles, in personal human situations, in pianissimo, that something is pulsating that corresponds to the prophetic pneuma, which in former times swept through the great communities like a firebrand, welding them together.
>
> If one tries intellectually to construe new religions without a new and genuine prophecy, then, in an inner sense, something similar will result, but with still worse effects. And academic prophecy, finally, will create only fanatical sects but never a genuine community.

'The Disenchantment of Modern Life' by Max Weber

Although 'science' is waved about like a cudgel today, real science is simply just a tool. It's really just an elaborate system of measurement. I actually have tremendous respect for science, but not much for 'Science', if you get my meaning here. What we are actually seeing is the emergence of an atheist *religion*. It's nothing new and it's not a religion with a great track record for self-replication. See, what the Randi's and the Schirmer's and the Dawkins' won't tell you is that atheism and skepticism were all the rage during the decline period of Ancient Rome.

If you want to scare the shit out of yourself, read up on the decline of Rome, particularly during the late Imperial period. It will be like looking in a mirror. Everything this country is going through today, they went through. This is one of the primary reasons that I argue that History is cyclical and not linear. The comfortable cosmopolitans of the Roman Empire were not stupid. I'd say most were smarter than the average American. They even had slaves with high degrees of education. And they too embraced reason and atheism as the hallmarks of a modern civilized Roman. They too became obsessed with fitness and business and pleasure.

How did that turn out? Well, exactly how it is today: birthrates plummeted far below replacement-rate among the educated, but much less so among the superstitious masses. Their religious leaders used demographics as a weapon, and realized that they would one day overwhelm their refined rivals by force of sheer numbers. And, of course, they ultimately did.

So if you "believe in science and reason," then you have to acknowledge the fact that this reductionist, atheist mindset has been a death-knell for cultures, going back thousands of years now. The science has been *done*, people. Atheism is the religion of the graveyard. And now the same patterns are repeating themselves, as predicted time and again. The canary in the coalmine is pop culture, the last thing that Americans still did better than anyone else.

So, in other words, our pop culture sucks because our *culture* sucks. And it sucks because we're focused on all the wrong things, and we mistake self-aggrandizement for self-actualization. We've been sold a bill of goods, only the goods were routed to China and now we're stuck with the bill. We're all trapped on the same ride, the only difference is that some of us realize it.

Note: This rant turned out to be quite prophetic, it's just the collapse took a bit longer than I thought it would. Then again, the implosion we're now seeing is all the more devastating for having been kicked down the road all those years. As it stands, I doubt we'll see pop culture ever come back at that scale ever again.

WELL, THAT SUCKED

BEFORE WE WALKED INTO THE NEW JERSEY RENAISSANCE Kingdom — this year has a *Pirate* theme, God help us all — we were approached by a woman who was ranting on about how horrible and what a ripoff it all was. She seemed pretty irate, but we chalked it up to the weather being ghastly.

The RenFaire definitely sucked this year, but no more than usual, I suppose. They all seem the same to me — inept, goofy, cut-rate — but any break from the relentless ennui of NJ suburbia doesn't need to try too hard to divert me for an hour or two. Maybe the weather just naturally makes you all the less forgiving of it all. My daughter loves it and my boys used to enjoy it as well, so it became a kind of tradition for Father's Day. Maybe next year we'll save the money and try the big one in upstate NY in September.

I was struck by what a bad idea it is to plan these things in the horrid NJ summer, considering most of these people are wearing about 35 pounds of clothing. Maybe other RenFaire's try a little harder, but I was also struck how little effort is put into this particular version.

The NJRK is basically a grammar school field day, only with sweaty, well-nourished underachievers who don't seem particularly motivated to create anything like a convincing or authentic environment. They seem much more interested in the excruciating type of mock-comedic theater you see a lot at cons, so long as it doesn't distract them from their Wii's or Taco Bell. There was the usual Madrigal choir but no one — not one single person — was attempting to sing in harmony, and no one knew how to project. I was standing about 20 feet away from a choir of about 20 people and I could barely hear them.

It's easy to rag on RenFaire people, but I think the concept can be reasonably entertaining if done well. It can be a good family outing that can offer a nice kind of geeky vibe, if run by people who aren't simply out to take your money and force you to listen to their wretched British accents, which seem to be drawn solely from repeated viewings of *Monty Python and The Holy Grail.* But these people need to try a little bit — well, a *lot* — harder, especially when the weather is so assaultive.

WHAT'S INTERESTING IN THE LIGHT OF THIS PARTICULAR BLOG is that the original concept of RenFaires was to recreate the time of Queen Elizabeth I. Which of course is when England fell under the sway of occultists like John Dee and Edward Kelley, as well as Rosicrucian/Neo-Templar master schemers like Francis Walsingham and Francis Bacon. Not to mention Shakespeare and Marlowe. Those were heady times.

You'd think people who claim to be fixated on that time period might trouble themselves to do a wee bit more research so they could offer up something besides face-painting and beanbag tosses. So much of the curvature of world history came be traced to the Renaissance, when the idea of a worldwide 'British Empire' was first conceived. At the same time, Shakespeare was creating the prototype not only for mass media, but also the English language as we know it today.

Soon after, we had the King James Bible, which would shake all of Christendom to its core, and then Freemasonry and its attendant revolutions. So even in as humble a setting as a RenFaire, you have the Mysteries lurking behind the curtain. All there for the taking, if you bother to look. So you NJ Kingdom people, a word of advice: try to spend less time in the off-season at White Castle and Wicca meets, and a little more time in the library.

Don't get me wrong, I'm rooting for these people. But just because you can make a nice costume doesn't mean you have a competent fair.

Sorry: a competent *faire*.

CHEETO EATING SURRENDER ZOMBIES

THE WALKING DEAD HAS BEEN ONE OF THE GREAT SUCCESS stories in geekdom. It's been racking up huge ratings on the AMC Channel — a one-time clearinghouse for Hollywood inventory that was repurposed as the boutique basic cable channel, with shows like *Mad Men* and *Breaking Bad* — and record sales for its comic books and trade paperback collections. It's made its creator Robert Kirkman fantastically rich, in an age when millionaire comics auteurs are largely a thing of the past.

The Walking Dead is essentially a serialization of George Romero's first two zombie films, namely 1968's ground-breaking *Night of the Living Dead* and its 1980 sequel, *Dawn of the Dead*. Zombies have fixtures of pulp entertainment for ages, but were always also-rans in the pop-cult sweepstakes.

Romero's low-budget films were cult classics, but the 'Zombie Apocalypse' theme that he essentially created didn't truly resonate with the mass audience until *The Walking Dead* brought it all into the mainstream. I often wonder how Romero feels about that. It's all dovetailed with zombie chic, which has been all the rage in geekdom, with zombie parties, zombie raves, zombie parades, you name it.

Curiously, the horror subculture which birthed the Zombie Apocalypse fetish is pretty much dead in the water. Vampires have been 'tweened to death, torture-porn, the post-*Ringu* remake craze, and the mockumentary fad have all played out their string, and monsters and slashers and *Alien*-clones fell victim to changing tastes and the inherent narrative limitations of the form. So why are zombies so hot these days?

I used to have zombie nightmares when I was young and alienated. Looking back, I see it as a kind of egocentric terror; that I was the only thinking human being in a world filled with undead automatons. I was an early fan of the comic, but it got old fast, since the power of the zombie apocalypse narrative tends to dissipate as it drags on. I never thought it rose to the level of the original *Dawn of the Dead,* or even the remake. Plus, the zombie myth is a hopeless, defeatist fantasy and I don't need any more of those in my life.

I believe it's precisely that defeatism that is so appealing to today's beaten down America. As with all apocalyptic fantasy, people who watch it always imagine themselves as one of the plucky survivors, not one of the poor bastards who gets ripped in two before the station break. The popularity of the series shows that there is no vision out there, no concept of the future. Aside from the crippling inequality that is putting all of us who aren't hedge fund pirates under enormous stress, the dominant intellectual fashion these days is a straining towards utter nihilism.

Out of a misguided reaction to the symbiotic relationship between religious fundamentalism and corporate hegemons during the Bush Era, it's all the rage now for young geeks to run around bigging up 'Science' as a substitute religion, even though at its core, true science is simply a form of measuring physical phenomena through a process that reduces everything to its component parts.

Yet those same corporate hegemons control the application of science in its near-totality, and are using it to help establish a broad-spectrum dominance that will stand beyond all challenge. The same figures who are waved around like Medieval saints by gullible geeks are in fact all bought-and-sold-and-paid-for whores for the corporate elite. They have no choice at all if they want a living wage, an audience and access to a well-appointed laboratory.

Which is why we shouldn't be surprised when those same vassals run around preaching the elite's worldview, albeit a politically-correct variant thereof: Life is meaningless, the Universe has no purpose, and nihilism is the only sensible philosophy. In other words, back to the Existentialist suicide culture that rose with the most recent triumph of 'the Rational'. That this is the worldview often espoused by sociopaths, tyrants and serial killers seems to escape everyone's notice.

So why should we be surprised by the popularity of the zombie, given that it's an inevitable by-product of the surrender culture now being pushed by the Nihilist revival? Defeatism is fool-proof. You can't control a positive outcome, but you can ensure a negative one simply by giving up and surrendering. Thus the ego is protected.

Once the skepdicks feel they've done away with the Paranormal (or dreamed up enough plausible denial to keep the geeks on the plantation) and the atheists feel they've destroyed Christianity (or until the Fundamentalists begin a serious pushback), the next step is destroying any kind or Science or technology that promises a different future than the Stalinist gulag state that the A+ crowd so desperately strains towards. It's already happening, with the Peak Oil crowd and the crypto-Luddites in obscure academic posts, who are unilaterally deciding the limits of science, harshing on the mellow of Starfleet Academy applicants everywhere.

Just as the skeptics and debunkers were seen as passé and old-fashioned by the Nü Atheists, so to will the atheists be seen by the inevitable rise of the Nihilist, the terminus of the culture of defeat. Central to the Nihilist worldview is that all human endeavor is pointless. And soon the Nü Atheist movement will be controlled by the same elements that took over the New Left in the Seventies, which will inevitably to the same internecine warfare that is the true passion of the Nihilist. That process has started in earnest already.

Although ever-optimistic liberals in America still believe the Republicans will come to their senses and fall in line with Obama's (read: "Wall Street's") agenda, already we are seeing a movement to a new kind of ethnic nationalism, one that will dispense with the niceties of the Bush Era. How will the PZ Myers' and Bill Maher's respond once the debating ends and fists and bullets start flying? Whose side do they think the cops will take?

Hmm, come to think of it, maybe *The Walking Dead* isn't sci-fi. Maybe it's some kind of allegory for America's inevitable future under all the false dichotomies that dominate political conversation. If those who don't subscribe to the Punch and Judy show don't start speaking up, it may yet come to pass.

Note: Damn. Was this piece ever prophetic. Sadly.

KINGDOM OF THE CULTS

NOWADAYS IT'S TEMPTING TO DISMISS ALL CULTS as intelligence cutouts. I've been known to entertain those notions myself now and again, but I think the real litmus test as to a cult's authenticity is how the authorities react to them. If a cult ends up getting plunger-fucked by The Man, it probably wasn't a cutout.

Americans tend to see their government as essentially neutral when it comes to how you choose to conduct your life and associate with others (or at least we used to), but all you need to do is to step outside the commonly accepted social arrangements to see just how fast and hard the government can bring the hammer down on your skull. *Any* government, really. Organizing yourself to exercise independence from the System is not only frowned upon, it's usually crushed. Often with *supreme* violence.

So with cults making the news again, you can't help but wonder: is the transgression here the various crimes the cults might be accused of, or is it trying to organize yourself in opposition to the System at a time when that System is becoming more totalizing than ever before in my lifetime?

Now we're hearing about the arrest of *Smallville* star Allison Mack for the role of procuring sex slaves for her cult leader, Keith Raniere. But are we really supposed to believe no one knew about Raniere's dating methods all along? I remember reading about this particular cult years ago, even the branding business sounds vaguely familiar. Is all this some new revelation, or did the NXIVM cult forget to grease the right palms last month?

Don't forget we have the horrific example of the Branch Davidian siege and massacre twenty-five years ago, based on a raft of charges and accusations that have since been proven to be deliberate lies. David Koresh and his Davidians weren't my cup of tea either, but I can't help but wonder if the long, flame-throwing arm of John Law wasn't searching around for examples to be made, so they moseyed on down to Waco and pinned the tail on that particular donkey. Maybe things got out of hand, maybe they went strictly according to plan, who can say? I guess we'll never know. Sucks to be you, Branchers.

That was a different time, and you had a lot of folks slapped into reality by the Gulf War and its aftermath. And a lot of those who were looking around, not really liking what they saw much, and wondering if maybe there was another way. In that regard, it really wasn't much different than what the hippie counterculture — meaning the real hippies, not the LARP hippies of Laurel Canyon *et al* — found themselves dealing with. Former Sixties radical John Sinclair put it rather bluntly when asked in the early 90s what happened to the Movement. "We got our asses kicked, man," Sinclair glumly replied.

So you may notice that there seem to be all kinds of cults out there these days, usually flying beneath the radar of the mainstream media, who seem primarily fixated on sniffing each other's farts and pretending they're afraid of Trump. But breakaway communities? Well, if so, they're keeping a low profile. Quite wisely, I might add.

The Rajneeshpuram saga back in the 1980s really said a lot about America, and about how successful communities are built and how they decay. Those old Oregon cowboys who got themselves so worked up about the Osho nuts were ultimately all the descendants of cultists themselves. Remember, the Old West wasn't won by nice, obedient, bourgeois types. It was won by religious fanatics, many of whom were fired up by the Third Great Awakening.

You see, nothing truly meaningful ever gets done without belief and faith. It's only the power of belief in something greater than the mere self that inspires the kind of sacrifice needed to overcome the kinds of hardships and tragedies that any great enterprise requires. Once you lose that fire, it's only a matter of time before your culture finds yourself circling the drain. Argue all you like, but the data is in. The Science is settled.

The documentary *Holy Hell* —about the rather-odd Buddhafield cult that sprang up in Eighties Los Angeles — shows exactly how this process works. Buddhafield was relatively benign as cults go, and no one can say that its members didn't have the time of their lives for an enviably long time, at least judging from all the video evidence.

I didn't really get the 'hell' bit in this particular story, certainly nothing even on the same planet of People's Temple or the Manson bunch, and the cult still seems to be going strong in Hawaii. But when you believe your guru is a living god, it can be a real bummer to discover he's just a cracked actor getting on in years. Yet, it was the cult's devotion that this weirdly charismatic ex-gay porn star that inspired some pretty impressive feats. Would they all have been sitting around watching TV and snacking on Yodels and Doritos without his inspiration? Maybe not. But then again, probably yes.

Sadly, the problem with cults is that that wonderful dopamine tsunami eventually subsides, and you eventually realize that the rest of the world isn't marching lockstep behind you.

EXCEPT FOR THE FACT THAT IT WAS ACTUALLY A CORPORATE concentration camp created and run by Masonic bankers in London, Plymouth Plantation really wasn't any different than Rajneeshpuram. The rural folk of Oregon just weren't accustomed to the kind of fanaticism that brought their forebears to those hills any longer. They forgot that it was the hot fire of faith alone that literally moves mountains and makes the deserts bloom.

I very much sympathize with the original citizens of Antelope's desire to be left alone and unmolested by a literal army of sex-crazed Californians and their Indian overlords, but at the same time I can't help but feel a deep sense of unspoken regret among them as well. Maybe it's the kind of regret you can see among war veterans, who miss the excitement and camaraderie of the worst days of their lives.

Mind you, a lot of the natives you see interviewed are indeed the kinds of dipshit hicks that people in New York or San Francisco think everyone outside their city limits is. They just sound *ignorant,* and I can't help but think the real problem up there were the women not wanting their hubbies getting any big ideas about serving themselves up a heapin' helpin' of some kooky cult quim, seeing as how it seemed to be women who were doing most of the driving with the campaign against the cult.

Of course, since this particular operation was actually being run by a sociopathic terrorist and all, their opposition was on-target. But the point is that the Oregonians and the authorities gave a lot of lip service to religion, but it didn't seem to be very deeply felt. And maybe that's the real problem in our sick, dying culture today. You can blame all your woes on the system, but if you're not willing to make the sacrifices needed to change it, then tough titties, as Sheela once famously said. Comfort or revolution: choose one.

I DO HAVE TO ADMIT TO A CERTAIN WEAKNESS for the cult experience, having seen it from the periphery as a wee wane. Ironically, this was a cult that can be *provably* shown to be a CIA operation, but that doesn't mean it didn't look incredibly exciting and utterly enchanting to a young, naive laddie such as myself.

See, the Jesus People movement didn't strike me as some intelligence cutout, it looked like the real deal to my young eyes. It looked like religion beyond religion, and it gave you the distinct impression that Jesus' arrival was imminent, if it hadn't already gone down. I still vividly remember seeing all the Jesus People reverberations at the Nazarene college my mother attended, and seeing the young Jesus hippies tuned into a channel I could only hear from a distance. It was so powerful and numinous that it haunted my dreams for a very long time. It just seemed like the way it was supposed to be. Sadly, it wasn't. Hey: I was not only highly impressionable at the time, I was hyper-vigilant. Sue me.

I'm not sure if that experience explains my later fascination with Heaven's Gate (AKA the most hardcore Trekkies ever). It seems odd because the kids I saw at Eastern Nazarene seemed so free and cool and beautiful to my innocent eyes, whereas the Gate's 'Away Team' seemed dumpy, dorky and defeated. But I've no doubt that a lot of the Gaters started their journey to Rancho San Diego in the same fiery cauldrons of the Seventies Jesus People revivals.

And after that high wore off, they ultimately found themselves mesmerized by a charmingly-fruity music professor-slash-mental patient, his ditzy hausfrau co-messiah, and their bonkers flying-saucer faith.

But Heaven's Gate's story doesn't seem in any way tragic or sinister to me. They come across as a fairly Orthodox Gnostic cult (if there could ever be such a thing) who took it as far as they could, saw the big hammer that the Panopticon was fixing to bring down on all of our heads, figured it wasn't going anywhere good, then took their chances with this whole "comet" business blowing into town.

It's tempting to write the Away Team all off as delusional nutcases, but don't forget the biggest UFO flap of modern times was going down a few miles down the road while the Gaters were packing their celestial bags. I doubt Applewhite's paranoia was justified, in that I don't think the FBI cared about what a bunch of sci-fi nerds with marginal skill-sets believed in. But I'm sure they were being monitored, given they were doing their web-design work for military clients.

Just as I know people who I take seriously who won't write off Osho as a fraud, I have heard from folks over the years who will defend Scientology and argue the cult's bad reputation is purely because of government aggression. Not to mention the CoS' surprisingly-cogent brief against Big Pharma and SSRIs. It's the Devil's Dilemma, isn't it? A rapacious cult — with all its weird links to crazy ol' Al Crowley and his cohort of pervs — versus an industry that is responsible for so much death, misery and oppression.

So, realizing we live in a fallen world, I should point out that even our cult leaders are flimsy and cut-rate in these times. Maybe I'm just a cranky old coot, screaming at those newfangled cultists to get off my lawn. But weren't cults so much more exciting and alluring back in the day, Mabel? Osho and his bunch with their johnsons and their dirty pillows flapping away in the Oregon breeze? Now *there* was a cult. Reverend Moon with his flower-peddlers and mass marriages? *There* was a cult. That big Odin-looking fuck Father Yod, with his barely-legal harem and his vegetarian bistro? Now *there* was a cult.

Sadly, the system seems to be marshaling its forces to build its own cult: the pseudo-socialist Woke suicide-cult that seems to swarm like flies over shit everywhere you look these days. Time was that cults arose in *opposition* to the System, but I guess that's why we have all these fall-guys in Washington these days; to create the barest veneer of an illusion that this new death-cultism is somehow rebellious.

Of course, the management-class Woke death-cult is not even remotely rebellious. Not even by a million light years.

INFINITE BELLICOSITY IN INFINITE CONFLAGRATIONS

J ESUS. I REALLY DON'T KNOW WHERE TO START. I watched the two-part opener of the new *Star Trek* series, and I'm still wondering if I didn't hallucinate it all. I'm still wondering if I didn't have some weird flashback and find myself in an alternate timeline where Star Trek is very slick, very costly recruitment propaganda for some alternate-reality, militarized space agency. Oh wait; I forgot. We already have a militarized space agency in *this* reality, called the "Space Force." And its insignia draws heavily on the Starfleet logo. *Now* I get it.

Just how militaristic was the pilot for *Star Trek: Discovery*, then? Well, it's the most flagrantly-militaristic SF I have seen since in a very, very long time. So much so that it actually veers perilously close to doctrinaire fascism.

First of all, forget the prefab debates over "diversity." That was all just a master-class lesson in Knowles' First Law ("Whenever a controversy over symbolism erupts in the media, it's usually disguising another hidden symbolic message altogether.") There's no real diversity to be found on the Discovery; every individual impulse is subordinated to authority. The only conflict among the crew is how genocidal they should actually be. This is the fetishization of uniformity and the worship of empire. This is the *Star Trek* I always saw the potential for, but hoped would never come.

L ET ME BE ABSOLUTELY CLEAR ABOUT THIS: the *Star Trek: Discovery* pilot is nothing else but a balls-out glorification of preemptive war and technocracy, the militarization of women and the demonization of individuality. Peacemakers and diplomats are not only seen as weak and naive dupes, but as virtual traitors who get what's coming to them. Just *how* vitriolic is this new Trek? Well, look at it this way: the insufficiently-warlike science officer is revealed to be a member of a race who exist only to be *hunted and eaten.*

I'm not kidding.

We see yet another makeover for the Klingons, who are more inhuman and grotesque than we've ever seen them. They are irredeemably alien, sporting bizarre costumes and mouths filled with huge, sharklike fangs. And despite all the diversity window-dressing, most of the Klingons are not only very dark-skinned (and played by predominantly black actors), they are actively racist towards light-skinned Klingons. They're also religious fanatics driven purely by emotion, where our Starfleet heroes are Dawkinsian wet-dreams of cold rationality. Yet the Klingons are also responding to what a reasonable person could argue were aggressive actions by the Federation; installing military equipment near their border, invading their sovereign territory, and killing one of their citizens.

However, the Klingon's real transgression seems to be "clinging on" to individuality, thereby resisting the joy and glory of wearing the ostentatiously-Masonic Starfleet uniform, which reduces all diversity and difference to an easily-manageable singularity of mind and purpose. Hence, we're subjected to excruciatingly long and ponderous scenes in which the Klingons growl about their worship of "Light" and argue about who will be their new "torchbearer," since Michael — yes, her name is *Michael* — does away with the old one.

Never mind the *de rigeur l*udicrousness of five-foot tall women beating up trained soldiers who are literally three times their body-mass, the blatant symbolism along the way just makes your jaw drop. How blatant? Well, the entire two-parter actually takes place in the solar system of a binary star. In fact the second part is titled "Battle at the Binary Stars." So, my guess that we would be seeing some Sirius symbology in this series was right on the money. But the unconscious takeaway of this seems that one day the troublesome binary (or "chaos" as the series trailer has it) will be resolved through Synthesis to the harmonious Starfleet Oneness.

Yeah. It's not your imagination. This is our pop culture circa 2017.

So how does this all work as drama? Well, it has its moments, even if those moments are all shamelessly-manipulative, emotionally-speaking. The writers pull out some fairly-effective tricks from the agitational-propaganda toolkit, even if all they are essentially doing is re-staging *Deep Space Nine's* far-superior "Sacrifice of Angels." I can't begin to imagine how much they spent on this production, but every single penny is up on the screen.

However, the acting is uniformly terrible. I realize that's almost a gimme with any *Trek* pilot but still, you notice. The woman who plays Michael — no, seriously; her fucking name is *Michael* — is not only a terrible actor, she's really not much of a screen presence either. When she isn't pouty, she's cranky, and she looks about as tough as the Keebler Elf. But I don't want to single her out; everyone else is equally as terrible. And it's not really her fault her character is the mariest Mary Sue who ever sue'd. It's the shitty writing.

I didn't use to worry much about the fact that *Star Trek* is basically propaganda advertising for a socialist military dictatorship, because I didn't really see it reaching an audience that I was particularly worried about. But today, with the ubiquity of witch-hunts and ideological struggle sessions taking place on college campuses every day, I actually am starting to get a bit concerned about all this predictive programming about young vanguards erasing the past and incinerating those who cling to it. Particularly with all the crypto-Masonic symbolism this kind of stuff is glazed with.

Ordo ab Chao, bitches!

YOU'LL FLOAT TOO

THERE ARE A NUMBER OF DIFFERENT PRODUCTIONS of *The Little Mermaid* being worked on right now. Four different films, a ballet, a live TV show and a traveling production of the Disney musical. But what is The *Little Mermaid* all about, really? I mean, when you really get down to brass tacks? It's really about a young girl entering another reality, our reality in this particular case. After a traumatic experience. With the aid of *sorcery*.

I've written a lot about the Descent to the Underworld, a theme which famously plays a very central role in *Stephen King's It.* I'm not giving away any spoilers here, you can see it all in the trailers. The earliest version we have of this myth concerns Inanna, the prototype for Atargatis and as such, the ultimate prototype for mermaids. Inanna descends into the Underworld with Enki (god of the waters, among other things) to confront the king and queen of Hell and rescue Dumuzid (or Tammuz), her shepherd-boy consort.

We see a variant on the Descent in the first (meaning "real") *Stranger Things*, when Sheriff Hopper and Joyce Byers travel to the Upside Down to rescue Will. *Wonder Woman,* the biggest hit movie of 2017 so far, is a beat-for-beat retelling of Inanna's descent, done with such on-the-spectrum obsession with detail I can't help but wonder if the film isn't actually a devotional text. And the real-life Amazons themselves were based on the Hittite priestesses of Atargatis, aka the Big Mermaid. *Alice in Wonderland* and *The Wizard of Oz* are variations on the theme, as is *The OA*, which is essentially an explicit Mystery cult narrative based on The Rape of Persephone. So yet another traumatized child crossing dimensional barriers. Kind of a thruline we're looking at here.

Twin Peaks is a variation on the theme, based on Orpheus and Eurydice. In that particular myth, Orpheus descends to the Underworld to rescue his consort Eurydice, who was killed while fleeing from a satyr. Orpheus is allowed to descend into Hades and rescue Eurydice, but only on the condition that he not turn back to look at her while leaving the Underworld. Since this is a Greek myth and everything has to end badly, Orpheus fucks up and does the one thing he's told not to do, so Eurydice is lost forever. Then he's murdered by a pack of horny Maenads, and his head and lyre float down a river before being enshrined in a temple on the Isle of Lesbos. *The End!*

In *Twin Peaks*, Cooper enters the Black Lodge — Hades, the Underworld, the transdimensional rift, yadda yadda — to rescue Annie Blackburn, but does so with insufficient courage. He loses Annie and is possessed by a demon. In *Twin Peaks: The Return*, Cooper returns to the Black Lodge to rescue Laura Palmer and change history — meaning he looks back — only to find himself back in the Black Lodge forever. *The End!*

We see variations on the Descent to the Underworld in all kinds of sci-fi narratives: *2001: A Space Odyssey* (with HAL's core as Hell), *Star Wars* (the Death Star), *Aliens* (the basement nest of the Xenomorphs), *Star Trek: First Contact* (the Borg-occupied engine room) and both *X-Files* movies (the underground alien ship and the underground genetics lab).

Well, this little comparative mythology lesson is absolutely scintillating, I hear you say, but what the fuck does it have to do with reality? Well, most of these descent stories deal with adults. It's a bit different with kids. So the question you really should be asking is how did all these kinds of stories become so dominant in our culture today? Well, let's get back to MKULTRA.

'MKULTRA' is like 'CIA'. It's more a shorthand for any number of bizarre human experiments the government undertook to try to control or alter the human mind, using drugs, weird tech, trauma, whatever. The cover story for this quarter-century, multimillion dollar enterprise was that it was all concocted to develop mind-controlled assassins and interrogation techniques. Which is all bullshit because the very term *assassin* comes from the Nizari sect, who were creating perfectly-functional mind-controlled assassins a thousand years ago, and pretty much everyone had perfected drug-driven interrogation techniques during WWII. I think the CIA's ambitions were infinitely grander.

MKULTRA was the brainchild of Allen Dulles, the first civilian CIA director. Dulles had a cushy post in neutral Switzerland during the Second World War. By a sheer stroke of coincidence, scientists in nearby Basel were experimenting with the chemical compounds that would ultimately become *lysergic acid diethylamide*. Dulles would also encounter the legendary Swiss psychiatrist Carl Jung, who was apparently treating Dulles' side action, Mary Bancroft, for a psychosomatic sneezing condition.

For a while, Jung and Dulles swapped notes through Bancroft, but later began to meet in person. Dulles wanted Jung to psychoanalyze Hitler, which we've since come to know as 'profiling'. Apparently, Dulles and Jung really hit it off, and the two would often engage in marathon gabfests. Dulles even gave Jung a fancy spy name: *Agent 488.*

As many of you know, Jung famously broke with his mentor Sigmund Freud (whom he saw as a father-figure and swapped patient-lovers with), and promptly lapsed into a full-blown nervous breakdown (or his "Night Sea Journey"). After which, Jung dove headfirst into the occult, particularly the blood-soaked mysteries of Mithras, which centered on the notion of spiritual transcendence through ordeal.

So what does any of this have to do with MKULTRA?

Well, Dulles was a very sharp guy. Jung probably showed him his beloved Mithraic Liturgy of the Paris Codex, which pretty much sounds like the account of a guy who was beamed aboard the Starship Enterprise while tripping balls on magic mushrooms. And by "pretty much," I mean "exactly."

I'm sure Jung pontificated about this all being evidence of the collective unconscious, and the hero's journey, and blablabla no one cares. But Dulles — who was pretty much only interested in finding things he could weaponize — probably read it for himself and said, "This sounds like some poor strung-out junkie got grabbed by a commando team and loaded onto a Flying Fortress. A damned *weird* Flying Fortress that shouldn't really exist in Ancient Egypt or Rome, but whatever." And his next thought was, "I'll have the boys back in Washington see what they can do with this. But first things first; one of those damned eggheads at Sandoz has got something he wants me to see."

Now, there's a meme out there that's been boiled down to *"the CIA created the Counterculture."* Of course, the CIA did no such thing. There already was a counterculture. What the CIA did was *weaponize* it. The "Counterculture," as we know it today can be traced back to early Twentieth Century Switzerland (surprise, surprise). I think you could make a pretty solid argument it dates even further back to the Burned-Over District or the Oneida Community a hundred years prior, but let's start with Ascona.

The Ascona Movement were hippies in pretty much every way that matters. They were into nature and ecology, vegetarianism and alternative medicine, the occult and paganism, feminism and free love. Ascona would have a major influence on the *Wandervogel*, the post-WWI German youth movement that wandered the countryside looking to get back to nature. Ascona luminaries like Otto Gross would in turn have a major influence on Jung. Certain ideas and practices of the *Wandervogel* were subsequently appropriated for the Hitler Youth, and the group themselves were abolished and outlawed as soon as the Nazis took power.

So one of the theses put forward by modern conspiracy researchers is that the American Counterculture was created in order to break up the family and destroy the social fabric. I think this is probably true. But what did they intend to replace it with? I can't say for sure, but I think an aggregate of some of the SF and fantasy we've been seeing for the past 70 years is a fairly reliable barometer of the intended endgame, so far as it goes.

And what we often see there are worlds of perpetual conflict, where children are taken from their parents and trained for whatever purpose has been chosen for them. If you think this all sounds like ancient Sparta, you're not too far off. Parents naturally want to shelter their children and protect them. Caretakers and teachers feel the same way, for the most part.

But, as with parents, those nurturing instincts aren't always a given. With the State? I doubt it's much of a consideration. This is why I never drank the Harry Potter Kool-Aid. Everyone looked at Hogwarts and saw some kind of Never-Never Land. I look at Hogwarts and see Sparta. With wands.

So what the Hell does this have to do with *Stephen King's It*? Well, what the novel is really about is a group of children who are essentially deputized (and given an occult weapon) by an external authority (the space-turtle) to risk their lives fighting an existential threat (Pennywise). Children who are then prematurely *sexualized*, by the way.

Similarly, *Stranger Things* is also about a group of children who are literally deputized (by the sheriff) to not only go up against an existential threat, but also against men with automatic weapons. We see this over and over again in children's fantasy, and for the most part, it's harmless. But now these themes are being increasingly presented in more realistic settings, and with graver stakes. I'm not saying that these aren't examples of effective storytelling. The point here is that too often we take knee-jerk stances on things — based in increasingly-obsolete Boomerish assumptions — and fail to ask ourselves is this inert or benign thing being *weaponized*? Are those perfectly-innocent castor beans or is it a dose of ricin? Because there's a difference between the two.

Here is why this worries me. I don't think this old trope of traumatized child turned interdimensional travel agent — again, which we read about in *It* — is just fantasy. I think some people actually believe this, have believed it for a very long time and want to weaponize it. I also think there are a lot of people who think the Spartans were on to something. I think there are a lot of people who think the only problem with kids today are their goddamned parents. If it weren't for parents, we'd be a super-race by now. Just ask the X-Men.

It's the reason I'm not exactly sure if *Childhood's End* was just imaginative sci-fi or a business plan. What's that book really about? It's about a race of space demons who come to Earth and usher in a global dictatorship, in order that Earth's children might become post-human. The demons don't really give two shits about us, they just came for our children. Similarly, *Star Trek: Discovery* presents us with a child who is taken from her home, raised in the stringent regimentation of the Vulcans, and magically transformed into a five-foot tall waif who can kick ass on seven-foot musclemen.

But that's not the way it works in reality. Whatever we might see in the movies or TV, the plain fact is that deeply-traumatized children usually end up as deeply-traumatized adults. In the real world, seriously-traumatized children tend to grow up a lot more like Laura Palmer than Harry Potter.

THE LAST BARBARIAN

AMERICA DIES A LITTLE EVERY SINGLE DAY, but losing a Frank Frazetta just brings our culture that much closer to the dustbin of history. Why? Because there's something wild, free, and savagely self-confident about Frazetta's art, qualities that have been sucked out of our culture by political correctness, corporate team-building, pea-brained paranoia and discount store religion.

Frazetta was the poet laureate of untrammeled *Id*, and his art captured an America at the height of its powers, then chronicled the start of its decline. This is why the cultural elite might embrace a Robert Crumb or even a Jack Kirby, but Frazetta's work is untameable. You can't pretty it up or pretend it's not exactly what is: a face-grabbing immersion into lust and rage, a guiltless celebration of the human machine obeying its most primal impulses.

Despite Frazetta's classical training, his art is not so much Florentine Renaissance as *Etruscan*. There's no time for social or artistic convention; only sex, sorcery and swordplay. Plus, more sex. Indeed, if there's one word that best sums up Frazetta's work, it would be 'tumescent'.

Sex was Frazetta's muse. Testosterone virtually explodes nearly from every brush-stroke. His women — with their cat eyes, ample hips and thighs, their full, firm asses and modest busts — ooze an idealized Mediterranean fecundity, straight out of ancient Minoan or Egyptian art. And for every submissive barbarian moll, Frazetta served up half a dozen wild jungle girls and witchy women, all every bit as imposing as his men. No doubt Frazetta was inspired by the tough-skinned Brooklyn girls of his youth, as well as his strong-willed wife, Ellie.

Similarly, Frazetta's depiction of men seems itself invested with a distinct kind of erotic energy, which is kind of amusing given the fact that he often used himself as a model. Frazetta wouldn't be the first artist guilty of narcissism, nor would he be the first some might accuse of getting off on his heroes as much as his heroines. Like Kirby before and Richard Corben after him, Frazetta made no bones that masculine potency was itself the natural counterpart of the feminine sexual allure at the core of his vision. But there certainly is a polymorphous aspect to Frazetta's art; you get the distinct impression a Frazetta hero would screw anything that moved, just so long as he was on top. As with violence, lust is self-justifying in the Frazetta Universe.

No wonder Frazetta's work was so potent (and popular) in the smug, self-righteous Seventies; it was an antidote to the tedious, therapeutic liberalism of the time.

In fact, that pretty much describes anything of lasting value from that decade; Glam and Punk, cult cinema (horror, sci-fi, grindhouse), *Heavy Metal, National Lampoon, Hustler* and similar explosions of the repressed Id in an age of encounter groups, corduroy, and Jimmy Carter.

Frazetta also played a vital role in the revival of the occult and the arcane in pop culture. His paintings played a major part in the sword-and-sorcery revival of the Sixties, embodying the same atavistic energy that Robert E. Howard put into words. He did the same for Edgar Rice Burroughs' Theosophist superhero, John Carter of Mars. Frazetta burned an image of the Martian badlands into the brains of young readers before they even cracked the covers.

The same goes for the classic black and white horror comics Jim Warren put on the stands in the Sixties. When Warren needed an artist to summon the dark, esoteric powers of his classic books like *Creepy* and *Vampirella*, the first guy he called was Frank Frazetta. His was a primal, instinctual kind of pop esotericism, and was all the more resonant and lasting for it.

Not only did Frazetta capture that dark energy floating around the Ether at the twilight of the Aquarian Age, he also had the kind of gut-punching catharsis that Jack Kirby had brought to the table. The fury in his work is the same you saw in Jack: you get the feeling that both artists had more than their fair share of street fights back in the day. And maybe saw the back of poppa's hand one too many times for their liking.

But the influence is not limited to comic books and van art. I'd go so far to say that Frazetta was every bit as important to the evolution of the Heavy Metal aesthetic as a Jimmy Page or Tony Iommi.

Certainly the New Wave of British Metal bands like Judas Priest, Iron Maiden and Motorhead were heavily influenced by the Frazetta barbarian milieu (both visually and spiritually), and Southern metal band Molly Hatchet used Frazetta art on their first few album covers, just as countless other bands used bad Frazetta copyists for their own. Certainly Eighties metal wouldn't be the same, not without the overall barbarian aesthetic that Frazetta popularized.

And therein lies the problem: when a revolutionary artist comes around, they almost immediately inspire a wave of imitators who invariably degrade the aesthetic currency. What had been exciting and visionary becomes cliché. It inevitably gets to the point where all of the bad imitations sour the public on the original, and the baby is then thrown out with the bathwater. The process probably began with cave paintings.

What makes Frazetta's work so powerful was not only his dedication to craft, but also his fearlessness, its surrender to Eros and Ares, even Hades.

It's very much the artifact of a younger, more confident America, one less beaten down by political correctness and self-censorship. It's an America that was truly *alive*, with all the glory and heartache that entails.

We're not quite there yet, but we may be nearing a Frazetta revival. The honesty and potency of his art has survived the backlash inspired by all of the crappy clones. And the incredible depth of his vision still packs a tremendous emotional punch, maybe more so today since that kind of gut-punching eroticism is so rare in an age bogged down with crappy porn pretending to be art. Frazetta was a true American original, one I'm very much afraid we're becoming unable to produce any more of. Every time one of these giants leaves us, a gnawing feeling of anxiety rises in my gut.

As the Romans said, life is short but art is eternal. The man is gone but the work lives on. Like Kirby, Frazetta tapped into something very deep and primal in our souls. Time took everything away from him, but the work is bouncing around the 'Net and probably will forever. Frazetta channeled impossibly deep mythic streams at the core of human consciousness, even if the museums don't want to know about it. But I'll bet the farm his work outlasts pretty much everyone being shown at the Whitney or the Guggenheim. Art may be eternal, but bullshit is very, very temporary.

HAVEN'T YOU HEARD? BACCHUS IS DEAD.

I'M NOT NOSTALGIC FOR THE EIGHTIES, when I was in my teens and 20s. Actually, that's not *entirely* true; my high school years were pretty exciting and there were plenty of good times afterward as well. But I went from a year in cartoon school straight into a high-pressure work world, back when a cocky 20 year-old could walk off the street and get a job with a decent salary and health insurance if he or she tried hard enough. But that was back before NAFTA and GATT and all the other salvos launched against American workers, especially young American workers.

The *Nineties*, though; the Nineties are another thing altogether. I can't quite explain why. I suppose it was a question of my generational cohort discovering their potential and learning how to make things happen. Computers and the Internet had a lot to do with it, back when some of us were naive to believe they could be used as tools of personal liberation and not just probing tendrils of the global Panopticon.

The Nineties were also a time when Generation X made their mark on the culture and came into its own, in a way that hadn't really happened since the late Sixties.

T HE NINETIES STARTED EARLY, MAYBE AS EARLY AS 1988. Music was a huge part of this, particularly the driving New York hip-hop you seemed to hear bursting from every corner. Jane's Addiction's *Nothing Shocking* was the first album of the Nineties in many ways, followed by Nine Inch Nail's *Pretty Hate Machine* the following year. Those two albums staked out the territory, erasing the arbitrary (and frankly, absurd) distinctions between dance music and hard rock that had been calcifying since the mid-Seventies.

1990 was the touchstone, though, especially in New York City. To me, 1990 Manhattan is forever a landscape of dark beauty punctuated with erotic, phosphene bursts of otherworldly intrusion. It wasn't a safe space. It was a very dangerous city, but also a city alive with possibility.

I zealously prowled the city streets after work or during lunch breaks, hell-bent in digging out every cache of hidden treasure, every hidden record shop or second-hand book or magazine store I could unearth. Though I had ulterior goals in mind, I realize now that what was really driving me was a need to soak up the city's arcane energy, plugging straight into its sorcerous heart before its last gasp of magical possibility exhausted itself. Which it most certainly did by the decade's end.

Of course, Manhattan is also an open-air temple of sigils, icons and totems, most placed there a century prior by men well versed in the esoteric sciences. These were all playing on my unconscious, as they did everyone in the city. I was just a little bit more tuned in than most. New York's city magic dug so deep that the city eventually became the venue for my secret sun dreams, and remained so for a very long time. (I should also mention I spent most of this time working in the Big Daddy occult-obelisk of them all, the Empire State Building.)

There was also East/West Books, which served every conceivable spiritual or occult interest, and other, edgier shops in the East Village where you could find all kinds of books on Weirdness, conspiracy culture and underground politics. These places were usually stocked with all other types of arcana and contraband; tarot cards, drug paraphernalia, fringe porn. And in the middle of this came the last great cresting of the Rock n' Roll wave: the alt.rock explosion that followed in the wake of Nirvana. All of that music was dropping like cluster bombs during this whole period. It all came so fast that it was hard to keep up with.

My last full-time job in the city was in an art department on the 47th floor of the Empire State, and it was like an urban treehouse, with radios blaring in every room. And right on time, too: one instant classic after another dropped in our laps from Long Island alt.rock station WDRE, and later, Q-Rock when it (ever-so-briefly) existed as an alt.rock station.

For someone who'd been dialed into alt.rock since the late Seventies, it was more than validation: it was a *vindication*. Most of this the new rock music seemed to burst forth from the West Coast, Seattle most famously, but also California, which was once America's great laboratory for forward-thinking rock and pop, both as producer and consumer.

O F COURSE, ONE OF THOSE CLASSIC WEST COAST ALBUMS was Stone Temple Pilots' 1994 sophomore effort, *Purple*. I was initially deeply skeptical of STP, since their extremely derivative first album was hit-or-miss for me. They also came across as dickheads in the early days. But *Purple* felt like an instant classic, and plugged into Generation X's coming of age.

Like their contemporaries. STP bypassed cornball Eighties Metal to hark back to the late-Sixties and Seventies roots of hard rock, leavening the batter with punk/post-punk attitude and economy. They also had a truly great singer in Scott Weiland, who understood the value of light and shadow in hard music (the story of Nineties rock is ultimately a story of great singers).

Weiland was also like many of his contemporaries in another, less fortunate way. Drug problems were almost *de rigeur* for big name rock stars (legend has it that record company publicists would even invent drug problem rumors for artists who had none), but Weiland's generation came out of the cauldron of Hardcore whose thermonuclear intensity tended to deaden one's responses to normal stimulation. Weiland's addictions very quickly overshadowed his considerable musical talent, at least where the press was concerned. At first vital, lithe and aggressive, he became increasingly fragile and brittle as his demons had their way with him.

Weiland's bandmates reached the end of their ropes more than once, forming counterfeit STPs with new singers (Talk Show & Army of Anyone), before finally sacking Weiland. He was replaced with Linkin Park singer Chester Bennington for the short-lived MKII incarnation of STP. But all that accomplished was prove how much STP needed Weiland to hammer their abstruse modal riffing into actual songs with proper melodies.

Weiland had also formed a new band and began working the third-tier circuit, where he died. His performances had become famously erratic, with videos of disastrous misfires circulating on YouTube. But he often seemed just as able to summon some of the old magic, most recently at a New Jersey show I wanted to attend but missed. I'll never have the opportunity again.

It seems all too fitting that this Californian golden god would die the day after mass shootings at a Christmas party in San Bernadino. California has been a terminal patient for a long time, the longtime American Promised Land now being the land of the nation's worst poverty and inequality. Like Weiland at the end, California is now just a hollow shell of its former self.

In the early Eighties, San Bernardino was the setting for the Us Festivals, ersatz Woodstock's thrown by Apple cofounder Steve Wozniak. He used his fortune to hire every rock band of any importance at the time, presenting the festivals as a showcase for his vision of a brave new future driven by an embrace of Globalism ('Unite Us in Song') and computer technology. Sadly, things didn't really work out that way. Today, San Bernardino is a notoriously high-crime city in which even the shooting of thirty-one people wasn't seen by locals as overly shocking.

But it's not alone in its misery. California's once mighty middle-class has been decimated or sent packing to greener pastures. The state is now populated by a Feudal elite lording over the poor. Its very landscape seems cursed and forsaken by the gods, who regularly smite it with fire, earthquake, drought, and other natural disasters. So it's all too fitting that California's last great Dionysus finally succumbed to the years of self-abuse and heartache.

T HESE ARE TERRIBLE TIMES FOR MOST WORKING MUSICIANS, no matter how much propaganda you might hear to the contrary from the pirate lobby. The loss of royalties from recordings has forced many artists into grueling touring schedules simply to break even. No forty-eight year-old man wants to spend his life on the road, traveling from one small theatre to another mid-sized club, being forced to remember the glamour and good times of the gravy days. Don't let anyone tell you otherwise.

Make no mistake, the new order has no place for Dionysian ecstasy. There is no free expression as the term is generally understood anymore, there is only provocation and reaction. And a new generation begs to return to the safety and certainty of the daycare environment that formed their consciousness, such as it is. There's no place left for Dionysus anymore in this giant techno-Kindergarten being constructed for us every minute of every day.

Not even in the timeout chair.

BOWIE: THE STARMAN RETURNS TO THE SKY

T HE LEGEND IS NOW COMPLETE. The story has been told, its ending could not have been more perfectly constructed or executed. It's been said that the great ones know when to leave the stage, but the greatest also know *how*.

A little less than three years ago, David Bowie released what I called "The Last Rock 'n' Roll Album," and pulled off what some critics labeled the greatest comeback since Elvis in 1968 (with whom Bowie shares a birthday). Hardcore Bowie fans like myself were a bit nonplussed by the critical response to *The Next Day*. Not because we didn't appreciate the praise, but because we wondered where these critics had been hiding while Bowie had been making important music both onstage (The BBC Radio Concert, the *A Reality* DVD, for starters) and in the studio (*Outside, Earthling, Heathen*).

But *The Next Day* was a landmark in that no one expected ever to hear from Bowie again, certainly not after he suffered a coronary event onstage in 2004 that was followed by a very long and troubling silence. No one certainly expected him to return with an album filled with top-rank material designed to serve as an end-piece to the pop/rock phase of Bowie's career. Fewer still expected him to follow that up with *Blackstar*, an experimental, jazz-inflected post-rock masterpiece designed to serve as his epitaph.

That he had also been working on a theatrical sequel to *The Man Who Fell to Earth* (currently enjoying a sellout run in New York) at the same time as recording *Blackstar* while dying of cancer can only add to the legend, of a man not-quite-human, but something more than you or I.

What can and must be said is that Bowie runs through the lifeblood of this blog and all the other work I've done. I can still remember the effect hearing 'Fame' had on my young mind, how it seemed like a transmission from a far stranger world, a world I wanted to go to. The effect was only cemented by 'Golden Years' and 'Sound and Vision', which stood out like holographic intruders on the old daguerreotype of the AM radio Top 40 wasteland.

I had no idea how utterly alien this man was, how these albums that redefined the course of popular music seem to burst fully formed from his fevered brain to the literal astonishment of his collaborators. I had no idea how he spent countless hours immersed in his occult library, or skywatching for UFOs, all the while painting, writing in his journals, studying dance or boxing and later, appearing in more films than most professional actors, until such time as it came to lay down another indelible classic. It's not a stretch to say that music was being *channeled* through him.

It wouldn't be until 1978 that I'd really immerse myself in Bowie's Mysteries, and by the golden locks of Apollo, what a time it was to do so. I can still remember buying *Stage* at Jason's Music and Luggage (!), which seems unloved today but for me was like finally stepping into that parallel dimension. It was here I'd be initiated into the same mysteries that so bewitched Philip K. Dick, namely Bowie and Eno's synth-driven symphonettes from *Low* and *Heroes*. Dick was so enraptured by this music he saw it as some kind of alien transmission converted to vinyl through a kind of modern electronic alchemy. Bowie and *The Man Who Fell to Earth* had such a powerful effect on Dick's emerging Gnostic awakening that they became major players in the first allegorical exegesis of his spiritual journey, *VALIS*.

Not long after, I ended up with an eight-track tape of *Hunky Dory*, and not long after that, *Lodger* was released. All of a sudden the hand-me-down rock stars of the Sixties and Seventies seemed totally irrelevant; counter-revolutionary, even. There was a dividing line now, it was Year Zero. Punk, post-punk, New Wave and the rest were the new vanguard: the Great Wheel had turned. Only Bowie and his fellow travelers (Fripp, Eno, Iggy, etc) would seem relevant in the new regime.

But Bowie had other plans. He'd released his legendary string of classic albums under constant threat of financial insolvency, thanks in large part to the drain on his accounts by his management team, who burned through his profits either with their endless partying or by trying to launch the careers of no-hopers. Bowie had seen a new generation of artists getting rich off of his ideas, and now *he* wanted to cash in. During the sessions for 'Under Pressure', Queen sold Bowie on the benefits he could reap by dumping the moribund RCA for the ravenous EMI, who'd made plutocrats out of the glam foursome.

With an eye on the success The Rolling Stones and The Police were having touring large stadiums, Bowie set his sights on American superstardom. Bowie's sexuality underwent public revision, with him suddenly claiming to have been a 'closet heterosexual'. He entered the studio with Chic mastermind Nile Rodgers, and a new backing band which included Chic drummer Tony Thompson and rising star Stevie Ray Vaughn on guitar. The result was *Let's Dance*, a bonafide blockbuster that finally put Bowie in the top rank, where he and his fans felt he belonged.

A massive tour was planned, which saw Bowie playing American football stadiums and making sure he gave fans every penny's worth of entertainment. I saw Bowie on this tour, and while it was an amazing show, it also felt like something had changed. This was no longer *my* Bowie, it was someone else. A lot of fans felt that way. Suspicions were not dissuaded when Bowie rushed out *Tonight*, which featured two bonafide classics ('Blue Jean', 'Loving the Alien') and a whole lot of filler.

Signs that Bowie was as bored with his new role as his Seventies fans were were confirmed by a long (for the time) post-*Tonight* silence punctuated only by a few weak soundtrack numbers. He re-emerged in 1987 with *Never Let Me Down*, an album that tried too hard to recapture *Let's Dance's* formula and ended up burying some worthy songs under the histrionic production techniques of the time. He compounded the felony with the *Glass Spider* tour, a half-hearted return to the theatricality of the *Diamond Dogs* era, only with 100% less cultural relevancy, and with 75% more cringe.

Sensing he'd made all the wrong moves, Bowie tried to right the ship. He did a bare-bones greatest-hits tour in 1990 (I saw that one too), but aside from King Crimson frontman Adrian Belew, the backing band simply wasn't up to the task. Bowie then hooked up with Iggy Pop's old rhythm section (the Sales Brothers, as in Soupy's kids) and new guitarist Reeves Gabrels for Tin Machine, but it looked and sounded exactly like the overwrought midlife crisis it actually was. A reunion with Nile Rodgers seemed promising, but his new record company went bankrupt as soon as *Black Tie White Noise* was released.

It wouldn't be until Bowie gave up on grasping for the mainstream and got his freak back on that he'd rediscover his inner Bowieness. A soundtrack for the British indie film *The Buddha of Suburbia* got Eno's attention again, and they took to the studio to record *Outside*, a sprawling, deliciously-pretentious slab of 200-proof Bowie, replete with a ludicrous 'concept' based on transgressive art, millennial angst and ritual murder.

This was a favorite Bowie period for me, since he was just successful enough to be visible, but not so much as to be annoyingly ubiquitous. His band, with Zach Alford on drums, Gail Ann Dorsey on bass and vocals, longtime keyboardist Mike Garson and guitarist Gabrels, were hard, polished and just artsy enough to be interesting.

Unfortunately, it kind of came to a thudding halt in 1999 when Bowie's mersh instincts (or, more likely, record company pressure) got the better of him again and the dreary *Hours* was released. It was an attempt to appeal to the then-burgeoning adult alternative contemporary market, but Reeve Gabrels wasn't having any of it and bolted. Fantastic artwork, though.

Bowie played around with a few ideas before cutting *Heathen* (2002) with Tony Visconti, the producer of his late Seventies classics. Because of the realities of the new market or simple maturity, Bowie dropped the attempts to appeal to the dissipating younger market and made a classic *Bowie* album, a return to old-fashioned song-craft without any trendy bells and whistles. A new live band was assembled and Bowie began touring heavily. Unfortunately, the stress of the road on the 56 year-old performer resulted in the aforementioned coronary event, leading us back to the long radio silence.

Of course, part of Bowie's mystique is his lifelong immersion in the Occult. OTO member Peter Koenig first explored this in a highly subjective and rambling essay called *The Laughing Gnostic* (which I first read back in the old USENET days) and has been continually updated ever since. It touches on Bowie's repeated use of catchwords and imagery taken from occult orders like the Golden Dawn as well as his cocaine-fueled obsession with fascism in the mid-70s. But Bowie himself has always been cagey about his occult interests, preferring to keep an aura of uncertainty and mystery.

Less ambivalent is Bowie's obsession with UFOs, which dates back to his time as a UFO watcher in London and lurks throughout his entire recorded catalog; from 'Memory of a Free Festival' in 1969 to 'Born on a UFO' in 2013, and all points in between. Such was Bowie's alien mystique that legends surrounding Bowie, UFOs and ETs arose in the rumor mill, from sightings in the New Mexico desert to space aliens stalking the star, disguised as fans.

The Man Who Fell to Earth was science fiction, but one has to wonder how exactly an alien come down to Earth would operate in the real world. Given the immense stellar distances, he might not travel physically but through some form of astral travel, using technology we can guess at. He might take refuge in a human being, preferably a fetus in which the personality has not yet formed.

He may choose to incarnate in 1947 — the year of Roswell and Kenneth Arnold — and may do so in London, a world capital filled with people calling out to the stars. He'd fill that host with powers far beyond those of ordinary humans, and an insatiable need to experience as much of the world as possible, like what an international celebrity with a storming libido might.

But these powers may not be suitable for the human host and might begin to take their toll at a relatively early age, say in the host's mid-fifties. It might also lead to a relatively early death. But it might also rally the host for one last great burst of productivity, including an epitaph to its supernatural presence here on Earth. I mean, just total speculation here.

Those kind of things don't happen in the real world. Or do they?

FARE THEE WELL, PRINCE DIONYSUS

YOU DON'T NEED TO TELL ANYONE THAT DEATH has been running rampant this year, certainly not music fans of my generation. Lemmy, David Bowie, Keith Emerson, Maurice White — all of whom who made music that left a mark on me — have left us. Late last year we lost Scott Weiland, whose death wasn't a surprise, but marked a passing of an important cultural moment nonetheless. And now we lose another great Dionysian incarnation, Prince. It's really starting to get to me.

Prince first appeared on my radar when the video for 'I Wanna Be Your Lover' was played on *Don Kirschner's Rock Concert.* I wasn't impressed. It just sounded like ordinary disco to me, and I still resented how disco had forced out all the muscular funk-pop I loved in the early to mid '70s and replaced it with treacly, cookie-cutter mush.

Things changed with the *Dirty Mind* album the following year. The sound was leaner, harder, freakier. Prince's sexuality was raw and unapologetic, but also lacking in the kind of aggressive machismo that normally came with the territory. There was a complexity there, an ambiguity, a tension that gave the smut dimension and character. There was a thought process at work as well. It made for an interesting package.

Prince now seemed part of a new vanguard bringing back a lean, hungry edge to pop R&B, along with Rick James, The Gap Band, and Cameo, but also fit nicely with the more experimental sounds coming out of NYC. Controversy repeated the formula and got a lot of airplay on the predominantly New Wave/post-punk college radio stations I lived on.

1982 was the year the entire game changed. MTV broke through to the mainstream, bringing a whole new wave of acts with it and sweeping away most of the hairy cock-rockers of the Seventies that seemed to linger past their sell-by date. Many of the acts that replaced them were conspicuously androgynous, 'New Pop' acts from the UK. And at the same time, Grandmaster Flash brought Hip-Hop to the mainstream.

Prince essentially fused all these disparate impulses with his double LP, *1999.* He continued to fuck with boundaries — racial, sexual, musical — and it only made him more popular. He assembled a multiracial backing band with men and women, conspicuously Wendy and Lisa, his guitarist and keyboardist (who went on to a career of their own). He fused rock, pop and R+B so effortlessly you barely noticed the seams, and later did the same with jazz and Hip-Hop.

1999 would be a mere prelude to his monster, 1984s *Purple Rain*, which accompanied the film of the same name. Along with *Let's Dance* (produced by Chic's Nile Rodgers) and Talking Heads' *Speaking in Tongues, Purple Rain* seemed to offer up a distinctly new fusion music for the Eighties, one in which technology itself became an instrument. That album was everywhere that spring and summer, so those songs are burned into my experience of 1984. Which was a great fucking year.

Purple Rain was filled with startling guitar pyrotechnics but also ripe with gospel influences, particularly in the title track. Like Marvin Gaye, Prince struggled to harmonize the yearnings of the spirit with the needs of the flesh. There was Hendrix and Bowie and James Brown lurking in the mix as well. Sly Stone was there in spirit, but the cake and the frosting were all Prince's alone. He embodied Dionysus with his outrageous music and flamboyant persona but also Hermes, particularly in the first phase of his career when he was so eager to violate boundaries and categories.

Along the way Prince had written or cowritten drop-dead classics for other artists, including 'Stand Back' with Stevie Nicks, 'I Feel for You' for Chaka Khan, 'Manic Monday' for The Bangles and 'The Glamorous Life' for Sheila E. Sinead O'Connor hit the big time with her cover of 'Nothing Compares 2 U', a song Prince wrote for one of his many side projects. Interesting to note these were all female artists.

Prince made some more albums and another feature film, but I didn't reconnect with him until *Sign O' The Times*, the 1987 double album that felt like a solid return to form after a bit of creative and stylistic drift. From there on it seemed as if Prince's moment passed, and pop became a vapid, arid wasteland of hairspray and histrionics.

Prince entered into a long and protracted battle with Warner Bros. over creative control and famously renamed himself as 'The Artist Formerly Known as Prince', using an androgynous symbol as his identifier. He started his own label, Paisley Park. He initially shunned the Internet and went to war against YouTube over copyright infringement. More recently, he rejoined the Jehovah's Witnesses.

I may have lost touch with the man and his music but like so much else I am grateful to have been there when it mattered, when those early classics were hitting the street. To have been there in that intermediate period of 1980/1981 when Prince was struggling to forge a new sound and then to hear it bear fruit. I wish kids today could feel that kind of excitement.

THE MUSES CHOOSE BROKEN VESSELS

T HE 'ALTERNATIVE ROCK' EXPLOSION OF THE EARLY NINETIES was fueled by a wave of great singers. After a lost decade of cookie-cutter metallic shriekers and New Wave gurglers, there was suddenly an embarrassment of strong male voices revitalizing rock music. Most of these had cut their teeth on Punk and Hardcore, and subsequently learned to trim back the fat and excess that torpedoed their Seventies forebears. They also learned to step around the wretched excesses that ran the Eighties metal explosion into the ground; cookie-cutter sameness, image over substance, half-written songs, cliché piled on cliché.

Alternative rock would itself soon get watered down and Xeroxed into oblivion, especially as careerists figured out a way to counterfeit the formula (I'm looking at you, Candlebox & Seven Mary Three) and record companies signed up every pseudo-grunge band they could find. By the end of the Nineties it had all devolved into an obnoxious frat-boy rock (I'm looking at you, Limp Bizkit & Creed), that reached its inevitable apotheosis at the disastrous Woodstock '99. But before that all went down, some of the most vital and exciting rock music of all time was produced.

Today, Alternative Rock has taken its place in the Classic Rock canon. Tracks by Nirvana, Soundgarden, Stone Temple Pilots and the Red Hot Chili Peppers are snuggled in tightly between all the Led Zeppelin, Aerosmith and Pink Floyd cuts overplayed on FM radio. But five of the most remarkable vocalists of that era — Kurt Cobain, Layne Staley, Jeff Buckley, Scott Weiland and now Chris Cornell — are lost to us. And the nine-ton Tyrannosaurus lurking in the back of the concert hall is that modern plague, clinical depression. It's the witches' curse on Generation X.

C HRIS CORNELL WAS AN ENIGMATIC FIGURE among the Grunge pantheon. Kurt Cobain was the snotty punk, Eddie Vedder the self-serious poet, Layne Staley the tortured howler and Scott Weiland the Joker in the pack, Cornell was an entirely unique presence, as was Soundgarden. Tall and lean but possessing an odd, androgynous presence and an enviable black mane, he came across as aloof, Olympian. His piercing, multi-octave voice felt like a weapon, more like Apollyon the Destroyer than Ozzy Osbourne.

Soundgarden was perhaps the most effective translator of the power of early Black Sabbath yet, but were also brainy, difficult, challenging. They were unmistakably *heavy metal* but didn't shriek the usual ditties about dick size and date rape. It was pretty clear they had no time for that kind of nonsense, and they took as much inspiration from King Crimson and Black Flag as from Zeppelin and Sabbath.

Predictably, Chris Cornell's corpse was literally not cold yet before the modern ambulance chasers of the Internet were declaring it was obviously an Illuminati sacrifice. One hilarious YouTube video went on about how there was no other explanation for Cornell's death, that he'd have no reason to kill himself. Obviously someone who never actually listened to a single note of Soundgarden music.

Like Ian Curtis — who hung himself 37 exactly years before — many of Cornell's lyrics read like suicide notes. After all, this is a man who kicked off one of his biggest hits with the couplet *"Nothing seems to kill me/ No matter how hard I try."* Two of his other big hits — 'Black Hole Sun' and 'Fell on Black Days' — are practically master classes in the art of expressing the utter hopelessness that can overtake you when a depressive episode strikes. The same goes for Soundgarden's breakout hit, 'Outshined', practically a hymn about searching for a crack of sunlight while waiting a dire episode out.

Cornell was quite candid about his history with clinical depression. It wasn't just for a gloom-metal gimmick that Cornell laid bare his struggles. He'd had an adverse reaction to angel dust at age 13, and the frightening, dissociative experience, coupled with the trauma of his parent's divorce, plunged him into a severe depression.

Cornell was also a substance abuser, and dove headlong into an opioid addiction after Soundgarden split in 1997. It may well have come from a chronic pain issue, closely related to chronic depression. The real hell of opioids is that they rewire your brain, causing the natural processes that regulate depression and euphoria to atrophy. Depression can skyrocket when you stop taking them, since your brain basically forgets how to produce sufficient amounts of the neurotransmitters that manage your moods.

CORNELL APPEARED WITH SOUNDGARDEN at Detroit's Fox Theater the night that he died. Despite an incredibly shaky performance he seemed in good spirits to some, all too common with depressives resolved to suicide. But others thought he seemed irritable and unfocused, often forgetting the lyrics. He complimented the Detroit audience and then said, "I feel sorry for the next city." His wife Vicky would blame the tranquilizer Ativan for his death, which seems a bit unlikely. An extra Ativan or two is unlikely to induce suicide. But long-term use of it certainly might.

The problem is that people who obsess on suicide usually don't talk about it with people close to them, since they realize that confessing to it will very likely derail what they have been planning. And again, professionals will tell you that very often when a depressive has resolved themselves to suicide they can often seem very cheerful and upbeat, since they believe that their suffering will soon end. Unfortunately, everyone else's will soon begin.

So if a rich, talented, and handsome rock star can't find a reason to stay alive, what hope is there for the rest of us? Well, it's a lot more complicated than that. Aside from his struggles with clinical depression, Cornell was also beset by tragedy, losing people closest to him to early death. The first of these was his roommate Andrew Wood, the flamboyant singer for legendary Seattle band Mother Love Bone, who died of a heroin overdose in 1990.

Cornell was so shaken by Wood's death that he formed a *de facto* supergroup tribute with members of Mother Love Bone for the now-legendary *Temple of the Dog* album, which produced the grunge anthem 'Hunger Strike'. Temple of the Dog led to the formation of Pearl Jam, facilitated by the introduction of Eddie Vedder to Cornell by drummer Jack Irons, a member of the original Red Hot Chili Peppers who also played with Pearl Jam and Joe Strummer, among others. Strangely enough, Irons has had his own epic struggles with major depressive disorder. As did Joe Strummer, for that matter.

The Muses choose broken vessels. It's a Secret Sun truism.

Another body blow was the 1994 death of Kurt Cobain, a friend who died in time to cast a pall of existential darkness over Soundgarden's epochal *Superunknown* album, released a month before Cobain's death. So even as Soundgarden were enjoying their moment, death and tragedy revisited Cornell. It had to hurt, especially since Cobain had told Cornell that Soundgarden has inspired him to form Nirvana in the first place.

S UPERUNKNOWN WAS AN INSTANT CLASSIC, easily one of the best hard rock albums ever recorded, hammering you with one killer track after another. Along with Stone Temple Pilots' *Purple* album, Pearl Jam's *Vitalogy* and others, it established 1994 as *the* watershed year for Alternative Rock, despite Cobain's death. Their 1996 follow-up *Down on the Upside* was worthy, but failed to capitalize on its predecessor's momentum, and seem to showcase a band uncertain of direction and sense of purpose. No one was really surprised when Soundgarden broke up the following year. Oddly enough, the breakup seemed to go down almost exactly three years after Kurt Cobain's death.

But tragedy wasn't finished with Cornell yet. Shortly after Soundgarden broke up Cornell would lose another soulmate. He'd already lost two friends within the space of a few years, and in 1997, singer-songwriter Jeff Buckley drowned while swimming in a tributary of the Mississippi in Tennessee. Cornell would be haunted by Buckley's death, writing the aching tribute, 'Wave Goodbye' for his first solo album, and acting as a *de facto* curator for Buckley's posthumous releases. Cornell showed he was clearly still haunted by Buckley's passing when he brought the late singer's old landline phone onstage with him during his 2011 acoustic solo tour. This tells us a lot, since the 20th anniversary of Jeff Buckley's death was less than two weeks after Cornell's death.

That, along with the timing of Ian Curtis' own death by hanging, seems a bit too synchronized for Cornell's passing to be some kind of mad whim because he took too much Ativan. As painful as it might be to admit, it seems like this was probably a very long time coming. After all, this is the man who wrote 'Pretty Noose'.

S O IT SEEMS APPARENT THAT IT WASN'T THE ILLUMINATI, but in fact the demon possession of depression that took Chris Cornell away from us. With many of his closest friends gone, and the glory days of the Nineties more and more a fading memory in a world itself gripped by chronic depression, I can't say I'm surprised by the suicide ruling.

If there's any good to come of this tragedy it's to understand that depression isn't some kind of scarlet letter, it's an inevitable result of what one scientist called "the greatest blind experiment in history," the bombardment of our brains and bodies with every manner of stimulus and stress imaginable, 24 hours a day, 7 days a week, 365 days a year and then some.

TWO YEARS LATER...

B ECAUSE WHAT ELSE WOULD YOU POSSIBLY EXPECT, the new Sound-garden concert movie played IMAX screens for one night only, which happened to fall on my birthday. And because of course, the closest screen it was showing on happened to be in Elizabeth.

I really enjoyed the show and left feeling quite elated and invigorated, which is kind of odd given how mind-numbingly bleak the music was. I was rocking in my cushioned stadium-style seat quite a bit (on account of being an embarrassment) and came *that* close to head-banging on a number of occasions. On account of I am a sad, hopeless douche.

The band played extremely well (the show is from 2013), though they didn't really catch fire until the last third of the two hour and forty minute set. I also kind of got the feeling they didn't like each other all that much, the *King Animal* material didn't seem to inspire them terribly, and under other circumstances it might be depressing to see a bunch of middle-aged men a good two decades past their prime ignore each other for 160 minutes. But hey; it's Soundgarden. You take a certain level of misery for granted.

But given the hugeness of the screen I did get a good look at Chris Cornell, four years before his death, and was frankly alarmed by what I saw. He looked a man who had already sued his demons for peace and was searching into the far distance for his escape route. And searching hard.

He did liven up a bit halfway through the set and even told some jokes, but they were mostly angry and/or self-depreciating, if not actually self-loathing. After a relatively subdued but effective performance, the jokes were followed by some aggressive, old-school jam-kicking, which felt very much like a delayed attempt at self-exorcism. But after a full evening of staring into his ready-to-die eyes, and any number of lyrical references to self-harm, I have to announce that as much I love me a juicy conspiracy theory, I have a very, very hard time believing Chris Cornell was killed by anyone but himself.

I can't quite explain why, but I believe that Cornell probably had a history of serious sexual abuse and trauma in his childhood, and wasn't willing or able to express it openly. But I think the Cornell Foundation, created to help children in crisis, pretty much speaks for itself. I don't believe he fell onto that particular cause on a whim. I think it's very possible he was doing that work in order to lay some old ghosts to rest by helping kids dealing with the same problems. Sometimes it's the only way you can keep those hellhounds at bay.

Moreover, the way Cornell bonded with Chester Bennington, who was very open about his history of sexual victimization, strikes me as fitting the pattern as well. Cornell often said that a bum dose of PCP in his early teens sent him into a depressive tailspin, but I'm fairly certain he wasn't telling us the whole story. I'd reckon the drug simply kicked open some gates he forgot he'd closed, and broke out some demons who'd haunt him the rest of his life.

So, as much fun as it might be to speculate on hit squads operating out of certain Beltway eateries or kleptocrat foundations, the horrible truth is that childhood sexual abuse often leaves serious neurological scars that will never heal, and sometimes people just get tired of watching the fucking scabs ooze every damn day.

All I can say is that I have done my due diligence on the matter and saw nothing last night not entirely consistent with a lovely, gifted and sensitive middle-aged man losing his patience with a lifetime of pain. Mind you. I'm not saying he didn't brush up against some very bad actors in his life. Having seen for myself how demonic the music industry is from an extremely early age, I'd be shocked if he hadn't. I can only tell you that I looked into those pale gray eyes on a very large screen and frankly, saw surrender. And that was a good four years before he finally threw in the towel.

We may never know why, but there's no doubt in my mind at least that Chris Cornell was riding a train with a one-way ticket. And to be honest, I don't begrudge the man one little bit.

JEREMY SWIMS TO THE SIREN

T REVOR WILSON, BEST KNOWN TO THE WORLD as 'Jeremy' in the award-winning music video for grunge superstars Pearl Jam, drowned while swimming at a Puerto Rican beach notorious for its dangerous riptide in 2017. There seems to be something eerie and ominous about that fact, so let's try to sort some of the details.

As it stands, four of the five main Grunge gods are no longer with us. Kurt Cobain was murdered in 1994, Layne Staley of Alice in Chains died of complications from a longtime heroin addiction in 2002, Scott Weiland of Stone Temple Pilots died of a heart attack in 2015, and Chris Cornell died earlier this year. Eddie Vedder is the last remaining 'Voice of a Generation'.

But Trevor Wilson was also an important avatar for the formless rage of Generation X, an anger that would outwear its welcome as the grim early Nineties gave way to the go-go Clinton Years. But at the time he, Vedder and 'Jeremy' were everywhere. I mean, *everywhere*.

Mark Pellington — a late Boomer and early punk rock adapter — conjured up a serving of provocative iconography for the 'Jeremy' video, drawing on Biblical references of the Serpent in the Garden of Eden (Genesis 3:6) and a bludgeoning array of crosscuts and captions to immerse the viewer in a nightmare world of trauma.

B ILLBOARD TELLS THE STORY OF WILSON'S LIFE AND DEATH in its latest issue. It's a window into a short but privileged life, attending school at the elite Rudolf Steiner Waldorf School in Manhattan and taking acting lessons at Lee Strasberg. His mother was a chef for a number of celebrities including Sir Ridley Scott. After his 15 minutes of fame, Wilson took another path. He went from the University of Rome to an internship in Egypt with the UN. Trevor stayed on and ended up writing speeches for then-Egyptian president Hosni Mubarak's wife, Suzanne.

Wilson's death is eerily reminiscent of Jeff Buckley's. He had also a close call during a run-in with police previously in Egypt and survived, which perhaps gave Wilson the same false sense of confidence while swimming with friends at a beach with a reputation for dangerous undertows that Buckley had in the Wolf River Lagoon after a similar close call in Australia.

I've talked about "Jeremy" director Mark Pellington in the past, having mutual friends and having worked for the studio that repped his commercial work, Crossroads Films. My first encounter with Crossroads came when they expressed interest in a screenplay I'd written.

Sadly, Crossroads decided to go with *Jawbreaker* instead, that deathless classic that thrilled the hearts of dozens across this great land of ours. Pellington is also known in High Weirdness circles for directing a movie about a man who loses his wife after a brief illness (*The Mothman Prophecies* again) only to lose his own wife Jennifer to a brief illness shortly thereafter. I was told her death left Pellington a "shell of a man."

I've been giving an awful lot of thought as the involvement of MKULTRA in the lives of some of these ill-starred musicians, given that they were all the same age and profile of one person who I have zero doubt was in fact an MKULTRA subject, University of Alabama shooter Amy Bishop.

Seattle is a major hub for the military and other important sectors of the Establishment, and it's well-known that MKULTRA experiments were being done in Vancouver (at the Hollywood Hospital, of all places) just a couple hours drive over the border. Not conclusive in any way, but maybe a signal that there was more behind the collapse and countless deaths involved in Nineties alternative music than just drugs and money.

Certainly, the 'Jeremy' video gives off a very strong MKULTRA vibe, playing more like a chronicle of personal dissolution and dissociation than a simple suicide. I don't know how much of this is just style and how much may in fact be intent. The rock video format is usually inert and harmless, except when it's not. The form certainly has an unusual pedigree, not wholly unrelated to MKULTRA at all.

THE TECHNIQUES OF ROCK VIDEO as they came to be by the early Nineties were pioneered in the Sixties by Kenneth Anger, particularly with his groundbreaking films *Scorpio Rising* and *Invocation of My Demon Brother*. These films were made using grants from the Ford Foundation (a well-known CIA front) and Sir John Paul Getty Jr., the Jesuit-trained oil baron, and just happened to begin production at the same time Dr. Stephen Aldrich was firing up the infernal machines in the OFTEN offices.

Do note that these same techniques can now be seen all over television and the internet, not only in music videos but on TV shows and commercials. And on and on it goes. It makes me wonder how much David Lynch and Mark Frost might know, given that they were mining themes of black magic in the Pacific Northwest. There sure seemed to be quite a few serial killers based in Washington in the bad, old MKOFTEN days.

The world is far, far stranger than you can imagine.

REVOLUTION SOLD SEPARATELY

SOMETIMES THE GODS OF SYNC ARRANGE THINGS so that deeper, more subtle truths can make themselves known. It just takes time and patience to sort through exactly what these truths may be. Maybe we aren't meant to know these truths on a literal level, but then again the Gods of Sync never seem to lose any sleep worrying about trifles like literalism.

9/28/18 seemed to be one of those days when those gods arrange things in such a fashion as to unveil deeper mysteries. Aside from the ongoing train-wreck in the nation's capital — in which the festering sores of the Sixties continued to metastasize into melanomas that will soon destroy this country — Friday also saw the passing of Marty Balin, lead singer of The Jefferson Airplane and founder of the San Francisco acid rock scene, as well as the long awaited release of a box set of solo material from Clash singer Joe Strummer, who passed away shortly before Christmas in 2002.

All three seem intimately connected in an important way. The Clash in many ways seemed to me not to be the reincarnation of The Rolling Stones as many fans and critics claimed, but in fact the bastard stepchildren of The Jefferson Airplane.

T HOUGH UNFONDLY REMEMBERED AS THE BAND that evolved into the Eighties synth-pop atrocities Starship, the original Jefferson Airplane were acid-dazed outlaws who kick-started the Psychedelic Rock revolution. Both the Airplane and The Clash epitomized the scenes they emerged from, both mindlessly and hypocritically preached radical politics, and both were manned to the absolute brim with scions of the National Security State. And appropriately, one of Marty Balin's greatest compositions for Jefferson Airplane ('She Has Funny Cars') was featured in the first *Stranger Things* series, which as pure chance would have it, also uses a Clash song as a central plot device ('Should I Stay or Should I Go').

It seems Marty Balin single-handedly earned the credit and/or blame for the San Francisco music scene when he opened The Matrix night club with borrowed seed money. The story goes that Marty was inspired by Dylan going electric, but none of the local clubs would book rock music. So he created his own space and nearly every major psychedelic band played there.

The Airplane came about through a partnership between Balin and Paul Kantner, an Army brat who'd attended an elite military academy for high school. They were later joined by Jorma Kaukonen, whose family had traveled the world when he was young because his father had worked for the State Department. Bassist Jack Casady was originally from Washington, but I'm not sure what his family were involved with, on account of not having my copy of *Weird Scenes Inside the Canyon* handy at the moment.

Marty Balin was the driving force in the Jefferson Airplane, and the band's first two albums are largely centered on his songs and vocals. This is especially true for *Surrealistic Pillow,* which for my money is the definitive album from the late Sixties San Francisco scene. It features the group's only hit singles, albeit sung by then-new vocalist Grace Slick (formerly known as high society debutante Grace Barnet Wing). But one of those was written by her soon-to-be ex-husband and the other is essentially 'Bolero' with lyrics taken from Lewis Carroll, and the best songs on the album are all Marty's showcases.

Surrealistic Pillow encapsulates the striking parallels between the ancient Mysteries and the early days of the Aquarian Explosion. It's all so poignant, because things would very nasty very quickly for a lot of these innocents, as bad drugs and bad actors would flood the sunny streets of San Francisco very soon after. Whatever role Balin may had played in both the establishment of Jefferson Airplane didn't do him much good after the success of *Surrealistic Pillow,* however. He wisely dipped out when the band were recording *After Bathing at Baxter's,* an acid-fueled mess that's essentially unlistenable now.

Onstage, the Airplane were already a bonafide jam band, earning the rep with their blissed-out improvisations. LSD and other hallucinogens were all the hot ticket in town, and the Airplane's songs got weirder and druggier.

Offstage, the Airplane were already splintering into factions. Kantner and Kaukonen were wresting control of the Airplane from its founder, and moving the band towards a darker, heavier and more explicitly 'revolutionary' direction. Balin's melodicism was on the shit-list (particularly with Kaukonen) and other members refused to work on his songs. He eventually became a background singer in his own band.

Their fourth studio album, *Crown of Creation* (1968), reflected a trend towards science fiction and apocalypticism. It also featured 'Triad' which David Crosby agave them after The Byrds had rejected it. The Airplane loved 'Triad'; free love was their way of life, and Grace bedded all of her bandmates save Balin at one time or another. The Airplane then peaked in 1969 with their landmark LP *Volunteers*, which climaxed with the pile-driving revolutionary anthem, 'Volunteers (of America).'

Which is to say that after two sides of charming but staggeringly inept pseudo-songs, 'Volunteers' ("Look what's happening on the street/Got a revolution, got a revolution") cuts through the entire record like a laser cannon. Neither Kantner nor Kaukonen could ever hold a tune in a bucket, and Slick's shrill harpy routine had already gone stale, so it's left up to Balin to demonstrate what a real singer could do with a real song in this band.

But Balin seemed to suffer for the sins of the San Francisco psychedelic scene. He'd been sidelined in his own band and Bill Graham had taken control of the club circuit (and the Airplane itself, until Slick demanded he be fired). To make matters worse, Balin got knocked unconscious on-camera at the Altamont Speedway when he bravely (or foolishly) tried to stop some Hell's Angels pledges from beating on his fans with billiard cues.

The Airplane preached Revolution® in a way uncannily similar to today's hyper-privileged Faux-Left. Like the contemporary models, the Airplane were not only born and bred in the belly of the Imperial beast, they also became a pack of greedy, narcissistic, hypocritical, coke-head assholes working for what was then the largest music corporation in America. Which is exactly why Balin said he quit the band in 1970. The Airplane stumbled on for a short while after, but no on really cared.

WITH THE AIRPLANE IN SHAMBLES, Kantner enlisted an all-star cast of friends for a new project he named Jefferson Starship, which was essentially a virtual band used for a series of side projects before congealing into a real one following the release of 1974's *Dragon Fly*. Jefferson Starship failed to trouble the charts until Balin joined as a full-time member for *Red Octopus* in 1975. Balin's lusty 'Miracles' became a major smash and *Octopus* topped the charts for four weeks.

While Kaukonen and Casady playing small clubs with Hot Tuna, Balin served up a string of hits with Jefferson Starship, three of which made the Top 10 ('Miracles', 'With Your Love', 'Runaway') and all of which have become standards in the Seventies AOR canon. The Starship were now far more successful than the Airplane had ever been, thanks to the very same love ballads that exiled Balin in the Sixties.

That success was short-lived. Balin would express his frustration when one of his hits was played on the radio and the DJ said something to the effect of 'there's Grace Slick and Jefferson Starship'. Worse, Balin's last (and in my opinion, best) single with the Starship, the epic 'Light the Sky on Fire' failed to hit the Top 40, probably due to its association with the surrealistically terrible *Star Wars Holiday Special.* Slick had become a raging alcoholic by this point, and her behavior drove Balin to quit again in 1978, after Slick had a drunken meltdown during a concert filmed for German television.

And we all know what happened next.

Balin was replaced by longtime session vocalist Mickey Thomas and Jefferson Starship morphed into a generic arena rock band, before morphing again into the loathsome pop outfit Starship after Paul Kantner finally bailed out. I remember when 'We Built this City' first aired on WNEW-FM. I was working as a line cook for the real-life Tony Soprano (a story for another day) when Scott Muni dropped the needle on that stinker. I remember saying to my coworkers, "That's the worst pile of shit I've ever heard. No *way* will that ever be a hit." Of course, I was younger then and had a lot to learn about life.

The original Jefferson Airplane would briefly reform in the late Eighties and made a terrible album before splitting again. Kantner would later reform Jefferson Starship, and it and 'Mickey Thomas' Starship' would tour at each other over the next several years, forcing fans to decide which version of Starship they didn't want to go see versus which version of Starship they *really* didn't want to go see.

Balin drifted in an out of the new-model Jefferson Starship, but his daughter's health issues limited his involvement. His final days were horrible and sad, as he'd become incapacitated by what his lawyers argued was appalling malpractice at New York's Mount Sinai Hospital. On account of the ways of this world being evil and cruel. The band is currently fronted by the eighty year-old David Freiberg, who can still belt it out.

Oddly enough, Balin's Airplane co-founders Paul Kantner and Signe Anderson died on the exact same day.

WHERE HAVE ALL THE GOOD TIMES GONE?

WELL, IT'S THAT TIME AGAIN, FOLKS: time to mourn the passing of another giant. And also to mourn the abominably pitiful state our culture is in, particularly pop culture. Eddie Van Halen, arguably the most influential guitarist in Rock n' Roll history, passed away at the age of 65 after a long battle with cancer. It's a milestone worth noting, even if the strong, confident America that Van Halen once epitomized has been dead for quite some time.

The original — the *real* — Van Halen was such a brief moment in time that it's easy to forget how revelatory they were. It may be hard to see today, after the brand was tarnished by constant infighting, countless counterfeits and Gary Cherone, but the original Van Halen were like a beacon of light arising from the murk of the late Seventies, when Disco reigned, Rock was dying and everyone was miserable.

The late Seventies were a lot darker and uglier than people seem to remember. Sure, Jimmy Carter bogged the entire country down with his dreary church lady/schoolmarm energy, but the culture was being lit by the Black Sun of Son of Sam's New York. Studio 54, with its witches brew of wealth, nihilism and cocaine, was the Vatican of the new Plutonian Church.

But the early vitality of Disco had given way to cookie-cutter mass production, and soft rock was ruling the airwaves. By the time Van Halen rolled around, nearly all of the hard rock giants of the late Sixties and early Seventies — Led Zeppelin, Deep Purple, Black Sabbath, KISS, Aerosmith, The Who, Alice Cooper, *et al* — were either falling apart or in crisis mode. Faceless Midwest arena rock and Southern boogie bands temporarily filled the void. Then, out of absolutely nowhere came this firestorm of intoxicating masculinity, leaping and grinning and spraying its spunk all over an exhausted genre.

On the surface, they looked like any number of Led Zeppelin wannabes, but those comparisons evaporated as soon as you dropped the needle on their first album and an overamped car horn gave way to Eddie's quicksilver glissandos and David Lee Roth's yips and howls, which drew less on Led Zeppelin and more on Parliament and the Ohio Players. And in one of those moments where circumstance gives way to symbolism, Van Halen toured as Black Sabbath's support act in the waning days of the Ozzy years, and blew the tired titans off the stage. Every single night, by all accounts.

I first heard Van Halen when WBCN-FM played 'Somebody Get a Doctor', when their second LP came out. I had the same reaction I'd have four years later when I first heard the Cocteau Twins: what the hell did I just hear?

Was that some transmission from another dimension? How the hell do you make guitars *sound* like that?

Of course, I was an alt.rock true believer by then, and actually sorted my LPs into pre-punk and post-punk stacks. So the ELO and ELP went here, and the Siouxsie and Circle Jerks went there. But for me it wasn't about whatever idiotic ideology punks pretended to believe in, it was about cutting ties with the tired old sounds that had become so oppressive to someone who had been plugged into popular music since a very young age. I even slept with the radio on, OK? Leave me alone.

In a lot of ways, Van Halen was the musical equivalent of the first *Star Wars* movie. It was a blast of pure pop culture enthusiasm buttressed by astonishing technical expertise and the "what the fuck, let's try it" spirit of pre-Feudal California. It was pure Apollonian sunshine come to blast away the Plutonian darkness and enervation stalking the land, just as *Star Wars* blew away all the self-indulgent cocaine nihilism that the early Seventies rebel auteurs had surrendered to. It wasn't their fault that thousands of impostors arose overnight to poach on their land.

Inevitably, Van Halen were on the shit-list when Hardcore rolled around. All of a sudden there was a *new* Year Zero to pledge allegiance to and I wasn't having it. Sure, I shaved my head, donned my army boots and was up front at all the ages-shows, but I didn't go home and listen to Hardcore records, outside of a small few like *Group Sex, Bad Brains (ROIR cassette),* and *Fresh Fruit for Rotting Vegetables.* I tried, but the music made no sense in that context. It was situational and liturgical. Without the mayhem, Hardcore was just a blur. Plus, I was neck-deep in post-punk and Neo-Psychedelia, along with muso stuff like Al DiMeola and mainstream New Wave like The Police. And, of course, Van Halen.

I eventually got tired of the contrived theatrics of Hardcore, and by my senior year spent my time with my high school friends. They were all wilder than the self-conscious skinheads, who always acted like they were on camera. And *1984* ruled that year, especially during the summer. It was genetically-engineered to be played at the beach.

We didn't realize it at the time, but *1984* was the grand finale for Van Halen. Tensions between David Lee Roth and the Van Halen brothers had become un-tenable, despite all the fun and camaraderie you saw on MTV. Acting like you're having fun is hard work, and the responsibilities of a major rock band in the 1980s were spoiling everyone's backstage party.

So Dave was booted from the band and replaced with Sammy Hagar. This was unforgivable to me. Sammy was the *old* guard, having been kicking around since the early Seventies when he fronted Montrose.

And he projected that kind of tired, corny heavy metal machismo that we all thought Van Halen had come to mock and scorn.

Whatever the reality, classic Van Halen felt like they were throwing a party that everyone was invited to, and telling a joke that everyone was in on. I didn't realize at the time how much of that was Dave, and lo, the new model VH were just another competent corporate rock band. (In hindsight, I came to realize that Sammy was nothing like his obnoxious onstage persona, and seems like a good guy to throw back a few with.)

So I was Team Dave, at least for a short spell. He put together a band with Steve Vai (for whom the term "guitar god" seems inadequate) and Billy Sheehan, but it just wasn't the same. It all fell apart very quickly and it soon became apparent that Dave was losing his sanity along with his hair. The six-year long party was really over, and it was time to move on.

My hopes were raised when VH pulled the old bait-and-switch at the 1996 MTV awards, and put out the greatest hits with the very under-rated "Me Wise Magic." But the mask of the Van Halen brothers' smiling faces had long been discarded, and they very-shittily kicked Dave to the curb in favor of the walking charisma-vacuum men call Gary Cherone.

Red flags were raised across the fruited plain with the release of the new lineup's first single, "Without You," nearly two years after the MTV debacle. It sounded uncannily like a Sammy-era outtake, except how it wandered around in search of a tune or hook for four minutes before giving up the ghost.

I'm sure Gary Cherone is a nice person and all, but he just sounded like a bad Sammy impersonator. And he looked like the low-ranking hired hand he actually was onstage. Eddie was fully in control now, for not-better and much worse. All of which is to say *Van Halen III* was horrible, so much so that it got Van Halen dropped from Warner's, an event that seemed *unimaginable* once upon a time. As legendary a guitarist as Eddie was, he's no songwriter, and it was clear that Dave and Sammy had hammered his billion-dollar riffs into actual songs. And ran the band for him, to boot.

Of course, Van Halen tried it with Sammy one more time, but Eddie was a trainwreck, lost in addiction hell while in recovery from major oral surgery for cancer. The tour was a flop, so the band ended rehiring Dave. But a very sour note was struck when the Van Halen's 86'd the loyal and dependable Michael Anthony for Eddie and Valerie Bertinelli's son, Wolfgang. After many years of seeing an angry and kind-of-insane Eddie wearing the skin-suit of our beloved, smiling Apollo, it was just another sign that the great Eighties party was dead and buried and you could never go home again.

The new lineup produced 2012's *A Different Kind of Truth,* which was as close to classic Van Halen as it was ever going to get. But these weren't the alien strangers who seemed to burst forth out of absolutely nowhere to save us all from the Seventies any longer, these were a bunch of rather unpleasant late middle-aged men and a pudgy teenager.

Worse, Dave seemed to have left his voice, such as it ever was, in the same place he'd left his hair and his sanity. And he couldn't paper over it with young-dumb-and-full-of-cum bullshitting, chest-hair and acrobatics anymore. There was no escaping from the Twenty-First Century, after all.

L ooking back on these old VH videos is like looking at World War One footage or something. You see what you once took for granted: young, fit men, full of piss and vinegar and don't give a fuck confidence. Who are these strange creatures and what happened to the likes of them?

Can you imagine if you built a time machine and dropped these guys into the dystopic hellhole Southern California has become today? Can you imagine trying to get Van Halen on the radio? They'd be canceled as soon as the first blue-haired sicko SJW hatefreak hit the YouTube play button. They'd be thrown off every platform in existence, for the capital crimes of unapologetic masculinity and shameless self-belief.

The plain fact is it simply doesn't get less Woke than classic Van Halen. Sure, bands have been lewder and more offensive but more often than not, it didn't feel right or natural. Van Halen never tried to be anything, they just *were.* Every fiber of their being was a finger directly in the All-Seeing Eye of the Oligarchic nightmare this country has been becoming since at least 9/11. They were not only what we once saw as the masculine ideal, they were also irreducibly and unapologetically *American.*

No, these guys would be marked for elimination as soon as they popped their heads out of Pasadena. Antifa would shut down every show they booked.

Don't despair; I think Van Halen's time will come around again. You know how it goes: Hard times make strong men, strong men make good times, good times make weak men, weak men make hard times. We're nearing the dawn of stage four of that cycle and once circumstances restore the natural balance, strong men — and genuinely strong women, for that matter — will be looking for some good time music to get through the inevitable hard times.

NOT-SO-POPULAR CULTURE

MY FAVORITE FLOPS

BEFORE LAUNCHING THE SECRET SUN, I briefly toyed with the idea of a blog centered on metaphysically and spiritually-themed movies and TV shows called 'Metaphyction'. But I soon realized something telling about the films I wanted to write about; most of them were flops. Granted, a lot of them went on to enjoy cult status on video, but that didn't help them any at the box office.

The point of all this is that films that delve into metaphysical themes ('metaphysical' being a blanket term for most of the stuff we look at here) usually don't seem to do well with the multiplex crowd who make or break films these days, but often do much better with the shut-ins like myself who prefer to consume their entertainment in their own homes.

So, here are my favorite flops in chronological order. Which, barring a few outliers, comprise the list of my favorite films.

THE WICKER MAN (1973)
PRODUCTION BUDGET £500,000
BOX OFFICE (INT'L) $58,341

TO SAY THE WICKER MAN WAS A FLOP on its release is to reduce the term 'flop' to a trifle. This was a film that its studio hated so much that not only did they go out of their way to figuratively bury it in the theaters, they actually took the negative of the film and literally buried it (as landfill for a highway project). If it weren't for low-budget maestro Roger Corman, the film might have been forgotten. Always looking for product, Corman worked up a truncated cut of the film in the second-run/drive-in circuit, where it built up a devoted cult following.

As with many of these films, I prefer the theatrical cut to the extended version. Corman's old-school instincts served the film well, and cut out a lot of extraneous exposition that slowed down the action. The film draws heavily on James Frazer's *The Golden Bough* for historical accuracy and may also draw on the equally-unappreciated British film *Eye of the Devil*.

The Wicker Man is deeply pagan, while most of my other favorite flops are Gnostic, but the humor, the sex and the subversion (as well as the songs) have made this one of my all-time favorites. And I'm certainly not alone. And I must say that the ending was genuinely shocking to me the first time I saw, way back in the pre-Internet, VCR-powered Stone Age.

BLADE RUNNER (1982)
PRODUCTION BUDGET $28M
BOX OFFICE (USA) $27M

THE FIRST OF MANY BIG-BUDGET PHILIP K. DICK ADAPTATIONS, *Blade Runner* was hampered by a downbeat vibe and a overly competitive release calendar (this was the summer of *ET, Poltergeist, Tron, The Road Warrior,* etc). I had no idea at the time, since this was before our pathological obsession with box office grosses turned us into soul-dead bean-counters instead of fans. I thought it was the greatest thing I'd seen since the first *Star Wars.*

Of course, it's "weighed down" with Gnostic pessimism and metaphysical ruminations about what it means to be human, and a lot of critics chafed at the voiceover (which I loved, and still prefer), but it's still a master class in big-budget movie-making. The sparkly Vangelis soundtrack doesn't hurt either.

I miss the days before non-executives spent their Monday mornings brooding over grosses. *Blade Runner* is still an important movie that people still want to see for the first time, and it's still a movie that rewards repeat viewings. Can you say that about *Van Helsing* or *Transformers 3?* I think not.

THE HUNGER (1983)
PRODUCTION BUDGET: $10M
BOX OFFICE (USA): $6M

THIS MOVIE IS GROSSLY MISUNDERSTOOD, mostly because of *that* scene (if you've seen the movie, you know what I mean). But it's a downright startling prophecy of the AIDS crisis, which was still in its early days when the film was being made. It's also a powerful meditation on obsession and addiction, as well as a condemnation of the shallow, youth-centric culture that has only got crazy worse since the Eighties.

The movie was savaged, partly because of *that* scene but also because David Bowie was seen as a dilettante playing at acting. The fact that director Tony Scott (brother of Ridley) made his bones doing commercials in the UK didn't endear him to the wags, either.

None of that phased me. I loved this movie back in the day and I still love it. This is the modern-day vampire story Anne Rice wishes she wrote.

JACOB'S LADDER (1990)
PRODUCTION BUDGET $25M
BOX OFFICE (USA) $26M

T HIS MOVIE SPOKE TO ME ON SO MANY LEVELS — many of which are very painful — that it became one of the first movies that I obsessed on. I've watched it more times than I could count. As with *Blade Runner*, it's an object lesson in big-screen directing. And having read the original script I can say it's as much — if not more — an Adrian Lyne film as a Bruce Joel Rubin film.

Lyne used the opportunity to stoke his own William Friedkin obsession, something my fellow children of the Seventies will appreciate. But he also went out of his way to avoid horror cliché, creating a new visual vocabulary for demons and monsters that is still in use to this day.

Balancing out the existential terror is the abject heartbreak of a young working-class father who loses a child (played by a young Macaulay Culkin, for whom my first son was an absolute ringer for at the time) before being sent to the killing fields of Southeast Asia. Elizabeth Pena smolders with carnality, and several actors who went on to bigger things put in A-plus performances.

DARK CITY (1998)
PRODUCTION BUDGET $27M
BOX OFFICE (INT'L) $27M

W HILE THIS SCI-FI NOIR HAS GROWN IN STATURE on DVD, but it was a flop upon release. Again, I was oblivious because I was sold on *Dark City* as soon as I saw the trailer. Even then I saw it took the retro-noir vibe of the first *Batman* movie and actually wrote a real story to place it in.

Of course, a little indie art picture called *The Matrix* came along a year later and stole *Dark City's* premise and its thunder. Plus, its actual sets.

Some have been disappointed with writer/director Alex Proyas' career path since (I actually like *Knowing* quite a bit), but that's Hollywood for you. Multi-million budgets are not meant to be used to make quirky statements based in Gnostic cosmology, they're meant to rake in multi-million dollar profits in return. That they so often don't shows that nobody in show business knows what the hell they're doing, since it's impossible to say what will happen in the culture and the world during the several years you're working on your film.

DAGON (2001)
PRODUCTION BUDGET $4,800,000
BOX OFFICE (INT'L) €212,699

STUART GORDON'S ADAPTATION of "The Shadow Over Innsmouth" is a deeply divisive movie, even among Lovecraft fans (hell, *especially* among Lovecraft fans), but I think it's a masterpiece. Because I am a natural-born contrarian.

On the surface level, *Dagon* is just another B-movie gorefest, but as the credit sequence tells us, it's *below* the surface where all the real action is. Lovecraft's pagan-phobia was simply a stand-in for his revulsion towards the immigrant hordes descending on the Northeast, but Gordon takes an opposite tack: the Mystery cult initiation we see unfold is a revelation to a deeper gnosis. Our hero Paul Marsh is systematically stripped of all of the yuppie comforts he took as a birthright, only to find a much deeper and more powerful birthright he had no idea existed.

The creepy Medieval Spanish village is a nice stand-in for Lovecraft's Cape Ann (which is a yuppie hellhole nowadays) and Gordon's use of sex and violence is less juvenile than his other pictures. And the actress who portrays Uxia brilliantly encapsulates a whole powder-keg of emotions familiar to any woman who's found the love of her life.

MULHOLLAND DR. (2001)
PRODUCTION BUDGET $15M
BOX OFFICE (INT'L) $20M

INLAND EMPIRE IS ESSENTIALLY THE SAME FILM (though much, much grimmer and much more insane) but *Mulholland Dr.* gets the nod for all the sumptuous color and cinematography that the bigger budget allowed. David Lynch has always been the poet laureate of dissociation and dream logic, and for my money, *Mulholland* is his masterpiece.

Naomi Watts would go on to star in the remake of *Ringu*, but this is a much scarier film because it's real. It's about how Hollywood takes everything away from the naive and the dreamers (her character is Canadian, appropriately) and gives them nothing but cold concrete and a bullet to the head in return.

I'm not surprised Lynch has quit making movies, since *Mulholland* and *Inland* stripped away all of the lies and bullshit that Hollywood sells, and showed us the disease-riddled, reanimated corpse that hides behind the curtain, pulling all of our strings.

SOLARIS (2002)
PRODUCTION BUDGET $47M
BOX OFFICE (INT'L) $30M

I WAS LATE TO THE SOLARIS PARTY, since I didn't happen to catch it until it was on cable. I made up for lost time. Steven Soderbergh came of age at a time when Hollywood was on fire, and the storytelling tics of all the late Sixties and Seventies auteurs are all over his work. His anti-linear approach sometimes works, sometimes doesn't. It definitely works here. Artistically, at least.

I can only explain this film's very existence by the fact that it's essentially a James Cameron project, with Soderbergh hired on to supply the poetry. If all of Hollywood didn't live in mortal terror of Cameron, there's no way this brooding, atmospheric Astro-Gnostic meditation on death and loss would have been green-lit. Clooney might have helped seal the deal, and it's always great to see Natascha McElhone, even if she's weirdly lit in a lot of this.

THE X-FILES: I WANT TO BELIEVE (2008)
PRODUCTION BUDGET $30M
BOX OFFICE (INT'L) $68 M

G IVEN THE UNJUST DRUBBING THIS FILM TOOK, it's the only film on this list to ostensibly turn a profit at the box office. This film was a victim of bad timing, given that *The Dark Knight* (released the previous week) worked so hard to dredge up the 9/11 vibe that pulled the rug out from underneath the original series. Its time will come and people will come to appreciate how perfectly Carter captured the bleak vibe of the late Bush years, not to mention how brilliantly directed and filmed it all is.

THE NINES (2007)
BOX OFFICE (INT'L) $130,000

I DON'T THINK THE ESSENTIALLY-INDESCRIBABLE COMEDY-DRAMA masterwork, *The Nines*, was ever released outside the festival circuit, so don't be scared off by its paltry gross. The performances by Ryan Reynolds, Hope Davis and Melissa McCarthy are spotless, not to mention some stunning work by the precocious Elle Fanning.

The critics saw this as John August's Charlie Kaufman move, but it's much more interesting than that. It's also Gnostic as hell, but not in a stupid *Matrix* kind of way. Don't let that scare you off: unlike most so-called "Gnostically-themed" movies, *The Nines* is a hell of a lot of fun.

THE DELICIOUS IRRATIONALITY OF BURN, WITCH, BURN

CONTRARY TO WHAT MOST PEOPLE TODAY MIGHT THINK, the current wave of skepticism and atheism is nothing new. It's not even unique to our recent history. In fact, the dominant voice of the Establishment and the media in the mid-Twentieth Century was a cold, reductionist one, which had declared the final triumph of science and technology over every aspect of our lives, and the Earth itself. To the status quo it was just a matter of time before we lived in a Jetsons world, and all expressions of passion and irrationality would be erased by the inevitable march of Progress.

Aside from the Evangelical enthusiasts — who were a very small and marginalized minority at the time — the 'Death of God' movement had taken hold in the seminaries and the dominant religions were given over to an arid kind of ethical navel-gazing, stripped of any supernatural component at all.

Rock n' Roll had been thoroughly defanged, with its biggest stars either marginalized or sidelined. Some rock stars, like Buddy Holly and Eddie Cochran, conveniently met very early deaths in plane crashes and automobile accidents, as did *Rebel Without a Cause* star James Dean. Inert folksingers like the Kingston Trio and Peter, Paul and Mary were all the rage on campus, as was a hand-me-down pseudo-existentialist intellectualism. Ayn Rand was being pushed as a modern-day guru, and she dutifully celebrated the corporate CEO as the highest expression of Creation.

Freemasonry had been stripped of its esoteric and revolutionary impulses, and had reinvented themselves as Rotarians with funny handshakes. Even the though the parade of alien invasion films of the time would have you believing otherwise, UFOlogy was effectively quashed by the mid-Fifties, and the FBI was monitoring the few groups and researchers left standing. Groups like Jack Parsons' OTO branch in Pasadena had wilted and died under the growing surveillance state, as did the nascent Wiccan movement in the UK.

But the esoteric and the irrational were not dead, they'd simply been shut out of the conversation by the dominant consensus and a brow-beaten mass media. Just as it seemed the new Rationalism would triumph for good, counter-cultural energies would explode back into the mainstream and shake the world to its core.

The pressures of a suffocating conformity, the escalating militarism of the Cold War, and the sheer, oppressive boredom of mainstream entertainment ultimately shattered the staid rationalism of the Establishment and opened more Pandora's boxes than you can count.

BURN, WITCH, BURN (UK TITLE: NIGHT OF THE EAGLE) is a perfect sneak preview of this explosion. Based on the 1943 Fritz Lieber novel *Conjure Wife*, the film presents an insufferably smug college professor who dances on the grave of Irrationality, not realizing that its occupant is not only *not* dead, it's not even sleeping. It'll soon rise from its slumber and shatter his orderly, rational world to pieces.

Department S star Peter Wyndgarde is a revelation as the professor, and it's almost impossible not to see a young Richard Dawkins in his haughty, prissy performance. A man of science, the professor wages total war on superstition in his classroom, but to his horror soon realizes that all of his career triumphs and victories were actually literally conjured up by his doting wife, through the casting of magical spells. Worse still, the respectable college he teaches at is secretly controlled by a coven of witches.

The film argues, quite subversively, that reason and rationality cannot survive without unreason and the irrational, because life itself is profoundly irrational. Which is why the Existentialists were reduced to realizing that the only truly rational question that can be asked is whether or not you should commit suicide. Not really a healthy example to follow, wouldn't you say?

As history has proven time and time again, only the irrational seem to survive in this insane, fallen world. The Rationalists inevitably erase themselves. It's important to note here that the Existentialists eventually gave way to the Occultists in the early Sixties; *Being and Nothingness* passed into the endless night and the inevitable *Morning of the Magicians*.

Try as they might, the Rationalists have never quite managed to put the genie back in the bottle. And *Burn, Witch, Burn* is a brilliant foreshadowing of the rebirth of the Irrational, using the very tools and technologies that the forces of Reason were convinced would ensure the triumph of Enlightenment thinking and philosophy.

Janet Blair, who made her mark as a comedienne, is absolutely perfect in her role as the domestic sorceress. If you get a chance, try to catch the American release of this on Netflix, which opens with a very authentic-sounding banishment ritual. Was this just an inside joke or did the makers of the film know something that their audiences did not?

You know my guess.

HEAVEN'S GATE: THE ULTIMATE TREKKIES

FOR SUCH A SMALL AND OBSCURE GROUP, Marshall Applewhite's Heaven's Gate cult has had an outsized impact on the culture. Their mass suicide captured the public's imagination in ways that the far more grisly horrors at Jonestown, Waco and the Solar Temple did not.

And for good reason: Heaven's Gate better captured the zeitgeist of their time, with their obsession with technology and the Internet. By comparison, Jonestown was a relic of the Depression-era revival tent, the massacre at Waco was the inevitable end result of the CIA's Jesus Freak op, and the Solar Temple were some weird relic of the Old Europe, a bizarre and quixotic retreat to an imaginary past.

But Gate leaders Marshall Herff Applewhite and Bonnie Nettles became a media sensation a quarter-century before the events at Rancho Santa Fe, when a large group of their followers disappeared into the primeval forests of the American northwest smack dab in the middle of one of the most remarkable UFO flaps in history. They eventually emerged from their exile, only to go underground and become one of the strangest cults of our times.

Both the disappearance and the suicides had a huge impact on pop culture, inspiring this TV movie — which believe it or not, was a series pilot — *The Mysterious Two,* which recently popped up on YouTube. Produced in 1979 but unaired until 1982, *The Mysterious Two* is yet another 70s sci-fi potboiler that one can imagine Chris Carter and his producers soaking up while at college, since you can see pieces of it all over various *X-Files* episodes.

THE MYSTERIOUS TWO STARS none other than John Forsythe in the Applewhite role. Forsythe, then best known as the voice of Charlie in *Charlie's Angels,* was one of those classically-handsome Jewish actors who were cast as idealized WASP patriarchs in the Sixties and Seventies, when WASP dominance was already long since past. Forsythe is joined by a female variant of the type; Priscilla Pointer, the mother of actress Amy Irving, whom this writer had a serious crush on back in the day (this was concurrent with my Tatum O'Neal crush, which lasted into the early Eighties). Irving caught my eye in *Carrie,* and then my heart in *The Fury,* which made such a huge impression on me that I had recurring telekinetic dreams for a very long time afterward.

The Mysterious Two also features one Robert Pine, father of Chris Pine, the counterfeit-Kirk of the JJ Abrams counterfeit-Trek movies. It has some overly familiar TV faces such as Noah Beery and Vic Tayback, but also two other actors that would go on to far more resonant and semiotically supercharged roles, namely Jerry Hardin (best known for our purposes from *The X-Files*) and none other than Freddy Krueger himself, Robert Englund.

Their appearance not only anticipates more powerful and lasting pop-cult phenomena, but also lends a bit of frisson through the suggestion of black budget meddling (via Harding) and MK Ultra-type mind manipulation (via Englund).

Where *Mysterious Two* fails and fails quite spectacularly in its depiction of the kinds of cultists drawn to the Two's seductive charisma. The secret behind Applewhite's control over his cult lay not only in the man's powerful personal magnetism, but also in the deep and abiding fatherly love he felt for the lost and lonely souls who got pulled into his orbit.

T HERE'S A DIRTY LITTLE SECRET that no one wants to acknowledge about cults in general and Heaven's Gate in particular: they are often the province of nerds. The level of commitment and danger varies widely among the various sects — with a Jedi cult on one end of the spectrum, and Aum Shinrikyo on the other — but you will often find that the people most drawn to cults — young, alienated, awkward, misunderstood — are classic nerds.

My encounter with the Church of $cientology in the early Eighties (having been suckered into the personality test scam, of course) was also an encounter with hardcore nerds. Everywhere you looked in the interview room you saw well-worn copies of lurid sci-fi paperbacks, Hubbard's own and others. Seeing as how I'd just spent a week's pay at Newbury Comics when I met up with these characters, I felt very much at home. Luckily my (and Amy Bishop's) sci-fi lit teacher knew all about them, and told me to stay away. Since I'd adopted her as my maternal surrogate at the time, I wisely followed her advice.

No cult was as unabashedly nerdly as Heaven's Gate. Although the media, particularly the reliably-clueless geek media, tried to paint them as some unknowable pack of religious extremists, the Gate were nothing of the sort. Judging from the hours of tape the Gate recorded, they were an unusually pleasant and cheerful bunch of nerds. They were what happens to nerds when the frontiers of reality and LARP unreality begin to blur. I've been to enough cons and RenFaire's to see it all for myself. I'd bet anyone who's spent any time at all in fandom looks at those Heaven's Gate videos and shudders with a deep and indelible sting of recognition, as if looking into a faithless mirror image.

Harlan Ellison recognized the Gate for what they were, and worked up a typically misanthropic rant for *Newsweek* in which he struggled desperately to convince apathetic frequent fliers that there once was an idealized Golden Age of science fiction, where intrepid rationalists rolled up their sleeves and dared to ascend to the deep reaches of the cosmos from their typewriters. Sadly, all the essay ultimately proved is how delusional Ellison was about the genre and its audience, and how powerful a grip the self-aggrandizing fantasies of a tiny elite of older sci-fi writers had on his imagination.

YOU WON'T SEE THE VAGUELY ATTRACTIVE FACES of the *Mysterious Two's* stock character actors in the Heaven's Gate videos. You will see the same awkward, bespectacled men and mannish yet amiable women you'll see at any gathering of serious fans of sci-fi and fantasy. In fact, you'll see the same kinds of faces and self-effacing smiles you'll see in the *Trekkies* documentaries. So much so that if the producers of those films were honest, they'd make *Trekkies III* entirely out of Heaven's Gate footage.

Why? Because Heaven's Gate were in fact the *ultimate* Star Trek fans. They were so devoted to Gene Roddenberry's idealized world, especially that of *The Next Generation*, that they were willing to die to become part of it. How powerful was the Gate's connection to *Trek*? So powerful that one of its members was Nichelle 'Uhura' Nichols' own brother, Thomas. He must have been a kind of demigod to the Gate.

The Gate understood that the Trek Universe is deeply and irreducibly Gnostic. The Gate understood that Roddenberry's pretensions to atheist rationalism were just so much nonsense, a pathetic sop to the solipsistic SF royalty whose approval he desperately sought but never truly received.

And so Applewhite and Nettles' fluffy-bunny New Age Christianity evolved into a severe and rigorous Gnostic Christianity, in which the pain and senselessness of our world faded in comparison to the serenity and discipline of the Enterprise D. The Gate rightfully saw that there was no place in this world for idealists and dreamers, especially those drawn to cults.

At some point, the pull of *TNG* became so strong that Applewhite shaved his boyish grey mop into a Picardian buzz-cut. The cult chirped out Trek jargon during their everyday activities, and finally renamed themselves the "Away Team." They were determined to leave a world they were smart enough to realize was corrupted and take their chances with the USS Hale-Bopp.

The problem is that it's all pure fantasy. The reality becomes obvious after watching enough *Star Trek*: "Roddenberry's future" is that of a galactic military dictatorship, a kind of totalitarian socialism in which every moment of our heroes' days are spent in pursuit of the good and the worthy. And so it was with the Gate.

THE GATE WERE JUST PART OF THE WONDERFUL WORLD of high weirdness that the Nineties were chock full of. I didn't pay them much mind myself, until a nagging connection dug into my subconscious. Just a few days before the Gate hitched a ride on that giant mothership in the sky one of the biggest UFO flaps of our time was going down on the other side of Interstate 8.

Marshall Applewhite heard an alleged 'remote viewer' claim on Art Bell's show that a ginormous UFO was trailing Comet Hale-Bopp, and saw this as the great signal that it was time to beam up. The UFO meme was soon debunked, but at the very same time Applewhite and his followers were wrapping up their affairs, the Phoenix Lights were causing panic just a few hours drive away from their Rancho Santa Fe stronghold.

Did the Gate hear about the event? I haven't found any evidence yet that they did but the timing of the event — whatever you may think of the exact nature of the sightings themselves — is bone-chilling. The Gate were awaiting a giant UFO to come pick them up. And just as they were preparing for its arrival thousands of people were reporting a giant UFO in the skies over Phoenix, a hop, skip and jump away. It's all eerily reminiscent of the end of *Mysterious Two,* which quite prophetically takes place in Santa Fe, NM, or any number of similar sci-fi movies.

Fandom has become a religion unto itself, so the days in which fandom and traditional religion could be synthesized may be behind us. Which is not to say the kind of totalizing devotion we saw in the Gate is a thing of the past. It simply means that it will simply take a different form the next time it pops up. Like the Gate, it too will catch us by surprise, until we sift through all of the dire portents that we ignored.

TAKING JACOB'S LADDER TO THE ULTRAWORLD

T HE GODS OF SYNC ARE A CAPRICIOUS LOT, often dive-bombing into our lives with tantalizing morsels of interconnectivity that answer one question at the same time they ask a thousand more. And so just as a realization broke through the fog of my addled brains, these strange signals from the Ether dropped upon my head like tender little drops of cosmic dew. Subsequently, a recent attempt at rewatching *Jacob's Ladder* put the final pieces of the puzzle into place with this nutty fan theory about *The X-Files* that I've stewing over.

I've watched *Jacob's Ladder* at least a hundred times, and probably a lot more than that. I used to watch it, rewind it, then watch it again. Every night, for a quite some time. Actually, I think I just stopped counting around the hundred mark. That's how I roll when something trips those old OCD circuits in the old bean. There's something seriously wrong with me. I'm the first to admit it.

But having spent way, way too much time in the first decade or so of my life either hallucinating and/or experiencing perilously high fevers and/or having extremely vivid nightmares and/or suffering long stints in a very grim and dodgy municipal hospital, *Jacob's Ladder* seemed to resonate on levels I rather wish it did not.

If all that weren't enough, I used to have this recurring nightmare when I was a wee wane of being a soldier in some European forest. It always ended with some German soldier leaping out from behind a tree and carving out my guts with a bayonet. At one point I chalked this up to spending so much time in my childhood on the immediate outskirts of Fort Devens, then known as the US Army Intelligence School. Later, not so much.

So it's safe to say that with two close family members in the service during Viet Nam - and Fort Devens looming in the close distance like Mordor - that the military made for a powerful presence in my young and impressionable mind.

J ACOB'S LADDER WAS WRITTEN BY BRUCE JOEL RUBIN, who made his first big splash with his story for the 1983 film, *Brainstorm*. Significantly, this was Natalie Wood's last film before her death by drowning, a drama that also co-starred Christopher Walken. *Brainstorm* was released less than a month before *The Dead Zone*, in which Walken portrays a psychic who acquires his gifts after an NDE.

As you have all come to expect by now, *The Dead Zone* co-star Martin Sheen first came to prominence in *The Outer Limits,* in particular an episode in which deigned to tell some tales out of school concerning military MK programs.

It was originally scheduled to air two days after the JFK assassination. Sheen later portrayed Kennedy in a miniseries in 1983. *Brainstorm* also featured Louise Fletcher, the actress who won an Oscar for *One Flew Over the Cuckoo's Nest*, a film inspired by Ken Kesey's days as an MKULTRA test subject. Fletcher later went on to co-star on *Star Trek: Deep Space Nine* as Kai Winn, a priestess of the Prophets, a thinly-veiled incarnation of the Council of Nine. Why wouldn't she, right?

Rubin later generated some big dollars with his scripts for *Ghost* and *Deep Impact* but couldn't get any bites for *Jacob's Ladder*, which languished in studio slush-piles until British director Adrian Lyne — fresh off his mega-smash *Fatal Attraction* — took a cotton to it. Lyne really needs to be considered a co-writer for this film since Rubin's original script was quite heavily revised on account of not really being all that great (I'm generally a fan of Rubin's work but the original screenplay for *Jacob's Ladder* is pretty corny business).

Lyne took out all the Temptation of St. Anthony horned devils and what-not, arguing that audiences would just laugh at them. He then developed an entirely new visual vocabulary for the demons, riffing off the motions of helicopter rotors for the horrific seizures the demons display. Lyne also steals huge swathes of style and mood from *The Exorcist*, an obvious touchstone for this film. And, it must be said, a rather unsettling mind-control allegory written by a former military intelligence office.

SO I'VE BEEN PUZZLING FOR YEARS over this weird pattern that runs throughout the entirety of the *X-Files* franchise. And that's that every episode dealing with aliens and/or the series' 'Mythology' was paired in the running order with an episode dealing explicitly with mind-control, or mind-control program corollaries such as hallucinogens, cults, hypnotism and violent sexual fetishism. Not to mention eugenics and breeding program themes.

I'm not exactly sure what it ultimately means yet, but it's too consistent and obsessive to be coincidental. In fact, the Mythology episodes quite often fold in mind-control and related topics right into the stories, including the very first episodes of the entire series (one of which depicts Mulder undergoing mind-erasure treatment at a secret air base).

So if my hare-brained hypothesis is correct, and *The X-Files* is actually about two subjects involved in a long-running eugenics program, and the aliens and whatnot they encounter are either staged hoaxes and/or hallucinogenic delusions, then the *Jacob's Ladder* connections to the series suddenly take on much greater significance. Not only are Mulder and Scully being used to breed super-humans, they're also being used to hunt down runaway subjects of previous genetic experiments. They've simply been programmed to think they're all monsters or aliens or whatever to salve their consciences.

So your Toomses and your Flukemen and your tumor-tasters and so on are all eugenics experiments, that were either let loose into the wild or escaped. Mulder and Scully's job was either to bring them back in, or rub them out. All of the Paranormal stuff is programmed psychodrama that helps to shield the agents from the ugly truth, in the same way Jacob Singer's imaginary post-war life plays out to shield him from the ugly truth of his impending death.

So it's worth nothing that the essential plotline of *Jacob's Ladder* — combat soldiers in Viet Nam being used at subjects for hallucinogenic drug testing — was lifted lock, stock and barrel for the eleventh season *X-Files* episode, 'Kitten'. I can just picture the story meeting: "OK, we're getting near the end of the line here. If we're going to just flat-out rewrite *Jacob's Ladder*, it's now or never."

And in case you hadn't noticed the pattern, 'Kitten' is followed by 'Ghouli', which fully introduces us for the first time to young William Mulder, the ultimate product of the postwar eugenics program who is like every monster his parents ever battled all rolled into one. To sweeten the pot, one of young William's mental powers is — wait for it — *mind control.*

Oh, and exactly who plays the part of William? None other than Miles Robbins, son of *Jacob's Ladder* star Tim Robbins and Susan Sarandon. But that's not the only direct connection between *Jacob's Ladder* and *The X-Files*. The two even share supporting actors. Like Brett Hinkley, who played a mind-controlling Amish alien in 'Genderbender'. There's also Pruitt Taylor Vince, who co-starred in 'Unruhe' in the fourth season. This will probably come as a total shock to you all, but 'Unruhe' deals with — wait for it — mind-control drugs and techniques. I mean, what are the odds, right?

There are other weird details. Mark Snow's score to the *X-Files* episode 'The Jersey Devil' lifted the Bulgarian Choir riffs from the *Jacob's Ladder* soundtrack back when they weren't yet a cliché. *X-Files* director-producer Kim Manners later said he prepped for the episode 'Grotesque' (amazingly, about demonic mind-control) by playing that very same soundtrack.

There are the Faceless Aliens who look like the demonic anesthesiologist from *Jacob's Ladder*. There's other stuff, like the very-*Jacob's Ladder* hospital scenes in 'Kill Switch' and 'The Sixth Extinction'. There's Mulder's ice-bath in 'Endgame', as well as the inexplicable car explosion in *Fight the Future*. There's Emily's ascension in 'All Souls'. Probably loads more that haven't yet come to mind yet.

There's also the fact that 'Sveta' (from the scorching first installment of 'My Struggle') looks and sounds a whole lot like Elizabeth Peña in *Jacob's Ladder*, only considerably less sexy. No shame in that; there aren't many people who are as elementally sexy as Elizabeth Peña is in *Jacob's Ladder*.

So you can't help but wonder, if the events seen in *Jacob's Ladder* are all the fantasies of a drugged and dying soldier (also lifted by TXF in 'Amor Fati'), does that jibe with my theory that the events of *The X-Files* are all the result of the heavy mind-control programming that is either seen (or implied) again and again in that series? If so, the much-maligned (and admittedly dreadful) second and third installments of the 'My Struggle' storyline — which turn out to be a very *Jacob's Ladder* dream/vision — suddenly take on a whole new dimension, especially given 'My Struggle 2's' climax on a bridge.

Why? Because that episode and *Jacob's Ladder* were inspired by the Ambrose Bierce short story, 'An Occurrence at Owl Creek Bridge'. But that's Chris Carter for you, isn't it? Fractal.

THE ASTRO-GNOSIS OF EARTHLING

CLASSICAL GNOSTICISM TAUGHT THAT HUMAN BEINGS were celestial entities trapped by the insane, sadistic Demiurge on a prison planet, simply to soothe his wounded ego. The entities were emanations from the *Pleroma*, or the Fullness, and were cast out due to a terrible cosmic abortion. Christian Gnostics taught that Christ was a purely spiritual being who was sent to liberate the prisoners of the 'Blind Idiot God' and his Archons by bringing them the knowledge of their true nature and identity.

AstroGnosticism believes that human beings were the result of an alien consciousness, itself a vastly-potent spiritual energy, grafted through whatever means onto the biology of advanced primates. That human beings are trapped on a planet to which their intelligence and consciousness is not merely maladaptive but in fact anti-adaptive, since trying to exist in an admittedly beautiful yet unimaginably destructive biosphere leads to depression, insanity, mass murder and habitat destruction.

And for some reason, the most potent vehicle for the AstroGnostic narrative seems to be the unassuming low-budget sci-fi film. A classic early example is the Mormon sci-fi opus, *The People*. This TV movie, based on the Zenna Henderson novels, is deeply informed by LDS folk mythology, telling of a people whose natural superiority (based on the fact that they are stranded aliens) made them targets for persecution from their shaved ape neighbors.

A more successful AstroGnostic franchise are the *Witch Mountain* films, the two made in the 1970s and the recent, rather overblown remake. Those films are centered on the danger the two fallen angels face from a national security state intent on exploiting the children's powers towards their own ends.

The recent remake with the Rock didn't seem to resonate the way the original *Escape* film did, precisely because its expensive bells and whistles distracted from the quiet, intimate realism of the original.

Which is why yet another classical AstroGnostic narrative, John August's *The Nines*, went straight to video despite having Ryan Reynolds and Melissa McCarthy as its stars. Even so, *The Nines* might be one of the most potent AstroGnostic narratives out there, as well as one of the most explicitly Christian Gnostic variants thereof.

Y OU'RE NOT WHO YOU THINK YOU ARE is also the message of *Earthling*, a lost classic *Outer Limits* episode in all but name. It starts when Judith, a young high school teacher, experiences a devastating accident (and miscarriage) coinciding with a mysterious cosmic event that also effects a space shuttle mission. Upon returning to work, Judith meets a precocious new student named Abby, who takes on the hippy free spirit persona, complete with old Volkswagen van. Abby is also a sexually-aggressive lesbian, or presents herself as such, and attempts to seduce Judith while drinking with her extremely creepy father (played by Peter Greene, best known as *Pulp Fiction's* Zed) at a bar frequented by her teachers.

As Abby and Judith talk on the shore of a pond, Abby begins to reveal her and Judith's true nature, and the true horror of their predicament. They don't belong here, they are trapped here, and Judith is the one they are all counting to set them free. The documentarian intimacy of the scene gives it a dark rush, since we're not sure if any of this is true or Judith is actually alone in the middle of nowhere with a dangerous psychopath.

Abby soon plunges Judith into a netherworld filled with insanity, murder, and pregnant children, which puts Judith at risk of losing both her job and her husband. As with any effective AstroGnostic narrative, the protagonist is unsure whether her revelators are telling her the truth or are all murderous lunatics caught in the grip of a collective delusion.

Judith watches in horror as Abby attempts to murder a girl she tries to seduce. She sees Abby's father and another 'alien' bury an apparent murder victim at their remote farm compound. But Judith soon develops horn-like tumors on her head as the others have, a sign that their host bodies can't handle the alien presence inside them. Concurrently we see the devastating mental breakdown of the sole remaining survivor of the shuttle mission, the attempts to break through his amnesia with creepy hypnosis techniques, and his strange family (his father is played by William Katt, veteran of another AstroGnostic drama, *The Greatest American Hero*).

It all gets pretty graphic, but at the same time it all reminds me very much of classic *Outer Limits* as well.

I DON'T KNOW IF WRITER-DIRECTOR CLAY LIFORD was consciously channeling classic Stefano-era TOL, but if he wasn't then *Earthling* is all the more remarkable for doing so. *Earthling* captures the desolate mood of old-time *Outer Limits* in a way the *X-Files* obsessed Nineties revival never managed.

The very premise of *Earthling* draws back to Stefano's Cambridge Five allegory, 'The Invisibles', without its rather unsubtle anal-rape analogs. We have settings recalling episodes like 'Architects of Fear', 'Man Who Was Never Born', and 'The Mice'. And of course we have the dangerous Sapphic chemistry of 'Bellero Shield' and 'Forms of Things Unknown' (though that's not nearly as shocking as it was in the early Sixties). We even have the Allyson Ames-styled random radiance in the form of Jenny Shakeshaft's tragic character. Some videogame-damaged fanboys complained about the no-budget effects in *Earthling*, but that's yet another link to classic *Outer Limits*, as is the abstruse, modal soundscaping.

It's unfortunate that films like this always seem to fall between all of the cracks and end up going over the heads of pretty much everyone. But at the same time it makes their existence all the more precious in that people who get it, *really* get it.

THE OA AND THE METAPHYSICS OF TRAUMA

I F YOU PRESSED ME FOR AN ADJECTIVE FOR THESE TIMES, I'd have to go with 'bleak'. The Obama Era opened with so many big promises, yet ended almost exactly as they began; with a nation bogged down in war abroad and dangerously polarized at home. The Trump Administration and its discontents are only accelerating the process.

With huge swathes of the country written off as obsolete by the decision-makers on the coasts, any sense of national unity has terminally eroded. For the moment, the dispossessed have been kept pacified with entertainment and opiates, but there's a growing sense that the American experiment is nearing its completion. This is why you have the richest-of-the-rich planning their escape to hold-outs in New Zealand and other remote locations, exactly as Roman knights and aristocrats did when central authority began to collapse in the Western Empire. Not a sign of rude health, that.

Everywhere you look you're confronted with trend-lines pointing towards a number of crisis points; social, political, economic. We have all the technology in the world yet the future is starting to look a bit bleak.

T HE NEW NETFLIX SERIES THE OA IS CERTAINLY BLEAK. So much so that it makes bleakness into its own kind of poetry. The camera eye is relentlessly dispassionate and there's very little musical score to relieve the some-times unbearable tension. Cold, washed-out colors dominate the photography. This isn't Hollywood you're looking at here. And as such, it's not necessarily an easy series to watch. A lot of viewers didn't make it through.

The OA's central themes are death, trauma and captivity. The zeitgeist is captured in the person of a maverick scientist whose quest makes him into a monster, a callous and obsessive Dr. Frankenstein whose inability to feel basic human compassion drives him to murder, over and again.

The story is fairly simple, and for some viewers, a bit repetitive. A young woman named Prairie is saved from jumping off a bridge and is brought to a hospital. It's discovered that she was the adopted daughter of an elderly couple and she's been missing for several years. Her back is mottled with strange scars, and even though she had been blind since childhood, she can now see.

Brought back home to a dismally anonymous, semi-finished housing tract, Prairie pulls a group of misfits into her orbit with her otherworldly charisma: a drug-dealing thug and his sidekick, an honor student from a troubled home, a transgender in the midst of transition, and an emotionally-fragile, middle-aged high school teacher.

Prairie begins telling them her story, which starts in Russia: she was the daughter of an oligarch who fell afoul of the *Organizatsiya*. To get back at their parents, the mob arranges the deaths of her and other rich children on the way to school. In death, Prairie is confronted by a woman, who is apparently her guardian angel, who returns Prairie to life but takes her sight.

When her father dies, Prairie ends up in America under the auspices of a shady adoption racket. There her adoptive parents (played by Alice Krige of *Star Trek: First Contact* fame and Scott Wilson, best known today for *The Walking Dead*) discover her. But they soon find out she's extremely troubled, given to weird, visionary episodes during sleep, for which she's heavily medicated.

When Prairie reaches adulthood, she begins to imagine her birth father is still alive and travels to New York to meet him. But instead she's found by Hap, an anesthesiologist obsessed with near-death experiences who can somehow tell Prairie had an NDE when he hears her playing violin in a subway. Hap seduces Prairie into coming home with him so they can study her condition but instead she's taken prisoner in his basement. There she meets Hap's other prisoners, all stock middle American archetypes. She bonds with Homer, a young football player who died and was resuscitated after sustaining a fatal injury during a game.

As Prairie tells it, Hap subjects his prisoners to brutal experiments in which they are repeatedly killed and medically resuscitated. During one of the experiments, Prairie meets the woman from her childhood vision again and is told she has a great mission to carry out. Along the way, Hap takes Homer to Cuba to seduce a female musician who Hap wants to kidnap.

Desperate to fill long hours of captivity, Hap's prisoners begin acting out complex ritual dances, believing that they can cross into other dimensions by following an exact sequence of movements. The dances actually do seem to have palpable effects, as shown during two memorable scenes.

As she tells her story, Prairie's circle is increasingly drawn into her weird stories, forming a kind of cult around her. The stories have a hypnotic, transformative effect on her audience, redirecting them from potentially self-destructive paths. Prairie is also contacted by a journalist who wants to tell her story, as well as by a somewhat-sketchy FBI psychologist. Later, the latter will act as the linchpin, as it becomes increasingly evident that Prairie's captivity may have in fact been part of a much larger conspiracy.

And this is where the series will burn itself into your brain. In the end, we are asked if Prairie's stories are real, or are in fact the product of a gifted but damaged psyche who's been subjected to an unimaginable ordeal. Was her captivity in fact even more traumatic and damaging than her stories will say? Are her stories elaborate constructions meant to shield herself from an even more terrifying reality? It's a question quite often asked when people claim experience with alien abduction, MKULTRA testing, or any other socially unacceptable traumas, isn't it?

BUT THE SEASON'S CLIMAX DOESN'T LET YOU OFF THE HOOK that easily. We see inarguable evidence that Prairie is not just the delusional victim of an ordeal we're finally asked to guess at, but is in fact a prophet. One whose mission it is to avert a harrowing outcome for her small circle of followers and the larger community they represent.

In a lot of important ways, *The OA* is an arty, indie, more-than-slightly pretentious companion piece to *Stranger Things*. Both deal with suburban monotony broken up by the arrival of a female character possessing otherworldly powers. In both series, that character brings a group of misfits into her orbit, as well as an authority figure. In both series, we see horrific human experiments undertaken, and in both series the subjects of them cross over into other realities.

But *The OA* is as elitist as *Stranger Things* is populist, as cold as the other is warm. It's not perfect by any means; the series bogs down to a crawl in some spots and dials up the cringe-meter in others.

At the same time, it goes a little deeper into the esoteric spheres than *Stranger Things* does, taking issues like the mutability of reality by the horns and leavening the dough with some well-studied metaphysics. It's not easy work, but *The OA* is worth sticking with, especially given the formulaic interchangeability of so many series these days.

It's like nothing else out there. In the end, it leaves you asking questions about the transformative nature of trauma and the grueling reality of captivity and the need it creates to construct alternate perceptions of reality in order to cope.

And other questions as well. Like, why do some trauma and/or NDE experiencers emerge with heightened or changed abilities and perceptions? Why have mad scientists, like those involved with MKULTRA, believed that controlled trauma could lead to enhanced psychic abilities? Does that somehow *justify* their abuses in their own minds? Are NDEs tricks the brain plays on the dying, or objective experiences? Does the Paranormal work the way we want it to, or does it follow its own inscrutable logic? I can only assume that these are questions the series will address in its second season. It will if it's smart.

The OA isn't perfect, not by any means. I'm not sure it's exactly *entertaining*, even. But the way it chooses to address complex metaphysics, and at the same time ask uncomfortable questions, makes it important.

THE OA: YOU ARE BEING INITIATED

I WROTE ABOUT THE EXTRAORDINARY NETFLIX SERIES THE OA over the winter, but something about it kept nagging at me. I was so focused on the externals of the storyline that it didn't occur to me that what we're actually seeing here is a classic Mystery religion narrative, complete with a journey to the Underworld.

The OA has all the usual secret society tropes like death and rebirth, piercing the veil between dimensions, revelation within a cavern, an elite vanguard separated from society, super powers, transcendence through ordeal, and a Lord of the Underworld kidnapping a virtuous maiden.

Brit Marling isn't your typical Hollywood airhead of the week. She was class valedictorian at the elite's elite Georgetown University and an intern at Goldman Sachs (who later offered her a full-time position). This is an extremely intelligent woman plugged into the very upper reaches of imperial power. As is her main collaborator Zal Batmanglij.

It shouldn't surprise us then that she is involved with Sir Ridley Scott, who produced her feature film, *The East*, in which she plays an intelligence agent sent to infiltrate a ecoterrorist group. She also played an American enlisted to head Scotland Yard's PR department in the British miniseries *Babylon* (created by Oscar-winning director Danny Boyle). Add in her model good looks and you start to wonder if Brit Marling wasn't grown in some CIA lab somewhere.

Especially when you factor in the ever-present themes of secret societies, cutting-edge science, and espionage in her work. And particularly when you consider that her work seems to be initiating its viewers into the esoteric world of Co-Masonry.

Co-Masonry is essentially a system that allows women to become Masons, but has historically followed a more mystical path than regular Freemasonry. It was particularly popular in the Victorian Era, and had a lot of crossover with the Theosophical movement.

Which is why I see *The OA* as a fundamentally (Co-)Masonic show. I know; that sounds absolutely ridiculous. Or at least it does until you begin to break down the symbolism and place the series in the greater context of the writing team's catalog. And then you realize, oh wait; this actually is what I'm seeing here.

The OA tells the story of Prairie Johnson, a girl born to a Russian oligarch who dies when her school bus falls into a river and is sent back to the physical world by a mysterious spirit, who is for intents and purposes, a goddess.

Here we see classic secret society symbolism emerge, such as when she tells the boys that they should leave their front doors open as a signal they will be joining her new lodge. There's also the fact that 'The OA' was heretofore best known as the nickname of the more-Masonic-than-Masonry "Order of the Arrow," whose initiates are traditionally the same age range as Prairie's secret society. Think hard on that fact while you digest all of this symbolism here.

The OA's lodge also meet on the second floor, or the Upper Chambers, the traditional meeting place for Freemasons. The 'Five Movements' that Prairie's secret society enact more-than-faintly resembles a recital of standard Masonic Degree signals, performed in sequence.

We also see the recurring use of purple in *The OA*, which many reviewers have commented on. By some inexplicable fluke in the time-space continuum, purple is also the identifying color of 'The Local Council of Royal and Select Masters', also known as "Cryptic Masonry," whose logo also incorporates and O and an A.

THE OA IS IN MANY WAYS A FURTHER EXPANSION on Marlin and Batmanglij's previous explicit secret society narrative, *The Sound of My Voice,* whose movie poster depicts Marlin as Isis Unveiled. That film is similarly rife with Masonic symbolism; The Anchor, an important Masonic symbol, is called 'the sign of a Traveler'. As we've seen, 'Traveler' is a common Masonic codeword.

There's also the initiation ritual in which petitioners are blindfolded (or 'hoodwinked') and dressed in white pajamas, exactly as Masonic applicants are. Remember that Prairie herself was blind before she was initiated into the mysteries of death and rebirth in the cavern. What's more, the entire plotline of *The Sound of My Voice* hinges on an elaborate secret handshake that this particular secret society uses as a form of recognition. Which is remarkably similar to the OA's 'Five Movements'. Given Marlin and Batmanglij's elite pedigree and the pervasive secret society themes in their screenplays, I'd say that this 'OA' symbol is something we need to keep our eyes out for in the days ahead.

THE OA, SEASON TWO: THE THEATRE OF DEPRESSION

IS THERE SUCH AN ANIMAL AS THE THEATRE OF DEPRESSION? If not, there should be. Online technology has converted most of the industrialized world into shut-ins and introverts, which is to say it's depressing the shit out of the world.

The OA seems like a fine exemplar of the Theatre of Depression. Every character in both series is demonstrably depressed and seems to be processing that depression in various fashions, and coping with it in other fashions still. The OA herself is no less depressed but is also ridden with a savior complex, one that she then infects those drawn to her with. The question becomes how much is the OA is a projection of Brit Marling herself. Not <u>if</u> it is, mind you, but how much of it is. My guess is quite a lot.

The first series had Marling play the OA in her Prairie Johnson incarnation, the adopted Russian daughter of an elderly Midwestern couple. The anonymous housing tract that the OA uses as her mission field was a stroke of inspiration, as it showed the devastating effects that sixteen years of the Bush-Obama Syndicate has had on the American Heartland.

Life in the tract — like most everywhere else — has been erased of meaning or purpose by a distant and implacably-hostile ruling class, of which Marling is a shining product of, oddly enough.

The OA then recruits for her own private mystery cult, whose liturgy and rituals betray a significant degree of familiarity with the ancient versions of such. So it's not unreasonable to assume *The OA* is in fact an expansion of Marling and creative partner Zal Batmanglij's film, *The Sound of My Voice*, since it deals with many of the same themes, both seem to act as an outlet for Marling to analyze her own messianic tendencies. Where Marling ends and the OA begins is probably only something her analyst could determine.

But for me, the cult gathered by the OA were a lot more compelling than the OA herself, and a lot more compelling than the fellow prisoners who shared her ordeal in Hap's dungeon. For my money, they're still the most interesting thing about Part Two as well. The latter were all victims of circumstance, but the OA cultists were seekers searching after spiritual meaning. Their very ordinariness, their dreary suburban environment and the absurd stories they were so entranced by made for a fascinating, if not disjointed and terminally-pretentious, narrative. I wanted to know what it was about these people that would make them desperate enough to be drawn into this very troubled woman's very private world.

P ART TWO TAKES US TO A PARALLEL DIMENSION in which the OA has escaped death at the hands of the school shooter, incarnating as a version of Nina Petrova that didn't die and resurrect as a child. In this dimension, she's the apparent courtesan of a psychotic Silicon Valley billionaire named Pierre Ruskin, who's played as a cross between Pierre Omidyar and Elon Musk.

There's also a B-plot in which a private detective (with the dazzlingly uncreative name of 'Kharim Washington') is searching for a girl who seems to have been lured into the haunted house by a video game devised by Ruskin, who is also running a side project in which he harvests the dreams of female volunteers, which later plays a significant role in Kharim's story-arc.

That project was shepherded by a former British Intelligence agent who suddenly leaves the project when she discovers Ruskin's true intentions. Ruskin is also working with a psychiatrist running a high-profile hospital on Treasure Island, a place in which Hap and the rest of his prisoners come to inhabit following their dimension-shift.

Hap is psychotic as ever, and has deceived Homer into denying his other-dimensional identity and convincing him he's this dimension's Homer (who's an irritating dweeb, and comes across as a CRISPR-cross of Chaz Bono and Wil Wheaton). The third arc deals with the OA cult trying to cope in the aftermath of Prairie's murder. Steve — the violent, drug-dealing jock — has morphed into the truest of true-believers in the OA and her message. He's even recruited his new girlfriend into the faith. That all rings very true to me.

The others continue on in their own trajectories; Jesse is lapsing into an opioid stupor. French is still in denial, while at the same time cruising for older men on Grindr. Betty continues to fall apart emotionally and Buck becomes the conduit for a traveler leaving the OA's new dimension.

This contact sends the new five off on a pilgrimage to reunite with the OA, whom all come to believe has successfully incarnated in another dimension. However, Buck fails to tell his parents where he's going, which triggers an Amber alert and an APB on Betty, who is portrayed as a manipulative cult leader who has essentially abducted the youngsters, and not the hapless mess she actually is.

Most of the action takes place in San Francisco, and as such is a lot less interesting a setting for these dramas. Cultists and occultism are nothing new or unusual to the Bay Area, and the rarified air that Nina and Ruskin (and, of course, Marling and Batmanglij) travel through is hard for normal people to relate with.

Kharim's an interesting character, in many ways. He's apparently racked by guilt over his former career as an undercover FBI agent working the sleazy entrapment ops that are the only thing that fucking agency actually does, and Kingsley Ben-Adir is an appealing actor. But I couldn't stop myself from wondering if the character and his arc were actually necessary for the story, or were part of the old Gary 7 internal spinoff routine. And I can't say the second-line characters in this arc were particularly interesting or believable, either.

Another major peeve I had with this series was that the huge chunks of screentime in which the characters explain the story to one another sucked out a lot of that air of mystery here. The exposition in Part Two is very thick, viscous and generously-portioned, and I kept comparing it — unfavorably — to how Lynch and Frost explained next to nothing about very similar themes in the *Twin Peaks* revival.

Don't get me wrong, on the whole I enjoyed Part Two of *The OA* and recommend it, but I didn't feel like I had to go online and read other people's interpretations of what I just watched, never mind argue them, Why? Because Marling and Batmanglij go to such lengths to have their onscreen surrogates spell everything out in excruciating detail.

Even the ending — which some critics have bitched about — wasn't even *close* to a mystery to me. Why? Because the show's rules justified it well ahead of time.

B RIT MARLING IS A FASCINATING CHARACTER. She chose to veer off the elite-career Autobahn (Georgetown, Goldman Sachs, Hollywood) to go make weird, idiosyncratic films and a weird, idiosyncratic Netflix series, ostensibly driven by her own depression. Of course, a pretty strong argument could be made that she's simply taking the scenic route to the same ultimate destination.

And perhaps her messianic tendencies took her off-road as well, since merely being fabulously wealthy didn't seem to suit her emotional needs. It certainly wouldn't be the first time for gifted, privileged people like herself. If that's the case, you'd think she'd work a little harder in making her character as compelling in the second series as she did in the first. I never felt like the OA was a *mystery* I just had to solve in this series. She didn't come across as the otherworldly invader she had been before.

It all felt more than a little *Mulholland Dr.*, to be honest, only it's about a rich and glamorous woman struggling to remember how rich and glamorous she is. Plus, godlike. That's not really a character most people can relate to. I had no problem believing the OA was an incarnate angel in the first series. This time she feels more like Nancy Drew with a trust-fund.

Some have asked me about some of the symbolism dropped here and there, but I didn't really see anything to write home about. I certainly didn't notice anything that felt out of place in the context of the overall themes. Just the New Normal, is all. I did perk up a bit with the (very Lovecraftian) Old Night scene, especially since it was clearly Twinned to that operatic soprano. That was quite, oh, *tantalizing*, but it didn't feel like Marling and Batmanglij would (or could) stick the landing. It also felt a bit *Arrival*, for obvious reasons.

So Part Two of *The OA* is perfectly fine television and well worth a watch. It's nothing like the raging shit-show that *Stranger Things 2* was. I don't know if I'd go out of your way to see it, and I definitely wouldn't recommend you watch if you're feeling a bit blue. Go rewatch *Stripes* or *Grosse Pointe Blank* or something, and save *The OA* for when you're feeling better.

DREAMING OF ME

THE LEPRECHAUN

ONE OF MY BIGGEST INFLUENCES WAS GRAHAM HANCOCK, the pioneering alt.historian and explorer. I once attended a talk on his latest book, *Supernatural*, at New York's Chapel of Sacred Mirrors. Being a Carlos Castaneda fan way back in the day, I dug it. Yet at the same time, I was desperately hoping that people wouldn't use the book as motivation to go out and chug some ayahuasca for themselves. I see that kind of activity as the equivalent of deep sea diving or Antarctic exploration: best left to the experts.

Many of the details in Hancock's talk struck a chord with me. When I was a kid I would get respiratory infections all of the time. As a result I would get terrifyingly high fevers, often peaking at 106°F. As a result of that, I would often hallucinate, a lot. When I was 12, I got a particularly serious ear infection and was bedridden for over two weeks. Actually, I was couch ridden; I was so weakened I couldn't walk up and down the stairs. If I wasn't so incredibly sick it would have been Paradise: nothing to do but lie around and read comics.

One night during this illness, I awoke to a most peculiar scene. A leprechaun was sitting on a rock in the middle of the living room and there was a thunder storm flashing in the adjacent room. I call him a "leprechaun" only because he was small and bearded, and wore archaic clothes and a rope belt. But he didn't seem cute and charming, he seemed scary as hell. He was shouting over the noise of the storm in a language I didn't understand, maybe Gaelic. And at some point the ceiling opened up and gold coins rained from the ceiling. The noise was unbearable and I passed out.

The thing is, that *happened.* It wasn't a dream; it all happened when I woke up and stopped when I passed out. I remember it better than yesterday. I was painfully awake at the time. There were no coins on the floor the next morning, nor any burn marks on the floor or on the furniture in the dining room. But that doesn't mean the episode didn't have weight and mass and sound and sight and smell.

After Hancock's talk I waited in the receiving line and then told him that story. His face lit up and he nodded knowingly the entire time. He told me that my experience was basically identical to any number of the shamanic experiences he heard about in the field. He said that high fever seemed to throw the same filtering switch in the brain that hallucinogens did. I was very gratified by this response, but at the same time I wondered how the hell anyone could put themselves through that kind of thing voluntarily.

When I was a kid it all felt like I was literally going through Hell. Which is probably why I became so obsessed with *Jacob's Ladder.*

MY FAVORITE NIGHTMARES

I CAME TO A STUNNING REALIZATION OVER THE WEEKEND: my most vivid memories are of nightmares that I had as a child. By contrast, even a lot of significant episodes in my life are almost lost to me, appearing only as fragments. My memory has always been a bit impressionistic, constructed not necessarily from events but from their repercussions.

But compared to those nightmares, even this morning is invisible. I'm talking about a level of lucidity that approaches the holographic; memories that I can *inhabit*, virtual-reality style. Most of them transpired during a particularly miserable period in an unhappy childhood, but there a few that came much later, though they mostly harken back to the same period. And oddly enough, most of them share strands of commonality with abduction reports.

Not that I actually believe they were 'screen memories', or dissociative memories of abduction phenomena. The point here is the ability of the mind — particularly the mind of a child — to construct a reality that transcends reality. And a reality that seems to share a frontier with the world of high weirdness, something I was too young to understand at the time.

The hallucinations mostly came later; in fact, they began after a period of powerfully vivid dreaming came to an end, when I was about 9 or 10. It was then that I went, almost inexplicably, from suffering from chronic asthma to dealing with chronic ear infections, which brought on vertigo and the high fevers (105°F was pretty common), which switched on the DMT circuits in my brain. So I learned not only to distrust memory, but my body itself. I still do, in many ways. In fact, when I began my adolescent pharmacratic adventures, it was remarkable how familiar it all seemed. And accordingly, a lot of this came with powerful Synchronistic emanations.

One of my very worst nightmares occurred in a house that responsible and rational people believed to be haunted. So much so that a spirit medium was called in to 'cleanse' the house. I never saw or sensed anything there, at least not consciously. But according to the medium, it was a protective spirit. A family friend spent the night and mistook the entity for another houseguest, only to find out the next morning that no such person existed.

Weirder still, when the guest returned to her own house, it was crawling with snakes. *That* story stuck with me, believe it. The other weird commonality in many of these super-vivid nightmares was a weird kind of plasmic light show, similar to the electrical storm (for lack of a better term) in the Leprechaun hallucination. There are variations on it but it usually appeared indoors.

WORLD'S END: One of the earliest nightmares I remembered didn't include the lightning. My parents are still together, even though I'm probably about four or five. We're going to World's End Park in Hingham to fly kites. But my family leaves me in the car and go off and disappear. I'm sitting in the backseat, alone and afraid.

Then the car starts by itself, is put into gear and drives away while I scream for my mother.

> **Bonus factoid:** World's End was originally tapped to become the site of the United Nations building in 1945, before the Manhattan site was chosen.

CHANNING STREET: I'm five or six, and I'm eating supper in my father's basement apartment on Channing Street off Wollaston Blvd. But I'm also being distracted by the too-bright light in the kitchen nook. And for some reason I then focus my attention on the ketchup bottle.

Suddenly I'm lifted into the air in my chair and whipped around the room, like a hellish amusement park ride. My family doesn't seem to notice; they continue to eat their dinner.

> **Sync Log:** In January 2007, a pod of dolphins was washed up on Wollaston Beach, less than a block away from the Channing St apartment. "Nobody I've talked to can ever remember a mass stranding of dolphins in Boston Harbor," said Tony LaCasse, spokesman for the New England Aquarium. "These dolphins were completely out of their winter habitat."
>
> Bonus Sync: This is the same neighborhood in which the first mass pagan ritual was held by Europeans in the Americas, and was dubbed 'Mount Dagon' by the Pilgrims.

THE MUMMY: This one is similar, but here the lightning appears. I'm five or six, and in a room I don't recognize. The ceilings are very high and made of glass. It's dark outside and my grandmother is babysitting my older sister and I.

The light storm suddenly appears, but inside the room. My sister and my Nana go blank, like they were switched off. A giant enters the room. It looks like a weird combination of Frankenstein and the Mummy, but also almost like an alien. It's coming for me.

> **Bonus Sync:** I can't find the reference, but I've since read reports of aliens matching that description in UFO literature.

THE REN: It's a beautiful morning. I'm six years old and I'm in the hospital, but I think I'm about to go home. I look under the bed and I see myself, hiding under the bed. He/Me has a big smile on his face, but he's scaring the shit out of me.

I ask him who he is. "I'm your Ren," he replies, smiling.

> **Bonus Sync:** I found out much later that the Ren is part of the Soul in Egyptian religion. There's no way in hell I knew that when I was six.
>
> The Ren is part of the Book of Breathings, and respiratory illness was the reason I spent a huge chunk in my early childhood in the hospital.
>
> Amy Bishop spent a lot of her childhood there as well, for the very same reason. How's that for a coincidence?

HOLE IN THE WALL: I had this nightmare in the haunted house, but it took place in Braintree. My sister and I had switched rooms for some reason. I'm in her room, and we're playing with giant Disneyland-type cartoon characters. We're very happy, but it's time for me to go to bed. I open the door to my room, but there's a man standing there in the dark.

I knock on my mother's door, open it and stand by the hole my father punched in the bedroom wall before he left. But the lightning is flashing in her room, and she screams at me when I tell her there's someone in my room. I can't hear her over the sound of the storm.

Suddenly, a hand bursts out of the hole in the wall and grabs onto my arm.

> I remember this better than I remember my breakfast. I can still hear the man in the dark room breathing, and feel that hand's iron grip. Just thinking about it makes my throat close up. I can still feel that grip on my wrist, even now.

THE SECRET SUN: That's the first of the many dreams that gave this blog its name. I wake up in the middle of the night and the Sun is out. But it looks wrong; the shadows are too deep. There's a giant out there again, this time it looks like a robot. It looks as if looking for something, and I realize it's looking for me.

> **Bonus Sync:** As with Channing Street, there was an extremely weird dolphin death a few years back a literal stone's throw from my old house in Braintree in the Monatiquot River, hundred miles away from their natural waters.

KNOCK, KNOCK: This was the worst of them all, because it was the most plausible. It never fails to put goosebumps on my forearms, since I'm only 99.9% convinced it didn't actually happen, and I can't remember in the context of waking up in terror from it like the rest of them.

It's nearly nine o'clock at night. My mother tells me she has to run down to Weymouth Landing to the store before it closes. I ask here to take me with her, because I'm afraid to be home alone. She gets irritated and tells me she won't be long. She leaves and I sit in the kitchen alone.

Then a knock comes at the back door but I don't see anyone there. I'm scared shitless.

The knock comes again. I sit there terrified. Again. And then it stops.

Then all at once all of the doors and drawers in the house begin opening and closing by themselves, loudly, violently and rapidly.

> **Bonus Sync:** This is the same back door that my mother had nightmares about in the same exact spot I had the Leprechaun visitation. As I wrote in the Owls post: "Now, I have no reason at all to believe that my mother was an alien abductee, but there is one particular story I remember her telling me.
>
> "She said that just before I was born she put my sister down for naps and then would often take one herself. But my mother would have this recurring nightmare that a 'witch' was on the porch and was trying to come into the house while she was asleep on the sofa."

KNOCK, KNOCK, PART 2: It's October 1983 and I'm 17. I'm with my mother and step-father, watching television in the Leprechaun room. It's late and we're worried because my sister hasn't come home yet. The light show starts up in the next room, but I realize that it's a police cruiser parked in front of the house. Now we're in a panic.

There's a loud knock at the front door, I go to answer it.

I open the door and there's a uniformed cop on the porch. The only problem is that he doesn't have a face. Without saying a word, the faceless cop takes out his gun and shoots me in the chest.

> **Bonus factoid:** If you saw the *Intruders* film, you remember the scene when the utility workers come to the abductee's front door. That was eerily similar to this. Or at least it felt eerily similar to this.

THE PILOT: When I was a kid, my mother had a nightclub act. As a result the families of the performers kind of formed a big clan. We socialized, we summered together, we went on vacations together. However, one of our group — a fourteen year-old boy — was very suspiciously killed three days after Christmas, by a gunshot through the heart, at point-blank range. This cemented the suspicion in my young mind that life was just a string of miseries, interrupted only by sporadic bouts of horror.

In my dream, I return and bring my wife and two-year old son to meet his family. But they had changed in the dream: they're involved in some weird kind of witchcraft. There's a giant magic circle painted into the wall of their basement and they're all wearing matching tie-dye shirts.

They all keep looking at us very strangely and I quickly realize they've all come to believe that they could bring their son back to life by sacrificing another little boy, who would guide the dead boy's spirit back from the Underworld.

I them realize that they want to use my son as their guide. The next thing I knew, I am tear-assing out of the house with my son in my arms.

One of the sisters comes out of the house, points at us and screams, "Stop him! He has the Pilot!"

Note: This is all inspired by the usual pop ooccultism that was popular when I was spending time with these people and not anything they were actually involved in, at least to the best of my knowledge.

However, There's a lot more to all of this that I can't tell you about, some very unsettling and disturbing real-life events, more recently. But they have less to do with black magic, and more to do with flesh and blood bad elements operating in the area.

NO NEW YORK

THE TERM 'SECRET SUN' DATES BACK TO MY CHILDHOOD. It refers to a recurring dream I've had since I was very young in which the Sun comes out in the middle of the night, but only a select few know about it. I've written about this in the past, most recently in this post about my childhood nightmares. What I didn't tell you is where these Secret Sun dreams take place.

I actually coined the term "Secret Sun" sitting in the 33rd St PATH station one day in 1996, since I had to come with a name for a project. A woman was reading a Gabriel Garcia Marquez book that looked like it had an eclipse on the cover, and suddenly the phrase popped into my head. I've been never able to find the book cover in question, even after all these years.

ONE OF THE GREAT JOYS OF DOING THIS KIND OF WORK is when a certain word or phrase catches your ear and in doing so unlocks new doors or puts long-missing pieces of the puzzle into place. I thought of the phrase 'only a select few know about' the Secret Sun while reading about Jacques Vallée's theories of the other-dimensional realm ("Magonia") he believes UFOs and other manifestations of the Paranormal spring from:

> A second and equally widespread theory is that Elfland constitutes a sort of parallel universe, which coexists with our own. It is made visible and tangible only to selected people, and the 'doors' that lead through it are tangential points, known only to the elves. - *Passport to Magonia*, Jacques Vallée

And there it was: "*tangible only to selected people.*" Different phrasing, but the same basic idea. The Magonia that Vallée refers too comes from one of history's most interesting UFO flaps, this one from the reign of Charlemagne in the 10th Century CE. Just as today, Medieval France had bitter, acid-tongued skeptics, dunking on the rural bumpkins for their ignorance and credulity. Only the skeptic in question was an Archbishop named Agobard, ironically enough.

> But we have seen and heard of many people overcome with so much foolishness, made crazy by so much stupidity, that they believe and say that there is a certain region, which is called Magonia, from which ships come in the clouds.

> In these ships the crops that fell because of hail and were lost in storms are carried back into that region; evidently these aerial sailors make a payment to the storm-makers, and take the grain and other crops.

NOW JUST AS THOSE SHIPS IN THE CLOUDS belong to another world not our own, so too does the secret sun. These dreams usually take place in another Manhattan, unlike our own, filled with vast, hidden, endless suburban neighborhoods encircling the great skyscrapers.

But there are other clues to this Not New York; I often enter on foot through marshlands and leave through grand, sun-drenched highways with route names of probable numerological portent. This is another world with another Sun. I only ever remember one person from the real world appearing in these dreams. Back in February of 2006, I wrote to her about it:

> We took a shortcut through a marsh, and you made me carry you through the puddly parts. I explained to you that I still believed in chivalry.
>
> 'Anyway, we got lost and ended up in New York. Then it was 1:30. I asked you if the sun was always out in New York at 1:30 in the morning. You said yeah, and it was getting on your nerves. You're the first real person to appear in a Secret Sun dream, so you should feel highly honored.

And strangely enough, I had another marsh dream which I wrote to another friend about the following month:

> I was walking with my father to his house and we got lost in a church basement that opened into a marsh. We went upstairs and found ourselves on the deck of the Starship Enterprise. Data was reporting on the bird flu crisis. All I wanted was to do was get to my father's house, so we left the deck and were back in the swamp.
>
> Data and some female officer came with us to my car. I said "Data, I hope to hell you know how to drive, because we just want to get to my dad's house." I turned around and Data was holding a gun to my father's head. I asked what him what the hell he was doing.
>
> He responded, *"You are when it's going to happen."*

I think the dream was a protective wish-fulfillment, because my friend was in the midst of a serious cancer scare and my subconscious associated hospitals with danger. In fact, she appeared in another Secret Sun dream not long after. It wouldn't be until many years later than any other real person would guest-star in one. But what struck me with this *Star Trek* dream and the recurring Secret Sun dream is that the marsh was a *gateway*, a physical door to another physical world.

I've since read that it's long been believed that swamps are exactly that.

IT'S NO GAME

NOT TO BE TRIFLED WITH

MOST PEOPLE DON'T REALLY BELIEVE IN THE SPIRIT WORLD, and that even includes a lot of people who say they do. Because if you really <u>do</u> believe, you will treat the spirit realm like you would a fallen power line during an ice storm. Only it's even more dangerous precisely because its effects aren't as apparent. I realize I can sound like a scold when it comes to this stuff, but that's not because I'm a killjoy. It's because I care about people, and because early life experience taught me that spirits are most definitely not to be trifled with.

I've talked before about how my mother was a professional musician when I was growing up. She had a performing company that played the big nightclubs in the area, one of which was owned by the Irish mob. She had three main partners, two singers and a costume designer. They had kids of their own so we kind of formed into a tribe of sorts, and spent a lot of time together in my formative years. We all used to spend summers together at a vacation cottage in Gloucester, right up the Old Nugent Farm Road from Good Harbor Beach. Sometimes it could be downright magical, like when I was on the beach and first heard 'Waterloo'.

Seeing how this was the early Seventies, we were also playing with Ouija boards and having séances and all that kind of stuff. We all used to walk down to Calvary Cemetery at night and do séances and ghost-hunts and stuff there, particularly in the summer of '74 when *The Exorcist* was all the rage. And as it happens, that was the absolute worst place we could be doing such things.

First of all, we were smack dab in the heart of Lovecraft country. Some researchers have named Gloucester as the real-life Innsmouth, with its town hall generally acknowledged as HPL's model for the Esoteric Order of Dagon lodge. Second, Gloucester was the site where the township of Salem was originally settled, before the townsfolk moved to find more fertile farmland.

And worst of all, Calvary Cemetery was on the eastern border of the old Babson Farm, where one of the strangest Paranormal events in Colonial American history took place. In the summer of 1692, old man Babson spotted two mysterious figures he thought were soldiers marching around his land. That number grew to three, and then six, and rumor spread they were French spies. The local militia spotted the figures and tried gunning them down, but their targets moved unnaturally fast when taking fire.

A local minister by the name of Reverend John Emerson reported on the bizarre events to no less than Cotton Mather, the prominent Boston clergymen who'd become world famous that very same summer for his work for the prosecution of the Salem Witch Trials.

Emerson wrote:

> "Babson saw three men walk softly out of the swamp. Being within two or three rods of them he shot, and as soon as his gun went off they all fell down. Babson, then running to his supposed prey, cried out unto his companion...'He had killed three!.'
>
> But coming about unto them they all rose up."

So yeah, a *really* bad idea holding séances on that particular spot. We were just dumb kids, but the powers we were trifling with didn't care, the same way the electrical socket doesn't care how old the kid sticking the butterknife in it is. And so it was that one of our clan would be killed shortly before year's end, shot through the heart under extremely suspicious circumstances. Circumstances, incidentally, that involved the US Army Intelligence School, formerly known as Fort Devens. And unfortunately, the trouble wouldn't end with his death. Not by a long shot.

That was Lesson #1. Lesson #2 would come some years later, and also involved cemeteries.

The night Hurricane Gloria made landfall in the US, two of my rocket-scientist roommates decided it would be a really excellent time to desecrate a grave. The big idea was that it might have old jewelry in it that they might be able to hock. Did I mention these guys first met in jail? Do I even need to?

Anyhow, the would-be grave-robbers brought some others along with them to the cemetery, all of whom were either in the middle of a bad acid trip or coming down from one. So you not only had all the hurricane overhead while a couple of idiots dug up a grave, you also had some human antennas plugged straight into the nether regions of the spirit world. How the entire neighborhood didn't go up in black flame that night is still a mystery to me.

Anyway, the two ex-cons dug up the grave and popped open the casket, but found nothing but some poor soul's earthly remains. Not content with mere grave desecration, they decided to move on to defiling a corpse and played a game of catch with the skull. Apparently they then thought to themselves, "You know would be even more excellent? If we brought the headstone from this defiled grave back to the house and kept it under the stairs." I think they might have spent the rest of the evening sticking their scwheens in the light sockets. I'm not sure, I'll have to check my diary.

Mind you, no one knew anything about magic or the spirit world back then. But they might as well have just burned the house down anyway, because everything there got really weird, dark and ugly, almost immediately.

And it stayed that way until our landlord showed up one fine day with some hired goon and a Rottweiler and chased everyone home at the time out the door. The would-be grave robbers weren't even there by that point. The bad mojo they kicked up drove them out months before that. Believe it or not, one of them would ultimately end up as a director on a long-running TV series. Hollywood, am I right?

Anyway, my future wife and I had a chat with the old woman next door as we left the witch house for good. The woman said she recently had the FBI holed up on the second floor of her house, since they were allegedly running surveillance on the house down the street. The only problem was that you couldn't actually see the place in question from her house. Moreover, the entire time we lived there I never saw a single soul go in or out of that house.

However, we did have a guy in and out of *our* house who the FBI might have had more than a casual interest in. Let's call him "the Warlock." He was a part-time retailer for drug traffickers out of Philadelphia and a full-time New Age mystic. And as Fate would have it, he first showed up at our house the night of the hurricane. He was there because one of the trippers called him and asked him to come over because she was starting to freak out and needed some mystic TLC. This guy had a real mystique about him, it must be said.

The Warlock also had some loose affiliation with the Grateful Dead that I could never pin down, and at one point had spent a week up at Hunter S. Thompson's place. He said Thompson didn't sleep the entire week, and spent most of his time screaming and hollering at everyone and shooting at trees. Much to my chagrin, the Warlock started coming over to work my telephone with his clientele. His idea of speaking in code was telling them he had something that "smelled good" when he was selling coke. Fucking moron.

Later, it occurred to me that our landlord — who was otherwise a very cool guy — freaked out so bad because he caught wind of the fact that the Feds were next door and he had a bunch of hippie-punk degenerates living in his property. My wife and I filed charges against him and took him to court. He got hit with a big fine and looked rather miserable that day. Did I mention the landlord was an absolute dead ringer for Robert DeNiro as Rupert Pupkin in *The King of Comedy?* No? Well, he was.

Anyhow, the Warlock showed up at the very big and very old house where my future wife and I were living, and asked if he could rent a room. I said that was fine, just as long as he didn't keep any drugs in the house or do any dealing on the phone. I told him the local cops had absolutely nothing to do in that town (except harass black folks unlucky enough to be driving through), and I didn't want them paying us any mind. He said that was OK, since he was working on a book and was trying to leave dealing behind.

So this cat decided one day it was time for me to be initiated as a warlock, and built a rather impressive stone altar out in the woods, literally overnight. He had the blade and the chalice and the rest of it, and burned sage and frankincense and waved his arms around and chanted a bunch of shit I didn't understand and don't remember. Then he had me stand at the altar while he dashed off into the forest.

I guess the idea was something was going to approach me or possess me, but I just stood there feeling like the stupidest asshole in the world. Seeing him pop his head out from behind various trees only made the cringe worse.

Did I mention the property we were living on had been in my wife's family since the early 1700s? I didn't? Well, let me just put that out there because of, y'know, *ancestor spirits*.

So the Warlock then disappeared for a little while. I think the Dead were blowing through town, or he went out west for the Rainbow Nation gathering or whatever. We didn't hear from him until he called from the hospital and asked us to pick him up. We did so and were shocked to see his face smashed up, his nose and cheek were broken, as were all his front teeth. It was the night of the 18th of October, 1986. I remember the day very well because there was a full moon.

So we ask him what happened and he tells us how he wiped out on his bicycle and landed on his face. I asked why he was on his bike, and he said he was going to the bus station. My hackles arose immediately, so I asked him where he was taking the bus to and he said Philadelphia. Then I flipped out, and said, "So you were going to Philly to meet up with your connection. Which means you were going to do exactly what I fucking told you not to do and keep drugs in this house. You fucking got what was coming to you."

I think I also pointed out that I was a Moon Child and it was a full moon, bla bla bla whatever. Which was really quite bold of me, because I idolized this guy at the time. Soon after that, he took off for good, leaving his rent and share of the phone bill several months overdue.

So do I think the Warlock got his face smashed in because he was messing around with very old and very easily-offended spirits in those woods? Well, let's just say I wouldn't be surprised, with the timing and all. Let's also just say I would never want to put myself into a situation where I was doing rituals in a place I knew absolutely nothing about, messing with spirits that may well not appreciate being trifled with. That never ends well.

BORNE IN FLAMES

IN 2008, I WAS INVITED OUT TO JEFF KRIPAL'S first 'Superpowers and the Supernormal' symposium at Esalen, on the recommendation of Roy Thomas, the legendary Marvel writer and editor. Strangely enough, I had just interviewed Chris Carter for *The Complete X-Files* book the day before I flew out. Roy and I had worked together before, and had long conversations in the dining hall about the Silver Age of Marvel.

Since my presentation was on 'The Synchro-Mysticism of Jack Kirby' we also spoke quite a bit about Kirby and his relationship with Stan, as well as Ditko. None of this was academic to Roy, since he was often caught in the middle of the struggles between the three titans of the Marvel Age, and was Stan's go-between with Jack after he left for DC in the early Seventies.

The trip turned out to be a turning point for this blog in other ways; I met, spoke to and listened to presentations by Jacques Vallée and Bertrand Méheust (whose presentation on UFOs was every bit as synchromystic as mine on Kirby).

All of this was pretty eye-opening since I hadn't given much thought to the UFO topic in 10 years at that point. Like many other people, I'd followed the 'nuts-n-bolts' approach to a dead-end, lost interest and moved onto other things. When I tried discussing old sightings and reports and such with Bertrand, he looked at me like I was a pitiable thing, hopelessly trapped in a useless paradigm. It would take me a little while before I understood where that look was coming from.

But it would be Russell Targ's presentation which would set an unconscious fire that I'm just now coming to understand. As some of you may know, Russell was the director of the remote viewing program at the Stanford Research Institute for many years and worked with people like Ingo Swann and Joe McMoneagle.

But if I was apathetic about UFOs in 2008, I was downright dismissive of remote viewing. My previous exposure to RV came through Art Bell and Ed Dames (the basis for the Kevin Spacey character in *The Men Who Stare at Goats*) and all of the rest of it, so basically my impression was that 'RV=disinfo hoax'. Russell quickly disabused me of that notion. He's not the hoaxer type (neither is Ed May, who presented on RV in 2009) and his presentation had me spellbound. What sealed the deal for me was a test he ran, where he produced a brown paper bag with an object in it. The group was to try to picture and then draw the object. I drew the silhouette of its profile my first try (it was an unusually shaped apple corer) and one of the others (a regional MUFON director, oddly enough) actually named it.

Not psychic spy grade stuff, certainly, but enough to capture my attention. And then the High Weirdness started.

Soon after I flew home, a 'freak' electrical storm in Humboldt County started a raging series of wildfires that tore down the California coast, raged throughout Big Sur, and licked at Esalen's gates for days before dying out. I should note that myself and a couple other Esalen newbies were feeling very weird and emotional the week we were there, for reasons I can't explain.

Shortly after that, I started getting all these weird phone calls from a state prison in Florida. I didn't know anyone in jail in Florida. And when I answered them, all I could ever hear was a completely unintelligible robotic voice.

Then one horrible day in August, two large black dogs that no one had ever seen before stormed into my yard and murdered one of my cats, while my new neighbors watched in horror. The dogs then ran off, never to be seen again. The neighbors were too afraid to get of their car so they honked their horn until we came out of the house.

I called the cops. It took a single female officer over an hour to show up because there had been some major disaster in town somewhere, and all available squad cars were dealing with the aftermath. I should add that it was one of those days when the sky was just *wrong,* if you know what I mean.

To top it all off, I went out to the store for a couple things on the evening of October 13th. I returned only to find the street filled with fire engines and police cruisers. As I slowly drove down the street I realized to my horror that it was actually my fucking house that was on fire, and my wife and kids were sitting on the back of an ambulance, being attended to by paramedics for smoke inhalation.

Luckily, the firehouse is around the corner and the volunteers were in-house that night, so damage was contained to the bedroom. It could very easily have been much, much worse. Even so, I felt like I was living in a summer stock production of *The Mothman Prophecies*. If something was indeed trying to get my attention, mission accomplished.

IT'S NO GAME

THERE'S SO MUCH STUPID OUT THERE that sometimes it gets pretty hard to figure out which particular flavor of stupid takes the cake. But my vote goes to all these idiots who dick around with black magic in hopes of scoring virtue points with Twitter bluechecks. And by that I mean numb-nuts who screw around with hexes and curses in hopes of making some kind of political statement, however garbled. I mean, why not just try juggling chainsaws? It's probably a lot safer in the long run.

On the face of it, this little LARP is little more than silly and inert. What's more, I seriously doubt most of these people really believe in any of it. It's just a minor Millennial fad, really. Nothing to think twice about. Well, nothing for you or I to think twice about, unless we're hankering for a good smirk.

But here's the thing: these symbols and names have been around for a very, very long time. So for the sake of argument, let's assume that there may be spiritual entities lurking behind these spells and icons. Very, very old entities that have seen entire empires off. If so, do you really think they'd appreciate some hipster dysphorics constantly ringing them up and demanding that they take sides in some dumb-ass partisan pissing match?

And why do these fools always assume that someone like Trump or Kavanaugh don't have a bunch of conjurers in their own corners already? It beggars belief. I guess for the same reason they need to believe that no one might be throwing hexes back at their dilettante asses. Like maybe someone who actually knows what they're doing?

I realize these fake witches are totally programmed by the corporate media, but do they really think those Republican types actually *believe* in the religions they give lip service to for Bible Belt votes? And how often do these spells need to fail before these folks shuffle back to their Maoist macaroni-art or Anarcho-Syndicalist interpretive dance? I guess some folks just don't get the message.

WE SAW THE EXACT SAME KIND OF FOOLISHNESS back in the 1980s. The parents of these preening poseurs actually believed that Reagan and his coterie were all a bunch of Bible-bashing yahoos who were out to create some ridiculous *Handmaid's Tale* fantasy world. Risibly stupid, I know.

Still, you heard this line morning, noon, and night for years until former White House Chief of Staff Don Regan revealed that a San Francisco astrologer named Joan Quigley was the real power behind the throne, and that the Gipper couldn't even wipe his ass without her writing up a chart first.

And that was *Reagan*, who was raised in a far more innocent age and place than the current occupant of the Oval Office. Does anyone believe for a second that Trump isn't deep into some weird shit, or at the very least pays someone to be into it for him? A New Yorker, from a very weird and very connected family, who spent his career in Atlantic City gambling and Manhattan real estate? A guy who used to throw drag parties at Trump Tower, and taped his game show at the open-air Mithraic Shrine known as Rockefeller Plaza for a decade and change? I mean, get real.

NOW, I DON'T WANT TO GIVE ANY OF THIS NONSENSE more credit than it's worth, but it speaks to a larger issue that's been weighing on my mind lately. And that's the fact that more and more people out there seem to be acting as if they're demonically-possessed. To tell you the truth, it's actually starting to get a little concerning.

You can look it all in purely secular and psychological terms (and perhaps in most cases, you probably should), but that's just a question of your own personal bias. But the constant barrage of occult symbolism out there, overt or covert, isn't being shoved down everyone's throats for giggles and grins.

These symbols have also been around for a long time and have been pretty well road-tested. They *do stuff,* however you choose to explain how or why. Toss that in with all the divide-and-rule tactics — which are the worst I've seen in my lifetime — and you've got a handy recipe for a mass psychic meltdown.

As cliché as it might sound, it reminds me very much like ancient Babylon, particularly during the Neo-Assyrian period. And that's what troubles me, since even a cursory glance at some of the literature from that era depicts a population who were all teetering on the verge of a mass psychic meltdown. Demons were said to be absolutely *everywhere* at all times. And witchcraft and/ or magic were practiced by pretty much everyone. In many ways, that was the true religion of the people. Some great literature came out of this time, such as the more metal-than-metal *Maqlû* (from which Peter Levenda gleefully ripped off for his *Necronomicon*) and the *Šurpu*.

But you also had a corpus of laments that seem to paint the picture of a culture trapped in the teeth of the black dog of depression:

> My god has forsaken me and disappeared,
> My goddess has failed me and keeps at a distance.
> The benevolent angel who walked beside me has departed,
> My protecting spirit has taken to flight, and is seeking someone else.
> My strength is gone; my appearance has become gloomy;
> My dignity has flown away, my protection made off...

And we all knew how it ended up not long after.

Namely with a Persian fellow named Cyrus the Great blowing into town and making Babylon — the breathtaking envy of the entire world for centuries — his personal footstool. That's the thing with trafficking with spirits; they're fickle as hell. Or so I've been told.

Now, any random Babylonian kindergartener was probably better-versed in magic than these poor fake witch squibs with their sad Trump 'spells', but that same kid probably was taught to be a good deal more circumspect about using it. I have no doubt that these people don't actually *believe* in magic, because if they did they wouldn't be nearly as thoughtless about using it. Why? Because the only way you believe in magic is having experienced it and that usually entails a lot of having your ass kicked by it. That's my understanding, at least.

L ET'S JUST SUPPOSE THERE'S SOME ANCIENT ENTITIES with the power to change the course of history. Why the fuck would they care if you sat around and lit candles and blew smoke up their asses? What's in it for them? How exactly would you even get their attention? I mean, how did real witches get the spirit world's attention?

I hate to break the news to everyone who's thrilled to the feminist-vegan-Wiccan wisdom of Marjorie Von Wombat-Raven and Gertrude Silver-Squirrel, but real witches got themselves noticed by *killing* things and offering them up to whatever demon they were asking to throw a curse at their husband's mistress or catamite.

I mean, god-damned *housewives* thought nothing of slitting a lamb or piglet's throat at some minor ritual to some minor god or goddess at some minor shrine. You think actual witches settled for *less* than that? I mean, I realize *you* don't think that, but those Tumblrista feebs in Brooklyn seem to. So, yeah, the spirits are most definitely not vegans. Have I said that before? Well, it bears repeating.

That's what's so brilliant to me about *A Dark Song*. Sure, the gates get good and opened, but only after long, excruciating months of pain and terror. Angels and demons both seem to enjoy human suffering as much as they love blood and death. If you want them to fudge your cosmic tax returns you'd better be willing to pony up the pain, bitch. And no half-measures, either. Half-measures seem to earn you double the life-fucking, for some reason. Just natural facts.

You see, however you choose to define or explain it, all this magic shit has real consequences. It's not a hobby and it's not a game. Fuck around with it with imperfect courage and a lack of humility? Best-case scenario, you'll go insane. Worst case, you kill yourself. But only after everyone and everything you care about is destroyed.

But even if you approach it with utter dedication, there's still no guarantee it won't destroy you. There's a very long line of brilliant magicians — men with intellects that'd make Einstein or Hawking weep in desolate despair — who were annihilated by their commerce with deal-making spirits. Look it up if you don't believe me.

Again, think about it rationally. I fully realize that's a raging oxymoron in this case, but humor me; if you really believe there are powers that are able to overrule the laws of physics and causality on your behalf, what's in it for *them*? I mean, *why* would they?

The only reason I can think of is that *they're planning on eating your fucking soul*, only they're not going to let you know that until they've set their table and poured the Merlot. And again, if you want to take a reductionistic, psychiatric kind of POV on all this, be my guest. It all ends up going down the same hole either way.

DON'T GET ME WRONG, there really isn't an epidemic of dimwits screwing around with black magic out there. Not by any means. But there doesn't need to be for things to get good and fucked up.

Terence McKenna once said that a healthy society could only afford to have some minuscule proportion of the population seriously involved with psychedelics. I forget the exact figure, but it was something like .025% or something. Double that number to .05% and things got very shaky, or so the Bard seemed to think. For my dollar the exact same can be said about the occult. Which may be exactly why so many people out there seem to have become demon-possessed and/or ragingly psychopathic. You can only bend a paperclip so much before it breaks, if you get my meaning.

So, Tarot cards, Ouija boards, ritual magick, astrology? If you're not willing to give yourself completely over to them, I say leave it all to the adepts, the ones willing to accept the consequences if it all goes tits-up. And by if, I mean "when." Same way climbing skyscrapers and diving off cliffs can be quite thrilling to watch, but they're not really something you can *dabble* in. Absolute best-case scenario is that you just waste a lot of time and money and those pesky spirits pay you no never mind.

Call me a square, call me a stick in the mud, whatever you like. Go to town. But I believe any halfway qualified magus will tell you the exact same thing. Believe me, I wouldn't bother to say anything if I didn't care. I realize this sounds ridiculously corny, but I only want everyone to be happy and want everything to work out OK. I'm sure that will be my ultimate undoing.

TWO MAGICIANS WALK INTO A BAR...

TWO MAGICIANS WALK INTO A BAR, a fashionable new joint in Williamsburg with exposed brick walls and artfully-painted pipes and ductwork along the ceiling. They take a seat at a table near the back. The room is dimly but artfully lit, offering up a faintly conspiratorial atmosphere for the upwardly-mobile patrons enjoying the early Spring afternoon.

The magicians are old friends, but have gone in very different directions in recent years. The first magician orders the latest, hippest craft beer - a winter wheat number with a ginger infusion - and the other orders a black coffee. The jukebox is especially loud and obnoxious in this joint, but at least the music is good; a carefully-curated selection of vintage Sixties rock and Seventies soul.

"So I wanted to touch base with you and see how your work has been progressing," the first magician says, carefully sipping from his wheat beer, then carefully dabbing at the foam on hip lips with a cloth napkin. "I've been making some major strides with my own practices."

The other magician eyes his companion, careful not to betray a hint of skepticism. "Really," he says neutrally. "What kind of strides are those?"

"I'm working with some people I met on Facebook. They're working in a number of different modalities and doing some really exciting things," the first magician replies cheerily.

"What kind of modalities are those?" the other magician says, sipping at his coffee, struggling to disguise his growing unease. It's very good coffee and he's grateful to have something else to focus his attention on.

"Well, the dominant praxis is based in the Obeah tradition, but we're working in a number of different indigenous modalities and finding points of congruence among them," the first magician says, arthymically drumming his fingers on the table to an early Funkadelic number. "I'm considering becoming a priest in a Hoodoo coven operating out of Portland, which also incorporates Alexandrian and Chaos magic, as well as some Dianic and Tantric practices. I may have to leave the Golden Dawn order I'm involved with, though. It's considered an expression of vestigial imperialism in certain circles. It is, when you think about it. All of its rituals are based in Medieval European monarchial rites. But the Order is falling apart anyway."

"I see," the other answers, stirring his coffee, even though he takes it black. Staring hard at his cup, he asks, "And you don't find that problematic at all?"

A 'hoodoo coven', for fuck's sake. How do you join a coven in Portland when you live in Park Slope?

"What do you mean?" his friend replies, with more than a slight hint of indignation.

"Can traditions be divorced from the cultures that birthed them?" the other asks. "Can you just take bits and pieces at will like that? Isn't this just consumerism run amok?"

"What are you talking about?" the first magician says. "That's the way magic has always worked. Religion, culture, everything."

"What I'm trying to say is that you grew up eating Cheerios and watching *He-Man* and *Transformers* in the suburbs, not on a Haitian sugar plantation," the second magician replies. "I know where your parents live, their house would have been considered a lavish castle in the Antebellum South. Don't you think you're engaging in... *cultural appropriation* by assuming that Hoodoo or Obeah is yours for the taking? What dues have you paid to justify reinventing yourself as a Hoodoo man?"

"Listen, as a victim of late-stage capitalism, I — *we* — are all paying some heavy dues, especially with the current occupant of the White House," his table-mate replies, despite the fact that he is pulling in a mid six-figure salary as a systems analyst. "We have been robbed of our own ancient traditions. The patriarchal Abrahamic religions wiped out the indigenous faith of my Celtic forebears. I consider it an act of resistance to submit myself to a system that was birthed by the marginalized and the oppressed."

The first magician takes another sip of his wheat beer and practices his hard look, stung by the insinuation that he'd stoop to something as offensive as culto-spiritual appropriation. *Theft*, in other words. No better than a Eighteenth Century slave trader.

The second magician decides to let it pass. "What kind of results are you seeing?" he asks instead, trying to re-steer the dialogue.

"Results?" his friend replies.

"Yes, what kind of *results* are you getting from the work? Are you keeping a journal?"

"Sure. But this isn't like rubbing a magic lamp and asking a djinn for three wishes. This is about exploration, self-discovery, self-actualization. We're not doing this to make withdrawals from the spirit-world ATM."

"OK," the second magician says. Since when wasn't magic about results? Therapeutic New Age happy-talk was everywhere now.

A waiter approaches to ask if they want to order anything from the kitchen. The first magician orders zucchini sticks, his companion orders buffalo wings. The arrival was well-timed, since it broke the tension building between the two old friends.

"So what kind of blood sacrifices are you partaking in?" the second magician inquires and immediately regrets the slip, which immediately kickstarts his companion's pissiness again.

"Is that some kind of joke?" the first magician replies angrily. "We take it as a vow to do no harm to any sentient creature. I'm a practicing vegan now. Most of us are. I've had a lot of requests for curses; y'know, binding spells, even love spells. But we don't work that way."

"These traditions you're working with take animal sacrifice for granted. They have for a very long time. It's the currency of their spirit world. Hell, even Greek housewives brought sacrificial piglets and lambs to Mystery cults as the price of admission. At one time or other, every religion in the known world practiced blood sacrifice. It was the basis of temple worship in Judaism, all over the Mediterranean. Those Celtic forebears of yours didn't even blink at human sacrifice. It was the foundation of their belief system. Same goes with the Norse. Same goes for the Phoenicians, the Canaanites, Mesoamericans. I mean, why should these spirits or gods grant you favors if you aren't willing to give them something in return?"

"You sound like you're on a dangerous path, my friend," the first magician says, and begins scanning the room for a familiar face so he could get up and escape this conversation.

"Me? No. I'm not the one claiming to rewrite ancient traditions to suit my needs. Animal sacrifice is not an opt-out in those traditions, it's part of the code. Always has been. Civil rights battles have been fought in court over preserving these practices. But here's the deal; if you're not willing to make *some* kind of meaningful sacrifice to the these spirits, who've been expecting them for thousands of years, then at some point sacrifices will be made *for* you. And I guarantee that you won't like that."

An uncomfortable silence takes hold. Both magicians stare hard at their cups and consider their next volley.

"I don't know where all this is coming from," the first magician says, still studying the foam in his beer. "I was really looking forward to a meeting of the minds with you today."

"It's coming from concern for your safety and well-being," his friend replies. "Folk magic is not a hobby, it's not the latest boho fad. You and your friends are dabbling in systems that can't just be rewritten to suit the needs of post-industrial urban professionals. It's not a steam table at a buffet restaurant. These are not systems you can *curate*. You're dealing with the *premodern*, not the postmodern."

"What does that even mean?" the first magician asks.

"It means that things have rules for a reason. And these are systems that based in deal-making with spirits who don't really give a shit whether you live or die. Just whether or not you can be useful to *them*."

"You're being seriously overly dramatic," the first magician says, "I know people who've been working with these systems for years, and haven't experienced anything like that."

"Haven't they? Maybe they just haven't made the connection. The spirits don't usually send you emails when they decide to fuck up your shit. Well, if you know their language you'll most certainly get the message. But first you need to let go of the illusion that the Universe is constantly conspiring on your behalf."

The first magician scoffs and begins scanning the room again.

"Listen, if you want to pursue all this, I can't stop you," the second magician says. "All I can say is that you can't separate blood and sacrifice from religions that have been focused around blood and sacrifice for millennia. You can certainly try, but at some point blood and sacrifice will come into your life whether you want it to or not. You might be a vegan but these spirits are most definitely carnivores."

"What happened to you, man?" the first magician asks, testily. "You sound like some friggin' church lady."

"No, I sound like a magician."

ASK WHO'S KNOCKING BEFORE YOU LET THEM IN

YESTERDAY, I WAS CHECKING OUT SOME PODCASTS on the phenomenon known as 'Black Eyed Children'. My normality-bias would generally have me file the BEKs in with Slenderman and other creepy pasta icons of the New American Nightmare, so I was surprised to hear there's been some actual research on the alleged phenomenon.

One of the alleged defining characteristics of the alleged phenomenon caught my attention. These strange children — who some theorize are human/alien hybrids, others identify as interdimensional demons — usually show up knocking at your door and asking to come inside. As with the old vampire stories, they need *permission* to enter your home. The lore goes a bit soft when dealing with stories of kids who are invited in, but apparently nothing good comes of it.

I haven't done enough research on the BEKs to decide whether I believe it's an urban legend or genuine Paranormal phenomena, but I was reminded of my late night encounter with a luminous intruder back in 2010. And for some strange reason I started thinking about The Nine. What's that Kenneth Grant line? *"Jack Parsons opened a door and something flew in?"*

That was probably The Nine.

What did The Nine bring to those who answered the door when they came knocking? In the case of Andrija Puharich and Dick Price, not much good. In fact, both died violently, of suspicious head injuries. In other cases, the results are more uncertain. But the usual *"it was just a psyop"* explanations about The Nine really don't stand up to serious scrutiny when you look at the secretiveness, elitism and devotion attached to this group.

The hoax explanation doesn't really wash either, given its longevity. A serious look at this group seems to reveal that The Nine had a grip on some fairly influential people, for reasons that are still at best obscure. Certainly, The Nine's profile is pretty low these days, but it could well be that they've simply gone back underground, as they were for 25 years following the Round Table workings. It may well be that these entities have a much different concept of time than we do.

I started thinking about The Nine again after a recent rewatch of *DMT: The Spirit Molecule* and some reading on Dr. Rick Strassman's DMT trials. To be honest, I was a bit alarmed by this rewatch, being more familiar not only with the ancient Mystery traditions the talking heads in the film are constantly stumbling over, but also the negative aspects of the trials that the film somehow forgets to talk about.

So if you only know about the trial from the movie, you may not have heard that Strassman ended the trials because he believed he was opening doors that were better left closed. Here we see the flaw in New Age optimism, that every 'higher power' or other-dimensional creature is going to have your best interests at heart. Strassman's own research conclusively proves that is very much not so. Increasingly, his subjects began to encounter malignant beings some described as 'alien insects' and experienced bad trips.

DMT can be a very dangerous drug. The fact remains that the 'spirit molecule' does not always lead us all to love and light. It can open our eyes to terrifying realities too, and mark us with those experiences for as long as any beatific ones might. For that reason, we must think long and hard about using it in ourselves and on one another.

This documentary — rather, this long-form advertisement for DMT — repeatedly glosses over the negative potentials of the experience in favor of a string of New Age happy-talk. In my view, this fails not only the viewer but the drug itself, repeating the same mistakes of over-promising and under-cautioning made by Timothy Leary and his cronies in the 1960s. And we all know how that turned out.

Terence McKenna, another DMT evangelist, famously identified similar beings as 'machine elves' or some variation thereof, a term veering close to John Lilly's paranoid Solid State Intelligence. Not very comforting precedent there.

Where *DMT: The Spirit Molecule* fails, and where the more noble ancient Mysteries succeeded is that the former offers no moral framework in preparation for the psychonaut. Whereas the Mystery cults were all about instilling positive moral guidance in the initiate. This helped the initiate ward off anxiety and fear, emotions that are often your express tickets to a bad trip.

But back to those pesky entities again; when one person encounters an alien insect, it's probably a hallucination. When several people — under controlled experimental conditions — encounter these entities there's a good chance those entities exist somewhere outside our imagination. Then the party's well and truly over. You don't even need to believe in the objective reality of alien space insects for all this to work. You can believe they are just artifacts of the human imagination given form by powerful psycho-pharmacology.

Either way, the same rules apply: Find out who's behind those doors before you open up and let them in.

WAS FORT A FORTEAN?

WHAT WOULD CHARLES FORT MAKE of the current culture that flies his flag? Probably not much. Unlike most so-called Forteans today, Fort wasn't a dilettante. He was obsessive to the point of mania about collecting information. Someone might even call him a "hoarder" today. Or worse, a "tinfoil hat guy."

Fort wasn't a moderate in any sense of the word, he was a man of deep fixations, of passionate opinions, of radical convictions. And in spite of the fashionable agnosticism of the time, a man of deep-seated *beliefs*. Only belief drives a man to swim against a tsunami in the way Fort swam against the rise of materialist reductionism. It certainly came with a deep cost to him.

And yet Fort was deeply immersed in quantum physics while the giants of the field were just giving birth to the science. To him, it only validated his convictions that materialism was an illusion. Fort even knocked around a prototype of the idea of the holographic universe a century before physicists, albeit a primitive and literalist one.

Unlike many Forteans, who dabble in the 'weird' but reflexively defer to scientific orthodoxy, Fort saw science as the latest incarnation of the ancient priesthoods, mesmerizing a cowed public with arcane and inscrutable language, secret rites and boiling cauldrons.

Would that Fort had lived to see Hiroshima and Nagasaki, every dark warning and paranoid suspicion he ever had clutched to his bosom would likely have been confirmed. Fort condemned scientists (and believers in Scientism) for doing then what they do with absolute impunity today; ignoring and/or throwing out evidence that challenges the dominant materialist paradigm.

Fort wrote in *Lo!*:

> "Scientists, in matters of our data, have been like somebody in Europe, before 1492, hearing stories of lands to the West, going out for an hour or so, in a row-boat, and then saying, whether exactly in these words, or not: 'Oh, Hell! There ain't no America'."

The loathing was mutual. The high priests of Scientism hated Fort and his work with a urgent passion, all the more so since Fort was so meticulous and methodical in cataloging his contrarian data. Fabian Socialist HG Wells would write a scathing letter to Fort's supporter Theodore Dreiser, expressing the majority opinion among the materialist ascendancy of the early 20th Century.

Wells wrote to Dreiser:

> I'm having Fort's *Book of the Damned* sent back to you. Fort seems to be one of the most damnable bores who ever cut scraps from out of the way newspapers. I thought they were facts. And he writes like a drunkard. *Lo!* has been sent to me but has gone into my wastepaper basket. And what do you mean by forcing 'orthodox science' to do this or that? Science is a continuing exploration and how in the devil can it have an orthodoxy? ...God dissolve (and forgive) your Fortean Society.

How bitter, how ironic Wells' words sound, since even he would be forced to acknowledge that the scientific priesthood behaves exactly like the Medieval Church today (and when it had the power of the state, as it did in Soviet Russia, Maoist China and Cambodia, it enforced its will with roughly the same methods). Back then, Wells merely wrote with the disgust of a priest whose sanctuary of prestige and privilege had been invaded.

Knowing the history, Fort wrote of a endless game of musical chairs, reminding his readers that both science and religion were just vehicles of state power. Moreover, he saw them as forms of "witchcraft."

> Now that religion is inglorious, one of the most fantastic of transferences of worships is that of glorifying science, as a beneficent being. It is the attributing of all that is of development, or of possible betterment to science. But no scientist has ever upheld a new idea, without bringing upon himself abuse from other scientists.

This also cuts to the core of Fort's essential pessimism. Having read of the endless catalogue of pre-Arnold, pre-Roswell sightings, Fort was a UFOlogist before the term was coined But his cosmology feels more like *Hypostasis of the Archons* than *Hangar 1*. Here's we get to what is perhaps Fort's most famous quotation, one you'd be hard-pressed to get most 'Forteans' to agree with:

> Would we, if we could, educate and sophisticate pigs, geese, cattle? Would it be wise to establish diplomatic relation with the hen that now functions, satisfied with mere sense of achievement by way of compensation? I think we're property. I should say we belong to something: That once upon a time, this earth was No-man's Land, that other worlds explored and colonized here, and fought among themselves for possession, but that now it's owned by something: That something owns this earth-all others warned off.

Today, we're force-fed the extraterrestrial hypothesis when it comes to those strangers in the sky, but the length, depth and intimacy of this phenomenon suggest — to anyone willing to consider the implications of the evidence — that this phenomenon is a permanent condition of the planet and our species.

Fort wrote about this a century ago, but no one seems to be able to face up to this yet. Certainly not most Forteans.

Modern Forteans seem to operate in territory once occupied by Subgenii and Discordians, a dorky micro-culture of harmless entertainment, characterized by ironic distance and a total lack of commitment. They might have the external trappings of a counter-culture, but are actually animated by a reflexive conventionality no different than secularists. This isn't a judgment call, it's just a simple observation.

It's like the kind of thing you see manifested in 'Weird News' in sites like *Huffington Post*, where Forteana is really just a joke, a brief diversion from the mandatory scientist, materialist orthodoxy. 'Believers' are usually identified as suckers and bumpkins. Fort wrote:

> 'People with a psychological need to believe in marvels are no more prejudiced and gullible than people with a psychological need not to believe in marvels'.

This is not a position you'll see among many of the current branches of Forteanism, which sometimes seem bent on waging an endless crusade against 'believers' and belief. It's as if it's OK to dabble in this stuff for the lulz, just don't actually take any of it seriously. Certainly that's takeaway you'll get from *Fortean Times*, and other venues that constantly attack their ostensible allies but never question received authority.

Of course, attacking a powerless constituency like 'believers' is a cost- and consequence-free way of looking like a freethinking iconoclast, when in fact you're actually anything but. It's just not what I would call 'Fortean'.

Fort is like Philip K. Dick and Jack Kirby, admired by an audience who find their personal convictions a curiosity at best, and an embarrassment at worst. Fort was a humorist and was smart enough to give his audience some wiggle room, but on the really controversial issues he seems remarkably stringent (e.g., 'we are property'). In many ways his jokiness is gallows humor, a respite from his existential pessimism.

Jeff Kripal identifies Fort as a Twentieth Century Gnostic in *Authors of the Impossible*, and from what I've read of the man I'd say that's not too far from the truth. The question is how he'll be regarded when the upheaval comes and things now taken for granted face their existential dilemma.

IT'S ALL REAL. NOW WHAT?

THERE'S A FAMOUS EXCHANGE IN THE RECENT STAR WARS sequel *The Force Awakens* in which Han Solo announces to the young rebels Rey and Finn that the Force and the Jedi — mystical concepts that had come to be seen as superstitious nonsense by most people — were all real. That the legends about them were "all true." Han says, "I thought it was all a bunch of mumbo-jumbo," but that, "the crazy thing is that it's true. All of it." This is a great tagline for a popcorn movie, a rallying cry for all those would-be real-life Jedi out there. But there's a flip side to the equation, maybe one that a lot of people might not factor into their calculations.

Han's benediction can't help but remind me of a warning passed on by rocket scientist Ed Forman — close friend and confidant to Jack Parsons — to his daughter when she cracked open one of the magical texts Forman inherited from Parsons. "It's all real, it all works," Forman said about magic. "Don't touch it. You'll get yourself in real trouble."

Words to live by. You see, if the Jedi and the Force are real so too are the Sith and the Dark Side. If the Aeons are real, so too are the Archons. If Angels are real, so are Demons.

Consumer economics have conditioned we moderns to believe that we can pick and choose among an endlessly-expanding menu of options, and discard the bits we find problematic. But if you believe that magic is a science — or even a religion — then you have to follow its rules. Magic is like any other system, you can't go and randomly chuck out huge chunks of code and expect it to work properly. Look at how religions tend to collapse once they start trying to discard all the socially-problematic bits of programming: the Devil, sin, punishment and the rest.

MAGIC AS WE'VE COME TO UNDERSTAND IT TODAY is based in no small part on Medieval grimoires, a good number of which are essentially handbooks for coaxing the princes, dukes and earls of Hell into doing your bidding. This all dates back to Babylon when Pazuzu - yes, *that* Pazuzu - was regarded by magicians as a nasty but useful demon you could enlist in your wars against other demons. Babylonians had a *lot* of problems with demons.

Now, I don't know about you, but I can't really see a 'Prince of Hell' as a pushover or a soft touch. I'm thinking Princes of Hell probably drive a hard bargain for their services. Whether you see demons as objectively real or as unconscious projections doesn't really matter once they figure out where all your tender points lie.

Magic is "hot," or so they tell me, and we're seeing the kind of curatorial custodianship applied to it that a generation raised from birth on libraries of data available with a mouse-click reflexively apply to every single cultural epiphenomenon that bubbles to the surface. The scope and breadth of their ability to process and collate data most consider trivial or irrelevant can boggle the mind when viewed from a distance. But do they realize hot can burn?

Interest in magic seems inevitable to a generation raised on Harry Potter and Peter Jackson's *Lord of the Rings* films, which made magic so palpable and seductive. But one has to wonder if this is just the latest ephemeral obsession — like vinyl collecting or organized skepticism — or something more durable? The reason I ask is that I'm old enough to have lived through a couple of occult revivals now.

I can't question the facility or intellectual firepower of a lot of people who've applied themselves to magic, most of them are a lot smarter than me. But I do have serious reservations about the power of magic itself. If you believe that it's real and that it works, you have to understand that it's not something you can walk away from once you get tired of it. And magic is something that's fucked up the lives of some of the best and the brightest the world has ever known. The history of magic is like a Greek tragedy, a parade of incredible minds who paid a heavy price for trying to gatecrash Olympus. John Dee is a good example. Paracelsus is another. More recently, we have Crowley and Parsons. All of these guys were brilliant polymaths, and under different circumstances would probably be sitting in the history books next to the Newtons, Galileos and Einsteins. Unfortunately, it didn't work out that way.

I'm not trying to discourage interest in magic. I'm not trying to pretend that I could. What I'm saying is that I think it's a lot more powerful — and potentially destructive — than the fluff pieces in the lifestyle sections of mainstream media outlets would lead you to believe. Chalk it up to the power of suggestion if you prefer, but the results will probably be the same.

There could be entirely materialistic explanations for magic's reality; the power of suggestion (again) or the subtle and complex machinations of the Unconscious. But that doesn't make the effects any less real or potentially dangerous. If it's real and it's powerful then it can cut your fingers off, just like any power tool. Which is why I think anyone who takes magic seriously is better off in the hands of an experienced practitioner, someone who knows where all the bodies are buried and the traps are laid.

I bring all this up because magic — however you choose to define it — seems to pop its cheery little head up in times of chaos. And we seem to be tiptoeing on the edge of a volcano of chaos this country hasn't seen in a hundred and fifty years. Not just America, but around the world as well.

And this chaos is being stoked and manipulated by all kinds of players on all points of all different spectrums; political, cultural, economic, etc. You may have noticed that the spy war I alluded to shortly after the 2016 election has gone mainstream now, and we've been bombarded with all kinds of meme magic and agitprop ever since. I'm sure that will all end well.

CHAOS MAGICIANS SEE THE DWELLER OF THE ABYSS as a liberating force. And I'm worried that a lot of others may too, even if they don't necessarily acknowledge Chrononzon by name. The world may look much the same in your daily life for the most part, but you can just sense that spinning vortex at your periphery, can't you?

Yeats prophesied a Center that no longer held, and now it's *de rigeur* among the smart-set to 'rebel' against that Center. So much so that 'rebelling' is now mainstream. But how do you rebel against a Center that no longer objectively exists? Is it a meaningful gesture or just an empty ritual of a fading past, when rebellion had actual consequences? Maybe we'll come to learn that a collective Center is as important to the body politic as your 'center' is to your physical body. It will be too late by then, of course.

It's at times like these — when faith is lost in the old certainties — that Magic and the Paranormal poke their heads up from the sand. When the gods break their contracts it seems there are always ambitious understudies willing to do a little business on the side.

The Greek Magical Papyri date back to a time when the Empire was collapsing and religious conflict was erupting into street battles all over major city centers. Mesopotamia was the venue for a never-ending struggle of nations, and subsequently produced some of the most startling magic history ever recorded.

The grimoires arose during the times of the Crusades, against the backdrop of an epic struggle between Christendom and Islam. The spiritual supermarket of New York's Burned-Over District can trace its origin to the Great Disappointment, when everyone seemed to whip themselves up in anticipation of a Second Coming that never came. Similarly, the occult revival of the Nineteenth Century took place under massive dislocation, human misery and uncertainty, despite a large-scale Christian revival.

With societal and economic pressures building everywhere you look, it's inevitable that Magic is going to find a new audience. The questions then become what do that they want from it, how far are they willing to go to get it, and will be they be either willing or able to pay the piper when the bills come due? I'd say these are questions anyone who's considering taking up these arts spend a lot of time thinking about.

CALL IT WHAT IT IS

SOMETIME I THINK WE'D DO WELL to have a Vocabulary Police Force, who could keep important terms from being degraded from misuse. The New Agers are particularly egregious offenders when it comes to vocabulary abuse, as were the Religious Right before them.

Politicians are career recidivists, but academics might be the Ted Bundys of word murder. Their in-house jargon is so tortured and twisted it's a miracle they can communicate with one another. Maybe they just pretend to understand each other, throwing out an arcane blizzard of inexplicable buzzwords that would leave the most esoteric Kabbalist breathless with envy, hoping no one notices they just said absolutely nothing at all.

The entheogenic community aren't exactly innocent in the abduction and torture of the English language either. We hear the 'C' word — 'consciousness' — thrown around with such abandon, and used to describe so many wildly different psycho-physiological states, that it's no wonder that some Rationalists are driven to deny that such a thing even exists. Maybe they do so simply because consciousness happy-talk can be so goddamn irritating. But it occurred to me the other night that those would-be gurus who try to sell consciousness like its a consumer product are in fact selling themselves short.

It was a hazy, sultry night and the Moon loomed rather ominously. I was walking around with my spirit animal Linda and soaking it all in. For a very brief moment the 'C' word crept into my mind, but was chased out by a more potent term, one that I felt more aptly captured the state I was in at the moment: *communion*.

It occurred to me that I was in *communion* with spirits, ones I couldn't name or quantify. As soon as that simple yet powerful idea slipped into my mind I went with it and it made sense to me. It felt real and true. I realized that such a simple notion was time-tested and true, and amazingly untainted by those kinds of people who talk a lot but say very little.

I also began to think about how this communion wasn't a fully-conscious process, but a kind of wireless download that my unconscious underwent while my workaday brain took in the sights and sounds. I realized that this was nothing new, but something that people unlearn through socialization. That it's a process that comes natural to children, before school and television programs it out of them. Anyone with kids has seen this when they were young and at play, how they seemed to be tuned into channels you were blocked from, hearing music you or I can't. Maybe restoring those connections is the meaning of it all. It's certainly something to aim for.

I probably wouldn't have noticed all this had I not prepared myself over the years with my trance and dream work. Hell, the sync-work as well. I've noticed that I've really chipped away at that wall between the conscious and unconscious mind, and probably also between the mundane and spiritual worlds.

I also realized how much more compelling the word 'communion' felt than the usual vague talk about states of consciousness. It was direct, palpable, numinous. It didn't feel tainted by boring lectures or sales pitches. It was complete, self-contained and immensely satisfying. It was its own explanation.

Try it. Let me know how it works for you.

ANOTHER KIND OF LANGUAGE

ABOUT THREE YEARS AGO, I MARKED THE OCCASION of John Keel's death by writing about some of the strange, semiotic links I have with the Mothman. There were a lot of them, and these syncs seemed to pop up at such important turning points in my career. I'll recap here:

• My first full-time job was at New England Comics, whose first publishing venture was *The Tick* by Ben Edlund. The Tick's sidekick was Arthur, a literal moth-man. Edlund was later an executive producer on the short-lived Fox series *Point Pleasant*.

• My first comic series was *Halo: An Angel's Story*, published by Sirius Entertainment. Soon after it was published I was called into a meeting with Crossroads Films, who were interested in developing a film project based on the comic. Crossroads was also a big ad production house and their star director was Mark Pellington, director of *The Mothman Prophecies* feature film.

• My lawyer at the time also represented Doug TenNapel, creator of the *Earthworm Jim* video game. His publisher was Top Shelf, also my publisher when I was an associate editor at *Comic Book Artist* magazine. Doug was the first to attempt a feature film based on the Mothman saga, which he shot in Point Pleasant.

• Last and most certainly not least, my editor for *Our Gods Wear Spandex* was actually *from* Point Pleasant, West Virginia and grew up immersed in first-hand Mothman accounts. Coincidentally, our first meeting took place on the same block where my demon neighbor Aleister Crowley began his notorious *Amalantrah Working*.

Now, there is usually one clear takeaway with these kinds of compound synchronicities and that is *to pay attention*. It's an unusually reliable indicator that there is something waiting for you down the road these signs are pointing to. The problem is that I always misinterpreted the Signal. I needed to undertake a deeper study of John Keel, not the Mothman itself.

Keel was a one-size-fits-all theorist when it came to all things Paranormal. Ghosts, UFOs, psi, cryptids, gods and angels, you name it; to Keel they were all Ultraterrestrials (UTs) in disguise. Keel's UTs were a transdimensional race of natural born troublemakers who could manipulate sound, light and matter and could exist at any point of their choosing along the electromagnetic spectrum.

All of a sudden there's been a realization among people in the Paranormal community that maybe John Keel is right. Maybe UFOs aren't extrasolar, metallic spacecraft. Maybe it's another kind of intelligence that's been living among us all along. Another kind of intelligence that speaks another kind of language. My study of Keel has allowed to me to view some of the Paranormal weirdness that's intruded into my life on occasion in an entirely new light.

N EEDLESS TO SAY, WEIRDNESS HAS FOLLOWED ME around my entire life. There are a number of incidents I can usually corroborate but cannot prove (the Paranormal is by definition unprovable) and so haven't written about here. I'm perfectly willing to accept the visionary aspect, because in the end the question remains the same: how did the event change the course of my life? But if I were to explain all of these odd Paranormal experiences to Keel, he wouldn't even blink.

He'd also offer his own theology of predestination as well. I happened to be born at the tail end of a major UFO flap, and my expectant mother's recurring nightmares of a witch trying to break into the house while she was napping were no such thing, but simply garbled memories of encounters with a mischievous Ultraterrestrial. The fact that she later developed an owl obsession and the fact that I would have my own encounter with a "leprechaun" in the same exact spot several years later would be all the proof he needed.

What does fascinate me though is the lightning in the dining room during that encounter. Given the hyper-real nature of the encounter, and my heart-pounding, wide awake state at the time, I've developed a working theory on the event, which seems plausible to me given the fact that so many people taking ayahuasca and DMT have had nearly identical experiences. In my fevered state, the DMT switch was thrown and the great filter was turned off. I noticed something and something noticed me noticing it, in the words of the John Keel stand-in in *Mothman Prophecies*. So that something put on a little show to ensure I'd chalk it all up to hallucination. It reached into my mind, pulled out the racial memory of the Leprechaun and the gold coins, and placed that in front of the plasma show I wasn't supposed to see.

W HAT FASCINATES ME ABOUT GHOSTS is like the overwhelming majority of UFO sightings, they are *constructions of light*. So if in fact any of this exists outside of the human imagination, Keel could very well be right; this an intelligence composed of energy and not mass, and expresses itself primarily as light or plasma. I would only add that it also speaks to us, only the language is symbolic and synchronic, not verbal. I wonder now if my 'swamp gas' story should be reinterpreted in that context.

Let's wind the clock back to 1988. My wife, infant son and I were driving through the Great Swamp — the very same Great Swamp immortalized by Orson Welles in his notorious 1939 *War of the Worlds* broadcast — to go shopping at the now-defunct Pathmark superstore. It was a beautiful night and the skies were crystal clear.

But something caught my eye. I noticed three stars in formation over the tree line. They seemed to be a bit on the bright side, but nothing too out of the ordinary. But a funny thing happened and kept happening: every time we came to a clearing and were able to see the skies, the position of the stars completely changed. My wife and I were very interested in astronomy at the time; we had a giant, glow in the dark star map on our bedroom wall, I was doing some backyard stargazing with a telescope, and even named one of our cats 'Boötes'. So we weren't naifs when it came to the stars.

In any event, it was pretty freaky but we lost sight of them as got deeper in the hilly woods just outside the Great Swamp Road. We did our shopping and left the store.

As I was putting away the groceries and as my wife was strapping the baby in his seat, a man approached us. He was tall, bespectacled, heavy, unshaven and badly dressed. He spoke with a light accent which sounded Eastern European.

He said that he had some baby furniture he was trying to get rid of, as well as things like strollers. My back was up immediately — why did this guy have any of this stuff? I didn't see any kids with him. My Eighties horror movie imagination began to run wild on that particular speculation.

The creep spoke mainly to my wife, who was the one who didn't grow up in Braintree, and as such was more trusting. I looked over and saw a middle-aged woman standing stiffly against an old Ford LTD station wagon, looking at us with her arms folded tightly across her chest. My bad feeling only got worse.

I placed myself between my wife and the stranger and told him thanks, but we were all set. He backed off and away and said if we need anything he lived on the corner of such and such a street and we could drop by anytime. My wife told me he also offered to babysit, which sends chills down my spine just thinking about it.

I finished putting the groceries in the trunk and looked over at the Ford. The stranger was sitting there watching us intently while he smoked in the dark car. Even in the dark I could see the deep discomfort carved into his wife's face. We never saw either one of them again, but the creepy feeling stayed with me a long time after.

This was my 'swamp gas' story for a long time, a weird conjunction of a will o' the wisp sighting and a disturbing encounter with a stranger in a dark, empty parking lot. The problem is that when I was looking up images of swamp gas ignitions for this post, I couldn't find a single one that looked like the weird star formation we saw over the swamp. Nothing. Looking back, I don't think we were looking at methane explosions at all.

This is exactly the kind of story that would be presented as a classic screen memory of an abduction encounter: a young family driving down a dark, deserted road, strange lights in the sky and an anomalous encounter with a predatory stranger speaking in a strange accent. It's almost Betty and Barney Hill Redux. But there was nothing dreamy or vague about it.

That's not to say there wasn't something deeply strange about it all. Those strange lights could well have been some kind of communication, a warning that something was wrong, something bad was about to happen, so be alert.

It just came to us in another kind of language.

PARANORMAL STATE

AS I'VE SAID MANY TIMES BEFORE, modern discourse has produced a Bizarro lexicon, in which words that once had meaning either take on new meanings that have little to do with their original intent, or in fact have no real meaning at all. I think most of you know what I'm talking about here.

And nowhere is this more apparent in what book publishers call the 'New Age' market, a catch-all phrase which itself has been bleached of its original meaning. It can refer to anything from self-help gurus to alternative history to Spiritualism to the more-speculative corners of conspiracy theory (think Icke, David).

So whereas my original exposure to the New Age subculture had more to do with the occult, in only a few short years it'd come to represent people who were trying to construct a movement with no real historical roots, no doctrines or scripture, basically with nothing but a lexicon of buzzwords that they had stripped of any meaning at all. Words like 'spirit', 'energy', 'consciousness', 'shaman', 'metaphysics', 'light', 'evolution'.

I'd visit these meetings and see bored middle-aged to elderly women (and occasionally their even more bored husbands) toss these words back and forth as if they were passcodes, as if the words themselves had some magical power to bring them somewhere. Exactly where was never made clear.

One of these get-togethers was at the Lucis Trust, the subject of countless conspiracy theories. It was so cripplingly lame, so soul-crushingly boring — literally filled with stereotypical spinsters in tennis shoes, half-listening to two of the dullest speakers in human history — that I fled during the coffee break.

But the culprit here isn't the victims of the New Age; these people are usually good-hearted, well-meaning seekers. It's the vapid commercial culture that produces imitation religion, from the Lucis Trust to the Megachurch. It's no mystery that neopaganism became so alluring to so many New Agers; the problem is that the same rot quickly set in.

Paganism in the ancient world was primarily based in fertility, in about doing whatever it took to appease the gods to ensure a bountiful harvest. That was literally a matter of life and death. With the rise of organized agriculture and surplus economies came the Mystery cults and the philosophical religions, in which humanity put its mind to more abstract questions. I don't know how compelling fertility can be in the Monsanto era, but I'd obviously be the last guy to question the enduring power of those ancient archetypes.

All of this brings me to the 'P' word. I may be skipping over some steps in between because this is a blog and not *Time Magazine,* and breaking rules is my way of staying fresh. But the P word: what is the P word, you may ask?

It's yet another word that consumer culture has stripped of meaning, a word that describes waters I've swum in my entire life but still remains radioactive to me since hucksters often use it when they want the rubes to think they're saying something when in fact they're saying nothing at all.

You know: 'Paranormal'.

T HE TERM 'PARANORMAL' USED TO MEAN SOMETHING. In *Operation Trojan Horse* and *Messengers of Deception,* the descriptions of the 'Paranormal' have a definite and specific meaning, and a definite and specific source. Both authors argue that UFOs are an 'Ultraterrestrial' phenomenon that has been with us a very long time, and uses a telepathy-based technology so advanced as to be essentially magic to interact with humanity, and uses a series of disguises and deceptions for reasons we can only guess at.

Paranormal simply means 'beside what is normal'. That can mean a whole host of things, and include pretty much everything we talk about on this blog. It can mean psi, the occult, the netherworld, ghosts and related phenomena, hallucinogens and shamanic experience; basically anything outside the 9-to-5 grind. But the word has been appropriated by the kind of nonsensical Reality (sic) TV you see on SyFy: brainless mannequins running around with night vision goggles on, huffing and puffing for 40 minutes until they all get together and trade notes about what a waste of time it all was. Well, that's how I sum it up, at least.

But my negative association with the term isn't limited to that kind of Kali Yuga entertainment. It's also used by alleged UFO researchers who can't be bothered to do anything but the most superficial casework, so they throw around fashionable buzzwords like 'Paranormal' or 'trickster', simply because they heard someone else use them somewhere.

Or maybe because they don't want to violate their audience's normality bias, so the New Agey buzzwords become a more comforting alternative. Because if you listen carefully, they end up reducing it all to nothing; not even hallucination. So nothing is what it all adds up to.

In the modern 'Paranormal' marketplace, the Beast must constantly be fed so any kind of perspective or discernment is chucked out the window. Pretty soon it's all just static and chatter, and then the game becomes the 'debunker' game, especially since none of these Art Bell wannabes are equipped to deal with anything truly Paranormal in the first place.

They may have liked a couple UFO or Paranormal movies in some vague fashion, and decided to blog about it with their typical American sense of unearned entitlement. But they never stopped to think that their perfectly normal brains and perfectly ordinary world-views were completely ill-suited for the Paranormal in the first place.

I feel extremely protective of people who have had genuine Paranormal experiences, because I realize that the Paranormal is usually a side effect of death and horror, and experiencers are often traumatized by them. And the last thing they need are a bunch of douchebags making a mockery of a facet of life most people already dismiss.

ONE OF THE MAIN REASONS THAT I DON'T TALK about the Paranormal here, however, is that what we understand to be Paranormal is usually anecdotal and almost impossible to prove. Talking about the stuff we discuss here is hard enough without worrying about the Skeptics' constantly moving goalpost. And that's when I can put it all up there, with links and everything.

Even so, one of the most interesting experiences I had in the history of this blog actually started on Facebook, when I came home to report a very strange sighting of a ghostly figure I had minutes after I (well, my dog and I) actually saw it. I first described it as a 'ghost' sighting, though I later read a nearly identical story in a Jenny Randles book on alien contact.

That inspired a huge thread on my FB wall which led to the post itself. As I reported in that piece I'd find out the next morning after seeing this strange, white figure that there'd been a serious hit and run accident at the end of the street, and the police had put up an electronic sign calling for witnesses to come forward.

As I said, the Paranormal is a by-product of death and horror. You can't get one without the other. Not if it's real.

THE STRANGEST FEELING (THAT I'VE BEEN HERE BEFORE)

PAST-LIFE REGRESSION WAS BIG BACK IN THE 1980S. You had a lot of hypnotists and self-declared mediums exploiting the fad, telling their clients that they were Caesar or Cleopatra or Shakespeare in a past life. Somehow they were never a tavern whore, or a dung sweeper. The whole fad did what these things usually do, and made the topic of reincarnation a target for ridicule.

And so it goes with the degradations of consumer culture. Never mind that any number of very ancient religions practiced by vast amounts of people believe in the concept, all it took was a few hucksters on Oprah to sully the belief.

Or did it? It's one of those things that you'll find a lot of people believing in quietly, almost automatically. It always made more sense to me than an eternity spent in some cosmic realm. And it's one of those things I began to seriously wonder about when I looked back on my childhood.

I WAS A WEIRD KID IN ELEMENTARY SCHOOL. I was fixated on things from the 1930s and 1940s, like the old radio shows, which you could get cheaply on LP at the local discount store. I was obsessed with the heroes of the Golden Age of comics and the Pulps. Certainly a lot of those characters were being revived at the time, but the audience was most certainly not grade-school kids, in fact most of those revivals tanked pretty quickly.

I was so fixated on that Depression/World War Two era that I'd make my mother buy anything that had imagery from the period. I even made her buy Moxie (a soft drink from the period) when it was reissued. Unfortunately, it tasted like carbonated ass. Maybe they changed the formula.

It goes without saying that I was fixated on *The Little Rascals* and *Three Stooges*. Nothing unusual for a kid at that time, but I doubt many kids were fixated on The Shadow, or Edgar Bergen and Charlie McCarthy, or George Burns and Gracie Allen. I moved on to other obsessions eventually, and didn't give it much mind until I remembered a recurring dream I had, even after I outgrew my weird 30s/40s fixation.

In this dream — and there were minor variations on it — I was carrying a rifle and walking through a snowy forest. Out of nowhere, a man in dark clothing and a helmet charges at me with a rifle. That's usually how it ends. In some versions, his rifle had a bayonet. This could well be an artifact of the old war movies I used to watch, but why that one motif?

I've read theories that people who died violent deaths were more likely to remember their past lives in their next incarnation, and that some children would often suffer various psychological and physiological problems as a result of their past life trauma.

I don't know if that's true, but I had spent a huge chunk of my life — *decades*, actually — having nightmares every single night. The stories varied, but centered on two basic themes: I was being murdered, or someone was coming to murder me.

I often wondered if this was one of the reasons I obsessed on the movie *Jacob's Ladder*, and watched it incessantly back in VHS days (actually, I watched it like the sick, sad, obsessive bastard I am). That film has the main character attacked in a very similar fashion to my recurring childhood dream, although that takes place in Viet Nam, not in some snowy pine forest.

I remember having the dream taking place in a forest. A forest behind a house I later had a rather involved ream about transmigration, a dream I had before I began to consider all of this in the context of reincarnation. I don't know what the link is exactly, but it would later take on a more disturbing light when it crossed over to a real-world tragedy that received no small amount of national attention.

OF COURSE, ALL OF THIS IS EXTREMELY UNFASHIONABLE at the moment, just like everything else of real interest or value. But reincarnation was held as truth by millions long before the current vogue for nihilism, and will endure long after it is gone. Which is to say by this century's end, judging by current demographic trends.

As with so many things, trying to find a mechanism for reincarnation might require us to look beyond the realm of the senses and the limited worldview instilled by our conscious attention. To look at the world and the Universe as living organisms, not just dead voids inhabited by meat robots and bacteria.

Maybe one day a new kind of science will emerge that will move beyond materialism and nihilism, and all the other knee-jerk adolescent behaviorisms so prevalent today. Maybe concepts like reincarnation may one day be truly understood. In the meantime, it's best not to even try to figure it out. As it stands today, we don't have the capacity to figure any of this stuff out. And because we're generally a bunch of entitled narcissists, that leads us to pretend these things don't exist. And doing so is ultimately how cultures and societies die.

You know, like ours currently is.

WHY I HATE SATURN

A FEW YEARS BACK I CAME TO A DECISION: I would only pay attention to the major transits in Astrology. These seem to be the only things astrologers can usually agree on, and sometimes even then it's still a crapshoot.

Since I basically look as astrology as a kind of synchronistic timekeeping system, charting the cyclical and rhythmic nature of time and being, I usually have a bias for the meat and potatoes astrologers who look at the various movements and their 'effects', which I interpret as the movements and their *correspondences*. Give me at least the *veneer* of something I can wrap my head around.

Back in the Nineties, a Californian named Rob Brezsny kicked off a kind of touchy-feely Astrology in which the columnist would serve up a hybrid of Stewart Smalley-type self-affirmation sermon and hippie tone-poem (with generous dollops of PC bromide thrown in), necessitating the reader to parse the hidden meaning allegedly embedded within. Sometimes it worked, usually you cringed. And it all got reduced to the point of self-parody; you need look no further than the current atrocity in *TV Guide* (which once ran horoscopes by heavyweights like Patric Walker and Sally Brompton) to see just how low that particular blend can go.

Whatever the skeptics may say, I've found the astrologers I pay attention to to be as least as credible as the weather services, at least when it comes to these major transits and these effects. This recent Saturn transit is a perfect example. I've written about this before, but my mind is still boggling over it. After Saturn's transit through Cancer, I was assured that it would be 29 years before I had to deal with that kind of misery again. And lo and behold, it was less than *five*.

Saturn is transiting through Libra, and apparently was doing so through my 4th house? Something like that. My eyes tend to glaze over with all the charts and graphs. As I said, I try to look at the big picture. Apparently, Cancerians are more vulnerable to Saturn's malign influence since the planet rules Capricorn, which is on the opposite end of the Zodiac. Whatever the exact mechanics of all this are, I'll leave to the experts. All I know is that the *effects* were brutal.

Believe me, I realize that to some this all sounds like madness. And I realize that a lot of people like to chalk all of this up to the power of suggestion and all the rest of it.

The problem is that the power of suggestion can't influence outside events beyond your control (at least according to the rational point of view), nor does it influence events that occurred during previous transits when you were totally oblivious to all of this. It just doesn't work that way.

Either way, when Saturn was transiting through Cancer it was kind of like living with a physically-abusive alcoholic; you never knew what kind of nightmare was going to come at you next. I ended up in the hospital quite a few times, and things just generally went to hell. This recent Saturn-in-Libra thing was more like walking around with a fifty-pound sack of wet sand on my back. Everything just ground down, like driving a car with four flat tires. Of course, the daily burden of managing a severe chronic pain condition doesn't make any of this any easier.

I wish I could say it was all a blessing in disguise, but I just don't see it at the moment. The Saturn-in-Cancer transit did actually presage a major reinvention, leading to the books and this blog and all the rest of it. But then Saturn shows up again and basically shits all over everything I worked so hard to build. So what's the hell's the point? I'm trying to make sense of it all, but the jury is still on their lunch break.

MAYBE THIS IS THE POINT WHERE I PEDDLE A BUNCH of rehashed Nietzschean twaddle about the glory of struggle and overcoming the odds. Nietzsche may have been a genius but he was also just another shut-in closet-case momma's boy whose brain was rotted out by syphilis. So maybe that doesn't do much in the way of applications.

We've been sold this bill of goods about the glory of hardship and redemptive qualities of struggle, predominantly by an over-privileged class of parasites who've never experienced a single day of real hardship in their lives. But the fact is that these narratives are all both deeply subjective and *highly* mythologized, and the sooner we dispense with the new *ubermenschen* archetype the better. It's all fine and good to overcome the odds and all the rest, but it's no way to write policy.

So maybe if there is a lesson in all of this, it's that suffering isn't some political issue that can be resolved, or some question of ideology that can all be wished away by some magical force like the gold standard or the hidden hand of the markets.

Sometimes shit just happens. Sometimes it's written in the stars.

FOR THE FAITHFUL NOT-QUITE DEPARTED

WHEN I WAS A KID, I REALLY TUNED into the whole Holy Week thing. Aside from Christmas, it seemed to be the only time of the year when there was an actual *story* being told, a compelling focus for all the ritual and interminable sermonizing we had to put up with all year. Easter was a story of resurrection, a story that long predates Christianity. It's probably one of the oldest stories we have. I understood the resurrection story, its power and its emotional appeal.

But there was something else that struck me about Holy Week. Our Sunday School met in the chapel for much of Lent into Easter, and the chapel was like a secret, hidden mini-church in which kids ruled. There were these little vent windows in the stained glass displays and they were usually left open, since the chapel tended to get awfully warm. And I would sit by the window and take in the intoxicating wholeness of Spring. That drug never left me.

When I was a kid I spent most of my playtime outdoors, often exploring the woods behind our neighborhood. I walked to school until I got to ninth grade. I tuned into the sights, sounds, and perhaps most importantly, the *smells* of the natural world in a way adults are incapable of. I was able to process all of this sensory input in a way I would never be able to again, because everything was rich, new, unknown and alive.

Spring also meant baseball, which we residents of Red Sox Country took as religion. Baseball meant Little League, when Watson Park turned into a city of kids every evening. It was there that I was first initiated into the deeper mysteries of Spring, when I met a pretty girl and we gave ourselves over to the rites of Venus in a dry patch of ground among the bulrushes. It couldn't possibly have been more archetypal.

There are lots of theories about the Easter story: It's just a rewriting of the passions of Pagan fertility gods. A double died on the cross, or the death was faked. It was a mass hallucination. Jesus' ghost appeared to the Apostles. Plus, that old standby: aliens. I'm not going to argue the point here. It's beside the point. The Easter story spoke — and speaks — to generations of people who have experienced loss and more than anything wish that loss could be undone.

WHEN I WAS EIGHT YEARS OLD, I lost someone very close to me, someone who died far too young. And died violently. It happened three days after Christmas, just because Fate is a sadistic bitch. (I still remember playing with my new GI Joe Training Center in the basement when my mother called me upstairs to break the news.) In many ways, my childhood died then and I spent far too much time trying to claw it back later.

It was as if this boy was touched by the gods, everyone thought so. Even adults recognized the power of his charisma, his natural charm. He was a natural-born leader, other kids just naturally fell in behind him. His death tore a hole through my world. Things I took for granted were going to change, and something important was going to be taken away from me. So his death wasn't just a single tragedy, a focal point in time. It was to have repercussions for my entire human ecosystem.

The dead boy haunted my dreams for years. You know how it is; you lose someone and they return to you in your dreams, explaining that it was a big misunderstanding, they were still alive and well. In one dream, he came back dressed like an astronaut. I met him by the grape orchard in my neighbor's yard. He told me didn't die, he'd just had been up in outer space. How's that for symbolism?

So yeah, the story of a charismatic young man rising from the dead — and returning to his friends and family — had tremendous resonance for me. Add in the magic of Springtime, which promised a rich banquet of baseball and Cheap Trick records (and hopefully, girls), and you're looking at a magic potion that Medieval alchemists would have sold their souls to brew up.

DEATH HAS RE-INSINUATED ITSELF into my human ecosystem. A while back, I told Gordon White that I could sense Death's presence, and felt like it had entered into a holding pattern over my head. This was shortly before a family member was diagnosed with cancer, which he beat into remission like the tough little bastard he is. But that was a false dawn, seeing Death has taken a number of trophies from my human ecosystem since then, nearly all at far too young an age.

So I know a bit about Death. More than I would like to.

I also know about the not-quite departed. Those whose passage to the other side is blocked for one reason or other. I spent a lot of time in a house where the not-quite departed had taken up residence and had to be encouraged to leave by a professional medium. There was a time in my life when everyone I knew either knew someone else who had a ghost story, or had a ghost story of their own.

The not-quite departed sometimes come back and try to make themselves known to us. I think this is more common than generally understood, simply because we don't usually recognize their language. For reasons we will probably never be able to explain, they can sometimes influence our physical environment, particularly through electricity. But that's just the stage show, like Jesus and his magic. The not-quite departed don't want to haunt our houses so much as our *souls*.

THE NOT-QUITE DEPARTED ARE SPIRITS with unfinished business on this plane. They were unloved or misunderstood, or they died unjustly, or too young. Of course, that describes half of the people who've ever died, but there seem to be other factors at work when the not-quite departed make themselves known to the living. Some think it's environmental; that geology plays a major role in these events. That very well could be, but we may also never know that for sure either.

Haunting is a pretty compelling explanation for the Easter story. You have the early death and the prerequisite geology angle with the stone tomb. You have the fear and guilt Jesus' followers felt making them more receptive to spectral influence, along with the conflicting stories, the violations of the laws of physics. Throw in some dreams, visions and fantasies, and you can wrap that thing up with a bow.

But again, that's not the selling point here. The pitch was that if you believed this story, *your* dead sons would one day return to you too. And for most of human history pretty much every family in Christendom were pining for a dead son.

Which makes me think that the dominance secularism is currently enjoying will be short-lived. Secularism seems to be feeding into anxiety and despair among a lot of people, which in turn is leading to an epidemic of early death, from drugs, suicide or misadventure. But this is a self-correcting dilemma. Trauma will inevitably lead people away from secularism; to religion, to magic, the New Age, whatever. This in turn will have a knock-on effect for the rest of the culture.

DEATH IS A FUNCTIONARY, A DELIVERY MAN. Something of the human essence keeps on trucking along regardless whether you believe it does or not. And I'm saying this at a time in my life when the peaceful eternal sleep of oblivion sounds awfully tempting, to be honest. All of which is to say is that as much as we think we can sanitize death and ignore the calls of the not-quite departed, I think the inexorable laws of nature have other plans for us in mind.

BENEDICTIONS

WHAT IF IT'S NONE OF THE ABOVE?

I'VE COME TO REALIZE MORE AND MORE that the world is nothing like we've been told it is. Like, *not even close.* I begin to wonder if, as the old song goes, "there's only a hair's breadth between us" and the powers and principalities we've lost the ability we once had to recognize. Then I begin to wonder if the epistemological chimeras we're conditioned to chase are all so much nonsense, no different from guessing how many angels can land on the head of a pin.

Take the whole Flat Earth thing: is the world flat or is it a globe? Well, what if it's *neither?* What if the question itself is completely irrelevant and has no effect whatsoever on how we really live our lives every day? Or take the eternal conundrum, "Are we alone?" Well, there are seven billion of us at last count. *No one* is alone. And if space aliens ever landed, I guarantee you wouldn't be able to stomach the way they *smelled.* Things would all go south from there.

And what if astronomy and astrophysics is all wrong and all rests on some fancy math games that we all agreed to abide by? What if all these infinite galaxies the Hubble is allegedly finding are just random globs of space-shit on its lens? Let's just pretend it's all real: what difference does it make anyway? It's all beyond our reach, and will still be so long after we're all gone.

So what if nearly all of our science - *especially* our cosmology — is all based on math tricks by clever hoaxers? We know the vast majority of experimental work being done these days can't be replicated. What if it's *all* just bullshit? We're asked every day to accept bold claims we have no way to test or falsify, in the same exact way that all the previous priesthoods forced us to believe their unprovable speculations. It's the same exact mind game, it's just that the specific ontology has changed.

Well, at least we know that physics is perfect, right? Well, that's all math, when all's said and done. What if the math is all wrong? I recently read a mathematician saying our math is bunk, and needs to be reinvented by AIs. So, where does that leave physics? I read recently that string theory is being written off as pseudo-science; what about the rest of theoretical physics?

But what if our reality can't be modeled by naturalist materialism or some kind of metaphysical speculation? What if it's something we can't even model at all? What if it just *is?* Asking questions like that, that's the *real* heresy, friend. That's when you really dive down the rabbit hole.

What if that *is* the Apocalypse, in the end? What if the hidden meaning of life is only revealed when you stop trying to pin made-up labels on everything and experience the world in all its fullness, wonder and mystery?

THE WHEEL HAS BEEN INVENTED

THE NÜ ATHEIST MOVEMENT IS ESSENTIALLY A PROJECT of the cultural Left. It's their *religious* project. Don't fall for the old trope that religion has to be theistic. A religion is simply a system of belief in a greater purpose that is used to bind a community together.

Communism and Nazism were religions; in fact they were consciously designed to be as such. You had your icons, your saints, your holy texts, your angels, your demons, it's just that the supernatural was taken out of the equation. And so it is with the Nü Atheist movement. Spend enough time reading atheist message boards and you'll see the same figureheads (Dawkins, Sagan) and holy texts (*God Delusion, Demon Haunted World*) invoked again and again.

Before Nü Atheism, the cultural Left tried for years to co-opt the old mainline Protestant denominations, in fact they did more than try. They were actually rather successful in seizing power in the various hierarchies of the Episcopal, Lutheran and Presbyterian denominations. The only problem was that as they instituted more and more explicitly postmodern reforms in the canon bylaws, the parishioners abandoned the churches in droves.

So we had a classic Pyhrric victory: the cultural Left seized power and invented all manner of square and spiral theological wheels, but soon found themselves ruling over an empty kingdom. And came next was the radical, irreparable polarization of American religion, with the Fundamentalists, Evangelicals and Pentecostals on one side, and secularists, agnostics and atheists on the other. In between are a handful of freaks and weirdos like us.

Now here we all are, with these violent forces tearing the social fabric apart at these opposing poles. If you're to survive and keep your identity and sanity in this clash of the titans, what's the best course of action? Well, let me get back to the detours.

In the early Nineties, I was working in New York, the Empire State Building to be precise. I was also going through a big Christian Mystic/Gnostic phase and reading all kinds of what my wife called my "Jesus books." I have to admit that I really didn't feel that overwhelming spiritual power that I felt in the Eighties when the New Age first hit me, but I think submitting myself to that kind of discipline was an important step in my overall development.

It was also the last days of my innocence, since I'd get online and have the misfortune of seeing just how ugly American Fundamentalism had become. Sadly, that particular discovery would end my church-going days forever.

Anyway, my work friends and I would often have our lunch on the shady grounds of The Church of the Transfiguration, a lovely little Anglo-Catholic Church off of Fifth Avenue, and from time to time I'd pop in for Mass. The ritual was as old-school as it gets: smells, bells, the priest facing the altar, the whole bit. I probably started drifting away by then, but there was something powerful and touching about a ritual that was nearly identical to that practiced a thousand years before. A wheel that works very well, thank you.

THE DECLINE IN CHURCH MEMBERSHIP OVERALL is a big story these days, though the media is missing the fact that a lot of Evangelicals who left their churches are forming home churches and private prayer groups. The same can't be said for the Mainline Churches. I wasn't raised as an Episcopalian — it seemed somewhat alien to me as a kid, trapped in a netherworld between Catholicism and Protestantism — but I'm fascinated by its travails, since its collapse has been the most dramatic.

Episcopal clergy have embraced every innovation you can imagine; gay priests are basically the conservatives there now. You've had Wiccan priests, Muslim priests, atheist priests, a Druid Archbishop — it's been a free-for-all. Nothing personal against Wiccans, Muslims or atheists who aren't Dawkinites, but all of this 'diversity' has obliterated the denomination ('decimation' is too mild a term), and now it stands on the brink of total and complete collapse.

For all its endless talk of 'inclusion', Episcopalians are almost exclusively white and old, and its membership is at its lowest level since the 1930s. Parishes are closing all across the country and directors are dipping into their endowments to keep the lights on. A lot of the blame for this is placed on the 2003 ordination of openly gay priest Gene Robinson as Bishop (who since retired), but I think what it really going on is A., the continuing polarization of the religious environment in this country, and B., the mind-numbing boredom and dreariness of your average Episcopal Mass.

I don't know who's running the seminaries these days, and my sample rate is admittedly small, but it seems that only the dullest speakers are allowed to be ordained in the Church. There has been a breakaway movement, a high-church schism that has split primarily over the gay issue, but also over doctrinal and liturgical issues that seem meaningless to people outside the church, but of vital importance to people *within* it.

The result is the 'Anglican Church in North America' which seems to be growing at the same rate the Episcopal Church is imploding. The ANCA is a 'smells-and-bells' liturgy church, and is 'right wing' only in relation to the ultra-ultra-left Episcopalians (the Baptists probably think it's San Francisco with incense).

And I have to admit it's of little interest or use to me personally, outside of the simple fact that they're growing when the Mother Church is dying. I study these things, which is why I'm poor. Though I do have to say if anyone believes that there aren't gay clergy in these new conservative churches — or in any religious body anywhere on the planet — then I have a Bridge to Nowhere I think you might be interested in buying shares in.

The media may not want to hear it, but I don't think the gay issue by itself would have caused the schism in these Anglican churches. The real issue is the fifty plus years of completely arbitrary — and often quite ridiculous — changes to Episcopal doctrine, liturgy and the rest. It was the constant reinvention of a wheel that most of the people thought worked just fine the way it was.

As with the zero-growth atheist birthrates, you can hurl all the invective you like. But if at the end of the day you can't pay to keep the lights on, all the radical theological innovations in the world won't really matter much outside the seminary dorm-room.

I COULD HAVE STAYED IN THE CHURCH and tried to inflict my crazy ideas on it, but I have too much respect for the institution to do so. I'd rather make my own way then try to force others to accept my bizarre and idiosyncratic notions. I don't understand why the Episcopal radicals didn't do the same when they had the money and power at their disposal to do. As it is, they dragged the entire organization down with them. That's what happens when you fail to recognize that the wheel has already been invented.

I left the Church physically because I left it spiritually; it no longer spoke to me. I loved church as a kid, but I loved the families and the fellowship and the beautiful old building and the places to explore and the history of it all. But one of my most profound spiritual experiences in church was a vision in which I was Thor trudging through a blizzard. The second was during a particularly beautiful Christmas Eve service in 1986, when Nina Hagen's "UFO" kept going through my head, and it and the votive candles hypnotized me to the point of tears.

Don't look now, but the Episcopal Church is on the phone: I think they want me to be their new Bishop.

YOU DON'T NEED THEIR PERMISSION ANYMORE

T RUTH (CAPITAL 'T') IS A POLITICAL CONSTRUCTION. You know it, I know it, everyone knows it. At the end of the day, what people accept as 'Truth' depends on their politics. Which in turn depends on their identity, or their perception of such.

There are some who will never question the official version of the JFK assassination, 9/11, the Apollo moon landings, Gulf War Syndrome, UFOs or any other topic you can name. No matter how compelling your evidence, no matter how shoddy or ramshackle the official version of events, certain kinds of people simply won't go there.

Which is not to say that alternative views are necessarily correct: there's a whole ton of alternative views I find every bit as shoddy as arguments you might hear on Fox News or read in *The New York Times*. I may even end up agreeing with the so-called Skeptics® on certain issues more often than not, though that's usually a function of their tendency to shoot at straw-men, to soften their audiences up for thornier and more troublesome targets. Which is a technique straight out of stage magic, by the way.

But I'm not here to sell you used worldviews from the mainstream or alternative media; I'd rather just try to encourage you to find your *own* truth. The mainstream and the alternative media have failed equally in my view, and the proof of the pudding is in the eating of the bullshit that the world is being force-fed every single day of the week. I just think that there isn't any reason to worry about the opinions or beliefs of a professional class and knowledge-based elite that doesn't care about you, at all. Actually, that's not *entirely* true: a frightening amount of them violently hate you and want you dead.

E VERYONE SEES A POLITICAL SYSTEM that is engineered to serve only the rich and the powerful; everyone realizes that the rest of us are being left to fend for ourselves. Everyone realizes that the so-called 'free market system' exists only to serve the executive class; that the 'hidden hand' of the so-called free market is actually the funny handshake of collusion, price fixing, money laundering and monopoly capitalism. The corporate media have been caught lying and covering up the misdeeds of the rich and powerful so many times that they have no credibility outside the professional class whose interests they serve.

Similarly, the scientific establishment isn't some Olympian overclass of aloof, disinterested monk-scholars; they're all bought-and-paid-for vassals of the corporate state. The so-called 'peer review system' is doomed from the start when not a single, solitary scientist will ever dare to step outside the bounds of orthodoxy for fear of ending their careers, literally overnight.

So why not take this unique opportunity to throw off the shackles of other people's expectations and pursue your own calling? Don't pursue it with 'skepticism' — a codeword self-sabotage and reductionism — but with rigorous *discernment*. Question your methods and your conclusions, but have faith in your instincts. And keep your goals in your sights at all times.

You might have heard terms like *"confirmation bias,"* or phrases like, *"extraordinary claims require extraordinary evidence."* Who's to say what extraordinary evidence entails? No, that's all just bullshit; it's only about skeptics moving the goalposts until they get their required result. If you want to use the skeptics to keep yourself honest, go for it. But if not, that's fine too. Either way, never make the mistake of looking at them as anything but a kind of hive-mind paradigm.

Always remember how screwed up these guys usually are (a fact which will burned into your brain if you ever spend any time among them) and if you like, do some digging on the dark underbelly of the movement. That in particular can be quite liberating.

You might notice I'm not endorsing or recommending any particular belief system or discipline. I wouldn't want to pretend I'm qualified to make those decisions. I would recommend that you do the requisite research and make sure that people you respect also respect you and take your pursuits seriously. But there is one other thing I'd strongly recommend: a dose of warrior spirit. Too many people interested in alternative pursuits are too reticent to fight for what they believe.

Unfortunately, there are too many people who want to take everything that's important to you away from you, just for a cheap thrill or a momentary ego boost. Are you going to let them?

WHAT I'M REALLY TRYING TO SAY is that you don't need their permission anymore, whoever 'they' may be. Corporate politics has failed you, Corporate Religion has failed you, Corporate Science wants to turn you into a robot. We've seen exactly where reductionism and materialism and hyper-specialization have led us; they've led us to a dead, cold, empty world.

There is most definitely a better way.

BE BRAVE

IN THE NINETEENTH CENTURY, CHRISTENDOM WAS ROCKED to its foundations by the breakthroughs in science and technology, largely financed and enabled by the deep pockets of the plunderous Imperial Age.

The once-placid and serene order of the Universe was called into question, and respectable middle-class intellectuals no longer could claim to believe in biblical inerrancy, or geocentrism or any number of comforting beliefs that had given meaning and certainty to Western peoples' lives since Constantine.

A small vanguard turned to occultism and mysticism to negotiate these treacherous new waters, but for the greater mass of people there were basically two doors to choose from. The middle classes pretty much ignored all the pointy-headed debates in the universities and carried on as before. This position became increasingly untenable with the rise of the mass electronic media. But you also had, for lack of better terms, a liberal reaction and a reactionary reaction.

The liberals embraced the new advances in science and politics and argued that the basic moral teachings of the Bible were intact. These stories were never meant to be taken literally, but were in fact allegories and parables. They'd point to the Gospels themselves to bolster this argument. At first, this was a bold move, a radical reinterpretation of the historical faith.

But over time this approach gave way to a kind of lame hair-splitting and evasiveness, a wishy-washiness and reflexive conflict-avoidance that came to characterize the so-called 'Mainline Protestant' denominations.

And of course, you also had the Fundamentalists. The literal interpretation of Scripture was often the province of backwoods Bible bangers, semi-literate 'Holiness' rabble-rousers who acted as entertainers as much as pastors. But one fine day the director of the oil monopoly Unocal decided backwoods literalism — with its reflexive worship of authority and hatred of anything remotely Socialist — might be good for business, so he secretly published a twelve-volume set of tracts that literally launched the Fundamentalist movement in America, appropriately called *The Fundamentals*.

The rest is a very sad and sordid history, as you're probably aware. One contingent lost its nerve and another lost its mind. I saw that post-Darwin split play out in real time, only I didn't realize it at the time. When I was a kid I took it for granted that pews would be filled every Sunday. But I didn't realize it was because we had a rock star preacher and a kick-ass youth program.

In 1980, our pastor left to accept a post at a big nondenominational church in Boston, so the bishop sent in a more typical product of the seminaries; a milquetoast little bureaucrat who brought in all the latest innovations that the Rockefeller-funded World Council of Churches were conjuring up. Almost overnight, attendance plummeted and the youth group was down to a mere handful. It was over.

And so it goes with liberal Protestantism in general. It's circling the drain.

I'm sure you had a similar situation at the end of the Pagan Age. The Roman Emperors throwing Christians to the lions did so not out of some cynical calculation; they did so because they were genuinely offended by what they saw as the Christians' impiety. Plenty of other cults — Isis, the Syrian Goddess, Bacchus — got as bad, if not worse, in earlier times.

On the other side, you had a host of philosophic cults who could argue against the reality of everything, except the alms they would philosophically coax out of your wallet. Many of these cults may have had more interesting ideas, but like Protestant reformers of the late Nineteenth Century many of them were almost predisposed against fighting their own corners with any conviction. The same could be said of the liberal establishment of the 1960s; they were so concerned with seeing every side of an issue they never bothered to argue their own. Of course, things today are a lot different — and obviously, a lot more polarized — than they were back then.

The same patterns continue, outside of politics and religion. Oftentimes people who are the most interesting thinkers never get around to learning how to argue their positions, and are often raised in environments where fighting your corner is seen as déclassé. But that's just a one way ticket to suicide, particularly in this environment.

T HERE'S A DEAD, USELESS AND OBSOLETE KIND OF MEME that is still hanging around. It's an old notion that really needs to be shot in the forehead and sent to the glue factory, and that's this old hairsplitting tendency, this tendency to argue against your own (or worse, your *friend's*) position in some pointless quest for objectivity.

I don't see that as mature and unbiased. I see it as self defeating, myopic and to be perfectly blunt: *cowardly*. It's also rather egotistical, in that the hairsplitter sets himself up as the arbitrator, the ultimate judge deciding whether an idea or a story is valid. Of course, as with the old liberals, normality bias is always upheld in the end. Which only makes me wonder if the judge has any real insight on the Mysteries at all, or is simply a tourist.

I've been around long enough to see how the self-appointed judges eventually evolve into born-again skeptics. I'm always surprised how shallow and literal their understanding of the Ineffable turns out to be. And that simply shows me that all the hairsplitting and all the "let's not get too carried away now" back-peddling was nothing but chickenshit cowardice all along, a fear of finding themselves in over their heads, discussing something they have no understanding of, or experience with.

Any kind of movement or subculture that gives people a reason to get up in the morning is about *passion*. It's about *intensity*. It's about *conviction*. It's about fighting to get your point of view across. It's about wanting to replace someone else's ideas with yours, come hell or high water. In this day and age, if you aren't passionate and committed about what you are trying to tell people, you won't even be ignored. Because you have to be *heard* to be ignored, and you won't even get that far.

So here's where I stand: You either believe in the spirits, or in Synchronicity, or in the Mysteries and the rest of it, or you don't. It's really that simple. You're either passionate about pursuing alternative models of thinking and consciousness, or you're not. So which will it be?

There's plenty of room for argument and debate that verges on near blood-letting; in fact, that's half the fun of it. But I have I no time for the hairsplitters anymore. I have no time for tired, old Bob Wilson bromides about "Chapel Perilous" or "reality tunnels" or any of the rest of it anymore. Because I know where that road ends. It ends like RAW ended, and that's not a place I ever want to be. I don't think it's a place *anyone* wants to ever find themselves, to be perfectly blunt about it.

This is a process that every person needs to undergo for themselves; it's been that way for thousands of years. But If people are constantly struggling to agree on the vaguest of baselines, then nothing can ever be accomplished, and everyone will just retreat their sanctums like a bunch of bitter old alchemists. And believe me, none of those guys died happy either.

So no matter how depressing and discouraging things may seem now, that does not mean they will remain so forever. History isn't the straight line we're all led to believe, it's cyclical and nonlinear. It has no "sides."

The fact that the current materialist modalities are so intimately identified with the misery and fear people feel today lays the groundwork for their own extinction. Especially this know-nothing, knee-jerk, reductionist denialism that passes for educated enlightenment these days. I don't know about you, but I wouldn't want my personal philosophy to be identified with the world as it stands today. And that philosophy *will*, mark my words.

THERE ARE OTHER FORCES AT WORK IN THIS WORLD. Very powerful yet subtle forces. They affect your life whether you believe in them of not. Hell, maybe even more so if you don't. If there's only one message you've ever gotten from reading this, that should be it.

I've lived the things I write about. I've used Synchronicity and all the rest of it again and again in a very practical way, and I'm always floored by the results when I tally them up. I wouldn't bother with any of it otherwise. What would be the point? I'm certainly not getting rich from any of this.

Yeah, it can get really difficult and incredibly frustrating, but once you get a peek behind the curtain, you simply can't pretend to believe the lie anymore. Pretending to do so will only make you miserable in the end. And maybe if you have caught even the tiniest glimpse of the Real, then maybe consider that that was for a reason. Maybe you were *meant* to do so.

So I say this to you all: *be brave.* Make a commitment and stick to it. Be patient and have the faith that your striving and suffering has a purpose. Have the courage of your convictions. Make the decision whether you want to die on your feet or die on your knees. Because there's sure as hell not going to be a third option on the menu.

Accept that people will reject and ridicule you, then accept that that doesn't matter. Accept that sometimes you'll have to do with evidence in lieu of proof, and with interesting questions instead of simple answers. Have the courage to accept what your senses tell you that you are experiencing, and don't worry about trying to drum up some pseudo-scientific explanation for it. No science is always better than bad science, believe me.

Be brave. Otherwise, you're just wasting everyone's time, worst of all your own.

THE WISDOM OF MYSTERY

A T THIS POINT IN MY LIFE, there is no doubt in my mind that human beings are "not alone." I'm not talking about *extraterrestrials*, mind you. I'm talking about entities that over the past millennia have been perceived or presented themselves as gods, spirits, demons, angels, fairies, Djinn, aliens, ghosts, poltergeists, and so on and so on.

These entities somehow exist outside the normal boundaries of Space/Time and are usually perceived according to the state of mind of the experiencer. I believe that these entities are part of a greater hierarchy which communicates with human beings through the manipulation of symbol and time, a process more commonly known as Synchronicity. This hierarchy is both an objective and subjective reality, in that it exists both within and without the human imagination.

I believe that most people are usually oblivious to these entities, and their forms of communication. With certain exceptions, I believe that these entities can only be perceived through a rather dramatic alteration of consciousness, some kind of break in the normal, everyday patterns of living. And it's a good thing, too. Because we're just way too fucked up to be plugged into that kind of power on a regular basis.

Now, these are all givens in my worldview. They're not issues I feel the need to debate, even though I realize a lot of people violently disagree with these beliefs. I don't care if they do. I care more about finding people who share these beliefs, and then disseminating them to others who are looking for something more than the usual mundane crap we have to deal with every day.

I've been studying all of this stuff long enough where I'm confident enough to make these kind of assumptions. What the exact nature or origin of these entities I'm talking about is totally beyond me. I'm only interested in the effect they have on the rest of us. I'm interested in how cultures wither away and die when they cut themselves off from this other world, the way atheist and secular societies inevitably stop reproducing, or reproducing at a rate sufficient to avoid extinction.

It's happened throughout history, and it's happening now. The numbers don't lie; a reductionist-materialist society is a dying society. History is filled with the names of dead nations and dead cultures, which is why atheists and secularists are so desperate to keep anyone from studying it, other than their politically correct mythology version thereto. I also have a pretty good idea that contact with this other realm is actively discouraged to disempower us, to keep us weak and confused and separated. Always has been.

In other words, there's a reason that all of the NGOs and foundations funnel so much money into the skeptic and atheist movements, as well as into their media amen-corners. Hell, I'll go one better and say that a lot of what passes for religion in this country is hardly any better than atheism itself.

A LOT OF PEOPLE WILL LOOK OUT AT THE VASTNESS of the Universe and feel insignificant. I find it has the exact opposite effect; it makes me feel *grateful*. I'm part of this unique drama. Whoever you are on this planet, you've been let into the cosmic VIP room. Think about that whenever you're getting all down on yourself.

It's been proven that people who strive towards a deeper connection with whatever it is you care to call it — the Infinite, the Ineffable, the Eternal, Doug, Ashley — are able to deal with crisis and major life challenges more effectively than those who don't. I don't think it's rocket science. It can be as simple as having a sense of mission, a sense of purpose. Or it could well be that we need something that unknowable otherness provides, the same way we need vitamins or sunlight.

I think it's the same with magic and myth, and all those other endlessly-discussed but poorly-understood phenomena; they open the mind to realities beyond whatever mundane problems the individual is dealing with, and create a sense of communion and community with something outside the self. I'm not exactly sure how or why all of it works, I only know it does.

So, no, I don't think all of the stuff I write about is inconsequential in times of crisis. On the contrary, I think it's *designed* for crisis, it arises *from* crisis and finds its fullest flowering in times of crisis.

L IFE IS NOT MEANINGLESS. There is a purpose to your existence. You're not alone. There are a lot of people looking for the same things you are. And the spirit world is real and is waiting for you to drop in and explore it.

I know that for a fact.

APOCRYPHA

THE MEANING OF "IS" IS ISIS

O N FEBRUARY 12, 1999, WHEN THE SUN WAS AT ITS APEX in the sky over the Capitol building, the United States Senate acquitted Bill Clinton on impeachment charges which were the culmination of various investigations that dogged the "Big Dog" throughout his term in office.

If you weren't there, it's kind of a long story. I suppose it all started with some bogus land deal the Clintons were involved in (are there any other kind in Arkansas?) then expanded into a sexual harassment suit filed against the Big Dog, which then went kerblooey when the Big Dog's DNA was found on the infamous blue dress of another one of his paramours, the voluptuous young intern, Monica Lewinsky.

After an eternity of contrived partisan wrangling and lascivious gossip, the whole charade ended the only way it was ever going to: with Clinton off the hook and his enemies in the Congress licking their wounds and/or looking for work.

Clinton was destined to be a one-termer before this ridiculous clown-show began, but then spent the last two years of his second term basking in record-high approval ratings. Now he chums around his adoptive family, the Bushes (George and Barbara often say the Big Dog is "like a son" to them).

But we don't care about all of that here, we're in it for the semiotics. And boy, the whole charade was lousy with them: truly fascinating parallels to all of the myth-themes we puzzle over. Where should we start?

How about here: in the Egyptian Mysteries, Osiris was trapped and murdered by Set, the god of chaos. Bill Clinton was entrapped by Kenneth Starr ("a star born of Fire"), who had him impeached.

Set had 72 co-conspirators, which parallels the "vast and organized Right Wing Conspiracy" Hillary Rodham Clinton spoke of: Bill Clinton had been in office 72 months when he was impeached.

The constellation of Taurus was seen as in opposition to Orion, which was identified with Osiris. Ken "Starr" brought his first indictment in May of 1998 (666x3), the month of Taurus in the Zodiac.

Monica Lewinsky came to the White House as a intern after the 1995 government shutdown, a kind of symbolic death that signaled Clinton's political rebirth after the disastrous 1994 elections.

Clinton got busy with Lewinsky in the Oval Office. Not much more need be said about that, other than its alignment with the Washington Monument. Clinton and Lewinsky never got around to the horizontal bop, preferring oral and manual stimulation. Any symbolic parallels there? As if you need to ask...

The Egyptian creator god Atum created the Universe by *autoerotic* means, both oral and manual. In ancient times, a Pharaoh's sex slave would often help her sovereign start his day in a similar fashion, in a ritual symbolic of the creation of the Universe by Atum.

In the ancient Mysteries, Isis cannot find Osiris' tubesteak so she magically creates one from the earth (or variously, wood). Speaking of which, remember the cigar incident? If not, go do a search on it. The rest of you can note that Isis uses the phony phallus to give Osiris the "breath of life" (*nudge-nudge*).

17s are everywhere in this ritual theater piece: Monica was subpoenaed on December 17, 1997, and Clinton gave us the infamous "meaning of IS IS" line during his January 17, 1998 deposition. Clinton then became the first sitting president to testify before a grand jury on August 17 of that year. On Aug. 17 of 2000, Starr's successor Robert Ray(!) empaneled a new grand jury that never went anywhere.

On November 19, 1998, Kenneth Starr outlined the charges against Clinton before the House Judiciary Committee. The very next day the first module of the new International Space Station (IS[I]S) was launched on the Zarya rocket from launch pad 333 at the Baikonour Cosmodrome in Kazakstan, 3,300 miles from the Giza Necropolis.

Zarya translates into "sunrise" or "rising sun" in English."Rising Sun" of course, is Horus in the ancient Egyptian pantheon of gods. "Horus in the Horizon" or more literally "Horus-rising," is symbolic of the transformation between the dimensions of life and death.

On the 16th of December, US and British forces dropped some bombs on the 33rd parallel (Iraq, to be precise). The House Impeachment took place on the 19th of December. Thirteen (13) House managers ran the farce.

December 19th was the day Licinius abdicated his role as Roman Emperor. It was his wedding to Constantine's half-sister in 313 AD that served as the occasion for the Edict of Milan (which he co-signed), that set the stage for Roman theocracy. December 19th is also the day that Apollo 17 splashed down.

The Senate trial opened on 1/7/99, which gives us the requisite 17 and 9s.

After the 13 House managers spoke in the opening arguments, the next lawyer was Cheryl Mills. Here's what the BBC had to say about her:

White House Deputy Counsel Cheryl Mills, the first woman to address the trial, is widely regarded as <u>the shining star of the defense team,</u> and gave an effective presentation on President Clinton's behalf on the second day of defense arguments. A <u>33-year-old</u> African-American, she is known as a devoted protector of the president and first lady...

After opening arguments, there were three (3) witnesses for Clinton. Speaking of 3, in between the opening and closing of the hearings was the 33rd Super Bowl, which saw the Atlanta Falcons (Atlanta is on the 33rd parallel) lose to the Denver (site of the Masonic International Airport) Broncos. The final score was 34-19. 3+4+1+9=17.

There were at least five 33rd Degree Freemasons in the Senate at the time: Trent Lott, Jesse Helms, Arlen Specter and Strom Thurmond (all Republican) and Robert Byrd (Democrat). Like, Clinton, 33rd Degree Mason Albert Pike called Little Rock, Arkansas his home.

Clinton himself was a member of the Order of Demolay, the Masonic youth group named for the last Grandmaster of the Knights Templar whose oppressors - King Philip of France and Pope Clement - both died under suspicious circumstances not long after DeMolay's execution.

The King and Pope of this ritual drama — House Speaker Newt Gingrich and Speaker-Designate Bob Livingston — both suffered political "deaths" when their own indiscretions were "outed" during the trial, sending both men out of Congress (and probably onto greener pastures).

The exact nature of Livingston's indiscretion was never publicized, but it was widely reported he had been married for 33 years. He confessed on Dec 17, 1998. His successor Representative (now Senator) David Vitter was a client of the late DC Madam, as well as the Canal Street Madam.

And just like the three unworthy craftsmen of the Masonic Hiram Abiff ritual, Representatives Henry Hyde, Helen Chenoweth and Dan Burton were themselves humiliated when they were revealed to be adulterers in the press, thanks to the tireless efforts of Larry Flynt.

In the end, Monica's testimony during her 23rd time on the stand absolved Clinton, by saying she had never been asked to lie. This whole episode unfolded over a period of 13 months, from the first revelation of Monica Lewinsky on the Drudge Report to Clinton's acquittal. After the trial, Clinton emerged from the oval office and gave a press conference in the Rose Garden. It was the 190th birthday of Abraham Lincoln, whose own Vice President was the last Chief Executive to be impeached.

And they all lived Masonically ever after.

WHAT WE SPEAK IS SECRET

SYMBOLS ARE HOT THESE DAYS. The unprecedented success of a pot-boiling thriller about ancient codes and secret societies has made symbolism into a national obsession.

Just a few short years ago, symbology was only of interest to academics and white-knuckled conspiracy enthusiasts. But then one little novel opened up a hidden door into a secret world, and introduced ordinary folks to a universal language that is thousands of years old. The cat is now out of the bag: for thousands of years prophets, artists, madmen and poets have been speaking to us in a language that is both consistent and predictive.

But as conditioned as we are to recognize only the verbal — the *literal* — we have gone about our business while others have plotted, prayed, and postulated right under our noses. In addition to being nearly invisible to the uninitiated, this language has a profound effect on those who care to learn it.

Somehow, there is some dormant sector of the human brain that is activated when one immerses oneself in the study of symbology. This is particularly true when the language is used for religious or spiritual reasons. Unlike literal scripture, which is forever pointing to a forever elusive revelation, the immersion into this secret language seems to create its own spiritual reality.

Sometimes meditating upon these symbols seems to make them come to life and speak to you in ways you could never express or articulate. And often when you delve into this world of sacred symbology, the symbols take over and tell you things you never thought you would know.

But the symbols will escape your notice, or at least your conscious attention, until you are able to decode them. And in order to decode them, you must understand where they come from and what those who speak in symbolic language are trying to say. For there are secret languages, and then there is the Secret Language. And the science of decoding symbolic language is commonly referred to as *Semiotics*.

Human beings communicate in three basic modes: verbal language, body language and symbolic language. Of the three, verbal or literal language is by far the simplest and least complex. We learn a vocabulary and then use it to communicate with others. This language is specific and localized. There are several hundred languages and dialects being used by human beings on Earth.

Body language is often used in conjunction with verbal language. It consists of an astonishing array of gestures and expressions, and can even include things such as body temperature, perspiration and scent.

Body language is generally a criminally misunderstood form of human communication. People lie all the time with language. It is much, much harder to lie with body language.

Symbolic language lies somewhere in between. It is an artificial language in that it usually doesn't arise from the voluntary or involuntary responses of the human body itself. It can either be orally or manually expressed. You can speak in symbols — such as a code — or you can write, draw, sculpt or film them. And to those who believe that every artificially expressed communication can be broken down into symbols, even literal meanings can hide secret intent.

Yet for the most part, Semiotics is actually like a secret decoder ring for nonverbal human communication. The goal of this discipline is to ascertain exactly how (and why) nonverbal modes of communication can denote meaning. In semiotics, human communication is broken down into a series of 'signs.' This involves a type of reverse engineering of these symbols, and necessitates tracing the origins of commonly-used symbols in human communication, much as a linguist traces the origins of commonly used words.

These signs are then studied individually and/or grouped into symbolic systems. 'Signs' can include all kinds of objects and events, including image, gesture, body language, sounds, even placement of objects. But unlike Communication Studies, Semiotics con-centrates on *meaning* and not modes.

THE ENTIRETY OF HUMAN COMMUNICATION IS SYMBOLIC. These very words you are reading are a series of abstract symbols we've all agreed represent certain sounds, which we then agree represent certain concepts when used in various combinations. And ultimately, everything we see or hear symbolically represents something else.

When a baby sees her mother's face, a whole series of thoughts and emotions are triggered by it. Her mother's face actually becomes a symbol for those thoughts and emotions: comfort, food, love. The triggers become ever more complex and sophisticated as the baby enters childhood, adolescence, and adulthood.

Likewise, a word not only represents the thing to which it has been assigned, but also the implications and associations of both the word and its object. Even the shapes of the letters can have a Rorschach-type effect on our subconscious minds, as can their sequencing.

Semiotics may seem like some egg-headed European theory from the 1960's like Post-Structuralism, but the term was actually coined by the 17th Century philosopher John Locke. And the method wasn't unique to Locke: Plato, Aristotle, and Augustine studied the use of signs to denote meaning.

Yet the science didn't come into its own until the late Nineteenth Century, when the American philosopher Charles Sanders Peirce developed Semiotics as its own discipline, rather than as a subset of Linguistics. Peirce even believed that, "We cannot think without signs." And one of the best-known semioticians at work today - Umberto Eco - is also a popular novelist.

Semiotics has gone mainstream in the wake of Dan Brown's monster hit novel, *The Da Vinci Code*. The protagonist of that book holds the fictional title of 'Professor of Semiotics' at Harvard University. What Langdon does is better described as a form of *de-encryption*, since the symbols he is dealing with in the story are intentionally designed codes. But he calls upon his understanding of symbology to decipher the maddeningly complex clues thrown at him by the fictional "Priory of Sion."

The Da Vinci Code bears a close resemblance to Umberto Eco's own hit novel, *Foucault's Pendulum*, which dealt with a lot of the same esoteric topics and also showcased the art of symbological de-encryption. But Eco took a far dimmer view of the occult underground that Brown seems to champion, and subsequently, *Foucault's Pendulum* wasn't nearly as successful as *The Da Vinci Code* has been.

DAEMONS IN THE DARK

I MAGINE THAT YOU'VE BUILT A TIME MACHINE. Imagine you enter that time machine and abduct English-speaking pilgrims from the rocky shores of Plymouth, Massachusetts. Imagine you take the brightest citizens you can find and show them your television and your cellphone and Google Earth, things we all take for granted today. How would you explain any of it? How would you explain satellite feeds and wireless internet?

How could you even begin to explain these things to people - separated by a mere moment in geological time - who have no concept of electricity, never mind microchips? Can you imagine the terror, the confusion, and the myths they would create to explain such an experience? No matter how hard you tried to explain these wonders, your poor abductees would have no context at all to process any of it. Even the most serene sounds and images would seem to mock their entire conception of reality.

You wouldn't necessarily need a time machine. There are still isolated tribes in the Amazon, the great heartland of Mother Earth, Stone Age peoples who have been sheltered by millions of square acres of impassible jungle. There have been flyovers of film crews, which surely has caused a great deal of confusion among the tribes. What context do they possibly have for a helicopter or airplane in their conception of the world? These surreptitious flybys must seem utterly magical and mysterious. Or more likely, demonic.

And then there are the cargo cults of the South Pacific, who came face to face with technological society during the Second World War. Cargo cults have become a bit of a cliche in UFO circles, but they and the isolated tribes serve as a more effective metaphor for those of us who subscribe to heretical ideas on flying saucers.

We breathe the same air these tribes do but for all intents and purposes we live in two entirely separate worlds. But would we - *do we* - behave any differently when confronted with a bewildering superior technology?

I 'M ONE OF THOSE HANDFUL OF WEIRDOS who believe flying saucers are real physical objects guided by intelligence, but do not believe they are filled with spacemen from another planet. I believe these things for the very same reason; too many people have been witnessing these things for too long for a truly reasonable individual to dismiss them all as illusions.

But the fact that so many people have seen so many UFOs for such an incredibly long time effectively rules out extraterrestrial vehicles, at least for me.

I loved *Star Trek* more than anyone but the distances between stars are huger than we can imagine. And even if an advanced civilization *has* mastered the warp drive, I don't think they'd come here and behave anything like flying saucers have since prehistory.

Let's go back to those poor abductees from Plymouth. If we were to try to explain our technology to them, we would have to use their modes of language, and here we would inevitably lapse into symbol, simile and metaphor; "It's all kind of like this... or it's as if... or it's like that, you see." It wouldn't be easy. And you can be certain your abductees would see it all as the Devil's work.

Human beings fill in blanks with imagination, and when faced with superior force, those blanks are invariably painted black. As much as we want to believe in angels, I think most of us are afraid that all those higher powers are exclusively demonic. This speaks to the fragility of the human condition. In the end, this world kills us all.

But based on what we know about flying saucers, it's hard to justify these fear projections, even following the liberal rules of evidence in UFOlogy. A skeptic would argue this is because the UFO phenomenon only exists in the human imagination. And perhaps they'd be half right.

Just as I can't find any compelling evidence that UFOs are interplanetary vehicles, neither can I find much proof of recent physical contact with physical "aliens," as we would commonly understand such a thing. The fact that there's been such of variety of creatures reported in these accounts — particularly before the Grey archetype took hold in the media — argues *against* the literal, physical reality of these experiences.

But there is compelling evidence that *something* is going on and has been for a very, very long time. Most people familiar with UFOlogy know that men in black showed up before, if not in a different context, particularly in America. There's a long tradition of encounters, told in the most sober of fashions, with beings good, bad and indifferent as angels, demons, fairy folk, and on and on and on. Local cults would often spring up commemorating these encounters in pre-Christian times.

THERE IS AN ANCIENT KEY that can unlock this puzzle. "Abductees" and "Contactees" have often described their encounters as terrifying, but I've yet to see any compelling evidence of actual physical harm. And these contacts also remind me of ancient contacts that were enshrined into the Mystery religions of the ancient Mediterranean, so much so that terrifying initiates in order to prepare their minds for contact with divine beings became common practice in many cults.

There are of course other explanations for this phenomena -- night terrors, sleep paralysis, and so on — but even without those cases you still have an interesting corpus of contact. You may be familiar with the many parallels between fairy lore ("fairy" being a catch-all phrase here for any number of supernatural but non-divine beings) and modern abduction accounts; the focus on sexuality and reproduction, the hybrids.

Some might use these parallels to dismiss it all, but I see it as confirmation that contact is taking place in an artificial environment that behaves a lot like our modern conceptions of Virtual Reality. How predictable that the gods of the ancient Mysteries insinuated themselves into our modern conception of Virtual Reality from the start: witness the Loa and Orisha manifesting themselves in Cyberspace in the work of SF novelist (and VR theorist) William Gibson.

Or note that the most popular VR narrative of our time - *The Matrix* - also features MIBs as the heavies (as does its prototype, *Dark City*). Both films are also drenched in Mystery symbolism as well. One day we might see it all as a return to first principles.

There are greater mysteries though, ones which the men in black phenomenon raise. Our current concept of physical reality is a reductive, artificial construct, created to facilitate a common consensus that allows the day-to-day responsibilities of life to be seen to. There are conscientious objectors to this construct though, just not ones you can lynch or toss in prison.

THROUGHOUT HISTORY WE'VE SEEN ACCOUNTS of beings and objects which appear and disappear at will, often in front of large groups of ordinary citizens, sometimes in front of cameras. They don't care whether or not anyone believes in them or can even explain them. They do whatever they want and don't worry much about the consequences.

The UFO isn't so easy to explain away, though not for lack of trying. But these anomalous beings are a different story. I've encountered a couple of them myself, and the lingering question in my mind is still *"what the fuck was that?"* But the fact that other people across time and geography have had identical experiences leads me to believe it was not my imagination.

One thing people who have these experiences can speak to is how random, and well, totally *irrelevant* these encounters can be. They usually explain nothing, they accomplish nothing, they confirm or deny no deep-seated need; they just are. Dreams can usually be traced to psychological urges, hallucinations less so, but still seem to fit into some larger psychic context. Encounters with what UFO heretics call "ultraterrestrials" usually make no damn sense at all.

A ND THEN THERE ARE MEN-IN-BLACK. There are a whole host of explanations that can easily explain the phenomenon as gov't agents, pranksters, or simple hoaxes. But what matters is not the encounter so much as the *result*. What was the result of this encounter? If it radically changed the course of a person's life, chances are pretty good that something important is at work. If they scare people, they just as often as not scare them into a heightened awareness of deeper realities than the shampoo commercial reality the snitches and debunkers demand we all be forced to live in.

I'd go even farther: I think we'd sooner trust the reality of a demonic encounter than an angelic one. In fact, a lot of people are inclined to interpret angels as devils in disguise; leading their victims to disaster by hypnotizing them with pretty promises. In contrast a man-in-black seems to be a WYSIWYG proposition.

But ask yourself, are these MIBs doing God's or the Devil's work? Warning a witness not to talk about their sighting, not to pursue the matter at all? To some people that can be seen as a nasty business. But those of us who've seen how UFOlogy can consume or destroy lives, by becoming a career-killing and wallet-draining obsession, aren't quite so sure. Reporting a UFO or abduction experience can open a person up to constant abuse and ridicule, which paradoxically often deepens the UFO obsession.

Would a devil really try to steer a poor soul away from that road? The more I read the MIB lore, the more I'm reminded not of devils, but of those stern-faced angels in Sodom, darkly warning Lot's family of the hellfire about to rain from the Heavens.

If you really take the time to see past the skeptic-believer dichotomy, the UFO phenomenon takes on the feeling of theatre, a high theatre in the skies. The high weirdness of the entire UFO drama, the juicy bits that the fading nuts-n-bolts crowd dismiss out of hand, starts to feel less anomalous than typical the more you really look at it.

If you dispense with the pulp sci-fi trappings and set your sights before 1947 on the timeline, what at first seems bizarre and ridiculous starts to make a lot more sense.

Many of the old UFO legends - the men like Kenneth Arnold and Aime Michel, not to mention John Keel and Jacques Vallee - dispensed with the invader from Zeta Reticuli mythology and came to realize that UFOs and their aftershocks have been our intimate companions since we lived in trees and caves. But this exegesis is a lot less comforting than the idea of space saviors to the believer, and heart-stoppingly terrifying to the debunker.

W E ALL HAVE A NORMALITY BIAS. In fact, for nearly twenty-five years I dismissed what some would see as a classic UFO encounter as a "swamp gas" sighting with weird after-effects. And for good reason; I happened to be driving through the Great Swamp of New Jersey, once immortalized in Orson Welles' *War of the Worlds* broadcast.

But it wasn't until I actually researched swamp gas (or foxfire, or Will o' the Wisp, or faerie fyre, or take your pick) that I realized there's no way it could have been swamp gas. I was my own debunker: I latched onto some weak, lame-ass excuse, one that didn't hold up to serious scrutiny and set it all in stone. I realize today I did so because the experience was pretty unsettling, and not unlike any number of men-in-black encounters (see page 268 for full story)

So even if we (rightfully) mistrust Space Brothers and Fairy Godmothers, we still operate under the assumption that pleasant events help us and unpleasant events hurt us. For my money, that's a dangerous view. Encounters with men-in-black or the like might be scary, but if they lead to a more holistic view of reality — maybe even a more cautious or *skeptical* one, if you will — then perhaps we should think about these things a bit differently.

I tend to agree with the view in High Weirdness circles that nothing entities like men-in-black say or do should be trusted or taken at face value. But if these encounters are frightening or intimidating, that only means we should treat these experiences all the more seriously.

It could well mean that somebody — or something — is trying to get your attention. The least you can do is pay it.

AN DUBIOUS INTERVIEW WITH A MODERN MONK

DUBIOUS MONK: *How long have you been writing?*

CK: Since I was a kid. I started out writing my own comics, then song lyrics, then these long, elaborate scripts for a very Blade Runner-influenced comic book project. But the artist went off to school and I was nowhere good enough at the time to draw it myself. I did a year at the Kubert School, then got a job in New York as a staff artist, so I spent my nights playing in bands and writing songs, which is a great way to learn how to play with words.

I got on the Internet fairly early and did a lot of writing on AOL boards, often on Gnosticism and Mysticism. I published a 'zine in 1994 called *Clash City Showdown* that morphed into one of the first websites on the band. There wasn't anything happening in the local musical scene at the time so I started work for my first comic series in 1994, and it was published in 1996.

That series got the attention of some movie people including Kevin Smith, and I spent a few years doing the Hollywood run-around, which was kind of excruciating. I also did some writing for a Jack Kirby fanzine which ultimately led to my association with *Comic Book Artist* magazine, which won the Eisner Award five years in a row, which is basically the Oscar for comics.

I self-published a book with all my Clash material in 2004, which got the attention of an editor for one of the big rock glossies in London. That eventually led to the *Lucifer Rising* cover feature, which was the best-selling issue of *Classic Rock* and given the current magazine market, probably still is. That in turn led to *Our Gods Wear Spandex*, which in turn led to *The Secret Sun*.

DM: *What prompted you to write the "Lucifer's Technologies" series and what do you hope readers take away from it?*

CK: Well, I'm glad you asked. That series began as nothing more than a filler piece on the *Lucifer* TV show, which is based on a comic series I was a big fan of. I was really busy with my freelance work at the time and just needed something to post on the blog to keep it current.

But here's the thing: sometimes forces outside you take control and you become nothing more than a vessel for stories that want to tell themselves. So as Fate would have it, the project I was working got put on hold so I suddenly found myself with a lot of time to write. And suddenly all of this information on the Lucifer archetype and the postwar tech boom started raining from the sky and dropping right into my lap. Connections I'd never seen anyone else make were demanding that I chase after them.

It was actually kind of a grueling and unpleasant process, very similar to what I went through with the *Secret Star Trek* series. Staying up all night reading reams of material; books, pdfs, websites, etc. I'm not sure I'd recommend the experience. Eventually I broke the Lucifer history off into a separate series.

DM: *What role if any, does magic(k) play in your life?*

CK: A very cautious and respectful one. I ended the *Lucifer Rising* article with a quote about magic from Jack Parsons' friend Ed Forman: *"It's all real, it all works. Don't touch it. You'll get yourself in real trouble."*

My earliest experiences with magical rituals were amateur productions on the face of it, but they had extremely grave consequences for some of the people involved. I learned from a very early age that you don't play around with this stuff. It's not the toy some people make it out to be these days.

So most of my "magical work," if you want to call it that, is about divination. I do a lot of sync work that I don't publish on the blog. I work with the Tarot in a very ham-fisted and indelicate way, but seem to get the results I'm after. I work with the UFO Tarot, which is probably one of the most opaque, sophomoric and confusing decks out there, but we seem to hit it off.

DM: *You write a lot about pop culture, metaphysics and science fiction. You have written about the occult roots of rock and roll as well as comic book superheroes and are currently dissecting Netflix new series Stranger Things on your blog. What do you suppose occult currents are doing in the context of modern music, art and science fiction these days?*

CK: Doing what they always do: animating them, giving them resonance. A lot of our pop culture comes from Nineteenth Century occultism, whether it's superheroes or zombies or science fiction. We take it all for granted now but it's all rather new. Sixty years ago most American kids would be reading *Hardy Boys* and *Nancy Drew* mysteries and watching Westerns and family sitcoms on TV. Even shows like *Superman* were hammered into a very inert pabulum in which a character who is essentially a god was reduced to fighting gangsters and rescuing puppies. The fact that all these occult themes are so well-established in pop culture is a symptom of niche marketing and audience atomization but also a symptom that our society is in serious trouble and that most people today feel vulnerable and marginalized.

I essentially said in *Our Gods Wear Spandex* that superheroes — which are actually the apotheosis of esoteric philosophy — are so popular these days because most people feel like the kid being bullied in the schoolyard, the archetype of the superheroes' audience in the first place.

DM: *After reading your blog, it seems you experience a fair bit of synchronicity and high strangeness. As an author, do you suppose that you attract these phenomena? Which is to say, are you "getting their attention"? "They," of course, being spirits or non-physical entities.*

CK: It's the other way around. I had started writing about this phenomena because I've experienced so much of it. And the writing is an attempt to understand it, to put it into some kind of recognizable context. I was born in the midst and the thick of one of the biggest UFO flaps in history, one that both Jacques Vallee and John Keel both reported on in some detail in *Passport to Magonia* and *Operation Trojan Horse*.

When I was a kid and my parents split up my father's house was so haunted that a medium was actually brought in to deal with it. Which goes to show how extreme the problem was, since my father didn't go for the Paranormal. At all.

And the high strangeness portfolio certainly seems to be growing in the past few years, which seems somewhat counter-intuitive to me. So I guess the blog and the rest of it are simply reinforcing the loop. It's all a result of an obsessive process of evidence gathering, which lead to all kinds of connections that would later inform the work I do today. I have this major OCD thing for evidence, since I feel you can find yourself in very dangerous waters without it. You can find yourself in dangers *with* it too, but at least you'll have some kind of anchor.

DM: *Of all the books you have written, do you have a favorite? If so, which one?*

CK: Well, probably *Clash City Showdown*, since that's the only one I had any control over. One of the reasons I've concentrated on blogging and haven't published anything in a few years now is that I've been frustrated by the restrictions I've had to deal with ever since my first comic series twenty years ago. Publishers are very pennywise and pound-foolish when it comes to page counts. I can't be constantly worrying over the word count as I'm writing. Economy is important but some-times you need space for your ideas to breathe.

DM: *Do you draw any parallels between the art of writing and the art magic?*

CK: Yes and no. I think there's a lot of very loose and facile talk about writing and magic, but it starts to feel a bit precious after a while. Magic and writing are two very different disciplines and are after different outcomes. Writing is still essentially about the exchange of information through ordinary means and magic is still essentially about influencing outcomes through extraordinary ones.

Writing can wield its own kind of magic but it's important to understand the lines of demarcation do exist, and neither writing nor magic is served by promiscuously blurring them.

DM: *What advice do you have for young authors just getting started today?*

CK: Learn how to write lyrics. It will teach you three vitally important elements in writing, and that's rhythm, economy and color. There should always be a pulse to your writing, a backbeat. You'll find it helps the process in ways you couldn't imagine.

Economy is another essential tool in the Internet Age, since there's so much competition for the same eyes and ears. Studying and writing lyrics will also help you to punch up your prose, and add a color and texture that puts more zing in the reading.

DM: *Who are your personal heroes, in writing and life in general?*

CK: I don't know if I really have any heroes anymore. I don't know if this is a function of age or a reaction to the crushing realities of the so-called New Normal, the grim, everyday world of oligarchic control and contrived chaos.

The world today reminds me of the original *Rollerball* film, in which a sport to specifically engineered to instill the sense of futility of individual effort — and of heroism itself — in the masses. It's amazing how prophetic those dystopian Seventies sci-fi movies were.

There are a lot of people I admire, but I suppose the people I will take as heroes will be the ones who can figure out how to lift the Globalists' Sword of Damocles from above all our heads.

DM: *Any interesting projects coming up on The Secret Sun or other creative outlets?*

CK: Well, I do have a novel series plotted out and most of the first book has been dialogued. I'm very excited about this project, the question remains if it's the best way to get back in the game.

Another reason I've concentrated on blogging, since I can publish whenever and whatever I want to, depending of the time available. I've been very punk rock about putting all work out there for free on the blog, but blogging is a very ephemeral form. Even the very best work tends to evaporate fairly quickly. Books still matter, which is a good thing. I do want to get back in the game, but I'm leaning towards self-publishing given my prior experiences.

THAT WAS THE GEEK
THAT WAS

THE DEMENTED 13: THE SECRET SUN HORROR HALL OF INFAMY

I T'S ONE OF LIFE'S PARADOXES: a lot of my favorite movies are generally classified as Horror, but Horror as a genre usually bores me. It's kind of the same way with me and heavy metal. See, the problem when you get to my age is that you've heard and seen it all before. And usually heard and seen it done a lot better. And nothing sucks quite as hard as bad Horror or bad Metal.

When I was a kid, the local grindhouse (The Strand, in Quincy Center) used to run double features of all the usual slasher and gore pictures. For a buck or two you had the privilege of sitting in a cold, grimy shitbox with greasy floors to watch kids slightly older than yourself get hacked to bits. I'm here to tell you that it all got old pretty quickly.

Hellraiser came along in the late Eighties and kicked off the torture porn sub-genre, but that never grabbed me on account of me not being a sociopathic sex-pest. Then *Scream* came along in the Nineties and kicked off the meta-Horror craze, but I was too old to care at that point.

Of course, *The X-Files* dipped into the Horror wellspring on a biweekly basis, and its sister show *Millennium* was essentially a spin on *Se7en*, with a healthy portion of *Red Dragon*. And both were heavily influenced by *Silence of the Lambs*, which is just highbrow Horror with pretensions to art. The boundaries between Horror, thrillers, and science fiction tend to get awful squishy.

But even if 99% of the genre has nothing for me, the economics and culture of Horror allows a certain amount of freedom to get really weird, as well as delve into the questions that preoccupy me. Namely, what do people put their faith in, how did those beliefs come about and how do those beliefs influence their behavior.

I T'S WHY THE TWO SUB-GENRES OF HORROR that interest me most are Folk Horror and Occult Horror. Both center on belief, and how belief can drive otherwise conventional people to do things they otherwise would not. Occult Horror tends to focus on devil-worship and black magic and Folk Horror usually centers on remnant or revanchist fertility cults, but again, the lines of demarcation are not always fixed.

So here's a sampling of some of my very favorite Horror movies. Some bleed into sci-fi, others into the thriller bin, and some aren't really all that scary, but all have a lot of meat on the bone when it comes to themes, concepts and subtext. They're movies that make you think, which is all any artist can ask of his audience.

QUATERMASS AND THE PIT (1967)

I HAVE A SECRET TO SHARE: Quatermass films and serials may present themselves as science fiction, but they're really straight-up Occult Horror.

Quatermass isn't really a scientist, he's a demonologist and an exorcist. The aliens are not any different than the demons of a hundred-thousand penny-dreadfuls and Pulps that came before, at least half of which Nigel Kneale surely read. All of the sci-fi trappings are just that: trappings. Window-dressing for the quasi-rationalist mindset of the time.

Quatermasss and the Pit is simply an old-school "curse of the forbidden tomb" narrative, no different than *Blood from the Mummy's Tomb* or *Raiders of the Lost Ark* or any number of Lovecraft stories. Quatermass even consults with old Christian texts locked away in a monastery.

I haven't confirmed it yet, but my guess is that Kneale got the original idea from the excavation of a Mithraic temple a few years before. The same temple now housed in Bloomberg's London headquarters. You can watch the film or the late Fifties serial it's based on, they're both floating around out there. Both make for very high-quality viewing.

THE MEPHISTO WALTZ (1971)

THIS IS ONE OF A FLOOD OF OCCULT-THEMED POTBOILERS to arise in the wake of *Rosemary's Baby,* and boasts a pre-*MASH* Alan Alda and an off-the-charts gorgeous Jacqueline Bisset. It was made by TV super-producer Quinn Martin, which is why it has the feel (and cast) of an early Seventies TV movie. Only with boobies.

That said, this is a well-rendered occult thriller worthy of classic Dennis Wheatley. The satanism isn't the moronic Anton LaVey cringe you'd expect but something altogether quieter and more sophisticated. And all the more unsettling. Alda plays a reporter assigned to interview a legendary pianist played by Curt Jurgens and soon finds himself lured into the older man's creepy, culty world. The film also takes an interesting sharp left turn: the first act focuses on the Alda character and the rest of the film on the Bisset character.

As with all good Horror, there's a distinct subtext of class politics at work here. Alda and Bisset are the working class strivers who the Jurgens character and his circle regard only as objects, as resources to be exploited. This is integral to their philosophy of evil; the inability to honor the lower classes as truly human. Gives the ending an extra kick.

SIMON, KING OF THE WITCHES (1971)

I DON'T KNOW WHAT THIS FILM IS CLASSIFIED AS, but it's a horror story as far as I'm concerned. It's a real-life horror story about how the Occult can lure very intelligent and capable people into its sticky web, by dangling the ever-elusive promise of apotheosis. And so it is that after mastering the magical arts, our hero finds himself living like a rat in a storm-drain and scraping for cash by offering his services to the rich and jaded. One of these writes him a bounced check and kicks off the grim proceedings.

Simon is a horror story of what happens when Hubris meets Nemesis. It's also a movie anyone thinking of fucking around with witchcraft should watch. Hopefully it will change your mind.

I strongly get the feeling this film influenced Alan Moore's creation of John Constantine, and I'd bet Grant Morrison gave it a spin or two. It's also incredibly well-rendered and realized, and Andrew Prine absolutely *owns* every single inch of the scenery he gnaws on.

GOD TOLD ME TO (1976)

OH, MAN. OH, MAN. OH, MAN. MAN. OH.

Oh, man.

God Told Me To is one of the most insane spectacles ever put to film. Larry Cohen basically collects every fringe idea circulating during the grim, grimy mid-70s, throws 'em into a pot and comes up with a movie unlike anything else before and probably after. Interested in elite cults, mind control, alien abduction, hermaphroditic hippie messiahs, urban blight, Catholic guilt? Well, you're in luck, because it's all here and it's all fucking crazy.

Robert Forster was originally cast in the starring role but Tony LoBianco owns it. This is a Big Apple story, set and filmed in a city that seemed to be on the verge of total collapse. You can't even begin to imagine anyone but the earnest, sad-eyed LoBianco driving it.

God Told Me To premiered shortly after the first Son of Sam shootings and seems to metaphysically converge with them, on so many Maury Terry-worthy levels. I don't remember if Terry mentioned this film in *The Ultimate Evil*, but if not, he should have. Keep your eyes peeled for Andy Kaufman in a small but pivotal role.

INVASION OF THE BODY SNATCHERS (1978)

W HEN I FIRST SAW THIS AS A WEE WANE I thought it was the most terrifying movie ever made. As a matter of fact, I think the same today.

Why? Because it isn't just a scary movie, it's a dead-on prophecy of the Woke pod-people plague that in large part unleashed their earthly infestation in the same city (San Francisco) the film is set in. This is all very sci-fi and cinematic - and very, very Seventies - but it depicts all too well the process unfolding all around us today. Today's pod-people even have a near-total stranglehold on vital communication systems, the same way as depicted in the film.

I suppose that's all old news for a lot of extremely online people these days, but that doesn't make it any less true. If you haven't seen this movie, watch it now. If you have seen this movie, watch it again now.

THE VISITOR (1979)

G OD TOLD ME TO IS INSANE, but generally coherent. This absolute bath-salt-absinthe-bender-delirium-tremen of a movie is insane too, then also generally even more insane. This is *Jodorowsky-level* celluloid insanity, only without the hippie self-consciousness and winking irony.

And *The Visitor* is even more insane, because with its standard-issue Hollywood cast — John Huston, Glenn Ford, Shelly Winters, Mel Ferrer, Lance Henriksen — you get the sense that Guilio Paradisi thought he was making mainstream cineplex fodder but was too batshit/bugnuts to fully grasp how utterly incoherent and hallucinogenic it all is. You may feel like you've dropped a heroic dose halfway through it. If in fact you did drop a heroic dose, it will probably sober you up.

The plot? Does it matter?

PHANTASM (1979)

Y EAH, 1979 WAS ONE OF THOSE YEARS. Kind of a precursor to 1983. In fact I see them as twins in some strange way. It's hard to say why when it comes to Horror, because most of the movies released in the genre in 1979 suck. But then again there's *Alien, The Visitor, The Brood, The Quatermass Conclusion* and this no-budget movie, which seemed to come out of absolutely nowhere and blow everyone's mind.

Like the others I've mentioned, *Phantasm* not only fucks with genre, it does the same to reality. *Phantasm* is essentially a Lynch-worthy meditation on the power of nightmare and hallucination, so much so that those inner turmoils start to overwrite reality.

Weirdly enough, I didn't even see *Phantasm* until it came out on VHS a few years later, but I felt like I had. I generally don't have a good memory for stories and plots, but I felt like this movie was exactly as I remembered my mental image of it being, and that's even the scenes beyond the ones they showed in the trailer. I almost felt like I'd lived it. Or more disturbingly, dreamed it.

JACOB'S LADDER (1990)

L ONGTIME READERS KNOW ALL ABOUT ME and this film. If you're new to The Secret Sun and need a sense what I'm all about, all you need to know is that I've watched Jacob's Ladder a least a hundred times and probably a lot more than that. In other words, there's something seriously wrong with me. I accept it. It's my lot in life.

This is yet another movie that got quite a lot of hate back in the day but has since become a cult classic. But it's one of the few Hollywood movies to deal with MKULTRA seriously at the same time it's also a long-form meditation on the Catholic concept of Purgatory. Adrian Lyne also single-handedly created a visual template for demonology that heavy metal video directors have been exploiting ever since.

Jacob's Ladder anticipates the dream-reality magic of *Lost Highway*, *Mulholland Dr.* And *Inland Empire*, at the same time it pays visual tribute to *The Exorcist* and grungy urban realist movies of the early Seventies like *The French Connection*.

DAGON (2001)

I 'M BEGINNING TO THINK THE ONLY WAY you can adapt Lovecraft is to basically *not* adapt Lovecraft. What I mean is that you need to kind of take his concepts as suggestions and then construct your own story out of them, the way Alex Garland did with *Annihilation*. Stuart Gordon did that a lot, but this kind-of sort-of adaption of "The Shadow Over Innsmouth" is the most effective example of it.

And unlike Lovecraft, Gordon was interested in women so he gives them major roles in the story.Gordon got his financing from Spanish investors so he sets the film in rainy Galicia.

That was a wise move, because the Cape Ann of Lovecraft's time is long gone: his original model for Innsmouth looks like Paramus with seagulls now.

A lot of people hate this movie — nearly everyone I recommended it to got very angry at me, mostly on account of the extreme gore — but I think it's an unheralded classic of Occult Horror.

THE MOTHMAN PROPHECIES (2002)

WHAT I SAID ABOUT HP LOVECRAFT holds especially true for Keel. Though maybe it doesn't, seeing that Keel didn't write fiction (even if a lot of people think he did).

The Mothman Prophecies book is one of the most confusing and unsatisfying things I've ever read, though I'd probably have thought differently back in the Seventies. Happily, Richard Hatem and Mark Pellington took Keel's batshit blizzard of rumors and anecdotes and built a coherent narrative out of it. It helps that they're backed up by a solid cast. Gere is suitably morose and bewildered, Laura Linney is immensely sympathetic and appealing, Wil Patton does his whole Wil Patton thing, and Alan Bates tears into his role with a gusto unseen apart from any Al Pacino performance of the past thirty years.

However, this film is especially valuable in that the Bates-Keel character gives the viewer a very useful primer on the malicious and untrustworthy nature of ultraterrestrials. Pay special attention and rewind as needed.

THE BOX (2009)

THIS RICHARD KELLY PICTURE GOT ALL KINDS OF HATE when it came out, which just absolutely baffles me. I can only guess everyone was still feeling cheated over *Southland Tales*. Or maybe everyone just wanted another *Donnie Darko*. Or maybe it was Cameron Diaz's very flimsy Southern accent.

Kelly set out to make a 1970s kind of drive-in movie and I think he succeeded admirably. For my money it also succeeds on a philosophical level, exploring the seductive power of Evil and its consequences. It also has atmosphere to burn and was filmed in a lot of neighborhoods near my old church.

I hope he continues to make films. David Lynch is getting on in years and Panos Cosmatos isn't exactly what you call prolific. We need more of this brand of dream-reality cinema.

MANDY (2018)

D O I REALLY NEED TO SAY ANYTHING more about *Mandy?* It's simply one of the greatest cinematic achievements in the past quarter-century and folds in so many ideas, themes, archetypes and modes you could spend the rest of your life unpacking it. It's everything I could ask for in a horror movie and will strike chords with *Hellraiser* and *Evil Dead* fans, though it's infinitely better than both.

Nic Cage is at his Nic Cageiest and makes his *Wicker Man* performance seem deadpan in comparison. But it works to the point that there is literally no one else, alive or dead, worthy of playing this role. The supporting cast are all absolutely flawless, the direction and cinematography makes *Twin Peaks: The Return* look an old *Doctor Who* serial and the music is cosmically attuned to the madness that unfolds as you sit and watch, spellbound.

So what exactly is *Mandy,* when all is said and done? *Mandy is* simply the alchemical distillation of a half-century of Grindhouse cinema, sprinkling in tinctures of all the greatness hiding in those unlovable movies with none of the mindless dreck.

THE DROVING (2020)

T HIS RECENT ENTRY IN THE "NEW FOLK HORROR" sweepstakes might seem a bit slow for some, but I see it as a parable on fighting dragons too long, as it were. As former SAS man Martin, Daniel Oldroyd utterly *inhabits* the role of an ostensible everyman searching for his beloved sister, who has gone missing in the Lake District and is presumed dead.

But we soon discover that Martin isn't quite the everyman we first thought, and by the film's end we realize he's every bit a monster as the monsters he's hunting. Even more so, really. The transformation is gradual but total, and offers up very effective commentary on the dehumanizing effects of wars of choice.

The folklore here was all concocted for the film, but you will believe every stitch of it, particularly when Martin's journey meets its ultimate destination.

THE YEAR THAT BROKE REALITY

NINETEEN EIGHTY-THREE HOVERS LIKE A WRAITH over all of my work and I've never been quite sure why. All I know is that I sensed something definitively change in the spring and summer of that year, even if those changes have only become apparent in the past few years. But I can say for sure is that something somehow seemed to have entered our world from somewhere else. I've never been able to define it and I can only try to track it by what you might call a process of elimination. It's harder than it sounds.

So, I hear you asking: what exactly happened in 1983 that was so earth-shaking? Well, how about the birth of an obscure little venture called the Internet? That "earth-shaking" enough for you?

No? Well, how about the dawn of the Cellphone Age? The first cellphone went on sale that year. How about the premiere of a plucky little upstart of a software suite called Microsoft Word?

Or maybe a little something called the Macintosh computer, which put a weird-ass whiz-kid from the Bay Area on the wider world's radar?

Starting to get the picture yet? Weird, right?

Cold War v1.0 nearly got hot on a number of occasions in 1983, what with the downing of Flight 007 on the first of September, the Soviet Nuclear False Alarm that same month and the provocation of the Able Archer war-games in November.

Note that all three of those potential armageddons were caused by malfunctioning computers. Something to bear in mind as Cold War v3.0 starts to heat up.

THE NEW AGE MOVEMENT, which has since become so ubiquitous and totalizing no one even notices it anymore, first came to the mainstream's attention in 1983 with the publication of proto-manic pixie dream-girl Shirley MacLaine's confession of crystal-clutching faith, *Out on a Limb*. Note: the character of Chris McNeil in *The Exorcist* was based on MacLaine.

The New Age would inspire a firestorm of reaction from conservative Christians throughout the Eighties, cut-and-pasted vestiges of which are still floating around the Internet. But by the end of the next decade all but the most traditionalist denominations would be recast in the New Age's mold, particularly the megachurch and Prosperity Gospel movements.

And in an irony so delicious it could only arise from a totally broken reality paradigm, the Christophobic corporate media are now the ones squirting out kittens over the New Age. Specifically, the growing overlap between it and the QAnon movements, both of which are disproportionately peopled by middle-aged/late middle-aged women. As was Theosophy (AKA "New Age v1.0"), incidentally.

H IV WAS REPORTEDLY ISOLATED/IDENTIFIED IN 1983, and AIDS went from a loose constellation of symptoms grimly-nicknamed "the gay cancer" to an officially-diagnosed syndrome. The fact that AIDS first raged amongst an isolated population that participated in the CDC's Hepatitis B immunization trials seems to have been forgotten. As has the widespread use of toxic party drugs like amyl nitrates and fuck-knows-what-the-hell cocaine and heroin and ketamine etc etc etc were being cut with. Not to mention the dangerously immunosuppressive effects of zinc deficiency brought about by excessive ejaculation.

I'm sure it's all an oversight. You forget things, I forget things. It's part of being human.

R OCK MUSIC WAS THE ABSOLUTE EPICENTER of youth culture in 1983 so it's only natural that the Us Festivals — held on a sun-seared hellscape in California's godforsaken Inland Empire — were conjured up as an aborted attempt to wed rock music to the emerging *Les technologies de Lucipher*.

To that end, Apple cofounder Steve Wozniak 33° set up air-conditioned tents where heatstroke-dodging young GenXers could browse the latest in digital devilry, not realizing the abuse and/or overuse of which would ultimately atrophy the minds, bodies and souls of much of their progeny. Not to mention their own future earning potential.

Feudal lords and barons would bankroll major festivals and carnivals to keep their serfs and sharecroppers pacified, so it's only natural that the moguls and khagans of the nascent Horned Caliphate would do the same.'Caliphate' in the Thelemic rendering of the word, of course.

T HE SEEDS FOR 1983 WERE PLANTED A VERY LONG TIME AGO, and the process that flowered that year first began to bloom in 1979. So it's no surprise that two pictures that best encapsulated the elusive energies and forces that emerged in 1983 were actually produced in 1981. Said films, *Liquid Sky* and *Wavelength*, look at the same phenomena, but from Manhattan and Hollywood POV's, respectively.

The former was largely shot in a five-block radius between Danceteria and the Koreatown brownstone penthouse the film's lead lives in. The latter is largely set in Laurel Canyon and the mysterious Lookout Mountain complex that will be familiar to Dave McGowan readers. The energies emanating from both locations would start to spread all over the world in 1983.

HOW WEIRD WAS 1983? It was so weird that David Cronenberg released two movies. The only other time that happened? 1979, of course.

Videodrome might seem more than a bit dated today, but only if you don't transpose the basic themes Cronenberg was exploring from the cable TV age to the social media age. It's actually more timely now than it was in 1983, if examined in that context.

The Dead Zone is an excellent film on its own, but has become all the more important in light of what we now know about the remote viewing programs running at the time under the aegis of INSCOM, or the US Army Intelligence and Security Command. That connection isn't explicit, but hovers over the film all the same.

Consider the fact that both *The Dead Zone* and *Brainstorm* were released within weeks of each other and that both starred Christopher Walken, even though *Brainstorm* had also been made in 1981 and was shelved after the drowning death of co-star Natalie Wood. Then consider that *Brainstorm* was directed by Douglas Trumbull, who was responsible for many of the special effects in *2001: A Space Odyssey* and *Close Encounters*, and was based on a premise written by Bruce Joel Rubin of *Jacob's Ladder* and *Deep Impact* fame.

Then consider that the Esalen Institute played a major role in the making of *Brainstorm*, and looms over many other films that year. Then remember that Esalen was being run by the Council of Nine channeling cult at the time. *1983*, everyone.

WarGames came out in March and neatly anticipated the aforementioned apocalyptic near-misses a few months later. It's also the first major exposure the early hacking underground got, at least that I can recall. The film's female lead Ally Sheedy first grabbed me by the attention when she guest-starred as a very naughty schoolgirl on *Hill Street Blues,* also in 1983. Later she'd star in a very 1983-worthy — and microbe-themed — episode of *The Outer Limits,* along with Peter Proud himself (that's Michael Sarrazin, for you non-geeks).

The Hunger, based on a Whitley Streiber novel, was released shortly after AIDS had been declared to be an identifiable syndrome but has since been seen to be a prophetic allegory of such. But it also coincided with the rise of Goth as an identifiable subculture (as opposed to just a subgenus of post-punk).

Bauhaus, who perform *The Hunger's* opening theme, didn't stick around to capitalize on first-wave Goth, having split after their underwhelming 1983 LP *Burning from the Inside*, recorded while Peter Murphy was stricken with pneumonia. A disease, incidentally, that would come to grim prominence beginning in 1983.

NINETEEN EIGHTY-THREE WOULD HAVE AN IMPACT both on Whitley Streiber and the world with the start of the Hudson Valley UFO wave, which lasted for several years. Streiber would document his own UFO wave in his Hudson Valley vacation home in the 1987 blockbuster *Communion*. That book would make alien abduction a household world and later be adapted into a film starring — you guessed it — Christopher Walken.

Last but not least, there's the 1983 film to end all 1983 films, even if it was released in early 1984. Or as I like to call it, "1983's spillway." The zeitgeist had shifted rather decisively by springtime, which is why it was pointless to do any *Stranger Things* sequels in the first place.

My friends and I vibed heavily on this film even if we had a Bostonian aversion to Mohawks, which were strictly for poseurs. But Harry Dean Stanton is at his Harry Dean Stantoniest, Emilio Estevez's flat-top deserved its own onscreen credit and Olivia Barash radiates so much high-frequency Ally Sheedy energy that I actually thought she *was* Ally Sheedy.

Either way, *Repo Man* effectively depicts how something else had entered our reality in 1983, even if it does so in the context of farce.

AND THAT'S REALLY THE POINT OF ALL THIS: something from outside our reality entered into our reality and began the slow and deliberate process of rewriting it. I have no idea what it is or where it came from, or if it even came from anywhere. I just know it's kind of a 'Call of Cthulhu' deal where the artists and the sensitives had been dreaming it and documented those dreams in songs or stories or whatever.

In a historical sense, this is all happening with frightening speed. Even the most clueless normies can sense that something is very, very off, even if they haven't a clue how or why.

So it's no accident then that three of the most highly-charged filmic presentations of the past decade are based in 1983.

The first of which is *Beyond the Black Rainbow*, written and directed by Panos Cosmatos ("the Cosmic Pan"). The specter of Esalen looms over the proceedings as you'd naturally come to expect. A lot of people have told me they have trouble with this film, to which I can only say put on your big-girl panties and fully enter into its dark, labyrinthine mysteries. It's required viewing here.

Stranger Things — meaning the first series and not the dumpster-fire/clown-orgy sequels — obviously lifts a lot from *Beyond the Black Rainbow*, on account of lifts a lot from everything. But that is precisely its genius.

If you want to know what 1983 was really all about, the first *Stranger Things* is a good a place to go as any. I've done a number of rewatches and it still blows my mind how a couple of dopey Millennials can capture that ephemeral 1983 essence so well. Of course, there are at least a dozen writers and producers listed in the credits, and my gut tells me that first-wave GenXer Shawn Levy was probably the man behind most of the *Stranger Things* magic.

Dunno what happened with the second and third seasons, which give you less an Eighties vibe than a hobo-throwing-up-in-your-mouth vibe. But as I said, they were surplus to requirements anyhow.

Finally, Panos Comatos — the poet-laureate of 1983-ology — stepped back up to the plate with *Mandy*, which brilliantly captures how the spiritual milk of the Aquarian Age had gone rancid by that time. Maybe that played a part in whatever happened in 1983, I don't know. But it's definitely something I think we should find out for sure.

TIMOTHY LEARY'S STILL DEAD

LONGTIME READERS KNOW THAT one of the biggest influences in my late teens and early twenties was Carlos Castaneda. Whether or not those stories are factual (and the general consensus seems to lean towards the "not"), they were genuinely magical in and of themselves for me. I learned a more important lesson in Castaneda's storytelling techniques than in anything Don Juan did or did not say. The books cast their own spells, regardless of whether or not they were true accounts.

Though it was Jack Kirby's work where I first encountered the numinous power of the psychedelic storytelling mind, it was Castaneda who first showed me how it could be done simply with the power of the written word. Maybe that's a power that every good writer wields, but it was Castaneda who really put me smack dab in the middle of the magical environment he was constructing. Not only did I believe every word, I *experienced* it.

Maybe the magic wore thin as the stories dragged out (well, more than maybe) but *Tales of Power, The Eagle's Gift, A Separate Reality* and *The Teachings of Don Juan* are still major touchstones for me.

Another huge influence on my younger brain was Timothy Leary. Not his Sixties LSD evangelism, mind you, but his Eighties pimping on behalf of the potentials of the Internet and Virtual Reality. Of course, Virtual Reality has yet to truly materialize, at least in the William Gibson sense. But it was an interview with Leary in the Twentieth Anniversary issue of *Rolling Stone* that turned me onto Gibson and the nascent Cyberpunk movement.

Being primed for the experience by Cyberpunk novels and Leary lectures, I can honestly say my first year on the Internet was itself a psychedelic experience. We're talking a 2400 bps hayride straight to America Online, but it was like a shot of liquid sky straight into my cerebral cortex. Maybe it was just the potential of it all I was buzzing on, but the first time I signed onto AOL (sometime in September of '93, a pivotal month in my personal timeline) I saw my future. Or rather, I *felt* it.

I was also very excited about the Cyberpunk/New Edge movement and was a huge fan of *Mondo 2000,* but if your subculture is accessible enough for Billy Idol to hitch his wagon to it, you know your basic operating philosophy is fundamentally flawed.

One thing a lot of do-it-yourself shamans — including Leary — didn't seem to understand is how rigorous and structured the ancient psychedelic traditions were/are, and how much sacrifice and suffering was called for.

To Leary and his compadres, LSD seemed to offer an instant workaround all of that. Instant shortcuts were very much part of that Space Age zeitgeist, something we've all learned to be far more skeptical of today.

I also blame Leary for popularized a drug most people aren't really equipped to deal with, and a drug that did as much — if not more — harm than good when it was cut with speed and strychnine and God knows what else. Once the Summer of Love ended with a thud, a lot of shattered psyches faced a long, cold winter.

A LAN WATTS NEVER SINGLED OUT TIMOTHY LEARY in his lectures on psychedelics, but it's clear he didn't approve of mainstreaming LSD or psychedelics in general. And, the hidden hand of the Company is all over Leary's bio, a fact that a lot of his friends have had a very hard time coming to terms with, including RAW.

I *want* to believe Leary was compromised, and was cornered into a situation that forced his hand, but there's the problem of MKULTRA lurking in the shadows here, no matter how ridiculously the program has been mythologized.

I don't think the Gottlieb boys knew from psychedelia; they were more concerned with developing neural weaponry. Since then, we've seen a parade of more demonically-effective psychotropic pharmaceuticals, and no one seems to be talking much about creating psychic spies anymore.

A whole host of powerful neural tools were suppressed largely out of political and cultural concerns, meaning that a bitter and destructive generational split in the Sixties created a backlash against potentially-useful compounds that honest doctors and therapists should have had access to, as well as individuals and groups involved in serious research and exploration. That's the way it was in the early Sixties, but something screwed it all up.

Sadly, Timothy Leary played a major part in the screwing.

PHILIP K. DICK'S YEAR OF THINKING MYSTICALLY

W HAT'S THE DIFFERENCE between madness and mystical thinking? It's a question that needs to be asked. For me, it's simple: the difference is the *result*. Usually, it's the only yardstick we have at hand.

It's funny: people seem to muddle through on the edge of total incompetence all around us, and everyone lets it slide. It's not until a person begins to commit thought crimes — ie, they begin to question commonly-held assumptions on the nature of Reality — that their own competence is called into question and held to much higher standards than their peers.

If you challenge the dominant reality paradigm you will receive an invisible but yet indelible scarlet letter on your forehead, and the most pathetic, most incompetent, most imbecilic people will be free to mock, ridicule and harass you with utter impunity. Hell, they'll be *rewarded* for upholding the sacred virtues of conformity, tedium and entropy that the Serious People™ want to blanket the world in.

But once in a great while, a magical thinker somehow transcends all of that and is accepted into the Invisible Pantheon. This can be a curse; this pantheon is filled with people whose works are admired and praised yet utterly ignored.

Serious People™ find it necessary to purchase the works of these thinkers primarily as a kind of magical talisman that will bestow on them the Badge of Seriousness®, which signals to other strivers that they are fit sexual partners, pliable employees and acceptable dinner party guests.

So when you see copies of *Finnegan's Wake, Pet Sounds* and *There Will Be Blood* on someone's shelf, don't be surprised if they look remarkably new and unmolested. And whatever you do, don't point out that art is meant to be *experienced* and understood, not simply purchased. There is no greater *faux pas* in middlebrow circles than questioning the magical powers of status-minded consumerism. Fuck with that at your own peril.

Mystical thinkers only reach the Invisible Pantheon once they're safely dead and are no longer at risk of saying inconvenient things about Reality. Critics will praise their work and compare it to other safely-dead Mystical Thinkers, though only in the context of literary criticism or anthropological observation.

Philip K. Dick is one of these. You see him compared to Borges a lot, as if Dick needs the Argentine's posthumous endorsement to be taken seriously by Serious People™. Dick's religious obsessions are particularly inconvenient, but enough Serious Critics™ have granted him absolution on this count that it's overlooked.

Dick's transformative experience — the 2/3/74 event — is generally overlooked by Serious People™, though it's often recounted with the requisite sadness, head-shaking and tut-tutting. Poor soul; had a schizophrenic break, don't you know. Seeing pink beams and hearing messages in Beatles songs Must have been all that mystical bullshit that did his head in.

Now, mystic beams of pink light might seem like the definition of pathological delusion, but speaking as a parent, I can tell you there's no result more important than the life of your child being saved a painful death from an undiagnosed ailment. We can question the agency of the beam — it could well be a manifestation of Dick's own unconscious, which detected that there was something not quite right with Christopher — but the supernatural doesn't like to operate like that.

In order to deal with the supernatural you have to speak its language and face it on its terms, not yours. At the same time it has a funny way of tailoring itself to its audience; for religious people it calls itself Miracle or Revelation. For Ray Kurzweil, it calls itself the Singularity. For so-called skeptics, it's anomaly, which needs to be promptly-but-quietly deleted and the deletion meticulously covered up.

Dick was a bit all over the place in his religious heterodoxy, but knowing how words work he left a record as to what the supernatural *felt* like.

"March 16, 1974: It appeared - in vivid fire, with shining colors and balanced patterns - and released me from every thrall, inner and outer. "

March 18, 1974: It, from inside me, looked out and saw the world did not compute, that I - and it - had been lied to. It denied the reality, and power, and authenticity of the world, saying, 'This cannot exist; it cannot exist.' "

March 20, 1974: It seized me entirely, lifting me from the limitations of the space-time matrix; it mastered me as, at the same time, I knew that the world around me was cardboard, a fake. Through its power of perception I saw what really existed, and through its power of no-thought decision, I acted to free myself. It took on in battle, as a champion of all human spirits in thrall, every evil, every Iron Imprisoning thing."

Dick really knew his religious history and called upon it to describe his experience, which essentially was the experience he'd been working up to for years prior. Same goes with Alan Moore; he didn't suddenly go from being a stockbroker to becoming a wizard. He'd been playing footsie and making goo-goo eyes at magic for some time before taking the final plunge. But Dick had been a basket-case prior to 2/3/74, so if it was a psychotic break like the Serious People™ would have us believe, it was the strangest psychotic break I've ever seen.

This was an *integrative* experience for Dick, not the disintegrative collapse you'd associate with psychosis. Dick cleaned up his act, and got his house in order, leading to having his work optioned by Hollywood.

2/3/74 produced *results*, of the psychic kind (Christopher's hernia) and the take out the garbage and balance the checkbook kind. I realize this doesn't fit with the narrative put forward by the dominant paradigm, but not everyone ends up like Jack Parsons (though his JO buddy certainly did pretty well for himself).

Carl Jung had a nearly identical experience to 2/3/74, and it inspired him to change the face of popular psychology. He was no less a mystical thinker than Moore or Dick — or Parsons, for that matter — and the only downside for him seemed to be dodging the brickbats of the Guardians of Mediocrity (that's mainstream academia for those playing along at home). Whatever guise it takes, Mysticism can often produce some positive results for its suitors, providing they don't try to bend the supernatural to their own will.

From my reading that always ends badly, for all involved.

ANCIENT ALIENS BURIES THE LEDE

A NCIENT ALIENS IS NOW IN ITS SEVENTH SEASON. I usually record it, but don't watch it that much anymore. It's gotten to the point where it's not telling me anything I don't know already, and having been on the other side of the camera a number of times, I know how the game is played.

What's very clear with the *Ancient Aliens*-style of interviewing is that the producers are looking for soundbites. They will prompt the interviewee to repeat the question in their own words and then give the required answer. I speak from experience. And anyone who's watched a number of episodes of *Ancient Aliens* probably can recite the answers along at home.

I've sometimes defended *Ancient Aliens*, but the fact of the matter is that I have a *lot* of problems with it. But I'm also mature enough to realize that any criticisms I have of the show are irrelevant. It is what it is. It wouldn't be aired around the clock if people weren't watching it, and it wouldn't have been renewed six times if it wasn't making money.

Compared to the original two-hour specials, *Ancient Aliens* is running on fumes, content-wise. It makes for pleasant enough background noise from time to time, but hasn't told us anything new for a while (*The Satanic Conspiracy* episode, while misleadingly titled, did have some good information on the Watchers). But this latest episode on superheroes was something else. Not only did it have the stock answers that you could hear on any episode on any topic, they blew the lede in a major way.

As I've been writing about since this blog went live, comic book superheroes didn't just materialize from the ether like tulpas as the *Ancient Aliens* cast of regulars repeatedly suggested, a good many of them were created or co-created by Jack Kirby. And the ones he didn't create or co-create, he had a hand in, like Iron Man and Spider-Man.

And Jack Kirby is a guy who was not only doing stories about ancient astronauts a long time before Erich Von Daniken, he was using AAT as the basis of the superheroes he was creating, beginning with *The Inhumans* in 1965. Kirby was so obsessed with AAT that it consumed the latter part of his career; three of his titles for Marvel in the 1970s were built around the theme, and he did a number of other AAT projects after he left comics for animation.

What's more, his prescient "Face on Mars" story from the late Fifties showed a distinct Theosophical influence with its ancient extraterrestrial civilizations, demonstrating he may have been exploring the same material that inspired Edgar Rice Burroughs for his own Mars material.

But aside from Kirby, you also had Otto Binder, who was not only one of the great writers of the Golden Age of Comics, he was also a prolific sci-fi writer, the editor of *Space* magazine, and the co-author of the classic AAT text, *Mankind, Child of the Stars*. Binder is not as well known as Kirby is today, but he wrote the Captain Marvel comics, which at the time were Superman's number-one rival on the stands, selling upwards of a million copies a month and inspiring a number of spin-offs.

It's really too much to ask at this point; a tiger doesn't change its stripes. And in a way, I'm glad Kirby wasn't drawn into the reductionist POV of *Ancient Aliens*, a show which does its best to make none of these old stories seem alien, as in *god-damn-what-the-fuck-you've-gotta-be-kidding-me* alien. It's just more naturalism, more materialism, more shopping-mall-American-midnight.

You see, materialism doesn't lead to a nation of scientists, rolling up their sleeves and boldly pressing at the frontiers of human knowledge. It leads to a nation of YOLO hedonists, drinking Jäger shots from each others' navels while running the Visa bills deep into the red at Cabo and Ibiza. Materialism gives us Kardashians, not Carl Sagans.

I could be wrong, but *Ancient Aliens* comes across as a show for people who've never had an *alien* experience, for people who've never tripped balls or ripped at the coffin lid of Infinity, or for people who've never had such an experience forced upon them.

It's just the same old, same old: mind-blowing mystical experiences (which nearly all of those ancient texts describe) reduced to a 1980s Saturday morning cartoon. It comes across as a show for people who haven't had their worldview shaked and baked. It's a show that takes the magical and makes it mundane, that takes the psychotronic and makes it pseudo-scientific.

I want to defend *Ancient Aliens,* I really do. But I can't. This was a golden opportunity — a major architect of today's pop culture who was also obsessed with ancient astronauts — and they blew it. Just blew it. I'm sure Gerry Jones told them about Kirby, I'm sure their other comics guests probably did as well. But what do we get? The same exact soundbites you hear on every other episode.

Go back and watch all the AAT documentaries from the Seventies, with Rod Serling and William Shatner and Leonard Nimoy and so on and so forth. Even if you don't believe a word of it, that stuff still holds up as entertainment and still kicks ass. And you definitely get the feeling that those motherfuckers were *experienced,* in the Hendrix sense.

THE SPACE BROTHERS ARE RUNNING A LITTLE LATE

S YFY IS FINALLY GETTING AROUND TO ADAPTING Arthur C. Clarke's classic novel, *Childhood's End*. It's one of those books that feels as if you've already seen it onscreen, probably because its plot points have been hijacked so many times by so many writers. It's a foundational text, not only in modern science fiction, but also in modern UFOlogy'. And I write this from the perspective of the Post-Postmodern age, where "modern" implies "archaic."

Which is why I wouldn't have signed off on this project if I were the head of SyFy. It's great science fiction, but it's of its time in a way many — perhaps *most* — of Clarke's books are. They speak to a confident, muscular liberalism, the certainty of linear progress, and the unalloyed benefits of world government. Some might argue that *Childhood's End* has a downbeat, indeed *apocalyptic* ending, but it's actually just Darwinism writ large, the inevitable macro-evolution of an undifferentiated blob as a cosmic certainty.

Childhood's End is a kind of Globalist fairy tale, a myth for the heady days of the early postwar era, when rational discourse in the Hall of Nations would solve all of mankind's problems. Only religious backwoods bumpkins, with their knee-jerk paranoid delusions, stood in the path of our new utopia.

But *Childhood's End* also stands as an artifact of the early days of the UFO era, when apocalyptic fervor was grafted onto the burgeoning phenomenon. Ironically, evidence for UFOs then was minuscule compared to what has been amassed today. But that's part of the process: the imagination takes over and fills in the blanks when facts on the ground are missing. It's the power of human expectation to project onto the Great Unknown.

Most of this was processed through science fiction, and not taken seriously or literally. But it persisted as a question in the public's mind, reaching its apotheosis with Spielberg's *Close Encounters of the Third Kind,* one of the most explicitly mystical works of popular art of the past century.

Then as now, the UFO phenomenon is/was primarily one of constructions of light, ones that predominantly *hover* instead of fly. And usually hover in place in ways that seem to defy the laws of physics, I should add. Observers as diametrically opposed as Philip Klass and Jacques Vallee made note of this, as do careful study of witness statements.

Some researchers have begun to wonder if the resulting contact scenarios weren't in fact hallucinations caused by some kind of stimulation of the temporal lobe by these mysterious lights. It's a fascinating theory that only deepens the weirdness of the phenomena, even if diminishes the messianic fever that once surrounded it.

Given the avalanche of garbage that surrounds the topic, it's tempting to dismiss the UFO issue all out of hand. Certainly the endless territorial pissing matches among UFOlogists are a major disincentive against looking any further into the issue. Until, of course, it reaches into your own life.

Despite a lifetime of skywatching, I had only one borderline encounter until this past year, when first my son, then my wife and daughter and myself encountered these mysterious constructions of light. My son had the presence of mind to record his; we were driving so we weren't as lucky. But all I can say is that we saw two classic orange orbs and they seemed to be moving under intelligent control. They also seemed to be bothering conventional aircraft, another hallmark of the phenomenon.

I can tell you that the reason that these thing look so blurry and indistinct on film is because that's how they look in the flesh. The word that keeps going through my mind to describe them is "unwholesome." I don't make any claims as to their nature or origin, all I can say is that people everywhere have seen these things forever. Take it as you like.

Unfortunately for *Childhood's End,* there's no real UFO culture to market the film to, at least not like what you saw twenty years ago when you had a large and active UFO convention circuit. I think that's because the subculture it exists in has changed, with a lot of conspiracy people falling for the whole Project Blue Beam psyop and many others no longer having the kind of quasi-religious expectation of our Space Brothers that emerged out of the early New Age movement.

A lot of this is the function of the post-NAFTA, post-GATT uncertainty economy, one in which the real unemployment rate hovers in the teens (as one honest Presidential candidate has pointed out), not the five-percent fiction floated in our increasingly-Soviet news media.

In a strange way, this all reminds of the early Christian movement, which we know from texts like *Contra Celsum* went through a long wilderness period of its own, and also emerged during a time of great social unrest. Strange as it sounds, it makes me wonder what the future holds for the UFO issue, given that we are living through a bad Roman Empire LARP at the moment as well.

A scholar studied the period and determined that the Christian movement was not only marginal within the Roman Empire, it was vanishingly small, right up to the end of the Third Century CE. His estimate had the Christian population at less than one-half of one percent (0.36%) circa 200 CE. Religious scholar Bart Ehrman estimated that it was no larger than five percent of the Empire at the time of Constantine, a figure other historians have confirmed.

The 0.36% number fascinates me. Having been raised in a serious Christian environment, it contradicts everything I was taught about the early Church. We were told Christianity was an oppressed majority kept down by a tiny, decadent elite, who knew every word of it was all true but suppressed the Faith so they could carry on with their immoral lifestyles. 0.36% also sounds about right if you were tallying up the amount of people who follow some kind of UFO belief system today.

Better still, it's probably the exact percentage of the population that watches *Ancient Aliens* religiously, as it were. *Ancient Aliens*, curiously enough, seems to have to moved away from couching all of their arguments in Saturday morning cartoon sci-fi and are moving towards a distinctly more supernatural worldview, more like the superior Seventies material that originally inspired it.

All this came to mind when a UFO debunker recently compared the Apostle Paul to the UFO movement, a comparison that sounds specious to everyone but Valleean-type Magonians. The mysterious light, the disembodied voice, the radical change? UFO reports are filled with those kinds of things.

I still have tremendous respect for Paul as a religious visionary and polemicist. But it has to be acknowledged that Paul, like many of the Early Church, believed the Second Coming was imminent, despite what modern apologists may say to the contrary. This fact also contradicts theories that Paul was invented centuries later by Roman propagandists. Which can't help but remind me of *Childhood's End*, and the messianic UFOlogy it was inspired by.

I wonder; did the Church have a strong kickoff but lose steam as it became apparent that Christ was not coming back in the believer's lifetime, just as it's become obvious that Disclosure is not imminent, or that the Space Brothers aren't about to land? Like UFOlogy, early Christianity thrived on a culture of Apocalypse. What happened when it all failed to materialize? The comparisons might seem spurious, if not downright insulting, until you study the distinctly Magonian texts of some of the Christian groups whose arguments didn't win out in the big Roman councils.

I don't know what the future holds for Humanity or for the UFO issue. As I've argued repeatedly, the best way to look at UFOs are as a surveillance program, in the Fortean tradition. Its mysteries and enigmas all seem to fall into place in that context. But until something somewhere changes dramatically, I don't see the kind of mythology expressed in stories like *Childhood's End* gaining much traction in the public imagination.

The apocalypses we believe in today are the dystopian variety, the miserable hell-on-earths of the zombie shows and the rest of it. A critical look at our popular culture tells us that we are a tired, broken, beaten-down people. Even our apocalypses have been downsized.

NEVER MIND THE MAINSTREAM

I WAS VERY PASSIONATE ABOUT MUSIC when I was a kid; punk and post-punk bands, particularly. It was a very hard passion, since these bands almost invariably threw themselves into the music industry Cuisinart at one point or another. I actually dreaded turning on the radio, since a lot of these acts began selling out in earnest.

The worst part about it all was reading the music papers and seeing the tortured rhetoric spill out of so many of my former heroes' mouths, as they sought to recast the soft rock, disco and pop pabulum they'd declared just months before they would erase from the charts as somehow now being "progressive" and "revolutionary." It was worse than painful; it was *humiliating.*

Of course, the sellouts weren't at fault for marching to the record industry's dictates: it was *their fans' fault* for not recognizing the revolutionary intent of serving up more of the same old crap that'd created the need for a New Wave in the first place.

Some of these acts scored hits, but most of them bombed badly. Most not only failed to win a mainstream audience, but usually alienated the considerable fanbases they had already acquired.

So when I was working on *The Secret History of Rock and Roll,* I came to have a new admiration for heavy metal culture. Not necessarily the music, mind you (I was more a hard rock fan and there's a very big difference between the two), but most definitely for the networks of bands and fans that grew and thrived despite almost-universal contempt from the mainstream, and particularly from the mainstream media.

Rock critics went out of their way to pour scorn on Metal when it split off from hard rock in the mid 1970s, which is not to say critics were all that big on hard rock either. But the critics had absolutely no effect on Metal. All they achieve was delegitimizing rock criticism. And not only in the eyes of Metal fans, but in the eyes of all the other new subcultures the entrenched, aging Boomer critic-class hated and feared, and that includes most of post-punk and synth-pop.

So a few years back some of the big English glossies put out collections of old clippings from the British music papers on the bigger bands and movements of the early Eighties. And what these cash-ins ultimately proved was how uniformly hostile the critics were to the bands that people still care about today.

I remember reading the papers back then and learning to distrust journalists at a very early age. I remember going to concerts and watching the audience explode in cathartic bliss, and then reading some sniffy dismissal of the show in *The Boston Phoenix* or somewhere. I also came to realize that the acts the critics cared about were comprehensible only to the critics.

Metal alone didn't make rock criticism irrelevant, but it certainly helped. And for fans of Metal, the only criteria that matters is whether or not the bands bring the noise. Metal culture not only exists *outside* mainstream acceptance, it exists in *defiance* of it.

Reading about the history of the ancient Mystery cults, I learned that heavy metal is actually very ancient indeed. Literally the *only* difference between ancient and modern Metal is electricity. The ancient headbangers dressed up like Spartans, played huge metal stringed instruments and used all sorts of things (including shields) as percussion. Anything to make a fucking racket.

And ancient Greek philosophers tripped over each other in writing orgasmic paeans in honor of the ancient metal gods like the Korybantes, Dactyls and Kouretes that read like clippings from back issues of *Kerrang.*

All of this came to mind when I was reading a Fortean site doing what so many Fortean sites do, and that is wringing their hands about how best to surrender their principles to the mainstream.

Concurrently, I saw a major alt.researcher complain about being dismissed as a "conspiracy buff" by some douchebag academic archaeologist, to which I replied that academia is never going to accept anything outside its orbit, and there is no halfway on which to meet them.

Those people are no different than the rock critics of the early Eighties, attacking all the important bands of the time while heaping praise on acts that absolutely no one remembers today.

The Fortean in question also said that people interested in anomalies needed to unite under an umbrella term like "Anomalism," (*gag*) to which I replied that anomalies are mere symptoms, what needs to be discussed and sought after are the *causes*. Like the nature of reality itself.

I've also been thinking about Gnosticism and those academic types looking to replace the liberal Protestantism of their youth with a mildly exotic variant. I was listening to a roundtable of "modern Gnostics" recently, and while all the individuals involved had all the proper credentials, they made Gnosticism sound like a particularly arid variant of Methodism.

I couldn't even make it halfway through the talk. It certainly didn't sound like the do-or-die Gnosticism of the Mandaeans, or Cathars, or Druze, or even the early Mormons. It sounded tamed, like one of those radio-ready singles from one of those former Punk rebels of the early Eighties. It won't ever make any fresh converts. It won't even keep most of the stale ones in the fold.

Maybe the basic temperaments of your average metalhead and your thoughtful Gnostic are just too different, but I think those of us looking to question the assumptions of our reality consensus have a lot to learn from the take-no-prisoners, my-way-or-the-highway attitude of your average metalhead.

The Establishment - the *Mainstream* - has no interest in compromising, and there's no point in pretending otherwise. So stop worrying about what those who have already sold their souls think. There is a viable and ancient and endlessly fascinating alternative to the prevailing consensus. A alternative that offers up lots of evidence for those willing to take the time to look.

SO MUCH TO ANSWER FOR

UNLIKE MANY FIRST-WAVE PUNKS, Johnny Rotten actually was a product of the working class. Born to Irish immigrant parents and raised in a dumpy flat on the wrong side of London, yet possessing a keen intellect and a biting wit, Lydon's rage against the pampered classes was no pose.

And so it was that Johnny was too stroppy and insolent to pretend that national hero Jimmy Savile wasn't a particularly noxious kind of evil.

Savile's predilections were always hiding in plain sight, it's just that no one wanted to notice how much attention he paid to little girls on his various television programs. England needed an Irish wise-ass with absolutely no fucks to give to point out that not only did the Emperor have no clothes, he was also diddling very young children all over the British Isles.

It's mind-boggling in hindsight, given how extravagantly psychotic and demonstrably-lecherous Savile was, but mass media conditioning is a very powerful thing.

Lydon was absolutely fearless and possessed of an uncanny magnetism and charisma in his prime. One interviewer complained how intimidating it was to talk to a man who fixed his unblinking stare on hapless journalists, making it clear he thought they, their magazines and their entire profession were ridiculous. He did not suffer fools gladly, nor protected predators.

Lydon was also an early version of the current Joker archetype in very many ways, and I wouldn't be surprised at all if Heath Ledger studied his performances when prepping for *The Dark Knight*. Ledger had definitely studied Jaz Coleman — an admitted acolyte of Lydon's — but I see a lot of Johnny Rotten in his performance as well.

So let's talk about that time when the cassette played Poptones.

IN MANY WAYS, YOU NEED TO UNDERSTAND THIS MUSIC to understand The Secret Sun. Even though I was immersed in comics and mythology at a very early age, it wasn't until I discovered Post-Punk that it all began to click for me.

I spent my childhood not only reading comics and the like, but I also kept my radio all the time, even when I slept. I developed an extremely intimate relationship to music. But it wasn't until when bands like Public Image Ltd (aka PiL) rolled into town that I began to truly appreciate the power of music to create landscapes in the mind. Which is a kind of magical power all its own, isn't it?

The point of this is that I spent quite a lot of time in the summer of 1980 getting very, very high and imprinting — hell, *engraving* — PiL's *Second Edition* into my unconscious, and it was a literally life-changing experience. One of the great lessons it offered was that anything can be taken apart piece by piece and reconstructed in ways not only more to your liking, but in ways that activate sectors of your psyche you never knew that you had.

PiL was formed in the wake of the Sex Pistols split. John Lydon was always frustrated with the Pistols' musical conservatism (at its core , their music was a stripped-down, revved-up version of the Rolling Stones) and enlisted a Dub Reggae bassist (Jah Wobble) and a Prog Rock guitarist (Keith Levene) to really tear things up.

They began by creating a dissonant, angular version of Punk, then a weird kind of Dub-Funk with *Metal Box* (AKA *Second Edition*), and after firing Jah Wobble, made an album based entirely around aggressive drum patterns (*Flowers of Romance*).

These two albums are legit magical totems for me. They exist in a very deep and primal unconscious space, essentially of their own volition. It's interesting to note that PiL were all toying with the occult at the time they made this music, which would later result in a haunting that drove Lydon from his lodgings and into a hard bed in a coal shed (this event would later be immortalized in the harrowing "Under the House").

A number of stories have circulated as to the song's meaning but I remember reading back in the day that "Poptones" is being sung from the point of a view of a murder victim ("you left a hole in the back of my head") whose body has been left in the English countryside.

There is something very deep and strange about this song, something that still gets under my skin. If there had been another "rock" song that put the bassline so front and center — particularly such a weird and confrontational bassline — I can't think of it. It's like an infernal machine casually winding its way through a subway tunnel, an effect only heightened by the fact that Keith Levene is playing guitar parts he admittedly lifted straight from "Starship Troopers" by Yes.

I had never heard anything even remotely like this at the time, and I'm not sure I've heard anything quite like it since. It arrived like some Lovecraftian invader into a musical and cultural landscape much, much different than our own, and planted strange seeds in its new environs. Rock critics compared it to Can, but those happy German hippies never unleashed anything nearly as eerie and inhumane as this.

"Poptones'" lyrics may not mention Ian Brady and Myra Hindley - the so-named "Moors Murderers," who raped and murdered several children in the Manchester area in the early Sixties - by name, though "hindsight" may certainly be an unconscious slip. But the theme of a body left in "foliage and peat" might very well have been inadvertently inspired by them. And I certainly hear strange echoes of "Poptones" in the Smiths' lament for Brady and Hindley's victims, "Suffer Little Children."

It's not obvious at first: The Smiths come across like comforting voices at a funeral, whereas PiL come off like jaded coroners at a crime scene. But the delicate guitar arpeggios in both songs make a strange beauty out of unimaginable terror.

Both songs take their time wandering around a single chord, and both feature a deep, heavy, modal bassline and mournful vocal. It's almost as if the crimes Morrissey is singing about are so much more real and profoundly horrible that they have to add that much more beauty to compensate.

It's interesting to note that both Lydon and Morrissey are from Irish Catholic families, particularly in light of revelations that have emerged about the Church since. Lydon had held a particular animus towards the institution after the local parish priest had been too drunk to come read Lydon's beloved mother - a devout practicing Catholic - her last rites as she lay dying.

The Moors Murders story also has a very Catholic flavor to them - specifically the child-hating, Jansenist heresy that took root in Britain and Ireland before coming over to Boston in the Nineteenth Century — as I saw in HBO's docudrama, *Longford*.

It was a very strange synchronicity for me; I had been out walking at night listening to PiL, and *Longford* greeted me when I got home. Something was triggered deep in my subconscious, and a connection that some admittedly may not sense was made. The poisonous climate of child hate and sexual psychosis that is the true legacy of religious extremism has created more monsters than you can name, but Hindley is certainly near the top of the list.

The title "Longford" refers to Francis Pakenham, the deeply religious Anglo-Irish Lord Longford who spent his time volunteering as an advocate for prisoners. A well-intentioned but profoundly gullible and delusional man, Longford may well be the *"bleeding heart, looking for bodies"* that Lydon was processing in "Poptones."As brilliantly portrayed by Jim Broadbent, Longford was used to dealing with ordinary criminals, but his traditionalist Catholic idealism was no match at all for the elemental evil of Hindley and Brady.

Samantha Morton puts in a wonderful performance as Hindley, but has no trace of her subject's ice-cold hate in her soft, delicate features. But we do see the decidedly erotic pull that Hindley had over both Lord and Lady Longford, and we see the destruction she wreaked on their lives from her maximum security prison cell. The wooly-headed idealism of the idle rich is also nicely contrasted with the instinctual revulsion of the poor when dealing with monsters.

The Moors Murders struck a very deep chord in a generation, as witnessed by "Suffer Little Children." Some processed the trauma in a different way. Throbbing Gristle dispassionately recounted the details of the crimes in "Very Friendly" and Crass attacked the tabloid obsession with Hindley in their song "Mother Earth," rightly pointing out how it acted as a convenient cover for the media's own murderous hatred and sexual predation.

But for many English artists, the shattering of the innocent certainties of childhood meant that all bets were off. Everything would need to be called into question. Those youthful terrors stoked by monsters like Ian Brady and Myra Hindley were baked into the darkness and rage that informed so much of British punk and post-punk in the Seventies and early Eighties.

TWILIGHT OF THE SPANDEX IDOLS

I T'S OVER. THE GOLDEN AGE OF SUPERHEROES, that began with the first X-Men movie, reached critical mass with *Iron Man* and *The Dark Knight*, then peaked with the *Infinity War* movies, is now winding down and wrapping up. The Zack Snyder movie isn't going to revive the genre, because the genre is exhausted and can't be revived.

Not only is the genre exhausted, but the very-costly CGI these films live and die on doesn't look nearly as impressive on a TV screen — even a large TV screen — as it does on the silver screen. In fact, the CGI looks kind of dopey and silly, and makes everything look like a Nineties video game.

Superheroes going all meta and self-parodic, like you see with *The Boys* and *WandaVision*, is always a strong indicator of a cycle's end. Marvel began publishing a self-parody in 1967 after the so-called Silver Age had peaked creatively and began to ebb. Superhero parodies were also big in the mid-to-late Eighties as *Watchmen* and *The Dark Knight* put the Canonical Age of Superheroes to rest.

Parodies — often unintentional — rose up again in the mid-Nineties after the market crashed and the first wave of self-cannibalizing retread superheroes that rose in the wake of the Canonical Age's end crashed on the rocky shores of a pandemic of retailer insolvency.

Comic book sales have now gotten so catastrophically bad that no one releases their actual sales figures anymore. Mind you, those figures have been artificially inflated for a very long time, to cover for the fact that there were never more than 250 thousand active comic-book fans in the US at any given point since the mid-70s. The nature of the specialty market — which cushioned publishers against losses by eliminating returns of unsold product — was enough to sustain a brisk and profitable industry for quite some time, even when you consider the periodic market crashes.

The class of TV superheroes aimed at a young female audience (mainly on the CW network) was never entirely healthy, but the shows are all cratering — hard — now. The writers and producers of these shows are like the addled heirs of old money fortunes, selling off the carpets and silverware to support their bath-salts and clown-porn addictions. All they've really done with their careers is burn down the mansions that reared them and salt the fields that fed them.

Publishers and producers alike are showing signs of panic and desperation in the face of encroaching economic oblivion, hence Hail Mary moves like arbitrary race/sex/gender swapping in hopes of finding new demographics to hawk their sloppy seconds to. You also can't help but get the feeling they — and anyone signing off of these surefire failures — are just trying to burnish their CVs with PC points for when they hit Netflix up for a pity deal.

The fact that so much hope is being placed on *Zack Snyder's Justice League* shows just how desperate things are getting. Joss Whedon's *Justice League* was a miserable failure that cost a lot of top execs at Warners their jobs. And in the surprise of all surprises, Whedon's long-rumored assholery is finally getting exposed, just in time to clear a social media path for the premiere of Zack Snyder's version of the JL.

Longtime readers know I'm a huge fan of Snyder's *Watchmen* (sue me), which I think underperformed at the box office for the same reasons his other DC movies did: his sensibility is too Nineties grunge and dark for the mass market, especially for families. So I'm not necessarily expecting his *Justice League* to suck. I'm just expecting it to be too dark for the audience HBO Max needs to pump up its subscription numbers.

Whedon took the reins on *Justice League* when Snyder suffered a family tragedy, in what was one of the weirdest moves in showbiz history. Kind of like Soundgarden replacing Chris Cornell with Weird Al Yankovic. Whedon ballooned the budget by reshooting like a drunken sailor, and it all came out like the sauerkraut ice cream sundae you'd expect from such mismatch of sensibilities. I'm sure the Snyder cut will be a lot better — and a lot more coherent — I just think it's too late.

THE STENCH OF FAILURE IS NOW WAFTING FROM THE GENRE, a stench that's very hard to wash off. *Wonder Woman 1984* was a flop at a time the studio could least afford it. The new *Batwoman* series is an absolute catastrophe, its latest episode barely squeaking by a half-million viewers. A planned *Wonder Girl* series was killed in the cradle. *Supergirl* was canceled, *Black Lightning* is about to follow, and *Swamp Thing* was axed before it could find an audience. *The Flash* and *Legends of Tomorrow* sputter on with absolutely no effect or impact on the culture.

Marvel seems to be very gun-shy about releasing *Black Widow*, not exactly a vote of confidence in a picture that was finished some time ago. And they're pinning their "Phase Four" hopes on a clutch of characters with no constituency or track record.

In fact, they're following in the footsteps of Marvel Comics in the 1970s, and adapting a lot of the characters launched to reverse the company's fortunes after the superheroes of the Sixties — the same ones who made billions for Disney in the 2010s — began to sputter in the sales department. It didn't work then; why should it work now?

I can speak to this with some authority, having created artwork for Marvel characters as a freelancer for 25 years. I was also a huge fan of The Eternals, Shang-Chi (AKA *Master of Kung-Fu*) and — of course — Doctor Strange as a kid, but I was a weird kid. None of these characters had much of a following back in the day, and they've all had series relaunch after relaunch over the years without much success.

Even this *Justice League* project harkens back to those decline years: the film frontlines Darkseid and Steppenwolf and the rest of Jack Kirby's 'Fourth World' milieu. Kirby created these characters when he left Marvel for DC, and despite the endless revisionism from his apologists they were miserable failures, sales-wise. They've since been given chance after chance to find an audience and they just never could. They're just not very interesting characters.

Jim Starlin, a death-obsessed Vietnam vet turned writer/artist who borrowed heavily from Kirby for his *Infinity Gauntlet* stories (Thanos is a shameless knockoff of Darkseid), finally figured out a good use for the Fourth World — as Justice League supporting characters — in the *Cosmic Odyssey* miniseries in 1988 and set the stage for their exploitation from that point on.

It's interesting to see the same characters launched after the Silver Age/Avengers characters crossover event "The Kree-Skrull War" was published in 1971 slated for Phase Four MCEU movies. "Kree-Skrull" established the prototype that gave rise to *The Infinity Gauntlet* twenty years later, and eventually reached its apotheosis with The *Infinity War/Endgame* films.

Of course, all of the friggin' lockdowns are just making everything worse. Comic book stores were already gagging for it before them, and I have no idea how they're keeping afloat now. Conventions — pathogen incubators in the best of times — have all been shuttered, and I doubt many will resurface even if all this bullshit ever does end. A open question, at this point in time.

I hate to see anyone suffer but I can't say I'm feeling too sorry for these people. Most of them — and ALL of them under the age of thirty — are mewling Globalist bootlickers, and accept everything the corporate media feeds them with a degree of quasi-religious submission the Taliban would find excessive.

So after dodging the Reaper more times than I can count, I think superheroes are finally finished as a cultural force at least for the foreseeable future. Superheroes belong to nations, not empires. They're the big brother who sticks up for you when you're getting picked on in the schoolyard. They first arose amongst the poverty and urban violence that followed in the wake of the waves of mass immigration in the early Twentieth Century, and went mainstream in response the rise of organized crime in the Prohibition era.

The heroes got a makeover in the run-up to World War II, with all the campy, fetishistic costumes (most of the first wave of superheroes wore regular street clothes, more or less). You had the whole Nazi-punching business in the early days of the war which bluechecks on Twitter love to post on their timelines, conspicuously ignoring the more problematic racist caricatures of... well, pretty much everyone else in pretty much all of the other comics of the time.

And those same bluechecks don't dare mention all the *Commie* punching, which you saw on those same comic book covers for the next couple of decades after the war ended. Same way they don't dare mention the inconvenient fact that those troops who stormed the beaches at Normandy in their pro-Antifa memes were fighting in racially-segregated militaries. But nearly everything Blue Twitter thinks, says and does is a deliberate lie.

Which is why we won't talk about all the grotesque, Klan-level racist caricaturing from those same heroic Hitler-punching purveyors (which seems to getting memory-holed on search engines), nor will we talk about all the blatant pedophilia in comic books, either.

Actually, psychologists like Josette Frank and Frederic Wertham and commentators like Gershem Scholem were talking about the rampant pedophilia in comic books — more like screaming to the rafters — in the Forties, Fifties and Sixties, respectively. And people listened, which is why Congress cracked down on the industry. That's all gotten memory-holed, too.

With the benefit of hindsight, it's nearly impossible not to get a snootful of pedo-ick looking at all the boy sidekicks of the Golden and Silver Age of superhero comics. It was particularly icky at DC, which Scholem might have been referencing when he declared the entire industry to be made up of kiddie-fiddlers. Of course, you can say the same thing about whoever came up with all the ancient myths superhero creators were lifting ideas from. The more things change, and whatnot.

I'm certainly not saying superheroes are going to disappear entirely, but I am saying their moment has passed. Nothing ever really goes away anymore, so they'll stick around in some form or other.

I largely stopped reading superheroes (conventional superheroes, certainly) after *The Dark Knight* and *Watchmen* first came out, because I didn't see any need for new stories. Frank Miller and Alan Moore had put the final touches on the archetype and there didn't seem to be any need to say anything further. And no one really has, possibly aside from *Kingdom Come*.

See, nothing really new has been said about superheroes since the mid-Eighties because nothing really new *can* be said about superheroes Same way nothing really new can be same about Westerns. They're both relics of a long-dead America, and exist only as nostalgia (Westerns) or as spectacle (superhero movies). And the mind-controlled minions streaming into the entertainment racket with cultural studies degrees are literally incapable of saying anything new or interesting about anything.

I'm not even saying that as a dig, it's just the way it is. Creativity - and basic, rudimentary talent, for that matter - runs counter to their programming.

In the end result, superheroes got a good century to speak their piece, same way the cowboys did. But they don't mean anything anymore, they don't matter anymore and they only exist to generate revenue for multinational corporations. And once that revenue finally dries up - which it's starting to - they'll retreat to the margins just like every other spent cultural force has. The process has begun in earnest and there's no stopping it.

Just like there's no stopping the impending collapse of the American Empire that reared them.

THE ILLUSIONS
FALL AWAY

YOU STILL DON'T NEED THEIR PERMISSION.

AGAINST MY BETTER JUDGEMENT I actually voted for Obama this past election. I hadn't planned on it, but my wife was insistent because of the issue with our insurance coverage. I knew full well it was a choice between effin' evil and really effin' evil, but what are you gonna do?

I didn't even vote in 2008; I realized as soon as I heard Obama was being backed by Sith Lord Pete Peterson that no good would ever come of him. Even so, I was worried that Romney would make everything worse by instituting austerity, cutting Social Security and Medicare, and ramping up the war machine in the Middle East and possibly against Russia as well.

It turns out that I needn't have worried at all, because Obama has done all of that for him. And now we see Obama out-Nixoning Nixon with ideological IRS hit-jobs and wiretapping enemies in the press. And that's on top of all the other Orwellian nightmares he's already out-Bushed Bush on.

It doesn't matter though, because Obama could stab young children on live TV and the Democrat zombies in the media would fall over each other, praising his knife skills and writing stirring think-pieces about how our brave President is creating a more sustainable world by doing away with useless eaters.

But that's not the point. The point is that identity politics — meaning quite ancient divide-and-rule tactics — are how the Wall St. faction that controls the Democratic Party has decided to wage political war against their Republican counterparts. The obvious agenda is to make sure that people are constantly fighting over symbolic issues so no one will notice that Obama is actually to the right of Bush on the issues that really matter, and *very* far to the right of Ronald Reagan, even.

"Social Justice," which is nothing more than a synonym for identity politics, has become the rallying cry because Obama and his party — especially his salad-tossing amen corner in the media — have completely given up on the concept of *economic* justice.

In other words, the middle class is to be wiped out — for good — by outsourcing, unpaid internships, and immigrant exploitation, no matter which party you vote for. You probably won't have a pension or insurance when you reach retirement age, and your kids probably won't be able to go to college. Upward mobility will be forever lost, like it is in California.

The good news is that you can use the magical totem of Social Justice to show your masters that you are an enlightened and progressive serf, and are nothing like those mouth-breathing, *regressive* serfs over there.

Of course, an integral part of the new identity politics program is atheism, and to a lesser extent, skepticism, atheism is perfect for the coddled children of hyper-privilege who comprise nearly the entirety of the so-called Progressive movement in North America, since they can finally play the victim. Oh poor godless me, Daddy sent me to a state university to major in Womyn's Studies, when I really wanted to go to Sarah Lawrence. I'm so put upon; it's God's fault.

Of course, atheism is not only *not* stigmatized in the bubbles they spend their entire lives traveling in, it's essentially *de rigeur*. If you're not an atheist, you'd better be a satanist or a witch, otherwise your career is toast.

So now they can point to some mouth-breathing yahoo in some deep red state somewhere and pretend that they are the victims. Better still, they don't have to worry about "people of color" at all, unless it's to browbeat an opponent about "white privilege." They can even (privately) huff-and-puff about how they are being *victimized* by POC, despite having lived lives of almost unimaginable comfort and privilege, since the atheist movement is in large part motivated by studiously-unacknowledged racial anxieties.

But some genius — and I'm thinking it was probably Obama's Svengali David Axelrod — realized that the best answer to the Religious Right (who were so influential primarily because they were reliable unpaid envelope-stuffers every election cycle) was the Atheist Left, because liberals have never figured out how to deal with religion.

The Left took over the so-called "mainline churches" and ran them all into the ground. I mean, atomic bombs have done less damage to their targets than the Left did to the churches they set out to "save." So why bother? Atheists make much more pliable consumers — and voters — if you appeal to their endless vanity and crippling insecurities.

So after spending twenty years on the Internet seeing mindless tribalism on the part of the Religious Right everywhere, I can now see mindless tribalism on the part of the Irreligious Left. So 'eff them all.

And while we're at it, 'eff all these Fortean farteans that constantly worry about what all these self-appointed arbiters of truth think of them. 'Eff those spineless cucks who ever-so-tentatively ask the Plaits and Randis and Shermers if it's OK to play with their little Paranormal toys for a while. Seriously, eff 'em. They're all cowards, traitors, and weaklings. They're of no use to anyone, not even themselves.

See, there's no point looking over your shoulder at people who will *never* accept you, and will never stop looking down on you, no matter what kind of worthy, schoolmarmish word-drool you might dress your "phenomena" up in.

There is no point in being your own debunker, because you just end up looking like a pussy and a sucker. The skepdicks just see you as weak and acco-modating, even if they occasionally pat you on the back for "being one of the more sensible ones."

Which is another way of saying they might occasional find you mildly useful if they can use you to attack your friends and allies.

You see, the real problem with High Strangeness or the Paranormal isn't really the evidence. The problem is that the people in the field who *should* speak up are too damn quiet and too busy worrying about the opinions of people who they'd be much better off mocking and ridiculing, just for the sheer fuck of it. The problem is *cowardice*.

I am old enough now to see where the Fartean road takes you. The Fartean highway of half-measures and unreciprocated compromise leads absolutely *nowhere*. And the road the atheists are all on only ever leads to one destination: total and utter despair.

So do this: fight tooth and claw for what you believe or find something else to do. Otherwise, you're wasting your life away.

"JUST AROUND THE CORNER."

E VERYONE IS A SKEPTIC AND A BELIEVER, when you get right down to it. Everyone has their own set of beliefs and disbeliefs. Everyone has had disappointments and experiences that teach them to be wary and untrusting. Oftentimes, you can scratch a skeptic and find a closet believer, and vice-versa. Sometimes the difference between a skeptic and a believer is just a few beers.

I used to believe in Progress, the inevitable linear march towards the future. Now, I'm not a skeptic so much as a very cautious believer. Or maybe just a wishful thinker. I see Progress not as a straight line, but a scribbly one. Things get better for some people, and get worse for others.

Until recently, Syria, Iraq and Ukraine were modern, industrialized countries with educated populations. Now they are disaster areas. But by the same token, the opposite can be said of many other countries who were mired in war and poverty thirty years ago, but now are forces to be reckoned with.

Like I said, Progress is not a straight line.

THE WESTERN WORLD ONCE BELIEVED IN PROGRESS towards Heavenly Salvation. The entire world was revealing itself and unfolding in such a way as to glorify Jehovah and lead to a paradise on Earth. With the Age of Discovery and the Industrial Revolution, those same exact expectations were simply transposed onto Science.

We have more sophisticated technology than ever before, but it hasn't led to Paradise, and most certainly not the stars. Silicon Valley isn't the engine of Utopia: it's the engine of the new Feudalism that dominates California, a state which went from being a middle class paradise to being one of the poorest and most economically stratified in the country, a place of grotesque inequality and near absolute-zero social mobility.

I'm old enough to have heard how the next world-changing technology is "just around the corner" but all we really seem to get are faster and smaller versions of things we already had.

• I remember seeing articles claiming that bionic limbs were "just around the corner" when *The Six Million Dollar Man* was popular.

• Virtual Reality was "just around the corner" twenty years ago, and it's still "just around the corner" today.

• Hovercraft as personal transportation was "just around the corner" around the same time. When's the last time you saw a hovercraft?

• Androids are supposed to be "just around the corner," but I feel like I've been seeing the same creepy Japanese fembot press conference on a tape loop since the Reagan Era.

• Transhumanism was all the rage a few years back, but now it's somehow landed on the "woo-woo" list.

Desperate Transhumanist true-believers look increasingly like electronics companies who went all-in on the Betamax format. We were hearing how uploading our minds into robot bodies was the way to achieve immortality, but now Silicon Valley is going for medical solutions for longevity. Sure, computer programs can beat grand masters at chess, but can they build a birdhouse and take out the trash as well?

Genuine Artificial Intelligence is supposed to be "just around the corner," but I've heard a lot of serious skepticism about that as well.

Of course, there's also the "Disclosure Movement," which forever keeps the illusion alive that the Government is going to reverse seventy years of policy and not only admit that UFOs actually exist, but admit that they are extraterrestrial spacecraft. That's always "just around the corner" too.

For guys my age, outer space is the biggest disappointment. *Star Trek* electrified a generation of kids who didn't have much else to look forward to, and then came *Star Wars*. But it seems like both have failed to stay relevant these days. I can't help but wonder if all this Flat Earth material out there is in some way a reaction to the broken promises of the space program, and of the better-living-through-technology paradigm altogether.

People my age grew up expecting there to be bases on Mars by now, and certainly some kind of colony on the Moon. But what if the space skeptics are right? What if outer space is an impassable hell of lethal radiation? Where do we go then?

It's not something I *want* to believe. I *want* to believe in the March of Progress. The alternatives aren't very appealing. I'd say most of the serious Apollo skeptics started out as serious space nerds. I'd also bet there are a lot of quote-unquote "believers" who are in fact skeptics, but are afraid to speak up.

Technology has solved many of the existential problems of the human condition (see irrigation, agriculture, medicine, air flight, etc). But technology also has a tendency to empower the worst of us to do harm to the best of us. It's why we may see ever stranger expressions of dissent from the dominant consensus, which preaches Progress and the salvational force of Technology. Social revolutions often spring from the most unlikely sources.

THE VENEER OF PROGRESS

R OD DREHER EDITS *THE AMERICAN CONSERVATIVE*. He's become a bit of a celebrity in Christian circles for pushing the so-called "Benedict Option," a philosophy which argues that modern culture has become so incompatible with Christianity that Christians need to disengage from it rather than try to transform it.

One could also argue he's trying to transform an exoteric religion into an *esoteric* religion. I just don't know if such a thing is possible without fundamentally changing the nature of the faith itself.

I was working on a post about Dreher, because he seems to think Gnosticism can mean whatever he needs it to mean whenever he wants to attack someone else within his own religion. In this case, he was attacking a nun who was pushing Transhumanism (it seems that the only places you see serious discussion of Transhumanism anymore are in religious circles).

For some reason I followed a link to another discussion where Dreher was unloading on the weird trend of atheists going for divinity degrees into order to facilitate "activist" work. I didn't care to read it into this any further until one of these atheists chimed in to annoy Dreher.

The atheist in question called himself "Schmendrick," which was all too appropriate, given the pile of absolute nonsense this clown spewed.

> As one of the millennial "nones" and with a friend who I'm also sure is a "none" at heart attending a Divinity School precisely so he can go into activism and social work, I can assure Mr. Dreher that for a non-trivial number of us, we search for meaning apart from the divine because divine metaphysics make no sense to us... all the supernatural stuff cuts against everything we see in daily life, which is a constant celebration of the power of naturalistic knowledge.
>
> Cell-phones, computers, the internet, advanced mathematics, space travel, self-driving cars, drones – the world of the young is filled to bursting with evidence that man can successfully understand, manipulate, and control the whole visible world (and huge swathes of the invisible one) without any recourse to mystery or supernatural explanations...
>
> If you want to re-sanctify the culture, the biggest hurdle is squaring the idea that the human spirit is fundamentally not of this world with the history of the past two hundred years, which rather decisively show that the human spirit is actually fantastically good at relating to and mastering this world.

WHERE DO YOU BEGIN? Even in the context of naturalistic science, this kind of thinking is so profoundly ignorant, narcissistic, and solipsistic as to be beyond the pale of reason. Does this Schmendrick realize that half of these modern wonders he cites here are *surveillance devices?*

Make note that this is the voice of wealth, youth, health and unimaginable privilege speaking. It's the voice of someone raised in absolute comfort and security, which is not the experience of huge swathes of humanity, even today. It's not the voice of someone whose father was killed by security services, or whose sister died of dysentery because there was no clean water, or whose brother was maimed fighting a bitter insurrection against a kleptocratic government.

It's not the voice of a terminal cancer patient or abuse survivor. It's not the voice of a laid-off steel worker who'll never find full-time employment again. It's not the voice of a single mother who takes a bus at 5:30 in the morning to work twelve hours in an illegal factory that pays below minimum wage and ignores all state and Federal safety and worker-protection regulations.

In other words, it's not the voice of the overwhelming majority of humanity, struggling to get through the day in an increasingly Social Darwinist world. It's the voice of someone who's been mediated their entire life by a corporate oligarchy which wants everyone to think and act the exact same way.

And our *"naturalistic knowledge?"* Increasingly, we're learning more about what we *don't* know than what we do, and we're learning just how limited our tools are in the face of that ignorance, and how our footprint on the planet seems to be confined more and more to urban centers, since our explorer spirit has largely been extinguished.

As to *"controlling the whole visible world,"* the fact is we don't really know what's in our forests, in our oceans, or be-neath the earth's surface, anyone who tells you otherwise is an idiot or a liar. The uncountable majority of the earth's surface has never seen a human footprint. The depths of the ocean may as well be on another planet.

"Mastering the world?" We've been enjoying a brief and unusual temperate period, one in which the unimaginable violence of the planet has been relatively restrained. But already we are seeing an increase in tectonic and volcanic activity (as well as related activity like sinkholes), activity against which all the self-driving cars in the world will be next to useless.

California and the Southwest continue to struggle against a historical, maybe even *prehistorical* drought.

We still see floods, monsoons, tsunamis and other disasters that take every scrap of technology, machinery and transportation we have and toss them in a septic stew that can form overnight and take years to recover from.

Huge chunks of the globe are currently experiencing war and political upheaval. There are epochal migrations underway that will bring political chaos and social unrest in their wake, and all of this is presuming that the superpowers *don't* go to war over the many flash-points that are presently flaring up.

And all this is during one of the Earth's more environmentally moderate periods. What would happen if Gaia got cranky? Or heaven forbid, our *Sun*? Every scrap of technology we have could be instantly rendered completely inert by a bad-enough solar storm. Who knows what could happen if we suddenly found ourselves faced with a magnetic pole shift?

Historians now believe that the so-called Dark Ages of Europe were brought about by a natural disaster that brought the once-formidable social infrastructure of the Roman Empire down to nearly Neolithic levels. People scraped by, but barely. A similar catastrophe today would end it all.

How brainwashed, how bamboozled these idiots are by the veneer of progress. Turn these gadgets off for a week and the Schmendricks of this world would all be curled into fetal positions, unable to speak or take in solid food. And this is what *Divinity* Schools are filled with? No wonder the churches are dying.

I WOULDN'T EVEN BOTHER TO ARGUE THE SUPERNATURAL worldview with a Schmendrick. The naturalistic worldview is dominant now, but it's inevitably going to fail, and we will all suffer the consequences of that. It's already failed to deliver on its most extravagant promises, unless you have a bungalow on the Moon you're not telling me about.

It's good this tool used a pseudonym, because sooner or later those words will come back to haunt him in a very special way. Count on it.

THE TECH DEVOLUTION HAS BEGUN.

HOLLYWOOD AND RIDICULOUS CGI FAKERY (like the Boston Dynamics parkour and Watusi hoaxes) have done exactly what *World of Tomorrow* propaganda did in the 1930s: quell worker unrest by stringing everyone along with the techno-utopia carrot. It's even more ridiculous today because the age of technological discovery is over — and has been for a while — and the Technological Devolution has begun, At least there were still genuine innovations to come back in the Thirties.

Think about it: we have (alleged) trillion-dollar companies and the best they can come up with are glorified bottle-rockets (that can't even reach the upper atmosphere) and Second Life-vintage cartoon avatars? And has anyone asked if Zuckie's latest scam has addressed the issue of VR sickness?

You can just smell the fear-stink and the flop-sweat out there in SiliCylon World. I'd be sympathetic if they weren't all so intent on destroying our economy, our industries and our way of life, just to filch a few more pennies out of our purses. The fact is that our technological infrastructure is bloated and tangled to the point of incoherence. We have massive public utilities reliant on ancient software and millions of households reliant on wooden telephone poles.

Believe me, I've had all too much experience with mass-scale power and internet outages for the past few years. I know all too well what's eventually coming for the rest of the country.

We're also experiencing a catastrophic demographic implosion all across the industrialized world, to the point that thousands of schools will be shuttered in the coming decades. Moreoever, IQ is dropping and autism-spectrum disorders are exploding worldwide.

And just to plop the cherry atop the shit sundae, Intersectionalist lunatics dominating the education system are conditioning today's students — already rendered listless and unmotivated by technology and pharmacology — that work ethics are patriarchal and math and science are racist. So, tell me: who exactly do you think is going to fix all these very complex machines and systems we depend on and keep them all running?

Answer? *No one.*

So is it really any wonder all these Big Tech tycoons are currently relocating to the South Pacific and/or inaccessible redoubts in the Rockies? They most certainly have access to information we do not. What are they not telling us, or at least not telling us out loud?

S O WHERE'S THE HOPE? Well, for my money the hope is where it's been every single time an empire has imploded before us: in the power of rediscovering the spirit realm. In the power of people to turn away from the crass, crappy and commercial, and come together to cooperate. To stop trying to dominate Nature — which is an utter and complete impossibility in the first place — and to learn to live in harmony with it.

I'm not saying it's going to be easy. Not even a little bit; trapped beasts like the current Beast System are always most dangerous when wounded and cornered. They're not going out without doing their damndest to take a shit-ton of us with them. But the alternative is continue to drift along with the tide like flotsam, and that's a surefire recipe for horrific failure.

In the meantime, what you can do is seek after the spirits. They are most definitely real and most definitely out there waiting for you, when you're ready to take off the blinders and meet them on their own terms. If nothing else, they'll help strip away a lot of that unnecessary fear and anxiety that's an inevitable side effect of living in an insane world. Start at that foundation and build from there.

Like the man said, this is just a ride. A thrill ride in the coming days, to be sure. But you've been here before and you will be here again. The question now is how you choose to ride it out this time around.

IF THE THUNDER DON'T GET YOU, THEN THE LIGHTNING WILL.

A FEW YEARS BACK I STARTED RANTING ON INCOHERENTLY about some insane notion I had that an obscure dream pop diva was in fact the Sibyl — or the Oracle of the Apocalypse — of this age.

This wasn't exactly a sudden realization, it was something that I'd been pondering for over thirty years at that point. I can't blame anyone for not believing me: I didn't have a lot of data to work with and didn't yet understand how oracles had traditionally worked in antiquity (hint: exactly like this one does now — look it up).

The Apocalypse was admittedly a tough sell back in 2017. And it's such a loaded word anyway, dumbed down by decades of Hollywood and fundamentalist propaganda. However, I see the idea of an Apocalypse — literally "the Unveiling" — as fundamentally small 'g' gnostic. Apocalypses are times in our history when false realities fall away and the true hidden reality reveals itself. They're when the Great Wheel of the Tao turns.

Apocalypses (yes, *plural*) are not usually very pleasant times, largely because the ruling classes come to realize that they are about to fall like lightning from Heaven, only they don't have a parachute. That's not the sum of it, but a very important part all the same.

We'll probably experience a series of cascading natural disasters, real plagues and wars and rumors of wars in the next half-century or so, like all the times before. Not to minimize the inevitable suffering in store for all of us, but this is just a part of the process of renewal, in the same way fires renew forests by doing away with the deadwood and thatch.

We've been here before: I'd tag the Bronze Age Collapse and the mysterious climate collapse in the early Middle Ages in Europe, the Black Death as well as the microbial apocalypse in the Americas starting in the 15th Century, just off the top of my head.

But this time is different. Something else is at work. Something is happening outside what we normally think of as the natural world. I mean, I still think it's very much part of the natural world, but I'm the first to admit it doesn't rightly feel that way at the moment. For the time being, I've landed on the Shimmer from *Annihilation* to model it. It's a pretty clumsy model, but it's the best I got at the moment.

Most of you probably know what I'm talking about: something seems to be happening to space and time, in ways we all sense but can't put our fingers on.

A lot of people are talking about "the Timeline" and reality simulations and the rest of it, but I use the Shimmer as a metaphor because of how the movie version refracted all the information it processed and rearranged it, often responding to how people perceived it. Kind of like how subatomic particles are said to respond to our attention as well.

I think this is why everything is so incredibly fucked up and why it just keeps getting worse. There's no doubt there's major human fuckery afoot, but I think this phenomenon is accelerating it and making it even more fucked up. Have you noticed how the Globalists and technocrats have achieved absolute domination over every institution in America, but none of them seem to be very happy about it? Their toadies and camp followers are downright miserable, and for good reason.

We have an idiotic microcosm of the Shimmer in the distortion that social media refracts, and that's only getting worse. We have a mass of severely mentally-sick people with an unprecedented amount of power and control, yet every victory they get just makes them more miserable and unhinged. Everything everywhere is being thrown massively out of balance, fueled by an insane doctrine of "disruption" that's become dogma for Big Tech. Lucifer's Technologies, all right.

I think the misery and rage we see amongst the dominant overclasses is in part a result of the unconscious realization that everything they've worked for is about to be swept away. Like I've said, we're at the end of an Age, not the beginning. The technocrats, many of whom are well into the Spectrum to begin with, have been trying for years to cope with the gnawing suspicion that the sands in the Big Egg Timer in the Sky were slowly but surely falling away, and not in their favor.

This is where the failed parade of messianic movements emerged from: Techno-Utopianism, Transhumanism, and now Woke.

It sucks to have worked so hard to get to the big leagues knowing the game will be called before you get to bat. It's why these people who have always had everything feel like they've never had anything. So at the same time technocrats are planning smart cities, they're hedging those bets by building fortified compounds on South Pacific islands. There's such a sense of panic and terror, like they have to cram this brave new world square into the round hole of history.

It's already failing — miserably — and is only going to get crazy worse. Because the old codes they were programmed with no longer apply. I don't expect it imminently, but I wouldn't be surprised that this all ends up with a solar flare or pole shift that fries all these lovely machines and forces the world to start all over again.

S O, BE HONEST: can you look at what is going on out there and tell me it doesn't look apocalyptic? I mean, even just a little bit?

But like I said, it's more that that. It's like the change is happening not only on the atomic but the *subatomic* level. Things are refracting and reorganizing themselves in very subtle ways. No one has ever experienced it before, so no one knows what the fuck to do about it. I'm sure there are some whacked-out quantum guys who can offer up some theories, but I don't think there's any actual science about it. Maybe there will never be.

So maybe this is why the gurgly glossolalia and non-Euclidean harmonies of a manic pixie dream girl from way back in the day make such an appropriate prophecy for all of this. It's familiar but alien, all at the same time. Hark, the Angel's Herald sings, if you get my meaning.

But one thing I can say for this Shimmer thing is that it freed me from the quicksand of my past and the pipe-dreams of the future and landed me in the Now. And I'm getting a lot more information beamed into my brain from the Now, so to speak, than I ever had from the imaginary landscapes of the past and future.

It's how I realized that part of all this political insanity is because of people trying to conserve an imaginary past (conservatives) or progress towards an imaginary future (progressives). People are ultimately fighting in the streets over their fantasies. No wonder it all comes across like a LARP.

I'm nobody and no one's going to listen to me, but I think some Now would go a long way in bridging that gap. The Big Wheel is not going to turn, it's turning *now*. You know it, I know it, everyone knows it. And there aren't any road maps for the world we're heading towards, so maybe we should start coming together to share notes. It's time.

DREAMT OF IN
YOUR PHILOSOPHY

UNTIL IT HAPPENED TO ME

REPORTS ON NEAR-DEATH EXPERIENCES crossed my path this week, for very different reasons. These were very different stories concerning very different people and leading to very different interpretations, but in the end they both led me to my conclusion: the Paranormal is Personal.

Many in the establishment media have declared war on near death experience, primarily because disempowered Evangelicals have latched onto NDEs as proof of their interpretation of Scripture. Which is why the odious, elitist British newspaper *The Independent* recently ran a story of a man who died (twice!) and didn't experience anything at all.

This is hardly news. NDEs are the exception not the rule and the article deliberately avoids any discussion of the man's hospital treatment. If he was anesthetized it would explain his lack of any memory before being awoken.

What actually happened is that the man does not *remember* an NDE, which may well be a result of drugs or brain injury. But unfortunately, we may never know for sure even if he did experience anything, since the man in question is a radical, doctrinaire atheist. The political agenda of the article is made clear by his own testimony, though he's surely only preaching to the converted:

> *"I have always been an atheist, but I have always had a part of me that hoped there was a God or Heaven or something greater than us. I mean, who wouldn't want there to be a Heaven?*
>
> *"I am still an atheist, and now I know that there is no such thing as God or Heaven. At least not for me. My reasoning behind that is no God would ever put a person and family through such a experience.*
>
> *"I am an atheist, and always will be. But I believe that your belief is your belief. The only thing we can share is our own experiences and let people make up their own mind. People need to stop forcing their own beliefs onto others."*

That last statement is stupid, given the general live-and-let-live attitude of Near-Death Experiencers. It would seem the fellow is one of those types who thinks anyone disagreeing with him is an intolerable threat, a type we see all too often these days.

But there's an obvious paradox here: if you distrust the "Jesus led me to the Elysian Fields" stories of a devout Evangelical, why should you trust the "*I spent all my time in a void*" stories of the devout atheist, especially given the fact that there's no evidence for his story either?

One wonders what would have happened had he gone through the classic NDE. We've heard of these 'Road to Damascus' events, where onetime unbelievers are so shaken by an experience that it changes the entire conduct of their lives. Near Death Experiences are well known for having this kind of effect.

Which brings me to my point: there are people who are interested in Paranormal topics but I think people only come to actually *believe* in the Paranormal once they experience it for themselves.

Arch-Skeptic Michael Shermer is the likely heir to the Skeptic King crown once James Randi shuffles off this mortal coil. Despite the sex abuse scandals that seem to be obligatory with these types. Shermer recently made headlines when he briefly wandered off the reservation in response to the kind of Paranormal event that many people have experienced and once were taken for granted. In this case, it had to do with a grandfather's old radio suddenly working after extensive efforts to repair had failed.

To which I'd say Shermer is very easily impressed and really, really <u>not</u> qualified to pass judgements on the Paranormal.

But the point is that it happened to *him* and so it meant something. It was worth writing about, worth confessing to his fellow consensus reality-worshippers. Otherwise, Shermer would have shredded anyone else who made such a claim. If it happened to *you*, he'd be first in line to attack.

So you you really do have to wonder how many skeptics out there are simply sour grapes cases, bitter that the Paranormal Train never stopped at their station. I wonder how many of these are actually *incapable* of experiencing or even truly understanding the Paranormal, because of their brain chemistry or some other kind of physiological issue.

It's pretty well documented that a lot of people who can and do experience the Paranormal don't exactly lead splendrous lives, and usually had horrific childhoods.

Colin Wilson is an interesting case; he had his elite credentials in order, could write his own ticket on the Great British Sterility Express. But after delving into the Paranormal for his foundational text *The Occult* in 1971, Wilson confessed what is utter heresy to the system that reared him:

> "It was not until two years ago, when I began the systematic research for this book, that I realized the remarkable consistency of the evidence for such matters as life after death, out-of-the-body experiences (astral projection), reincarnation.

"In a basic sense, my attitude remains unchanged; I still regard philosophy — the pursuit of reality through intuition aided by intellect — as being more relevant, more important, than questions of "the occult."

"But the weighing of the evidence, in this unsympathetic frame of mind, has convinced me that the basic claims of "occultism" are true. It seems to me that the reality of life after death has been established beyond all reasonable doubt.

"I sympathize with the philosophers and scientists who regard it as emotional nonsense, because I am temperamentally on their side; but I think they are closing their eyes to evidence that would convince them if it concerned the mating habits of albino rats or the behavior of alpha particles."

I know where Wilson is coming from. I had such trouble with the Paranormal as a concept that it took me a very long time to define my own experiences as Paranormal, and even to realize that experiences I saw as mundane were in fact anything but.

But I believe true skepticism isn't just saying "No" no matter what, it's only saying "Yes" once you've satisfied the need for evidence. All the sloppy, evidence-free Paranormal stuff you see out there is just boring. It's just flat soda and stale bread. But here's an important point: I wasn't able to understand the context of my own experiences until I studied the experiences of *other* people.

So I do think there's a major shortcoming in the solipsistic approach to evidence *vis a vis* the Paranormal. Hoaxes and bullshit are pretty easy to sniff out after a while, and it's important to trust other people and not see everything through the prism of your own experience.

The Paranormal can be a contagion. If you know a bunch of people who have had weird experiences but haven't had one yourself, just think about this: the fact that you are attracting these people into your life is a Paranormal experience all its own. You are what is called a "strange attractor."

The same goes if someone close to you confides about a profoundly weird experience. You have become part of their circuit now. I'll leave you with this quote from Paracelsus:

Thus these beings appear to us, not in order to stay among us or become allied to us, but in order for us to become able to understand them. These apparitions are scarce, to tell the truth. But why should it be otherwise?

Is it not enough for one of us to see an Angel, in order for all of us to believe in the other Angels?

I LOOK LIKE I'VE SEEN A GHOST

I DON'T BLOG MUCH ON THE PARANORMAL. Not that I'm a disbeliever: in fact, I expect we'll be seeing more and more weirdness manifesting as everything continues to spin apart. Whether this is all a function of neurology, or interdimensional rifts or electromagnetic disturbances is hard to say, which is why I try not to spend too much time on the topic.

And normally I wouldn't talk about it here, but my pal Mike Clelland is a collector of these kinds of things, and insisted that I do. So with all of that prefacing, let me just explain what happened the other night. You decide for yourself what it all means.

It was around 10:45 PM, and I was taking my dog for a walk because I was feeling really wound up. We were walking down the street and a figure came out of the woods and stepped into our path about thirty feet in front of us. It seemed as if it was completely white, which I interpreted at the time as white clothing. It stood beneath an overhanging branch so its head was completely in shadow. It was maybe a bit under five feet tall.

I would have thought it was a kid cutting through the woods, who was startled when he saw us on the street, only it didn't react to us at all. It calmly came out of the woods and then stood under an overhanging branch, facing us.

It didn't make a sound the whole time; not a single sound, not even when it came out of the woods. No snapped twigs, no footfalls, nothing. This is a quiet summer night when every sound reverberates. It just stood there, facing us. Like it was waiting for us. That was unsettling.

The other weird thing is that my very loud, very excitable Collie puppy didn't bark, even though I saw that she saw it too. If it were a person or a animal, she would have barked her brains out, especially in a situation like that. She just stood there staring at the figure, like she was studying something new and interesting. She didn't seem to be frightened; fascinated, rather.

We looked at it for about a minute and then I backed her away, and said, "C'mon." I got a very weird vibe once I started to process it. Granted, it was nighttime, but we were fairly close and I couldn't make the damn thing out, only a white figure that somehow didn't seem completely solid. It didn't move the whole time.

I did pull out my cell phone in a vain attempt to light the scene, but it was hopeless. It stayed there as we walked away and I didn't hear anything as we turned the corner. At all.

About a block away, a strange and totally unfamiliar thought came into my head: "I've just seen a ghost." I've become aware of how I'm imposing a narrative familiarity on this event, which was really a lot weirder than I'm able to communicate. The word "ghost" is reductionist; it calls to minds a host of images and cultural associations that really don't communicate the strangeness of this encounter.

I went home and told my wife about it. She was fascinated, and walked over to the spot looking for it. And while she looking around, our black cat Tricky came jumping out of the bushes and scared the hell out of her, exactly like some horror movie fake-out. And the next morning, my dog woke me up by barking her head off, almost like a delayed reaction from the previous night.

Later that morning, I drove down the same street on the way to drop off some papers. When I got to the corner I was startled by a large electronic traffic sign, which indicated that a serious hit and run accident had occurred the other day and the police were looking for tips. I haven't heard yet if the victim died.

THIS NEIGHBORHOOD HAS AN INTERESTING HISTORY. As I've written, there's a lot of weird symbolism around and there are six cemeteries in walking distance of my house. At the end of the street in question is a house built on the lot of an earlier house in which a firefighter died during an arson fire a year after we moved in.

A couple summers ago, a young woman walked from the nearest cemetery into a speeding commuter train. The strange thing was that she wasn't even from the area. Not even the same state.

It's these kinds of syncs — recent tragedies and violent deaths within a short distance of this encounter — that make me think a bit more seriously about an event I might otherwise file away as a curiosity. I mean, that's classic ghost stuff, right?

And plus, there's the whole thing with Aleister Crowley being buried not too far away.

Y'know, *that*.

MESSAGES FROM THE OTHER SIDE

I DON'T BELIEVE IN THE PARANORMAL — or certain aspects of it, specifically — because I find the various books or TV shows on the topic so wonderfully convincing. I do so because of my own experiences, and because people I trust have told me about their own experiences with powerful and unusual phenomena.

For instance, I knew a lot of people when I was young who had first or second-hand experiences with hauntings. It probably wasn't everybody, but it sure felt that way at times. New England seemed to be a hotspot in the 1970s. Some of the stories still retain their numinous potency.

Before our own sighting this summer, I knew a handful of sober-minded people who had UFO experiences, which they were able to report with clarity and without undue agitation. That personal connection goes a long way on my ledger. Longer than the testimony of some creepy debunker who spends all the time he's not indulging God-knows-what-paraphilias talking about things he claims not to believe in.

That doesn't mean I dive into the Paranormal deep end without my discernment floatation device. Or that I give equal weight to all phenomena. That's an express ticket to Nowheresville, Jack. It simply means that I take serious reports seriously and don't toss out evidence simply because I refuse to accept anything beyond the reach of naturalism and materialism, which are religious philosophies whether they cop to it or not.

In the end result we're really looking at *data* — whether it feels that way or not — and making personal judgments from a preponderance of such. One event, or even a series of events, is never going to move the needle. It's the accumulation of data over time that determines your attitude towards the Paranormal, however you choose to define what is a rather annoyingly nebulous and badly-abused term.

I bring all this up because of a series of strange events that have arisen within the past couple weeks following the recent death of my father-in-law, Charlie. To be perfectly frank, I was more than a little hesitant to blog about them since not only can't I provide evidence these events occurred (I have a bit of a hangup for evidence), I only witnessed one of them personally.

But Mr. Gordon White, whose wisdom I always value and usually defer to, thought it was important to blog about it precisely because other people have experienced these kinds of phenomena, and would appreciate whatever validation I can offer by reporting what's been going on in the aftermath of Charlie's death.

Charlie's passing was unexpected but not exactly shocking. He'd been in relatively good health and in good spirits prior to his death. What's interesting in light of some of the phenomena in question is that he was involved with computers very early on, working on mainframes in the 50s and was a very early adopter of personal computers.

He lived a long and interesting life, and passed away suddenly in his bedroom at the age of 85. No long, excruciating illness, just a relatively painless exit at home with his family. We should all be so lucky.

Indeed, the recent weirdness seems focused on computers. The one event I witnessed was straight out of a Hollywood remake of a superior Japanese horror movie: my wife's phone (a Samsung smartphone) started flashing on and off and started calling up totally random pages and images. She said nothing like that had ever happened before. It hasn't happened again since. Words don't do it justice, believe me.

The kicker is that her sister reported the same thing with her phone. Well, it must have been a problem with the phones or the network, right? Um, wrong. They have totally different phones and use different carriers. My wife also says that she was getting random email notifications but no email, and equally random friend request notifications but no friend requests. Again, she said she'd never experienced this before.

Other strange things happened. She and her sister were scanning and printing photos for montages for the wake, but kept having certain photos go missing and reappear. Of course, this could be the ever-popular alternate universe phenomena that all of us deal with when it comes to your car keys and important papers, which you deliberately and consciously put one place only to have them show up somewhere else later.

My younger son, who was helping Charlie with his autobiography, had some bizarre problems with his relatively new laptop last night. He'd talk to Apple, think the problem would be fixed, and then some totally random text screen would show up. It's still up in the air as of this writing.

The other day a Christmas tree ornament showed up in the middle of the living room. Big deal, it's Christmas, right? Well, sure, but we still haven't gotten the ornaments out of the attic yet.

The strangest thing happened at the wake. My nephew placed a glass on a table, several inches from the edge. No one was near the table. No one was moving around, no one doing jumping jacks or Karate forms. Somehow the glass fell from the middle of the table to the floor. Everyone stopped their conversations to look at the glass.

There were other occurrences, but that was stuff that got my attention. I told my wife and her sister to write everything down. Maybe most of it will have a rational explanation, maybe not. The thing with the wife's phone was truly weird. Neither of us had ever seen it before.

Gordon tells me that these kind of things aren't unusual, that many people have experienced them, they just don't talk about them. He believes — and I agree — that it's important to discuss these things when they pop up.

I'M PRESENTING THESE ANECDOTES as they were reported to me but I do think it's important to stay tethered while wading into these murky waters. If there are indeed otherworldly communications at work, you should know which are genuine and which are not. If the dead are taking the trouble to contact us they probably have something important to say. It might be a good idea to work out what that is exactly.

I remember that the clock that belonged to my great-grandfather stopped upon his death and was never able to be repaired, even by an expert clockmaker. The arch-skeptic Michael Shermer reported a similar event with an old family radio, and it made such an impression on him that he was willing to risk excommunication from the Church of Suicidal Nihilism by talking about it publicly.

Let me just say that I'm not presenting any of this as definitive because to tell you the truth, I don't know what to make of any of it myself. But I'm willing to bet a lot of you out there have similar stories that you'd like to tell. We might get somewhere interesting if we had a body of compelling evidence of this sort to pore through, especially if we could get some documentation in the mix.

The irony is that this is the kind of thing Charlie would have scoffed at. Maybe that's the whole point, if indeed any of this were some kind of genuine communication.

Kind of like, "Hey kids, look, I was wrong. Joke's on me."

"AND THEY NOTICED THAT YOU NOTICED THEM."

HAVE YOU EVER SEEN THE MOVIE ADAPTATION of *The Mothman Prophecies?* It's an adaptation in theory only, really. It's not set in the Sixties, and the John Keel character has been split into two seemingly opposite poles; one played by veteran British actor Alan Bates and another played by Richard Gere, of all people.

The Gere character is kinda like Keel circa 1966, drawn into the mystery, excitement and allure of the Paranormal, and the Bates character is more the older Keel, who is very much a broken man, battered and bewildered by the endless enigmas one has to wrestle with when dealing with the world of Paranormality. And so the Bates-Keel character spends most of his screen time trying to warn the Gere-Keel away from the seductive allure of whatever is having its way with the good people of Point Pleasant, West Virginia.

The Gere-Keel asks Bates-Keel why these entities are fucking with him in this way, why they chose him, implying that he is somehow special, somehow "chosen." Bates-Keel regards Gere-Keel with a pitying look and simply replies that, "You *noticed* them, and they noticed that you noticed them."

And so it is. I think you can tell if someone has had a lot of experience with the Paranormal by their wariness and their weariness. Because one thing the *Mothman* movie definitely got right is that the Paranormal feeds off death and tragedy like rocket fuel. From what I can tell, the only way you can navigate its murky waters is to know where you really stand, and learn to resist the temptations these Powers, Principalities and Dominions can throw in front of you. Because if you start to play by their rules, you will most certainly lose.

I first noticed them a very long time ago. Not because I was especially perceptive or intelligent, but because chronic high fevers (and I mean *very* high: 105°F on average) rewired my circuits and allowed — or more accurately, *forced* — me to see things just beyond the frame, if only just barely and for fleeting moments at a time. There was also the thing with the house that was haunted and needed to be exorcised back in the Seventies, but that's a story for another day.

I can't say any of this has done me much good. It's not exactly something you can monetize, certainly not these days. And these powers seem to be extraordinarily jealous of your attention. The only thing that's kept me tethered to sanity, such as it is, is my policy of trying to nail down as much of the evidence as I can and to keep a healthy emotional distance from it all whenever possible.

That's helped quite a bit in 2016, a year which I'm quite amazed I survived.

2016 wasn't that way out of some random glitch in the causality matrix, it apparently played host to some of the heaviest space weather we've seen in some time. Pretty much the entire Solar System was in retrograde for most of the year. So if you felt like you were walking through mud, or breathing underwater, that wasn't your imagination.

They tell me retrogrades are challenging, but not necessarily negative. They can act as opportunities to dig into the hard drive of your life and do some defragmenting, so to speak. Since I invariably seem to get the full breakfast from the planets, I found myself too often on hold with my paying work. But having excellent stellar counseling, I decided to throw myself into my research, and what resulted was probably the most productive period yet seen on this blog.

But I also did a lot of personal research, trying to parse out some longstanding problems and their possible sources. I have a major mystery in my life, a period of time when I was constantly hospitalized. This in turn connected to a series of events, the exact nature of which I'm still trying to straighten out, but the effects of which I have to struggle with every single day.

Just when I was really getting sick of having to wrestle with these old demons — yet again — the space weather lifted and the devils let go. So a word to the wise: you can probably safely ignore your daily horoscope, but keep an eye what those big guys out there are doing. I've yet to see these planetary macro-movements fail to deliver what they promise. Or rather, what they *threaten*.

I wrote back in 2015 how we had close encounters of the first kind, with my son taking a short video of three UFOs that flew over the golf course where he worked and hovered — perfectly motionless — over the woods for some time. The video is short and low-rez, taken on an old iPhone at dusk. In classic Vallean fashion, the sighting inspired him to purchase an expensive digital camera with a telephoto lens. Of course, no UFOs have crossed his path since.

My wife, my daughter and I had our own sighting a few weeks later in New Hampshire, a stunning observation of two orange orbs harassing a Cessna that had taken off from a local airport. The orbs swooped around the plane a few times before splitting formation and flying straight over our heads. They most certainly seemed to me like they were under intelligent control.

We were so stunned we didn't even think to get pictures of it, though I doubt that they'd look like much given that we were in a moving car on a very well-lit highway. Still, I hate not being able to have documentation of these kinds of events. But as it happens that wasn't really necessary, since the sighting was essentially corroborated by a wave of similar events in the exact same area earlier this year:

One of the things I discovered during my retrogrades this past year is that my grandfather worked on the SAGE radar project. In other words the *real* Montauk Project, which went mainstream in a major way in 2016 when *Stranger Things* hit the world like a tidal wave.

I was thinking about that connection when I discovered this strange detail of history: no less a figure than Wernher Von Braun was basically smuggled along with his entire staff into my childhood stomping grounds of Quincy Massachusetts and housed a few hundred feet off the coast after the war. Meaning tiny little corner of New England — which was so crucially important in the first 11 years of my life — was ground zero for Operation Paperclip.

As Synchronicity would have it, a story popped up of a series of UFO sightings over Quincy not too long after I made that discovery. I caught wind of the story on what would have been my grandmother's 101st birthday. It was also almost exactly a year after our own sighting. The reason why I found this so remarkable was because of a photo my sister found when going through my grandmother's belongings after her death, of my mother, my sister and I at Easter.

A bit of background first: back in 2009 I wrote a short post called "Owls," which touched on my mother's obsession with the birds when I was growing up. Our entire living room became a virtual owl shrine with statues, figurines and prints. This room was interesting for another reason, because of a story my mother told me after my first son was born.

She said that just before I was born she put my sister down for naps and then would often take one herself. But she would have this recurring nightmare that a "witch" was on the porch and was trying to come into the house while my mother was asleep on the sofa. That was the same exact spot I had the leprechaun hallucination you're all so sick of hearing about.

In the photo, there's a circular patch of dead grass. The pattern is very similar to a famous UFO case from Kansas in the 1970s. This might seem like nothing, just some dead grass in an early spring yard, whoop-de-doo. But the thing is that it's *exactly* parallel with the old Owl Room. In other words, it's right where it should be *when* it should be.

Speaking of nightmares, I've had a few interesting experiences at night recently. I don't know exactly what to call them, they weren't anything like the dreams I've been having over the past several years. These were physical, tangible, extremely vivid, and cogent. Some weird spin on lucid dreaming, maybe? Who the hell knows, my brains are a mess.

Anyway, in one of these dreams I was back in our old house and had gotten up in the middle of the night. I went to turn the hall light on but it seemed as if the power were out. I took a half-step backward and bumped into a large figure, which then wrapped his arms around my chest. I tried to push back against him but he had these weapons in his hands. They were these metal rods with electrodes at the bottoms. He then pressed them into my chest and I felt a strong shock go through my body. I'd never seen anything like those rods before, but it just so happens they actually exist.

There was another dream; again, I'm not sure how to classify it. I was in my bedroom in the dark, trying to find something on a bookshelf. I went to turn on the light and all of a sudden some weird thing was on top of me. It felt like a child or a large animal, but I never saw it. There were a couple more like that, but you get the point. I did not enjoy them at all, in case you're wondering.

Then there was the *X-Files* reboot, which I'd written on extensively. But fiction bled over into reality after the last episode of the reboot aired: just as we saw in "Founder's Mutation," several thousand grackles appeared in our backyard-the day after the last episode aired. They stayed for five days and then flew off. Weirdly, I couldn't find out information on any other grackle flocks in any of the birdwatching sites (some of which get very anal about cataloging every SINGLE, SOLITARY BIRD someone sees). Then they returned. They'd been gone for weeks and all of a sudden they were in my backyard again. And just as before, they disappeared as soon as I recorded them. But just as in *The X-Files* episode, bad things did indeed happen when the birds gathered.

Very bad things. *Terrible* fucking things.

There's been a lot of death this past year, not only of celebrities but of people much closer to home. Too many of whom died way, way too young. It's been extremely difficult for me, and unbearable for the people I care most about. But I'd be remiss if I didn't mention that there hasn't been *unusual* activity connected to some of this tragedy. As it was last year, I might add.

I'm hesitant to go into specifics because it couldn't possibly be more sensitive, but let me just say that there has been some manifestation on a fairly significant scale, involving a number of different people, and resulting in phenomena such as object displacement, interference with electrical circuitry, and interference with computer interfaces in a way that was not only highly unusual, but also highly significant to the people in question.

Let me just say this was not an experience I ever want to repeat. There's a reason things like this usually pop up in horror movies. Because the entire experience was absolutely fucking horrible.

TONIC FOR
THE TROOPS

THE SYNCHRONISTIC PROCESS OF RE-ENCHANTMENT

TWO OF CARL JUNG'S GREAT CONTRIBUTIONS to the modern psychological lexicon were the terms "introvert" and "extrovert." These terms have been a bit dumbed down over the years, with introvert coming to describe shy, retiring wallflower types and extroverts describing loud, boisterous salesmen/politician glad-handlers. However, you can have outgoing introverts and vice versa.

The term introvert — which is the one we'll concentrate on since it probably describes most of the people reading this — can be described more succinctly as an individual whose life experience is filtered through his or her own internal narrative. Or more aptly, extroverts are those telling the story of their lives to others, and introverts tell it to themselves.

And again, there are sorts of caveats and amendments to add here and it's not really to be taken literally. Since most writers tend to be introverted, but let's forget them for now. Let's concentrate on the fact that introverts live a life of the mind, and not of the senses.

We understood the mechanics of all of this for a very long time, before the rise of consumer capitalism (and then the predatory/monopoly capitalism we have today) demanded that *everything* be commodified, that everything be reduced to a price tag. A price tag in a state of constant deflation, I might add.

The process of re-enchantment demands that the whole idea of a price tag on human experience be abolished. Magic is neither bought nor sold, it doesn't even respond to that kind of terminology.

And since Mysticism has traditionally been understood to be a harmonization of our inner reality and the invisible forces that control the flow and rhythm of our outer reality, the key is to learn the symbols that gravitate towards you and *stop to think what you are meant to do* once those symbols harmonize on the interior and exterior expressions of your life.

In other words, it makes no sense to study symbolism and Synchronicity unless you are going to eventually use them to steer the course of your life. And as the exterior expression of our lives becomes more hollow and impoverished, learning how to understand and then to surf the waves of Synchronicity is increasingly important. In fat times, introverts are always left out, always outsiders looking in.

Those folks on the borderlands between the inner and outer worlds abandon ship and ride the gravy train. In lean times, the equation is often reversed.

One of the reasons I wrote *Our Gods Wear Spandex* was that I understood that the mainstream was gravitating towards superhero fantasies — the same escapist fantasy of the harried nerds and geeks that normies either ignored or bullied in their school days — because they finally began to understand that they were nothing to the Masters of the Universe lording over them.

If anything they, especially if they are in the middle classes, are an irritant and an obstacle to the program of impoverishing and disempowering the entire world population so that the various plans and agendas could be put into place without delay or obstruction.

In the best-case scenarios, a lot of those put-upon kids were *saved* by heroic fantasy, whether superhero-flavored or not. They were able to enter into a parallel reality — an *inner* reality — where they weren't helpless or marginalized. Innovations like role-playing games and hardcore punk (as well as the eternal last refuge of the victimized sensitive, the martial arts dojo) offered practicable methods to exorcise those demons and reinvent themselves and their place in the world.

What I'm trying to say here is that all of the things we talk about here are often dismissed or ridiculed, but that's only if they are used for a kind of rank, escapist onanism. Synchronicity-spotting is just a stoner's game if it isn't A., applied to one's own life, and B., *used as a way to change one's relationship to the world outside.*

Sure, you can go to any convention, whether pop-cult or "New Age," and find a lot of hopeless cases who have shut out the world from their reveries. But you can find those kinds of people anywhere. And it's the people who shut out the world *inside* that end up doing more damage to themselves and the people around them. But we're not allowed to talk about that.

Even so, I know a lot of people who took that inspiration and changed the course of their life (often getting themselves out of some very difficult situations) because of those same stories. If you add in symbolism and Synchronicity to all of that and turn on new seekers to the mix, who can tell what will happen once that formula kicks in?

Re-Enchantment, probably. On a worldwide scale.

THAT'S THE SPIRIT

S PIRITUAL-BUT-NOT-RELIGIOUS IS A PHRASE that's become increasingly common these days. What exactly the phrase means depends on who lays claim to it. For some, it means they still believe in church teachings but prefer to sleep in on Sunday. For others, it means a belief in angels, reincarnation, and a host of quasi-Christian/New Age syntheses.

It's one of those times when language fails us, something that seems to happen more and more often when dealing with anything esoteric.

You could fill a dictionary with words whose meaning has been degraded, tarnished or even reversed in the past thirty years or so. Hyper-mediation is to blame, but our public discourse is even more so, never mind the dumbing-down process going on in our schools and on our TVs. Because of this, we have to use words *provisionally*, adding disclaimers like "but not religious," among many others. Some of us often have to devise something on the level of a *creed* to navigate the minefields of language we're faced with.

Unfortunately, even when all that is said and done, the concept of "spirit" itself is like quicksand.

It tends to describe either some kind of emotional state on one end of the spectrum, and a belief in ghosts on the other. Which is to say that some people find a self-construction of beliefs, practices and rituals to be comforting and others a belief in communing with disembodied personalities.

That's all fine with me. You'd be surprised how many people who claim to be "above all of that" simply construct a parallel analog thereto, whether it's based in science, or politics, or sports, or whatever. It's inevitable, since we either atomize ourselves as mere consumers in a mechanistic, material view of reality (an increasingly-popular option) or we find some way to tap into something beyond ourselves.

In that regard, what we call "spirituality" is the operating system software to facilitate that process.

You won't find very many long-lasting secular societies in history. Atheism may be painted in the media as the inevitable next step in the grand march of history, but it's actually a time-tested symptom of a declining civilization, one that surrenders to the comforts of materialism and urbanism and fails to reproduce itself.

We certainly saw this in Greece and Rome, as the Cynics and the Skeptics turned their backs on the old gods and the old ruling families gave way to more vigorous peoples from the East.

But at the same time, there was also a radical religious fundamentalism running a parallel track to the secular. In the case of Rome, religious extremism among the Plebeians and a nihilistic atheism among the Patricians ultimately led to Constantine, who tried to save the Empire but himself led to Theodosius, who drove the Empire into the ground Not a comforting precedent.

There's a myth among the "Brights," (as they call themselves), that secularism inevitably leads to Enlightenment, when it actually leads to materialism and Me-Generationism. Richard Dawkins is in fact the spiritual godfather of Paris Hilton and Kim Kardashian.

When there's nothing to believe in, why not indulge in raw hedonism and materialism? Why *not* create a culture devoted to nothing but sex and other tangible pursuits? Maybe 2% of the population (at most) will adopt "Reason" — whatever that means — as its new god, and the rest will look out for Number One.

Unfortunately, Fundamentalism is equally materialistic. Never mind the obvious example of the "Prosperity Gospel," if you get any Fundamentalist or Evangelical talking, the conversation will inevitably come down to politics, and politics only. Pentecostal and Charismatic types maybe a bit less so, but they too are often motivated by what "they" — "they" meaning "not me" — are doing in the here and now.

H OWEVER YOU CHOSE TO DEFINE IT, spirituality is an indispensable part of our operating system as a society because there come times when there's not much else to hold on to. We've enjoyed an unparalleled period of prosperity and comfort, but there are all sorts of indicators suggesting that period may be coming to a close.

Spirituality also inspires people to think beyond their own temporary interests and think about the future as well. The question then becomes which spirituality will emerge as the old ones wither, in North America and Europe, at least.

Many people rightly turn away from "spirituality" — and by God, I truly despise the word itself — since we associate it with people, values and ideas that make us physically ill. Whether its organized religion or ditzy aunties clutching their crystals, or whining gurus dispensing refried bromides on HuffPost, the word "spirituality" has a whole host of sick-making associations attached to it like lampreys.

But while I loathe its usual definitions, I also understand that it's a concept that no truly healthy — and sustaining — society can do without. But how that concept is disseminated in another question entirely. I'm reminded of how refreshing the concept of the "New Age" seemed in the early 80s before it was immediately hijacked by the ditzy auntie brigades.

In turn, neopaganism (sic) became appealing to some people, and then the pseudo-Gnostic mysticism of *The Da Vinci Code* milieu, and finally occultism became a refuge that your auntie couldn't follow you into. It's amazing how quickly things are used up and discarded these days; how queasy do you feel when you hear the term "consciousness," for instance?

The point being is that this operating system I refer to often needs to define itself, but by defining itself it becomes fodder for consumer culture. It's something that's happened to every counter-cultural movement in history, recent history at least.

But here's where evolution demands the negotiation. What a new spirituality — let's stick with "operating system" so I don't puke — needs to do is identify itself by what it seeks to accomplish and how it intends to go about that. The buzzwords might work in the old media context, when everything had to be boiled into soundbites, but new media allows room to breathe. You can describe your goals and your means without resorting to labels, if you so desire.

It's amazing how what is done around here is really no different from what the ancients did; the smarter ones who didn't take everything literally, that is. Symbolism and synchronicity were pretty much the primary tools in the esoteric kitbag even back then, often accompanied by various kinds of divinatory tools.

And it was understood that the gods or the angels or whomever spoke to people in symbolic language and that symbolically-charged coincidence was usually the means of transmission.

Then you add in the various meditation techniques, the augmentations (if you will), various types of scarabs or amulets and assorted systems of divination, and you understand that that ancient esotericism was a remarkably pragmatic undertaking, a way to understand the nature of the world, and use that understanding to get certain things *accomplished.*

I don't need to sell you on any of this if you've gotten this far, but this essay isn't about selling you something. If anything, it's about encouraging you to dust off the old books you bought when this was all new, then redouble your efforts and your commitment to the path you're already on.

Sometimes in the middle of a journey you tend to lose sight of where you came from and where you're going. Taking another look at the roadmap and the itinerary can be a great help if you have to stop and change a tire, or you run out of gas in the middle of nowhere.

Metaphorically speaking, of course.

WOULD YOU CARE TO TRANCE?

NEUROLOGISTS DO A LOT OF WORK STUDYING THE BRAIN and the effects of aging and maturity on its function. They don't tend to do much work in the way of consciousness, since the paradigm that dominates academia and the sciences doesn't even allow for the existence of such a thing.

So what I mean to say is that if you feel that the world has become cold, gray, dead, inert, hopeless and meaningless you're not imagining anything at all; the philosophy that arose in the Eighteenth Century has annihilated all meaningful resistance to its dominance so even the opposition to the ruling class is entirely materialist, reductionist, mechanical, dialectic, dead, empty, anti-human.

We're now stuck in this William Gibson Reality, only it's the shitty non-sci-fi books he wrote in the 2000s version of it. The attack on Sony Pictures was straight out of a Gibson novel (even the hackers' name) and yet another signal that the digital cuttlefish that controls information has a soft white underbelly that can be exploited to deleterious effect, and the danger only grows.

The Transhumanist movement and the Singulatarian movement have most certainly run out of gas in the past few years, but the promise of a mechanistic Nirvana lives on in their hearts.

I don't know how much currency it has in the greater culture; it seems that digital trivia and binge drinking (eg., distraction and oblivion) seem to be the preferred methods of deliverance for the Millennials.

The ubiquity of digital media has created a literal Borgsong, an inescapable static that is rewiring our brains every day (and our DNA, according to some scientists) But at the same time you can sense a growing discontent, a silent, simmering dissent that can't even identify itself, its gripes, its goals.

But if you know the psychology of repression, you know that makes it all the more potentially explosive. The corporate media gives constant voice to their pre-approved pseudo-dissenters, not a single one of who challenges the materialist status quo, but human souls today are starving and wounded, and henceforth unpredictably dangerous.

Timothy Leary once said we can't understand an interior process until we have an external model. The Cylons and their simpering toadies recoil at the truth of this, but the fact is that their Skynet is just an inferior simulacrum of our interior supercomputers, and non-local superconsciousness.

This isn't a belief on my part: it's a *conviction*.

Pseudo-reality is all about turning off this signal, using ridicule and pseudo-skepticism. And as it stands, consumer culture keeps people tranquilized enough not to care. But no student of history — or science — expects *any* status quo to remain in place forever. All drugs, chemical or digital, run the risk of tolerance and inefficacy, and we're just one medium-strength solar flare away from the whole system going down for good.

I know entheogens are being talked up again, but I've been working with hypnogogic trance for a number of years now and I'm getting to the point where it's as powerful as any hallucinogen, but seems to more reliably tap into what I can only refer to non-local consciousness. I can only describe it as a kind of remote viewing, in that I'll drift along in that fuzzy stream of semi-consciousness and then find myself in the middle of the ocean or on top of a skyscraper in a stark moment of clarity.

People might once have called these moments astral travel, in that I very often visualize — with great clarity — places I've never been or seen before. Whether or not these visions are real in an objective sense is immaterial, the point is the experience itself and the effect it has on bridging the conscious and unconscious spheres.

It's not always entirely pleasant in a soft, floaty kind of way, but it's often profound. And it's kicked loose a roadblock on my creative impulses that I've struggled against for several years now, so I can't help but wonder if these moments of shock are helping to rewire my unconscious mind in a way that it has become more accessible to my conscious flow, which is really what hypnogogic trance is all about.

So this form of meditation isn't just for kicks. I feel like I've turned back the clock on certain sectors of my own neurology, and that's vitally important for someone in my line of work.

How do you do it? It's almost laughably simple, but it requires a lot of experimentation on your part. What you need to do is sustain a state where you are semi-awake, able to access both your conscious and unconscious thought-streams. Similar to that state you experience after you've awoken from an afternoon nap.

I use a bunch of pillows to position myself so that I'm comfortable but in no danger of actually falling asleep. I recommend trance/ambient music and any kind of supplements that may relax you like Theanine, Valerian Root, St John's Wort. Again, you want to be relaxed but you don't want to fall asleep. It's simple but not easy, if you get my meaning.

The encouraging thing about the process is that it's accumulative in my experience, in that your prior results accumulate and contribute to future results. It's a *practice*, in other words, not like a drug. It's not really meditation, because the point isn't to quiet the mind; the point is to turn the power of the mind up as far as you can handle. But you're doing something meaningful, in that you're trying to *unify* the conscious and unconscious, sort of like a computer tapping into a network.

It's psychedelic as hell, far more chaotic and nonlinear than dreaming, and produces the occasional auditory hallucination (bells and tones, usually, but sometimes voices as well). It's gotten so I keep a notepad on my bedstand, since interesting little phrases and riddles frequently pop up during the flow.

My experience proves to me there's another network available beyond the conscious mind, though I'd really have to sit down and catalog the reasons why. I'd rather you experience this for yourself. If you're a willing psychonaut, get ready for a lot of work but also major dividends in the future.

TO THE MYSTIC

W HEN IT COMES TO THE QUESTION of transcending ordinary consensus reality, there are three basic solutions. There is the
Dispensationalist Solution (the Creator will suspend all of the complex and
interlocking laws that govern the Universe in order to reveal Himself to the
world), the Scientistic Solution (the laws of the Universe will be re-engineered
in order to facilitate the apotheosis of the cognitive elites) and the Mystical
Solution, which argues that "consensus reality" is a fictional construct based on
faulty and/or incomplete sensory information.

I think most of you know which solution gets my vote.

Both the Dispensationalist and the Scientistic paradigms are linear,
hierarchical, anthropocentric, and often, profoundly narcissistic. The more I
read about Transhumanism and the Singularity, the more it reminds me of
Sunday School, only with Kurzweil and his minions on the Creator's throne.
But those lessons I learned in Sunday School aren't exactly the ones being
taught in churches today.

The only thriving churches in the world today preach the "Prosperity
Gospel," which teaches that God - *the Creator of the Infinite Universe* - is a
magical genie who wants you to win that football game, buy that Escalade, and
generally bask in His endless bounty until the time He calls you up to come sit
by His throne so He might spend the rest of Eternity indulging your each and
every whim. I *wish* I were exaggerating.

Wesleyean theology didn't really pan out that way. Which is probably why
most churches don't teach it — or any other genuinely conservative Christian
theology — all that much anymore.

I wonder how many of these people know the Ocean, something I
recommend to anyone reading this. The Ocean is my mystic touchstone, my
metaphor for reality. It's the nursery of all life on Earth. It can provide food and
entertainment. It can moderate our weather and provide means of travel, but it
can also wipe us off the face of the earth. It probably will one day. A Mystical
worldview would teach us that we need to co-exist with the Ocean. We need to
stop dumping our shit in it, stop overfishing it, and learn how to get the hell of
its way when its on the rag. A decent tropical storm can make our most
powerful nuclear weapons look like a wet fart.

The Scientistic mind might dream of taming the Ocean one day, but only
because they only know the Ocean as statistics on paper. The Dispensational
mind doesn't care; the oceans in Heaven are tame as kittens and the
temperature of bathwater, since that's what suits the believer's temporal needs.

But the Mystical mind looks at the Ocean and sees both Creator and Destroyer. Or rather, *feels* it, since a *higher* perception unfettered by reductionist rationalism is the (or a) definition of the Mystical mind.

Rationalism apotheosizes itself as Scientism, which in turn leads to Transhumanism and the rest of that delusional bullshit. Digitizing our life processes seems like a nifty idea, if it were even possible, until a massive sunspot wipes out the grid, or something screws up the magnetosphere. Then there are earthquakes, ice ages, pole shifts, asteroids, and all of the other unforeseen events that laugh at our pretensions to immortality.

Being humbled can often tear away the blinders that prevent you from seeing the world as it really is. Having the certainties of life - an oxymoron if ever there was one - torn away can open your eyes to a deeper panorama. It doesn't come without a price, but it often comes with incredible rewards as well; a profound sense of wonder and connection not the least among them.

Scientism-leading-to-Transhumanism (which all secular-materialist thinking must inevitably lead to) and Evangelicalism are the only socially-acceptable viewpoints on offer in the media. You might have smatterings of watered-down Mysticism at the fringes (usually in the form of corporate New Age gurus), but that might in fact be a function of physiology, not censorship.

Those cursed/blessed with a Mystical view of the world usually have some internal condition, or some extraordinary experience in their history, that changed their basic perceptions of the world. Which is why a lot of them gravitate towards the arts; it's the only way they can express the Ineffable. Even so, there needs to be a renewed effort to communicate the Mystical/Sensitive worldview, since both the Scientistic and Dispensationalist ones are allowed to *impose* themselves on the rest of us in order to facilitate their own apotheosis.

The Mystical worldview argues that we don't *need* more, we need to look at what we already have in a new way. The Mystical worldview argues that nothing is linear, not even history. Everything is cyclical, everything is revolving. Everything comes, goes, and then comes again. The problem isn't with what we have, the problem is that we haven't figured out how to use it yet.

The Aliens and the Angels are all around us, waiting for us to scrape the illusions from our eyes and finally see them as they are, not who we think they should be.

THE INFORMATION

THE INFORMATION

Original posting dates of essays

PART FIVE

PART SIX

PART SEVEN

PART EIGHT

AND THAT WAS THE GEEK THAT WAS

The Demented 13	10.28.21
The Year That Broke Reality	07.03.21
Timothy Leary's STILL Dead	12.12.10
Year Of Thinking Mystically	01.07.11
Ancient Aliens Buries The Lede	08.23.14
Space Brothers Are Running A Little Late	10.29.15
Never Mind the Mainstream	08.03.15
So Much to Answer for	07.15.08
Twilight of the Spandex Idols	02.15.21

TONIC FOR THE TROOPS

You Still Don't Need Their Permission.	05.15.13
"Just Around The Corner"	03.08.15
The Veneer Of Progress	11.01.15
The Tech Devolution Has Begun	08.19.21
If the Thunder Don't Get You	01.11.21

DREAMT OF IN YOUR PHILOSOPHY

Until It Happened To Me	02.28.15
I Look Like I've Seen A Ghost	09.03.10
Messages from the Other Side	12.18.15
"And They Noticed That You Noticed Them."	12.30.16

PRAXIS MAKES PERFECT

Synchronistic Process of Re-Enchantment	11.07.11
That's the Spirit	09.26.11
Would You Care to Trance?	12.21.14
Synching to the Mystic	12.04.10

CHRISTOPHER LORING KNOWLES is the author of the novel *He Will Live Up in the Sky*, as well as the Eagle Award-winning *Our Gods Wear Spandex: The Secret History of Comic Book Heroes* and *The Secret History of Rock 'n' Roll: The Mysterious Roots of Modern Music*.

He is co-author of *The Complete X-Files: Behind the Series, the Myths, and the Movies*. He was an associate editor and columnist for the five-time Eisner Award-winning *Comic Book Artist* magazine, as well as a writer and reviewer for *Classic Rock* magazine.

He has appeared on ABC's *20/20* and VH1's *Metal Evolution* and several radio shows including National Public Radio and The Voice of America. He has also appeared in several documentaries such as *Wonder Woman: Daughter of Myth* and *The Man, The Myth: Superman*. He has also lectured on science fiction, mysticism and mythology at the legendary Esalen Institute at Big Sur.

He blogs regularly on The Secret Sun and other blogs.

Printed in Great Britain
by Amazon

83288512R00231